ISRAEL
TODAY
REVISED EDITION

יִשְׂרָאֵל בְּיָמֵינוּ

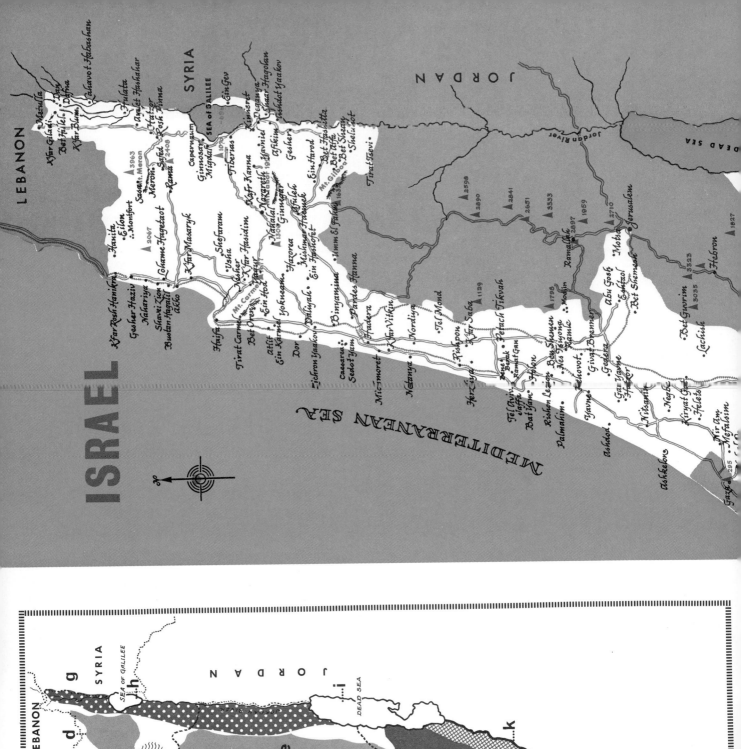
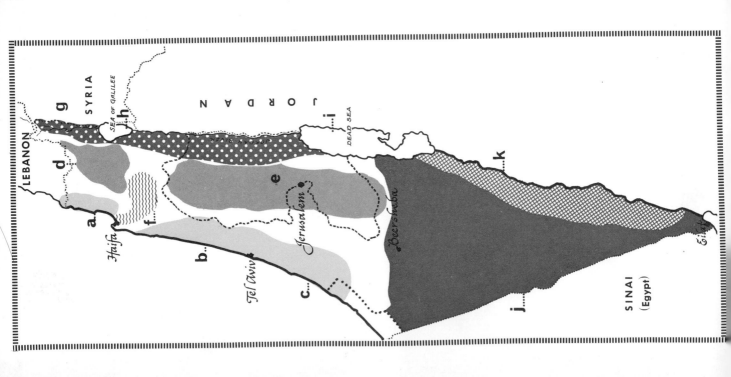

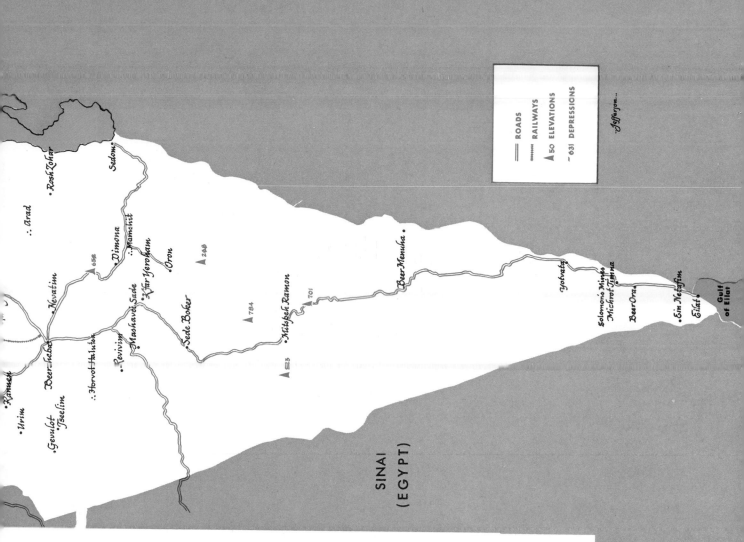

SINAI
(EGYPT)

Gulf
of Eilat

Roads / Railways / Elevations / Depressions legend box:

ROADS
RAILWAYS
▲ 50 ELEVATIONS
~ 631 DEPRESSIONS

The **Coastal Plain**, bordering the Mediterranean Sea for 116 miles, includes the Zebulun Valley (a) the Plain of Sharon (b) and the Plain of Judea (c). This region has a few small rivers, many wells, a temperate climate. It contains Israel's two largest cities, Tel Aviv and Haifa, and most of the country's people and industries. There are many citrus and banana groves, vineyards and vegetable farms in this area.

The **Central Mountains**. The Hills of Galilee (d) have some of Israel's loveliest scenery and many towns and villages, with mixed farming in the valleys and olive groves and newly planted forests on the rocky slopes. Jerusalem commands the Hills of Judea (e) most of which are in the Kingdom of Jordan.

The **Valley of Jezreel** (f) the "emek," separating the Hills of Galilee and Judea, is thirty miles long. Its fertile soil supports numerous farming villages.

The **Jordan Valley**. The Jordan River, with sources in Syria, Lebanon, and Israel, waters this deep, semi-tropical valley for 158 miles, 73 of them in Israel. After leaving the Huleh Valley (g) once swampland but now Israel's best farmland—the Jordan drops below sea level, flows through the Sea of Galilee (h) winds through the Kingdom of Jordan, and empties into the Dead Sea (i) the world's lowest point below sea level.

The **Negev** accounts for half of Israel's territory but barely one-fiftieth of her people. Though mostly barren but beautiful wasteland, with little rainfall, the northwest portion (j) has cattle ranches and wheat fields spreading farther south as water is piped in. Valuable minerals and chemicals are extracted from the Dead Sea (i). Beersheba, the Negev's capital, is a growing industrial city, and Eilat is the country's only Red Sea port. New towns and villages are flourishing even in the dry Aravah depression (k).

REVISED EDITION—1968

In the Six Day War of June, 1967, Israel occupied Arab lands on all borders, and united the two parts of Jerusalem into a single city. Jerusalem apart, Israel says she intends to keep some of the occupied territory, but the Arab nations must make peace directly with her in order to have any of it restored. A new map in Chapter 25, Page 300, shows both the old Israel and the occupied territory.

ISRAEL TODAY

REVISED EDITION—1968

HARRY ESSRIG and ABRAHAM SEGAL

יִשְׂרָאֵל בְּיָמֵינוּ

Design and illustration: Robert Sugar

Union of American Hebrew Congregations, New York

A Note About the Spelling and Transliteration of Hebrew Words.
The best way to read Hebrew words is, of course, in the Hebrew alphabet. For that reason, a great many of the Hebrew words appear in the text of *Israel Today* in Hebrew letters. For those who have not studied Hebrew, these words are listed at the bottom of the page in English transliteration. For the most part, the authors follow the original Hebrew pronunciation even when they spell the names of organizations, holidays, cities, etc., in English. For example, Beer Sheva is used in preference to Beersheba with the exception of the map at the beginning of the book. Since this is a book about modern Israel, the Israeli or Sefardic pronunciation is followed.

FOURTH PRINTING, 1968
REVISED EDITION

Library of Congress Catalogue Card Number 64–22869
Copyright 1964, by
UNION OF AMERICAN HEBREW CONGREGATIONS
Produced in U. S. of America

To
Rose Baskin Essrig
and
Sadie Weinstein Segal
this book is lovingly dedicated

EDITOR'S INTRODUCTION

We have felt for many years that the students in our Jewish religious schools were learning more about the ancient Israelites than about the modern Israelis. Indeed, our textbooks devoted more pages to our nomadic ancestors in the land of Canaan than to the present-day farmers and city-dwellers of Israel.

With the appearance of *Israel Today* we hope to provide for our students the proper balance between present and past—between history and the contemporary scene. The authors of this volume have also sought to strike a balance in describing the realities of present-day life in Israel. They give due credit to the chalutzim of all types, those who are working in the new frontiers of agriculture, industry, science, and the arts. By the same token, they point out shortcomings and problems that beset the young State of Israel and her people.

In preparing *Israel Today* the authors and the book designers have gone to great lengths to make this book interesting and attractive. They have included many novel features which entailed weeks and months of additional effort and painstaking care. All of the members of the Commission on Jewish Education who have been associated with this project since its inception present this book with a profound sense of gratitude and pride.

Dr. Samuel Grand

REVISED EDITION

Israel Today was first issued in the fall of 1964. Plans for thorough revision and updating were interrupted by the Six Day War and its aftermath. Hence, a full revision was deemed impractical due to unsettled conditions in the Middle East. But the authors have added a new chapter at the end, called "A New Israel?" on the Six Day War, its outcomes and significance. Throughout the book, in the margins, they have inserted recent facts and trends, later statistics, and other items of special interest. They have also revised various charts and maps.

We are gratified that the basic ideas of the book have stood the test of these intervening years and the spectacular events of 1967-1968, and that only a few factual items required alteration. This new revised edition permits *Israel Today* to continue to be of wide and effective use in our schools.

Jack D. Spiro

FROM THE AUTHORS

Dear Student:

Writing a textbook on Israel has been a hard job —but enjoyable too. Israel is an inspiring, exciting subject, and besides, we consider it a great honor to be able to explain about Israel to young people who will become members of the American Jewish community.

We had the help of many fine, worthy people and organizations. The late Dr. Emanuel Gamoran, who served as Director of the Commission on Jewish Education for forty years, suggested the original idea for our book. Dr. Eugene B. Borowitz, who followed him as Director of the Commission, helped get us started and suggested we write "the most exciting, most fascinating Jewish textbook ever produced." We probably haven't done *that*—but we *tried,* and we hope he likes the result.

Quite a few people read this book and gave us their opinions. In fact, they analyzed almost every sentence and suggested many corrections and improvements. We owe a great deal to Rabbi David I. Cedarbaum, Dr. Leon Fram, Dr. Toby K. Kurzband, and Mr. Samuel A. Nemzoff, members of the Commission, and to Mr. Moshe Aumann and Mr. Israel Meir, Consuls of Israel in New York City. These "readers," as they are called, helped us to say more clearly what was in our minds. We've used almost all their suggestions, and are glad we did.

Mr. Ralph Davis, Production Manager for the Union of American Hebrew Congregations, took charge of turning our typed pages into the printed volume you are holding. He is an expert of exceptional skill and experience. We don't know much about *his* part of book production but we certainly appreciate the way he understood *our* part and helped us do it.

We think this book has a "different" look, and we hope you like it. The art work and design were done by Mr. Robert Sugar under the supervision of Ralph Davis. He put together the pictures and drawings in such a way as to bring out the "adventure" of Israel—which is the main idea we wanted to put across. He also made many excellent suggestions to improve the book.

The book wouldn't exist at all if not for two special friends. Mrs. Julia Minor, secretarial assistant to the Director of Education, typed the various parts of the book several times, copied and arranged, kept track of things, and wrote letters. And not just with the patience and skill of an expert secretary, but with great intelligence and devotion. Her opinions, suggestions, and criticisms were always helpful.

And to Dr. Samuel Grand, Director of Experimental Education and Audio-Visual Aids, we owe perhaps the biggest debt of all. As Editor of the book, he took full command of the over-all project and paid attention to the small details. He gave us countless hours of his time. He has had many years of experience in creating and helping others to produce new films, filmstrips, recordings, and books. He knows both Israeli and American Jewish youth from first-hand experience, and we can't begin to tell you how much of this book really belongs to *him*, too. We have known and respected him for a long time, and now we admire him even more. He has taught us more than we can possibly explain.

(By the way, if you still find an error or a weak spot in the book, please blame *us*, and not any of our "helpers." We didn't always follow their suggestions. We and not they are responsible for the book.)

We are deeply grateful to Lazare Grunberg, and his staff for their painstaking care in reading the manuscript, the galleys, and the page proofs.

We obtained pictures and information from many sources, especially the Israel Office of Information, the Zionist Archives and Library, The Department of Education and Culture of the Jewish Agency, *World Over* Magazine, etc. The Union of American Hebrew Congregations, through its Commission on Jewish Education, was enthusiastically involved in this book all the way, in providing all the necessary help and especially in allowing us to express our own ideas in our own way.

All in all, we think our book had the best readers, designers, secretary, editor, and publisher that authors could have. Every one of them has told us that no other book has ever called forth so much effort from him. That's what Israel does to people!

Well, we hope the authors have also brought to their task the same enthusiasm and dedication shown by so many others. And if *Israel Today* in turn sparks the same feelings in *you*, all of us will be well rewarded.

Be sure to write and tell us (in care of the UAHC) what *you* think of our book!

Cordially,

Harry Essrig

Rabbi, University Synagogue
Los Angeles, California

Abraham Segal

Director, Union of American Hebrew Congregations
Department of Teacher Education

TABLE OF CONTENTS

ISRAEL
TODAY
REVISED EDITION

יִשְׂרָאֵל בְּיָמֵינוּ

In Israel you can climb to the top of Mount Carmel,
where Elijah challenged the false prophets in the name of the One God . . .
. . . and stand above the modern city of Haifa.

You can descend to the Dead Sea, the lowest point below sea level in the world.

You can see the ruins of the ancient synagogue at Kfar Nahum,

You can visit homes of the 20th century in Tel Aviv,
and homes of the 1st century in Qumran...

. . . modern libraries and schools . . .

. . . underground Arab potteries 500 years old . . .

. . . and Jewish farmers working their land.

You and Israel

You can fly from New York City to Tel Aviv, Israel, in about twelve hours aboard an El Al jet plane. Israel is close to you in other ways, too. This tiny land looms large in your future, as a Jew and as an American. *You* are part of Israel's story. You will discover why as you learn about the first Jewish State in 2,000 years.

An Exciting Land

Israel's story is full of adventure. Men and women dared to challenge swamps and deserts and enemies, to risk their lives for an ancient dream and a new way of life. They became new heroes and heroines in the long list in Jewish history.

What fascinating places you can visit in your imagination this year! Israel has hundreds of famous historic sites—amazing contrasts of old and new existing side by side. Israel's pioneers created the most unusual farming villages in the world, brought a "dead" language back to life, put a new spirit into the Sabbath and the Jewish holidays.

This land has been almost 4,000 years in the making. Wars and neglect ruined the country, but here it is, once again fertile and in bloom. "It can't be done," people said. "It's impractical, unnecessary." But Jewish pioneers went right ahead, to this very day. Farming in the desert, getting drinking water from the salty seas, fighting off five Arab nations, building an atomic reactor, blending one nation out of hundreds of thousands of immigrants from all over the world—nothing stopped the builders of Israel!

1

The World Is Interested

Since ancient times, this land has been a "bridge" for three continents. This birthplace of great religions is a "holy land" to Jews, Christians, and Moslems. It is the land where the Bible was created.

In some ways Israel is like a fortress, surrounded by hostile Arab countries. They boycott anyone who does business with Israel. Egypt keeps Israeli ships and ships carrying Israeli goods from the Suez Canal. Thousands of Arabs, who left their homes in Israel, live miserably in "refugee" camps just outside her borders—a most serious problem to Israel, the Arabs, and the United Nations.

Yet Israel has managed to "leap-frog" over the wall of distrust that surrounds her. The world's nations helped to create Israel, and many have promised to protect her territory from invasion. The United States, France, and England are her special friends. Some new nations of Asia and Africa eagerly use Israel's experience. She is a model, a "pilot plant" for other undeveloped lands trying to become modern and independent.

1967. With the Six Day War (see Chapter 25), France's policy changed, and since then she has no longer been pro-Israel, and has even become anti-Israel.

■ Since earliest times, soldiers, merchants, scholars have used this bridge.

There are no events in history so different in scale and yet so alike in their nature as the American Revolution in the eighteenth century and the establishment of Israel's independence in the present day and age.

—Abba Eban, former Ambassador
of Israel to the United Nations

Many lands have the same problems as Israel. How can farmers make ends meet? How to give medical care to the aged? How to educate children? How much should the government do for its citizens? Israel's answers to such questions may benefit all mankind. Her work on many scientific and industrial problems may help other nations.★

Israel is the only modern, democratic nation in an underdeveloped part of the world. She sets an example of social and spiritual progress—in medical practice, community living, labor unions, scientific research, social welfare. Israel's very existence shows that freedom and democracy work better than Communism does—a lesson that many countries today very much need.

Israel is not perfect. She is often criticized by other nations, by non-Jews—even by Jews and by Israelis themselves. Sometimes the critics do not know all the facts, or do not understand Israel's special problems. Sometimes they sincerely disagree with her. When she launched the Sinai Campaign against Egypt in 1956, for example, most of the United Nations voted against her. When Israel tried and executed the Nazi mass-murderer, Eichmann, again some of her friends did not approve.

★ Why is Israel especially able to help less developed countries? Why does she want to help them? Why do these countries turn to her for help?

1967. The Six Day War (see Chapter 25) came after a period of world silence on Arab, especially Egyptian, provocations. Afterward, many nations, led by Russia, branded Israel an "aggressor" and demanded her immediate withdrawal from Arab territory without an armistice or a peace treaty or guarantees of any kind.

America and Israel

Americans are curious about Israel, and follow events there with great interest. This is not surprising, for there are many similarities between American and Israeli history. In each, a land was settled by people who left the Old World in search of freedom and security. Both required pioneering under fearful hardships, a sharp break with the past, an open mind toward the future. Israel's founders, in many ways, repeated the struggles of America's Pilgrims, colonial settlers, western pioneers.

The government of the United States has constantly supported and strengthened Israel. All kinds of Americans—not just Jews—buy Israeli products: diamonds, cement, raincoats, steel pipes, chocolate, wine, stamps, and many others.

Try This: Write to a Christian friend, real or imaginary. Tell him in your own words why he should be interested in Israel and why he should help in supporting her.

Write to Israel Office of Information, 11 East 70th Street, New York, N.Y. 10021, for sample copies of the magazine, *Land of the Bible*. Look through them and figure out what things about Israel would be of most interest to American Christians.

America's churches also keep in close touch with Israel. Here their faith was born. The land has many Christian historic sites and churches. Many places in Israel remind the Christian worshiper of the life and death of Jesus, of his Apostles, and of other treasured events. Though most of the population is Jewish, Christians and Moslems have equal rights. Their holy places are carefully protected. American Jews and Christians find in Israel a common source of religious inspiration.

American Jews and Israel

Many Americans feel close to the homeland of their ancestors—Ireland, Italy, Greece, or Poland. They like to remember the language and history, the songs and dances and holidays of the "home" country, the country they love best next to the United States. It is a *family* feeling, the way one feels about a relative who lives far away but is still *close*.

We American Jews are no different: America is our country, but the Israelis are our brothers. When you see a newspaper headline about Israel, you feel pleased when the news is good, disturbed when it is bad. American Jews have a special pride in Israel—in her prestige among the nations, her victories over enemies, her progress in science and culture. We feel upset when Israel is in danger, when we think she has done something wrong, or when someone criticizes her. We feel responsible for Israel—for helping, protecting, defending her.

And so, we belong to organizations that help Israel—the Zionist Organization of America, Hadassah, ORT, the Pioneer Women, and others. Through these organizations we support many institutions in Israel.

American Jews have raised hundreds of millions of dollars in United Jewish Appeal campaigns to help settle new immigrants in Israel. Through Bonds for Israel we invest money in all kinds of Israeli "development" projects.

In our synagogues, too, we raise funds, sell her products, learn more about her situation. Each of our religious groups—Orthodox, Conservative, Reform—has its own special interest, its own special projects in Israel. It would be hard to name any American Jewish organization that is *not* concerned with Israel, one way or another.

The Jewish magazines in your home feature Israeli news. The Israel Philharmonic Orchestra tours our country. Israeli writers, artists, athletes, scientists, and political leaders frequently speak here—and are always warmly applauded. The International Jerusalem

■ (Top) Children's Forest, Ma'aleh Hahamisha, planted by children the world over. (Center) Greenhouse, Meir Shefeyah, children's village supported by Junior Hadassah. (Bottom) Hadassah —Hebrew University Medical Center, Jerusalem.

Examination is given here by the Hebrew University. We joyfully celebrate every anniversary of Israel's independence. Perhaps you have seen the exhibit of Israeli Children's Art which occasionally visits our cities. There are probably Israeli objects in your home—religious symbols, decorative pieces, and so on. American Jews of all ages visit Israel, to tour, study, or work.

Israel's Special Meaning

Israel has a special meaning for you as a Jew. It is "the Jewish national home"—the only place in the world where Jews are a majority of the population. There they speak one common language, have their own form of government, develop their own culture, regulate their own lives, observe their own religious customs. We accept Israel as "the Jewish national home" even though we ourselves may not wish to live there.

Israel has been a country of refuge for the dispossessed and persecuted Jews of the world. Hundreds of thousands of homeless Jews, who survived the Second World War and the Nazi concentration camps of Germany, found new homes there. The establishment of the new Jewish State in 1948 electrified the Jews living in poverty and misery in North Africa and other Arab lands. Thousands upon thousands of them flocked to Israel. Israel stands ready to welcome Russia's Jews, if the Communists ever let them out. Israel truly represents "the ingathering of exiles" that the prophet Isaiah predicted.

American Jews helped greatly in rebuilding a Jewish homeland in Israel and in settling refugees there. These tasks helped to unite the American Jewish community. Through Israel, we learned to work together despite our differences.

America and Israel are the two most important centers of Jewish life today. America has the largest, richest Jewish community in the world. Israel offers its Jewish citizens a chance to lead a completely Jewish life. From Israel, Jews everywhere may get inspiration, new

Try This: Your class can correspond with a class in an Israeli school. Write to the Jewish National Fund, 42 East 69th Street, New York, N.Y. 10021, giving your age and hobbies. You may write in English. Your class or school can "adopt" a class or school in Israel. For information write to Keren Hayesod, Youth Division, P. O. Box 583, Jerusalem, Israel. You can exchange gifts and letters with your "adopted" school, send them needed supplies.

1967. The most spectacular evidence of American Jewish concern for Israel is, of course, what happened with the Six Day War (see Chapter 25).

In celebrating the rebirth of Israel we pray, O Lord, that the whole house of Israel will unite to do Thy will. And, as we seek Thy favor for the welfare of the new State, so we invoke Thy blessings upon our country and upon all mankind. Hasten the day when the vision of Thy prophets will be realized: the Lord shall be One and His name shall be One in a world of universal justice, peace, and brotherhood. Amen.

—Prayer of Thanksgiving, Union of
American Hebrew Congregations

Try This: Hold a panel discussion with two or three pupils in your class. Some topics for the individual panelists: Several ways in which *I* can help Israel. Several ways in which Israel can help *me*. Some topics the class is going to study (check the Table of Contents) that interest *me* especially—and why. Some questions or problems in my mind about Israel that I'd like to have answered for me.

ideas. New Sabbath and holiday customs, our National Bible Quiz, Hebrew expressions, songs and dances, exchange teachers and youth leaders—these we have "borrowed" from Israel already. As the years go by, Jewish life in Israel will influence us even more.

The Jewish future has no meaning without Israel. This land was the birthplace of Judaism. Even when the Jewish people were exiled, they never forgot the land, never gave up their claim to it, never lost hope that they would some day get it back. This was perhaps the most cherished dream of the Jewish people for centuries—and it came true in our own day!

Every subject you study in your Jewish school connects somehow with Israel. Open your history book to almost any page, or your prayer book, or the Bible. Read any issue of *World Over* or *Keeping Posted*. Study your Hebrew lesson, or discuss Jewish affairs and current events, or review the age-old Jewish ideals of peace and justice. Celebrate the Sabbath or any holiday, or do some Jewish singing and dancing just for fun. You'll soon find Israel part of what you are thinking, saying, and doing.

The Bible actually comes to life in Israel. Children and adults, scholars and plain people, workers and high government officials, all study it regularly. It is a guidebook for archeologists, helps scientists find minerals, oil, and water. The Bible's social and religious ideals are part of everyday discussions and decisions.

The Hebrew language was once considered "dead." Yet it is spoken once again by a living people, used in books, newspapers, magazines, radio broadcasts, business documents, scientific work, music, art, sports—everything. We, too, are stimulated by the Hebrew culture of Israel. Many American Jews study Hebrew at some time in their lives; some even learn to speak and understand it. New works of scholarship, new poems, plays, and novels, keep coming out of Israel. The Jews were long ago named "the people of the Book." The Israelis are once again living up to this honorable title.

6

HAVE YOU WONDERED . . . ?

. . . about all the different names of Israel and the Jewish people? Here are some things you might like to know:

The Land. אֶרֶץ כְּנַעַן—The Land of Canaan, from the Canaanites, one of the main tribes living there when the Hebrews settled in it.

אֶרֶץ יִשְׂרָאֵל—Land of Israel, the oldest Jewish name for the land, used for centuries.

צִיוֹן—Zion, an ancient fortress or hill, used by the Bible prophets to stand for Jerusalem as a *spiritual* center of the Jewish people.

Judea, the name the Romans called. They called the people Judeans. The name comes from יְהוּדָה—Judah.

Palestine, another name used by the Romans, comes from the Philistines, a people who once lived along the Mediterranean shore and were Israel's fiercest enemies in ancient times.

מְדִינַת יִשְׂרָאֵל—The State of Israel, its newest name.

The People. עִבְרִים—Hebrews, earliest name used by our ancestors, probably meaning "Those from over (or across)" the Jordan River.

יִשְׂרָאֵל—Israel, Israelites, Children of Israel. Jacob received the new name of Israel after his fight with the angel recorded in the Bible (Genesis 32:29). The word Yisrael means "Prince of God" or "Warrior of God." The twelve tribes, descendants of Jacob's twelve sons, called themselves "B'nai Yisrael," Children (or sons) of Israel, or Israelites. Israel also became the name of the northern half of the country, when it was split into two kingdoms after the death of King Solomon.

■ In Israel, the Bible and the Prayer Book are so familiar they even get into "commercials"—like this ad for "Miracle Cleanser" using "Dayenu" from the Pesach Haggadah to describe its virtues. How do you feel about this kind of ad?

Eretz Canaan: אֶרֶץ כְּנַעַן   Eretz Yisrael: אֶרֶץ יִשְׂרָאֵל   Tzion: צִיוֹן
Yehudah: יְהוּדָה   Medinat Yisrael: מְדִינַת יִשְׂרָאֵל   Ivrim: עִבְרִים
Yisrael: יִשְׂרָאֵל

7

Jew, from יְהוּדָה—Judah, fourth son of Jacob, whose descendants became the leading and most powerful tribe. The Northern Kingdom (Yisrael) was conquered and destroyed, and this part of our people disappeared. The Southern Kingdom (Yehudah) was also conquered, but not destroyed, and its people survived as "Judeans" and later, *Jews*.

יִשְׂרְאֵלִי—Israeli, a citizen of the State of Israel.

> "Out of Zion shall go forth the law,
> And the word of the Lord from Jerusalem."
> —Isaiah 2:3

Why is "Zion" used here, rather than "Israel"? Why did the Zionist movement use the name "Zion"—instead of "Israel," for example—for the idea of rebuilding a Jewish homeland?

YOU'LL ENJOY READING

Understanding Israel ("Understanding Your World" series, published by Laidlaw Brothers)

YOU'LL ENJOY SEEING

Israel, an Adventure (film: Tribune Films)

Yisraeli: יִשְׂרְאֵלִי

chapter 2

Let's Explore Israel!

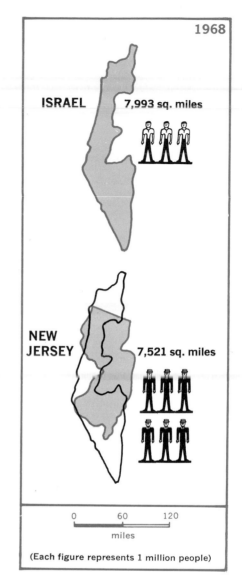

1968

ISRAEL   7,993 sq. miles

NEW
JERSEY   7,521 sq. miles

0   60   120
miles

(Each figure represents 1 million people)

A Small Land

So much has happened in Israel, and is still happening there, that it is sometimes hard to realize how *small* a country she is.

From north to south, Israel's longest distance is only 265 miles; from east to west, only 70 miles. On turnpikes, a car would cover these two distances in just about five hours and an hour-and-a-half. In clear weather, and if no mountains were in the way, a plane would have to go up only half a mile for the pilot to see both the east and west borders at the widest part—and only four miles up to see both the north and south borders at the longest part. And he'd have to watch his speed and location carefully, or he'd be across the border in no time.

Try This: Figure out how many Israelis there are per square mile (divide 8,000 into 2,800,000, Israel's total population in 1968). Then compare with the figure for your own state and city and for the United States. Compare size and population also.

A Bridge Between Continents

But size doesn't always measure importance. Israel's location has made her *very* important all through world history. Israel lies along the eastern shore of the Mediterranean Sea, at the western end of a region called the Middle East. Israel is the meeting-point of three continents, the quickest route between Europe, Asia, and Africa.

Traders and conquerors, scholars and explorers have traveled over this land for centuries. Surrounding countries always regarded it with greedy eyes. Sea-going nations to the west wanted to build caravan routes for land trade. Inland nations to the east wanted to use it for shipping and trading from the Mediterranean coast. Often Israel was the "expressway" for the armies of mighty empires, or became a "neutral" zone to protect their borders. This land was always being conquered and reconquered, enjoying independence for only brief periods of time.★

★ Why has world peace always been especially important to Israel—a matter of life and death?

9

All this made ancient Palestine a meeting-ground for many different ideas and customs. These influenced the Jewish people, and Judaism itself. In turn, the "bridge" helped to spread many Jewish ideas and customs.

Israel's location is still vital to other countries. After World War I (1918), Britain wanted to control it because it was so close to the Suez Canal, her lifeline to India. After World War II (1945), all the leading countries tried to gain influence in the Middle East. Russia wanted a warm-water seaport in that general region, and control in deciding its future. The Western nations, including the United States, wanted allies and bases, as protection against Russia.★

As a "bridge," Israel can be a trading center for Eastern and Western nations, a meeting-place for the culture and science of the two halves of the world. Her location helps her attract tourists, become prosperous, win more friends and influence many countries.

1968. For Russia's role in the Middle East before, during, and after the Six Day War, see Chapter 25.

★ Would you expect Israel to be more a Western or an Eastern (Oriental) type of country, in language, music, foods, attitudes toward life? (Hint: Is there a third possibility?)

1967. After the Six Day War (see Chapter 25), Israel occupied new territory formerly in Arab hands. It is not yet clear what will become of this added territory. But meanwhile, Israel's borders have been straightened out, she controls land where formerly Arab raids were launched, and she is safer from sudden attack.

★ Israel is tiny in comparison to all the Arab countries. Why then do they object to her, fear and hate her, want to destroy her? Why do the Arabs, despite their threats and warnings, hesitate to attack Israel?

Enemy Neighbors

Israel is surrounded on land by much larger hostile nations. Her border of only 600 miles faces enemy countries that refuse to accept her and openly plan to destroy her.

Three-fourths of all Israelis live in one small section, in the middle of the country. This region averages only twelve miles wide between the Mediterranean Sea and the country of Jordan. Except in the southern half, no Israeli settlement is more than twenty miles away from an Arab frontier. If the Arabs attack, as they did in 1948–49, the Israelis will have to win or be pushed into the sea.★

From the air, Israel is shaped something like an arrowhead. To us, Israel seems more like a fortress under attack. We wonder how Israelis have managed to build a whole new country, establish an independent state, develop a normal way of life. But they do not seem worried or nervous. They work hard to be ready to defend themselves, but are cheerful and confident. They have faith in themselves and in the land that has given them so much.

Land of Contrasts

In just a few hours, you can leave a wintry mountainside and go to a burning hot desert, then move on to a cool, breezy beach. For a short vacation trip, you do not have to choose between seashore, mountain, and desert—you can have them all. And any kind of scenery you want, too—big-city boulevards, or beautiful farm country, or ruins of ancient buildings.

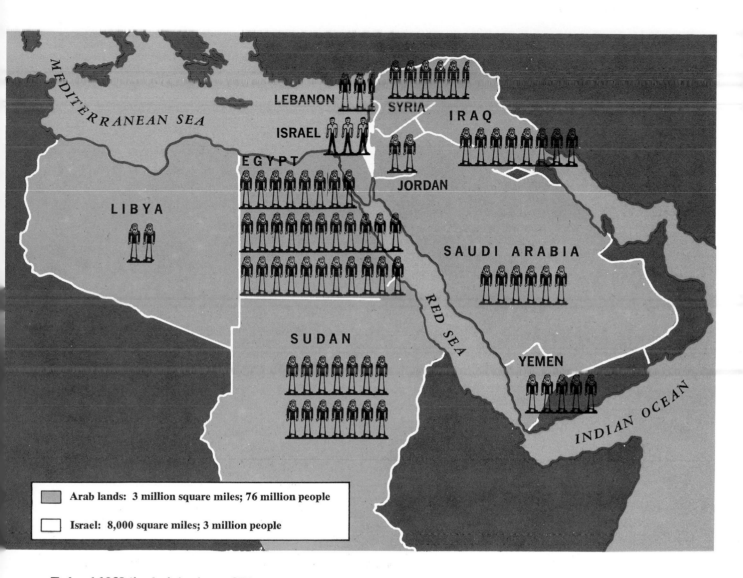

■ As of 1968 the Arab lands are 375 times larger than Israel and have 25 times as many people.

Israel probably has more different kinds of climate and scenery, for her size, than any other country in the world. In fact, Israel is like a miniature world—she has a little of everything.

Israel's weather is mild in winter and warm in summer. There are some unpleasant hot spells when desert winds blow from the east, and some uncomfortable places in the Jordan Valley and the Negev. But on the coast, cool sea breezes usually temper the climate all year round, even on warmest days. This part of Israel has often been compared to Southern California at its best. Snow falls only in the mountains, and then only once every few years.

11

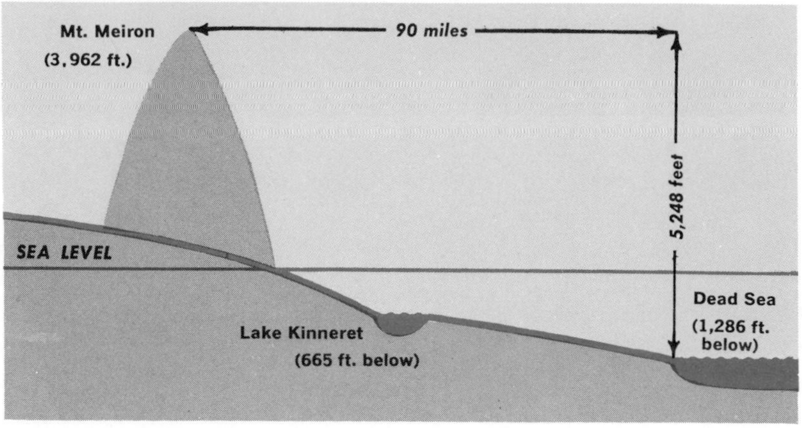

Mt. Meiron
(3,962 ft.)

90 miles

5,248 feet

SEA LEVEL

Dead Sea
(1,286 ft.
below)

Lake Kinneret
(665 ft. below)

■ Compare Israel's highest peak, Mount Atzmon (or Meron), with her lowest spot, the Dead Sea. The Jordan River drops sharply in sea level within a short distance. Though without big waterfalls, Israel has unusual possibilities for waterpower to turn dynamos and generate electricity.

Try This: Look up the weather facts for the different seasons in the region where you live. Then design a poster chart to contrast this information with Israel.

Like everything else in Israel, the rainfall varies greatly—heavy in the north, less and less as you go south, until finally, in the Negev, very little indeed. Rain in Israel falls only during one season—the four winter months—but usually a heavy layer of dew covers the ground every morning.

TEMPERATURE			
	At Tel Aviv (Seacoast)	At Jerusalem and Galilee	At Jordan Valley and the Negev
Coldest Month (January)	47-65° humidity 80%	40-55°	50-70° humidity 28%
Hottest Month (August)	70-90° humidity 55%	65-85°	80-105° humidity 35%

CLIMATE		
Spring	March	Cool. Brief, occasional showers.
Summer	April to September	Constant sunshine, warm. No rain.
Autumn	October	Clear, cool.
Winter	November to February	Cool. Heavy rains alternating with brilliant sunshine.

Israel's Cities

Israel's people are Jews, Christians, Moslems, of many different origins. Israelis do not look, talk, or dress alike. They do not eat the same foods, or observe their religion in the same ways, or have the same attitude toward life. What a job to form one nation out of them!

An easy way to start an argument in Israel is to praise—or criticize—one of her three main cities. Jerusalem, Tel Aviv, Haifa, each has its own loyal "fans."

Jerusalem's name comes from שָׁלוֹם—peace. Yet it is surrounded on three sides by enemy territory. In the War for Independence some of the fiercest fighting took place here. When it stopped, Jerusalem was in two parts, separated by the Israel-Jordan border. The "Old City"—the Arab section—is one of the world's oldest cities, with holy places of Jews, Christians, and Moslems. The "New City" —the Jewish part—connects with the rest of Israel only by a narrow strip of land.

But it doesn't "feel" like a border city with an uneasy truce hanging over it. After all, in its long history Jerusalem has been "conquered" thirty-six times and "destroyed" ten times—yet it's still here, still beautiful. The sky above is clear blue, many of the stone houses and buildings are a soft pink-gold, the cypress trees around the city are deep green. Floors in the homes are often made of light-yellow tiles; furniture is usually simple, and arranged for roominess. Jerusalem has a quiet oriental feeling, serious, dignified, steady—yet it's also a busy, modern city. In the bright sunny daytime, it's a beehive of activity—at night, it's dark and still and mysterious.

Jerusalem is more serious, more religious, than Tel Aviv or Haifa. Here people go to bed earlier. There are no sidewalk cafes, such as you see in Tel Aviv.

On Friday evenings, visitors tour the many charming old synagogues. They need a guide to get them in and out of the crooked little streets and byways, and to explain at each synagogue why the worshipers have their own special customs. Centuries of history lie behind the synagogues, built by Jews from distant countries in Asia or Africa. Jerusalem still observes the festival of Purim one day later than all other Jewish communities in the world, following an ancient tradition of "walled cities."

Shalom: שָׁלוֹם

1967. Israel, in the Six Day War (see Chapter 25), took over the "Old City" and Jerusalem became a united city under Israeli control for the first time in 2,000 years.

1968. Jerusalem's population: 265,000.

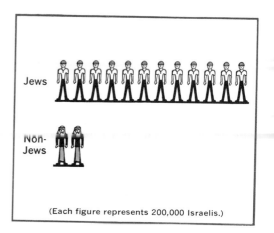

Jews

Non-Jews

(Each figure represents 200,000 Israelis.)

■ The only country where Jews are in the majority. Why should immigrants settle in towns and villages? Why must young people spend part of their army service working on the land? In 1948, half the people lived in big cities, a quarter in towns, and a quarter in villages. Has there been an improvement in 1968?

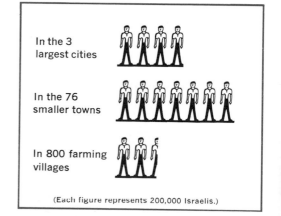

In the 3 largest cities

In the 76 smaller towns

In 800 farming villages

(Each figure represents 200,000 Israelis.)

13

Ten measures of beauty came down to earth; nine were taken by Jerusalem, and one by the rest of the world.

Talmud

Jerusalem

A Jerusalem שַׁבָּת—Sabbath, is world-famous for its tone of peaceful rest and holy joy. Jerusalem rests, not to play and have fun, but to pray and sing to God. The whole city takes its character from the many sincere religious Jews, who love the Sabbath as a "queen," and feel honored and delighted when "she" comes to visit them each week. The synagogues are full, the city is silent. But on Saturday night, after the worshipers have said "good-by" to the "queen," the whole population seems to pour out on the streets—walking, singing, visiting, talking.

On week-days, routine work goes on in the Knesset (Parliament), the government offices, the Supreme Court, the headquarters of many important organizations. The Hebrew University and its Hadassah Medical School make Jerusalem the country's cultural and medical center; the Bezalel Museum and Art Gallery make it an important art center. Jerusalem has brand-new housing projects, a district where the strictest Orthodox Jews in the world still follow every custom of their East European days, and modern factories and hotels. Favorite tourist spots are the Tomb of David on Mount Zion, and the grave of Herzl, the "father" of Israel—and the Bible Zoo, where every cage has a Bible quotation about the animal inside. Vacationers and tourists like the city for its cool climate and pleasant weather.

Something for everyone! And for Jews, something special. Ever since Temple days, 2,000 years ago, Jerusalem has been a symbol of Jewish unity, of the Jewish hope for "God's kingdom on earth" —a world of justice, freedom, peace. You, too, when you go there some day, will feel as if you are making a pilgrimage to a holy place. Long ago, Jewish poets called Jerusalem the "heart" of Israel —and the heart of Israel it still is today.

Shabbat: שַׁבָּת

1966. The Knesset moved into a beautiful new building. Other new buildings that year included the Harry S. Truman Peace Centre, and the John F. Kennedy Memorial in the Judean Hills.

■ **The campus of the Hebrew University. (Opposite page) Jerusalem "the Golden." Look up the official seals of Israel's cities in the latest "Facts About Israel," in the section called "Principal Cities and Places of Interest," and see if you can explain the symbols used by each city.**

14

Tel Aviv

In 1909, forty Jewish families in the Arab city of Jaffa went out to the sand dunes nearby, with shovels and a wheel-barrow, to start a city of their own. Today, Tel Aviv is Israel's largest city, with 400,000 people—one-seventh of Israel's population—and the most modern city in the whole Middle East. Jaffa has dwindled to a mere suburb or section of Tel Aviv.

Tel Aviv's people like speed, noise, new things—and other people. They do not stay home very much. They are always crowding the streets, going places, and doing things. Music is everywhere you go on the main streets—popular, jazz, classical, from radios, students practicing on their instruments, bands playing in the cafes. Hundreds of outdoor cafes, of all sizes, line the streets. People go to their favorite cafes not only to eat and drink and be entertained, but to play chess, talk politics, and even do business. Tel Aviv's many movie houses are crowded for every performance.

The sparkling city has spacious parks and boulevards, a splendid library, four different theaters, operas, and one of the world's best symphony orchestras. Israel's best zoo is located here, also a fine biological station, and Tel Aviv's own university. The people are

■ (Below and right) From camels to cars—the same spot in Tel Aviv, 50 years ago and today. Why are Israelis as proud of Tel Aviv's newness as they are of Jerusalem's age?

factory workers and merchants, young and old, world tourists and vacationing country farmers, serious artists and "characters." Visitors flock to this democratic, lively city. Tel Aviv thrills them or annoys them—but it never bores them. They think of it as Israel's "playground."

And yet, Tel Aviv has most of Israel's big business firms and banks, and almost half her factories. From its central station, hundreds of buses leave daily for all parts of the land. Many foreign embassies are located here, and most of Israel's book and newspaper publishers.

Three holidays have their own special flavor in Tel Aviv. On Chanukah, a giant menorah lights up atop the "Great Synagogue," for all the world to see. On Purim, the whole city turns out for a merry עַדְלְיָדַע—carnival, of spectacular floats picturing the Jewish past and present. And on Israel's Independence Day—יוֹם הָעַצְמָאוּת, the country's biggest parade marches here, where Israel's Declaration of Independence was proclaimed in 1948.

On Friday afternoons every store, shop, factory, and office closes down for Shabbat. The children watch for "Joshua and his trumpet"—one of the elderly bearded men riding through the streets in a car, blowing a shofar to warn everyone that Shabbat is at hand.

Friday nights are for family "get-togethers" and friendly visiting. On Saturday morning Tel Avivans—early risers on other days—sleep late. During the day, they walk about, visit the zoo, swim, and play on the crowded beaches. When night comes, everything "opens up"—cafes, movies, all the rest, almost with a "bang."

■ Tel Avivans of all ages relax at a sidewalk cafe.

Adloyada: עַדְלְיָדַע   Yom Ha-Atzmaut: יוֹם הָעַצְמָאוּת

★ Jerusalem is often compared to Washington, D. C., and Tel Aviv to New York City. What similarities do you see? As you read on about Haifa, think of another American city it can be compared to.

Tel Aviv is not as serious and dignified, or as beautiful, as Jerusalem—it is like a younger brother, full of energy, excitement, and pride.

Tel Aviv recently erected Israel's first skyscraper, thirty-two stories high, and built expressways to Jerusalem and Haifa. It also extended its beach farther out into the Mediterranean Sea—making new space for hotels, entertainment places, bathing facilities, and parks. And along with everything else to boast of, Tel Aviv is the first and largest all-Jewish city in the world.★

Haifa

One of Haifa's most impressive sights is a great glistening golden dome—the temple and world headquarters of the Bahai religion—surrounded by strikingly beautiful Persian gardens. Everywhere in Haifa are cool parks and gardens, gorgeous views. Flower beds decorate every street corner. Roads into the city are bordered by palm trees, the traffic lanes are separated by blooming shrubs. The city is clean—and has no slums.

This is Israel's most beautiful, most varied city. Its lovely setting in a landscape of plain, sea, and mountain reminds many visitors of Naples in Italy. Haifa began on the waterfront. As its population grew, the city moved upward along the side of Mount Carmel. Today it has three distinct "layers," each like a separate city, with its own special character.

The newest "layer," on top, is Har Ha-Carmel (Mount Carmel), a favorite vacation spot for all Israelis. They like the mountain air and views, summer hotels, sanitariums and rest homes, movies, high-class restaurants, quiet shady streets with fine homes.

On the slope of this beautiful mountain, about five miles from the city proper, is the new campus of Israel's Institute of Technology—the Technion—for training engineers and architects. However, the old school is still being used.

But with all its beauty, Haifa is also Israel's hardest-working city. The second "layer"—Hadar Ha-Carmel, "the beauty of Carmel"—has not only movies, hotels, and cafes, but also many business firms and government buildings.

In the earliest "layer" along the bay, smoke belches from the stacks of the country's biggest factories for making steel, oil, glass, cloth, chemicals, cars.

Nine out of ten workers in Haifa belong to the Histadrut. This remarkable labor union owns more than half of Haifa's factories, and has its own hospital, bank, adult classes, restaurants, newspapers.

Only in Israel

A favorite Haifa story tells of a man who wanted to marry off his daughter. He went to a marriage broker, who arranges such things, offering 5,000 pounds (then worth about $14,000) for a good "catch." The broker, looking through his files, mentioned a lawyer, rich and handsome, a doctor with a fine practice, and so on. But each time, the man shook his head and said, "Not good enough," or "Something better."

Finally, the broker burst out: "What do you expect for 5,000 pounds—a plumber?"

■ **Haifa Port Area.**

Even the garbage man or street cleaner walks the streets here with an air of dignity and pride. To Haifans, all Israelis are workers—the finest thing a person can be. The bus drivers have their own book club, and consider themselves as good as college professors.

Haifa's beautiful bay is the biggest, busiest seaport in the whole Middle East. Monster cranes run on tracks, swing out to load and unload ships flying almost every flag in the world. Israel's Navy is based here. Her trim fighting ships mingle with stodgy freighters and plush passenger liners; her uniformed sailors stand out among the dock workers, engineers, technicians of the harbor.

★ Israel's three cities have been given many other nicknames besides "heart," "playground," and "muscles." What seems true, and what not, about these examples?

Jerusalem   city of the past
                      sunset city   prays

Tel Aviv   city of the present
                      daylight city   plays

Haifa   city of the future
                      sunrise city   works

Haifa is the gateway to Israel for huge numbers of immigrants, the first sight they see from the water, the first Israeli soil they touch. Visitors, tourists, businessmen, diplomats come and go. Haifa's harbor is a place of noise and motion, lifting and lowering, entering and leaving.

In the middle of Israel's beauty spot—Israel's muscles!★

Israel's Towns

Israel has over 76 towns of varying sizes. Some of these—like Safed, Tiberias, Akko, Lod, Ramla, Beer Sheva, Nazareth—go back to ancient Bible times, or the Middle Ages. They have weathered old synagogues and churches, crowded Arab streets, tombs and other landmarks of ancient scholars and warriors. In 1948, these were all small, sleepy places. Today, they are much bigger and livelier. They have new homes, factories and mines, summer and winter health resorts, artists' colonies, airfields.

Another group of towns began as farming villages, as far back as 1878. In those days, Jewish city people, ignorant of farming, bought swamp land and tried to raise crops. They fought off Arab raids, lived through illness and hunger, dried up the swamps by planting trees—and succeeded. Today, these small plantations are sizable towns, famous for fruits and wines from surrounding farms, and for large factories, too. They have good beaches and lawns, modern schools, fine hotels, scientific laboratories—and some of the proudest names in all Israel: Petach Tikvah, Rehovot, Rishon Letzion, Herzliyah.

The suburbs of some cities have grown big enough to be considered separate towns. The best known, and actually Israel's fourth biggest city, is Ramat Gan, near Tel Aviv. This modern "garden city" is famous for both factories and parks. Its Bar Ilan University is a combination of American university and Orthodox yeshivah (Talmud academy).

Israel's newest towns have not "grown" naturally, but are carefully planned in advance by the government for a whole broad region. Kiryat Gat, for example, is the central town for over fifty farming villages grouped around it in ten districts. The whole region was laid out according to one master plan for farms and factories, roads, water and electricity, schools. A textile factory, for example, is located near farms raising cotton.

The whole Lachish region, where the southern Negev district begins, was selected to benefit from a pipeline bringing water down the length of Israel. Each village has a synagogue and the two first

■ Petach-Tikvah

■ Rehovot

20

grades of school; each district has a health clinic, and higher grades; the central town has a hospital, and still higher grades. For some planned regions of this kind, Israel has conducted international competitions among artists and architects. This new idea in "city planning" has attracted world-wide interest.

1968. Besides the Lachish Region, which now clusters 56 villages around its central town, there are 4 others in various parts of the country, all growing rapidly.

■ The farming village of Nahalal looks, from the air, like a wheel: community institutions in the center, surrounded in turn by homes, farm buildings, fields. Can you guess which of the three kinds of village described in the text would prefer such an arrangement?

Farmers of Israel

About 800 farming villages dot Israel's landscape, about 700 of them Jewish. Some are different from anything else in the world— a fascinating part of Israeli life.

In some farming villages people work their own land, buy their own seeds and tools, sell their own produce, live in their own house, take care of their own children. In other villages, the whole group owns all property. The village works, buys, sells as a group. All villagers eat together, and the children all live together, by themselves. In still other villages, a family works its own land and lives in its own house. But the whole village owns farm supplies and tools in common, and cooperatively sells the produce of all farms.

These settlements differ in politics and religious attitudes. You can try out different villages, join one, quit, join another. If you

Try This: Select one town and find out more about it for a report to the class. Stress unusual, exciting facts that show how Israel is an old-new land, or how it was created by daring, determined pioneers. Some books that will help: Comay's *Everyone's Guide to Israel;* Edelman's *Israel: New People in an Old Land;* Zeligs' *Story of Modern Palestine;* Jewish encyclopedias.

Divide the class into committees. See what each committee can find, in the books suggested above, about one of these fascinating places in Israel:

—unique villages: Ein Hod; Meir Shefeyah; Uriel

—places with exciting stories: Tel Hai; Mishmar David; Masada

—villages and towns with annual festivals: Dalia; Ein Gev; Meron; Modin; Zichron Ya-akov

—famous mountains: Gilboa; Tabor; Carmel

—places famous for Bible events: Eshtaol; Dothan; Emek Yizreel; Beth Shean; Sodom; Megiddo

—a miscellaneous group: what happened at Deganiah? Yavne? Atlit? Caesarea?

have enough people on your side, you can even start a new village of the type *you* want. Recently, for example, a community of Orthodox Jews, called Chasidim, who lived together here in the United States, moved as a group to Israel. There they set up their own Chasidic farming village.

Variety and freedom make Israeli farm life interesting and exciting, with plenty of competition, argument, and enthusiasm.

YOU'LL ENJOY READING

Habibi's Adventures in the Land of Israel, by Althea O. Silverman
Journey to Israel: a Pictorial Guide, by Ernest Aschner and Zachary Serwer
Jerusalem: Living City (Israel Office of Information)
Yerushalayim: a Reader, by Azriel Eisenberg

YOU'LL ENJOY SEEING

Israel: the Land and Its People (filmstrip series, Jewish Agency): This Is Israel; Galilee; Haifa and the Emek; Kinneret and the Judean Hills; The Darom and the Negev; Tel Aviv and the Coastal Plain
Jerusalem (filmstrip: Jewish Education Committee)
Window on Jerusalem (film: Mizrachi Women's Organization)
View-Master "Nations of the World" Packet on Israel (Sawyer's, Inc.)

chapter 3

Why the Jews Wanted a Homeland

■ 1900 years ago, the Roman Empire minted this coin to celebrate its "destruction" of the Jewish State.

Your parents lived through an event that many generations of Jews hoped, prayed, and waited for—the creation of Israel. All the odds were against it—yet it happened.

The "Dead" Land

In 70 C.E., the Romans "destroyed" the Jewish State, as the Babylonians had done 600 years earlier. They plowed the city of Jerusalem with salt so that nothing could ever grow there, and cursed it "forever." They built, in the city of Rome, a triumphal arch to celebrate Judea's downfall and to honor themselves as conquerors. Jewish independence was ended for all time—or so it seemed.

For almost 2,000 years Jews lived scattered in nearly all parts of the world—Babylonia, Spain, France, England, Italy, Poland, Russia, America. During this life of exile and wandering, especially in the Middle Ages, Jews prayed for God to send His Messiah to reform the world and lead them back to Palestine. But it was a futile hope.

"There is no greater service for the religious Jew to perform than to rebuild the ruins of the Holy Land."

Zvi Hirsch Kalischer (Poland, 1795-1874). Was the first Orthodox rabbi of modern times to work for actual return to Palestine ("practical" Zionism). He inspired the organization of Zionist youth clubs and aroused other Jewish leaders to join him.

"Children of Israel, be one band, and thus prepare yourselves for the redemption!"

Yehudah ben Solomon Hai Alkalai (Serbia, 1798-1878). Worked out a complete Zionist program long before the name Zionism was even dreamed of. At the age of seventy, he went to Palestine himself and founded a settlement society.

Palestine itself was ruled by others. Century after century, conquerors swept across the countryside, leaving destruction behind them. The land, neglected, became swamp and desert, suited only for primitive Arab peasants and a few Jews living on charity. How could such ruined soil ever support modern farms, modern cities?

The Turkish Empire held Palestine in a tight, unyielding grip. Jews were not wanted there. Then the Turks lost it in 1917, and Britain took over. The Arabs resented Jewish settlers, attacked their homes, and set fire to their fields. Britain hindered Jewish growth there as much as she could. Jews, too, wherever they lived, were divided among themselves. Many were not interested in restoring a Jewish homeland. Many opposed the idea altogether. Many wanted a homeland, but not in Palestine. And many were not sure *what* they wanted.

And yet the dream of centuries came true. Today, for the third time in history, the world has a free and independent State of Israel. Seldom has a people won such a victory over so many obstacles.

The "Impossible" Dream

You will have to use your imagination to feel like the homeless Jews of many years ago. Ever since their exile began, many centuries ago, they were without a land of their own. But though their State came to an end, they did not perish as a people. Strengthened by their own religion and way of life, they led a separate existence in many lands. They were without citizenship, equal rights, or equal opportunities. Wherever they settled, no matter how much they helped the country, they frequently suffered discrimination and persecution. Life was difficult most of the time, and sometimes almost impossible.

The nineteenth century brought a new age of daring thoughts and great adventures for mankind. New nations were born then, as in Asia and Africa today. In many lands the people revolted against tyrants, set up new governments. Each people loved its own land, its own culture and institutions, wanted to live by them freely. This was also a time of other "revolutions": the beginnings of democratic rights for all men, of modern factories and laboratories, free public education, equal rights for women, freedom for slaves.

All this stirred the Jewish people. They had never given up their hope of some day returning to Palestine. Now, toward the end of the nineteenth century, many Jews in Europe refused to wait for the Messiah to come and perform miracles. They wanted something done *now* for their homeless people. They, too, began to feel like a nation. They wanted the same right as anyone else to lead a life

If I forget you, Jerusalem, let my right hand forget its cunning. Let my tongue cleave to the roof of my mouth, if I do not remember you, if I do not put Jerusalem above my greatest joy.

—Psalm 137.5-0

of their own in their native land, to develop their own culture according to their traditions.

Today, this idea sounds quite sensible. We see the State of Israel celebrating one birthday after another, a full-fledged member of the family of nations. But a hundred years ago, *not* to wait for God's miracles was a revolutionary idea. Many, Jews and non-Jews alike, laughed at the preposterous plan of the Zionists. Return to their ancient land and make it Jewish again, with the help of the other nations? The Jews were *not* a nation—they didn't *need* a homeland, said the scoffers. And even if they did, why Palestine? Why not other places easier to obtain, easier to live in?

But the Zionists insisted that Jews needed and deserved their own land. Jews had *never* given up their ties to Palestine or their claim to it. This was the natural, logical place for a Jewish nation. There and only there, the Zionists insisted, could the Jewish nation be born again, as in the days of King David or the Maccabees. There and only there, could Jews lead a Jewish life that did not depend entirely on the decisions of other nations.

Try This: Look up two or three new Asian or African countries "born" since 1948. How do they compare with Israel in size, resources, population, allies and enemies, achievements? Do any of them have relationships with Israel?

The Great Hatred

In the 1880's, two great dangers strengthened the Zionist arguments. One was a new kind of anti-Semitism that became especially vicious at this time. Our people had enjoyed a wonderful feeling of freedom after the French Revolution of 1789. France gave the Jews all the rights of citizenship, and other European nations gradually did the same. But now, hardly a hundred years later, this very equality and freedom caused new prejudice, new persecution.

Our people had suffered from deep hatred during the Middle Ages because they were "different" in religious belief and customs. The Christian church leaders blamed the Jews for Jesus' death and for "stubbornly" refusing to accept him as the savior of mankind. But now, in modern times, a new element was added to the old dislike for Jews. Prejudiced people now regarded Jews as an inferior Semitic "race" threatening to "destroy" the superior "European" civilization—the very same idea Hitler used so criminally and horribly in the twentieth century.

Try This: Look up, in Jewish encyclopedias or history books, any of the following examples of false accusations and cruel laws against the Jews: Damascus Affair; Tisza-Eszlar; Polna; Kishinev; Beilis; the "May Laws." Does the existence of Israel today help prevent such events? If they happened today, what could Israel do about it?

25

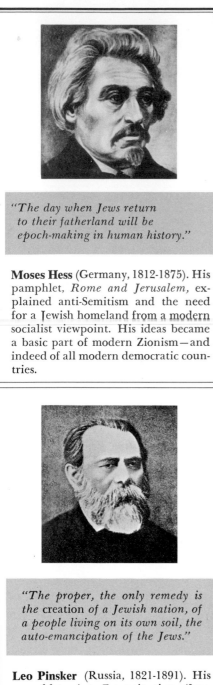

"The day when Jews return to their fatherland will be epoch-making in human history."

Moses Hess (Germany, 1812-1875). His pamphlet, *Rome and Jerusalem,* explained anti-Semitism and the need for a Jewish homeland from a modern socialist viewpoint. His ideas became a basic part of modern Zionism—and indeed of all modern democratic countries.

"The proper, the only remedy is the creation of a Jewish nation, of a people living on its own soil, the auto-emancipation of the Jews."

Leo Pinsker (Russia, 1821-1891). His pamphlet, *Auto-Emancipation* (freeing yourself by your own efforts), had a powerful influence on Jews, especially the youth. His challenging "Now or never!" appeal pumped new vigor into Zionist groups.

HONOR ROLL

Justice, fair play, equality were demanded by all right-minded people. But at the same time, anti-Semitic writers, politicians, and churchmen were poisoning the people's minds. Jews must be kept in their "place," not allowed to have jobs or become businessmen or enter the professions, not permitted to "mingle" or gain equal rights. In the Middle Ages, Jews were encouraged and sometimes even forced to turn Christian, to become like everyone else, and so end their "inferior" situation. Now, they were "evil by birth," by "something in their blood." They could only be enslaved or exterminated.

A minority everywhere, scattered among many nations, Jews were easy to criticize and attack. Who would defend them or speak up for them? They had no government, no army or ambassadors. The answer, said the Zionists, was a land of their own. Here, they would be a living example of Jewish ability and character, an answer to the false charges of the anti-Semites. Jews living among the other nations could no longer be called "different" or "homeless." A nation, a government, would speak for them, defend them, give them a home if they needed one.

The New Challenge

The other danger our people faced was assimilation—neglect of Jewish life and learning. The main cause of this was the new freedom. Jews no longer lived separately in ghettos. Jews, in many lands, could hold jobs or own business firms that once were denied to them. Modern life brought Jews and Christians closer together as citizens of the same country. Many differences between them were bound to rub off.

Some Jews left Judaism altogether and converted to Christianity, hoping thus to advance socially or in their careers. Others tried to imitate Christians in every possible way, hoping *that* would make them more acceptable. Still others lost interest in Jewish life and religion.

The Zionists were especially worried that the unique ideas and customs of our people might be lost as Jews forgot more and more of their heritage. Only a Jewish homeland in Palestine, they said, would preserve Jewish unity, Jewish character. Only there could true Judaism survive. And only there could Jews, as Jews, become a truly modern people like other peoples.

Zionism was a program of action for Jews who did not want other people to decide what should happen to them as Jews. Zionism was a political *and* a religious movement. Zionists wanted not only a

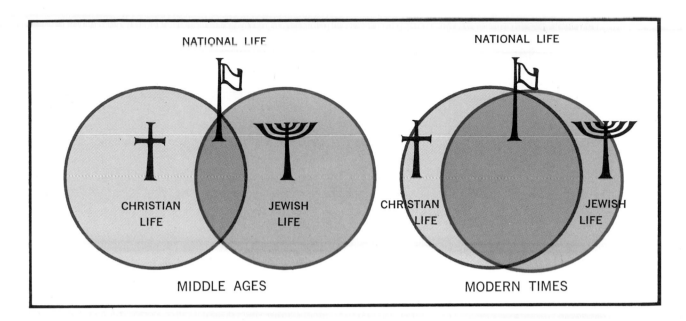

NATIONAL LIFE

CHRISTIAN
LIFE

JEWISH
LIFE

MIDDLE AGES

NATIONAL LIFE

CHRISTIAN
LIFE

JEWISH
LIFE

MODERN TIMES

Jewish State where Jews could govern themselves—they also wanted a land of social equality and economic justice according to the ideals of the Bible prophets and later Jewish leaders. Zionists were determined to revive Hebrew as the everyday Jewish language, to create a new Hebrew literature as Jews once did with the Bible and the Talmud.★

★ Why did most Zionists insist that the Jewish homeland could be established *only* in Palestine?

The Final Push

Toward the end of the 1880's, three out of every four Jews in the world lived in Eastern Europe—Russia and Poland. Russia was still a medieval, tyrannical country that did not grant freedom or citizenship to Jews. Instead, the government tried for a century to make life so miserable for Jews that they would have to turn Christian, or leave the country, or perish. The government forcibly moved Jews out of their villages and towns into overcrowded cities, imposed special taxes, banned them from the best jobs and universities.

The coming of modern industry also hurt the Russian Jews. Most Jews had earned a living as craftsmen and small traders. But now their little workshops were replaced by machines in the factories. Factory owners refused to hire Jews, giving preference to village peasants. Before railroads came, for example, many Jews were coach drivers, teamsters, innkeepers. Their jobs and business places were ruined by modern transportation.

Try This: You are a Zionist in Europe about the year 1890, arguing with two other Jews. One believes in complete assimilation, the other in revolutions to set up new governments. How would you defend your own Zionist ideas? With other pupils, present this debate for your class.

Peretz Smolenskin (Russia, 1842-1885). A widely-read Hebrew writer, he especially influenced Jewish young people all over Europe to become Zionists.

Sir Moses Montefiore (England, 1784-1885). He used his enormous wealth to support the new Jewish colonies in Palestine.

Edmond De Rothschild (France, 1845-1934). From 1890-1905, he supported financially nearly all the struggling young Jewish settlements in Palestine.

HONOR ROLL

Both persecution and poverty became worse when the Russian Tzar was assassinated by revolutionaries in 1881. The government blamed all Russia's troubles on the Jews. New laws in 1882 put crushing restrictions on where Jews could live and prevented them from moving anywhere within the country. They could not own mortgages or lease land. Without special permission, they could not enter a university or follow a profession. Riots, "pogroms," broke out against the Jews—murder and destruction were encouraged by the government. Life for Russia's Jews became absolutely unbearable.

No chance here for freedom or citizenship, as in Western countries. Revolutions were not succeeding against Russian tyranny—and would not help *Jewish* life anyway. Assimilation was no answer, either. There was no modern democratic life to be part of, and besides, the government wanted conversion or nothing.

The best answer seemed to be emigration to America, the land of opportunity. Between 1880 and 1914, two million Russian Jews escaped to America, and another million arrived by 1930. In fact, most American Jews today are descendants of this huge "wave" of East European immigration.

Misery and suffering gave Zionism its biggest "push." In 1881, the First Aliyah to Palestine began—the first groups of immigrants with definite ideas about the life they wanted to lead, the Jewish country they wanted to build. Inspired by Zionism, groups of Russian and other Jews began moving to Palestine, to "build it and be rebuilt by it."

Zionism in Eastern Europe now gained more followers. Many Russian Jews felt they could lead a normal Jewish life only in Palestine. Ridiculous or impossible as this seemed to anyone else, more and more Russian Jews believed in a Jewish state in Palestine—and dreamed of going there to work for it.

Honor Roll of Zionism

Many belong on this Honor Roll—Orthodox rabbis, socialists, physicians, Hebrew writers, small groups of hardy pioneers, a few wealthy and generous men, a few high-minded Christians—and thousands upon thousands of ordinary people. Some believed from the beginning in Jewishness and a Jewish homeland. Others at first favored assimilation or revolution. Then the 1840 pogroms in Damascus and the 1880 pogroms in Russia showed them the truth about modern anti-Semitism. Some said from the first that Palestine was the only possible Jewish homeland. Others thought any land would do, but later changed their minds.

Each in his own way, for his own reasons, out of his own experiences, came to the same conclusion and built the rest of his life around it. There must be a Jewish state, in Palestine, officially approved by the world's nations, and built literally from the ground up by Jewish workers.

These men wrote pamphlets and letters, traveled among Jewish communities to speak and plead for Zionism. They raised funds, started Zionist youth clubs. Some gave their own money to buy land and provide buildings and tools. Most important of all were the young people who went to Palestine themselves. They were children of the ghetto, of merchants and peddlers. Their hands had never touched a plow, but they meant to be farmers in a rough land, to reclaim barren soil, to establish model farming villages. Through crop failures, dry spells, illness, poverty, Arab attacks, they held on —until more settlers, inspired by their magnificent example, came to help.

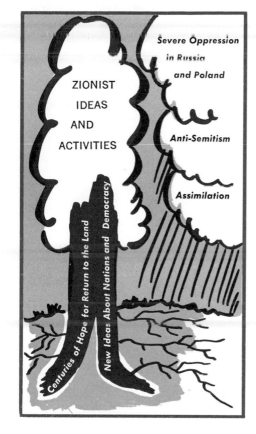

■ The "tree" of Zionism.

HAVE YOU WONDERED . . . ?

. . . where the name "Zionism" comes from?

It was suggested in 1893 by Nathan Birnbaum, a leader in the movement, to express the longing for return as well as practical action to win back the ancient homeland.

In the Bible, "Zion" originally meant the strong fort of Jerusalem which King David captured from the Jebusites. Later, the prophets and writers of Psalms used the name Zion as a symbol for all of Jerusalem, especially the Temple. This is what they meant when they said "The holy mountain of Zion," or "From Zion shall go forth the Law." "Daughter of Zion," of course, meant the whole land of Israel.

Later still, in the Middle Ages, "Zion" came to mean the whole Jewish past and future, the most precious memories and sacred hopes of the Jewish people. This is how the great medieval poet, Yehudah Halevi, used it, when in old age he wrote his magnificent "Zionide" poems—poems of sorrow and longing for Zion, the land and character and the ideals of the Jewish people.

YOU'LL ENJOY READING

The First Book of Israel, by Norah B. Kubie

YOU'LL ENJOY SEEING

Major Noah (filmstrip: Jewish Education Committee)

29

chapter 4

The Past Comes to Life

In March, 1960, an army expedition prepared to move through the canyons of a wilderness near the Dead Sea. Crack scouts flanked the unit. Helicopters whirled upward, hovered. Officers checked their heavy trucks, rock-movers, walkie-talkies, binoculars, electric generators, mine-detectors. A naval officer reported ready on his rope ladders.

The unit was not out on military maneuvers, a raid, or a manhunt. It was looking for ancient coins, arrowheads, pottery, documents. Nobody in Israel thought this a strange assignment for soldiers, or was surprised when they brought back a spectacular "find."

■ (Opposite) Archeologists explore caves and holes near Beer Sheva. How many of their tools can you identify? (Above, left) A bundle of ancient legal documents. (Above, right) Vessels used in ancient Roman religious ceremonies.

Israel's Favorite Outdoor Sport

Many Israelis spend their vacations searching fields and caves for ancient remains, or visiting a "dig" to watch archeologists at work. Thousands attend archeological lectures and conferences arranged by the government, the Hebrew University, and the Israel Exploration Society.

Farmers, construction workers, golfers, children—all watch eagerly for an old coin or piece of pottery. Israelis constantly write or visit the Hebrew University and the government's Department of Antiquities, to ask about a jar or piece of metal they have found. Important finds often begin when amateurs report a discovery to

31

★ Why all this intense excitement in Israel over the past? Why are Christians also deeply interested? Arabs? Historians?

the authorities, who then "mount" a full-scale search party. And whenever such an expedition is announced, hundreds of volunteers show up and beg to go along.

A do-it-yourself archeology book has been an Israeli best-seller. The Army has its own archeology courses, *required* for officer candidates. The Hebrew University may be the only college in the world where the campus heroes are the archeology students—because they get the first chance to volunteer for new "digs."★

You Are There!

In 1935, archeologists at Lachish, a few miles from Beer Sheva in the northern Negev, found a wall, a gate, and a room—and on the floor, many pieces of ancient pottery. Eighteen pieces had lettering on them, and became world-famous as the "Lachish Letters."

These letters were written 2,500 years ago, around 586 B.C.E., when King Zedekiah rebelled against the mighty Babylonian Empire. The prophet Jeremiah wanted to make peace with the Babylonians, to prevent total destruction of the Jewish people. But the people and their leaders did not listen to him. The Babylonian armies swept down over the entire country and besieged Jerusalem. Of all the cities of Judah, Jeremiah tells us (34:7) that only Lachish and Azekah remained as fortified cities.

The Lachish letters, written at the very moment of Jerusalem's fall, recapture for us the heartache of those fearful days.

An army officer named Hoshaiah is stationed with his men halfway between Jerusalem and Lachish, at a guardpost on the road to Egypt. Ya'osh, his superior officer at Lachish, keeps sending messages accusing Hoshaiah of showing confidential letters to members of Jeremiah's peace party—and of disobeying orders.

■ **This drawing from an ancient Assyrian relief shows Jews defending Lachish by hurling stones and flaming arrows at oncoming battering rams.**

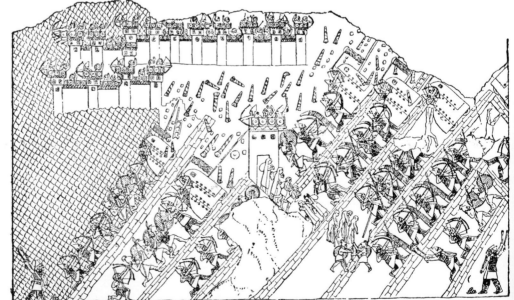

Hoshaiah writes back denial after denial. No writing materials in this last-ditch outpost—so he scratches his words on pieces of pottery. He sends a man with a letter, hoping he gets there—and that Ya'osh believes him. But back comes another biting criticism.

Alone with his men, not knowing exactly what is happening, watching smoke rise from distant Azekah and other cities, listening to rumors of destruction by the Babylonians—and death almost at hand. A "little man," powerless against the menace pressing on him from all sides, Hoshaiah begs Ya'osh for help, understanding, clearer orders. . . .

What finally happened to poor Hoshaiah? Trials in those days were held at the town gate, and court records were filed in a special chamber nearby—just the kind of place where Hoshaiah's letters were found. Was he recalled to Lachish to face court martial? Were the letters part of the evidence at his trial? Nobody knows. And was Hoshaiah judged innocent or guilty? What became of him afterward? Out of the distant past his frantic cry comes to us—but we don't know how it was answered.

But we do know that this Lachish region is one of the world's oldest battlegrounds. Here, Joshua attacked the Canaanites, Samson fought the Philistines, the shepherd boy David struck down the giant Goliath. Later, King David made Lachish the keystone of his southern defense system for the country. And now, in modern Israel, Lachish is again a keystone in the country's defense.

Here Israel planned a whole region in advance, to settle new immigrants in a more orderly way. It was also designed to connect the Jerusalem "corridor" with the Negev and strengthen the border against another Arab invasion. Major fighting occurred here during the 1948–49 war—a logical place for an enemy to try to split the country, and for a strong settlement to hold them back.

■ Hazor—one of Israel's largest and most scientific "digs." Why have the archeologists excavated in squares, and left thick walls between them? Read about Hazor in Joshua 11:10-15 and I Samuel 9:15.

Is the Bible Accurate?

Hoshaiah's letters show that events mentioned in the Book of Jeremiah actually happened. Such a find refutes scholars who question the Bible's accuracy about history and geography.

Thousands of clay tablets, other writings, household objects, tombs, monuments, sculptures—all agree exactly with Bible details about our ancestors' earliest homes, their travels, the way they lived. They prove that the Bible account of Moses and the Exodus from Egypt is based on facts. According to the Bible, Joshua conquered the town of Hazor, and King Solomon rebuilt it 300 years later. Hazor has been found, a Canaanite city destroyed, and an Israelite city rebuilt, at exactly the place and dates given in the Bible.

Try This: Start your own archeological map of Israel—on the bulletin board, or in your notebook. Mark Lachish, and beside it, print a sentence or two of your own about Hoshaiah's letters. As you read on, do the same for other great finds.

No archeological find has ever contradicted the Bible.

—Nelson Glueck, President of Hebrew Union
College-Jewish Institute of Religion.

Another Bible place often questioned by some scholars is "the pool of Gibeon," where King David fought a bloody battle with Saul's son. But archeologists found, at an Arab village called El Jib, near Jerusalem, both the name "Gibeon" and the pool itself.

Scholars once insisted that the Bible's measurements for King Solomon's various buildings are greatly exaggerated. At Megiddo in 1929, excavators found one of his huge stables, big enough for at least 400 horses. An exciting 1960 discovery, just outside Jerusalem, was an ancient fort. Archeologists had to dig down through a medieval church and a Roman bath-house to find it. It turned out to be the "palace" mentioned in II Chronicles 26:21, where King Uzziah lived out his life in lonely seclusion after being struck with leprosy.

Try This: Add the places just mentioned to your archeological map—again with a sentence or two of your own for each. To locate the places, ask your librarian for a Bible atlas.

Bible Detectives

Archeologists say they explore Israel with a trowel in one hand and the Bible in the other. The trowel is for digging in the soil, the Bible is to figure out *where* to dig. Neither job is easy!

Bible "detective work" means constant searching for references to unknown places, matching a phrase here and a phrase there, poring over maps, questioning native Arabs, reading and rereading reports of earlier archeologists—sometimes years of investigation before starting to dig. Archeologists looking in this way for King Solomon's mines gradually narrowed down their possible location to one specific region: Wadi Aravah (Valley of the Desert). This is a gigantic canyon stretching from the southern end of the Dead Sea down to the Gulf of Aqaba.

In 1932, an expedition explored the entire length and breadth of this region. At a place the Arabs called "Copper Ruin," evidence turned up of a huge copper mining center of Solomon's time and after, about 1,000–600 B.C.E. Diggers found iron and copper deposits, mines, and many small furnaces for refining the metal.

At Ezion-Geber, near the Red Sea, the expedition uncovered the largest copper furnaces of ancient times. Here the ore was manufactured into bricks and useful objects in an ingeniously constructed factory. Winds coming down the valley from the north blew directly

Try This: Want to play "Bible detective"? Here are verses from which archeologists deduced the logical place to hunt for Solomon's mines. Look up each one, and explain why they added up to the Wadi Aravah in the Negev:

I Samuel 13:19   Judges 4:11
Nehemiah 11:35   Numbers 21:9
Deuteronomy 8:9   I Kings 9:26
Genesis 4:22

Add to your archeology map of Israel. See your librarian for a good modern map.

into air channels, which forced a draft right into the furnace room. From the seaport, the factory's products were shipped all over the then known world. The whole region was one of the biggest metal-working operations of ancient times—"the Pittsburgh of Palestine."

Today, up-to-date mines, refineries, and factories repeat the whole operation. And from Eilat, Israel's modern port city, Israel again ships metals and minerals to the countries of Asia and Africa.

The Wilderness That Never Was

Exploring the whole Aravah canyon took many years. Meanwhile, archeologists investigated the rest of the Negev.

Could that dry, desolate country ever have supported civilized human beings? Tantalizing remarks in the Bible hinted that it did. In 1952, expeditions began exploring every single square mile of the Negev. Finds over the next few years proved that several different civilizations had once inhabited this wilderness.

■ Israeli soldier helps Hebrew University students search for coins and vessels of brass and copper. What military instrument is he using?

Two thousand years before Abraham, about 4000 B.C.E., an ancient people lived there, with farms, animals, shops for crafts and metal-work. In Abraham's time, too, about 2000 B.C.E., settlements thrived there. The most interesting of the Negev's ancient peoples were the Nabateans. Learning about them made a vital difference to Israel's plans for the future.

The Nabateans lived in the Negev for 400 years, from about 200 B.C.E. to 200 C.E. A prosperous people, originally from Arabia, they became the best water engineers in this part of the world. They built hillside channels to catch rain water and drain it slowly down to their reservoirs, losing hardly a drop. They walled off dry river-beds, to force spring rains to sink in instead of washing the soil away. They tilled large farms, supplying all their own foods. Over 300 of their towns, many protected by strong forts, profited from business with passing caravans.

The Romans eventually conquered the Nabateans and annexed their land. Later wars ruined the country. The Nabateans died out, and the desert sand slowly buried their cities and forts, their farms and waterworks.

Archeologists say only a few of the Bible's clues have been used so far, and great new discoveries are yet to come. The "manna" the Israelites ate in the wilderness after escaping from Egypt, the ruins of the wicked cities of Sodom and Gomorrah, Solomon's fabulous gold mines of Ophir, the five cities of the Philistines—can these be found? Only time—and archeology—will tell!

Try This: A second chance to play "Bible detective": look up these verses that led to the discovery of the Nabateans, and connect them as the archeologists did.

I Kings 5:5	I Kings 10:1-2
I Kings 8:65	I Kings 10:28-29
I Chronicles 26:10	

Add to your archeology map the Nabatean cities of Subeita and Avdat, with sentences of your own about them.

Pathways to Understanding

A few years before Israel became a state, dealers in antiquities, and Jewish and Christian scholars, heard startling rumors. Mysterious scrolls of ancient writing had turned up in the caves of Qumran, near the north end of the Dead Sea—in the Kingdom of Jordan, where Jews were not allowed to enter. But Hebrew University scholars managed to trace one scroll. They bought it through secret negotiations with an Arab dealer, on the very day in 1947 that the United Nations declared Israel an independent Jewish State. The writing on this scroll turned out to be 2,000 years old.

In the next few years, rumors spread of more scrolls being found. For Israelis, they were something "special." A Jewish State was being born. And these documents had been written and hidden away during the last independent Jewish State. They *must* belong to Israel! And so, even during the war with Arab invaders, the government and the Hebrew University tracked down seven of the scrolls—sometimes through luck, sometimes through patient detective work in many countries, including the United States. They raised the money to buy the scrolls for Israel.

The scrolls include Bible books, commentaries, psalms. One predicts a war between "The Children of Light" (Israel) and "The Children of Darkness" (their enemies). Another is an alphabetical guide to help beginners learn to read.

The scrolls were written about 100 B.C.E., and were buried in the caves about 150 years afterward. They were the "library" of a community of Jews—men, women, children—living at Qumran, about sixteen miles from Jerusalem. These people wanted to keep apart from the rest of the world, and devote their lives to study and worship. They were Essenes—a group you have studied in Jewish history—or a similar community.

The scrolls give us a clearer picture of such ancient Jewish groups. Before finding the scrolls, for example, historians knew nothing about these groups directly—only remarks about them in other books.

The Qumran Jews believed the end of the world was coming soon, and they must get ready for it by practicing a sinless life. They stressed cleanliness through purification ceremonies in pools of water, and celebrated a holy meal of wine and bread. They had no private property; everything belonged to the group. They ate, prayed, studied together—singing psalms, listening to the reading and explanation of the Bible. They wrote new literature about their beliefs, and about a great teacher who started their community—a new "chosen people," who had a "new covenant" with God.

The early Christians were at first a group within Judaism who conducted their lives much like the Qumran people. The scrolls show how Christianity was a "child" of Judaism—it grew out of Jewish life, was influenced by Jewish ideas.

What finally happened to the Qumran community? Why did they hide away their library of scrolls? Archeological evidence, and remarks in the scrolls themselves, give us a hint. Between 67 and 70 C.E., the Jews, in a war of independence against the Romans, were defeated only after bitter fighting. Roman legions besieged Jerusalem, and their patrols scoured the countryside. The Qumran community feared for its safety. The people decided to go north to Damascus, in Syria, to live with another group of their own faith. To preserve their sacred writings, they wrapped them tightly in linen, sealed them in jars, and buried the jars deep in hard-to-find caves. After the war, they thought, they would return, resume their quiet life of holiness and cleanliness. But they never came back— we don't know why. The writings remained hidden for nearly 1,900 years.

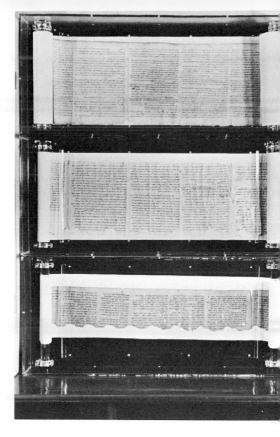

■ **Three of the Dead Sea Scrolls: (top to bottom) Rules of the community for meals, work, study; Book of Isaiah, written a few hundred years after he lived; commentary on Habbakuk, another Bible prophet.**

Try This: Look up Masora in Jewish encyclopedias and history books. Draw up a brief statement about the Bible scholars who took this name: when they lived, what they did and why, what we owe them today. How are they connected with the Dead Sea scrolls and the Lachish letters?

Add to your archeology outline map.

Operation Bar Kochba

The army expedition, with helicopters, mine-detectors, and walkie-talkies, gave Israel another thrilling adventure in Jewish history.

We have many legends about Shimon Bar Kochba, who led a Jewish revolt against the Romans in 132–135 C.E.—but few proven facts. According to the Talmud, Bar Kochba, through tough guerrilla tactics, captured fifty towns from the Roman legions. But Roman reinforcements poured in, and the Jewish fighters retreated, with their families, to caves near the southern part of the Dead Sea. The Romans blocked all valleys leading out of the wilderness and waited for the rebels to surrender or starve. Finally, when the Romans ventured in, they found only dead bodies in the caves.

Did all this really happen? Was there really a Bar Kochba, and were people really willing to die for him? Did Jewish families really hole up in the caves for weeks and months?

In 1952, rumors spread that Arabs were stealing across the Jordan border, "working" Israeli caves and making valuable finds. A Hebrew University archeological team made some "probes" over the next few years, and found remains of ancient food, clothing, tools, also a Roman army camp.

Then, in 1960, an anonymous tip came in from "an American friend," who had been in Jordan. The Arabs, he reported, were making their finds closer to the border. The University team moved into the wild, almost unreachable cliffs near Ein Gedi.

Here they found a vulture's nest built partly out of bits of parchment, papyrus, and phylacteries (Tefillin), with Bible verses and lists of Hebrew names. And a coin labeled "Shimon Prince of Israel" and "Herut Lirushalayim" (freedom for Jerusalem). They also found remains of clothing, food, arrowheads, human bones, and a chess piece, all dating from about 135 C.E.!

The "dig" invited danger from Arab snipers. It was a region of sudden dust storms and pelting rains, of freezing nights and scorching days, of poisonous snakes and dangerous falls. Cliffs were vertical, or leaning outward, without footholds or ledges. The job needed military discipline, plus scientific and engineering skill. So now the government took over, with a unit of ninety soldiers and eighty volunteers from the university and nearby farm settlements.

At first, they found only skulls, olive-pits, bits of parchment, an arrowhead, a coin. Then, deep under the rocky soil, they found a palm-leaf basket containing Roman objects, with designs of gods and animals deliberately hammered, and scraped away. Bar Kochba's fighters had raided the Roman camp, snatched their equipment, then tried to destroy "graven images" that violated the Second Commandment.

1968. The most spectacular archeological "dig" in modern Israel began in 1963 at Masada, site of King Herod's palaces and the last Jewish stronghold in the revolt against the Romans, 70 C.E. Excavators found synagogues, baths, manuscripts, etc. You'll enjoy seeing the Union of American Hebrew Congregations filmstrip on Masada, based on the book, "Masada, Herod's Fortress and the Zealots' Last Stand," by Yigael Yadin, Israel's leading archeologist and former Army chief.

■ Helicopters photographed openings too hard for Arab smugglers to see or reach. Then volunteers went down by rope from cliff tops. Men on opposite cliffs, equipped with binoculars and two-way radio, guided the dangerous journeys past bulges and overhangs.

■ **This letter establishes Bar Kochba's true name as Bar Kosiba. Look up the story of his name in a Jewish encyclopedia or history book.**

And in a deep hole beyond a narrow slit in a cavern wall, they found a battered goatskin bottle. It had belonged to a woman, for it contained beads, cosmetics, a mirror—and a small bundle of papyrus tightly tied with twisted palm-leaves.

Prince of Israel

Two months after the find, scholars published eleven letters from Bar Kochba to his officers written in Hebrew, Aramaic, and Greek.

Bar Kochba himself dictated these letters, 1,800 years ago, to scribes who wrote them on small bits of parchment. In one letter, Bar Kochba criticizes his commanders: "You and the people of Ein Gedi sit, eat, and drink the property of the House of Israel, but do not concern yourselves about supplies for your comrades in arms." In another, he orders that *lulav* and *etrog* be provided to the troops to celebrate the festival of Sukkot, and that the Levites are to be given a tenth of all fruits as required in the Bible. Another letter asks for more supplies, and orders the arrest of a certain person. "Don't forget," Bar Kochba adds, "he has a sword. Take it and send him to me." Still another letter mentions lovingly a certain teacher or rabbi, apparently famous in those days but never heard of before in Jewish history.

Some officer or scribe saved these letters, out of respect for Bar Kochba or for his military records. He took them along to the hideout in the caves. Then, knowing the end was in sight for them all, he hid them in a woman's kit, thinking the Romans would never search there. Or perhaps a woman collected the letters, and hid them away at the bottom of her own personal "bag."

Try This: You are one of the fast-weakening fighters in the Ein Gedi caves. Write a letter to Bar Kochba, explaining the situation, your raids on the Roman camp, and your reason for preserving his letters. Be sure to look up Masada in Jewish encyclopedias or history books, and refer to it in your letter —it would be in the minds of the dying heroes, as something similar happened there sixty-five years before.

Bar Kochba, in these letters, is exactly as the Talmud describes him: a man of action but of few words, tough, strict, efficient, with deep religious feeling, who sought the advice of learned rabbis, and struggled not only with the Romans but with his own followers.

The Bar Kochba finds were displayed in Israel's museums. The skeletons in the caves were given a full military burial as heroes of Israel. You can imagine the emotions of the Israelis, and of Jews the world over.

The Past That Never Dies

At Hebron, near Lachish, in 1961, a new building was going up on a hillside. A worker fell through soft ground into an underground burial cave. On the wall, someone had hurriedly scratched three human figures, two sailboats, and these words: "The Lord God of the whole earth, the mountains of Judah belong to Him, to the God of Jerusalem."

The phrase "God of Jerusalem" occurs just once in the Bible, in describing how the Assyrians besieged Jerusalem and conquered the country in 722 B.C.E. Was the writer someone escaping from the Assyrians, hiding out in a cave to avoid capture and death? Someone who scratched on the rock wall his defiant last words of faith?

A still later find is the oldest Hebrew letter in existence, dating back nearly 3,000 years. Someone had lent money to a poor farmer and had taken his cloak as security. Now, the moneylender would not return the cloak. The Hebrew peasant was asking his Hebrew prince—both of them *your* ancestors—to see that justice was done as the Bible commands. (Exodus 22:25-56; Deuteronomy 24:12-13).★

■ It takes Hebrew University expert, Prof. H. Bieberkraut, days of patient, grueling work with special tools to open an ancient scroll.

★ From these finds, what is there in common between the ancient and the modern people of Israel?

Finish up your archeology outline map of Israel.

YOU'LL ENJOY READING

Caves of Riches, by Alan Honour
The Great Discovery, by Azriel Eisenberg
The Land and People of Israel, by Gail Hoffman
Voices from the Past, by Azriel Eisenberg

YOU'LL ENJOY SEEING

Digging for Buried Treasure (filmstrip: Union of American Hebrew Congregations)

chapter 5

Israel's Wild West

■ Statue of a Warsaw Ghetto fighter stands before the water tower of the Kibbutz Yad Mordechai, whose fighters helped save the Negev for Israel.

The Magic South

Like America a hundred years ago, Israel has a wild frontier—but it's in the South.

הַנֶּגֶב—the Negev, a region of lifeless deserts, jagged mountains, and deep canyons, has the same magic for Israelis as the West had for Americans. The thrill of desert adventure, the challenge of taming a wilderness, the battle of man against nature, the heroism of the Negev's pioneers—all this fires the imagination of the entire country. For years, Israelis have had a favorite song—*Hay Daromah Le-Eilat*—Southward, Ho, to Eilat—just as Americans, lining up their covered wagons, shouted "Westward, ho!"

Winning the Negev

Long ago, this beautiful, rugged land was a place of caravan routes, mines, factories, homes. Later, it had cities, forts, even farms. But it was conquered in turn by the Romans, the Arabs, and the Turks, and was destroyed. For centuries, sun and sand took over. In this lifeless desert, only nomads lived, with their camels and goats. And that is how the Negev would still be if not for the courage and determination of the Israelis.

Under British control, Jews could not buy land there. Britain wanted the Negev for herself, to protect her military bases in the Middle East. But Palestine's Jews were already looking ahead. They set up three small settlements south of Beer Sheva to study soil and climate, and experiment with farming. In 1947, twenty-seven Negev villages had only six hundred Jews altogether. Then, while

■ American cowboys herd "dogies" in Israel. Two Texas cow-punchers, with graduate degrees in agriculture, have cross-bred American, Arabian, and Israeli stock for stronger, heavier cattle. On government ranches in the Negev, in the Galil, or near Haifa, farmers can "learn the ropes" in a six-months course, then start their own "spread." Purpose: more and better meat for Israel's families.

Hanegev: הַנֶּגֶב

	1948	TODAY
Arad	Rock, sand, and the remains of ancient buried cities	About 24,000 people . . . factories making porcelain, cement, marble, chemicals, knit-wear . . . modern hotel . . . rest-home for Histadrut construction workers
Beer Sheva	Small trading post on the desert rim . . . one paved street, a few meager shops, and one Jew — a doctor	"Boom town" capital of the Negev, grow-ing at great speed . . . about 65,000 people, housing projects, civic center, plumbing, pottery, glassware factories using the Negev's raw materials
Dimona	Ugly, desolate wilderness, site of town mentioned in Book of Joshua. The name means garbage or dump pile	About 19,000 people . . . textile factories . . . modern homes, schools, shopping cen-ters . . . the Negev's first vocational school . . . Israel's first atomic reactor.
Mizpeh-Ramon	Mid-point of the Negev . . . rock, sun, heat, and not much else	Cheerful town of over 1,500 people . . . paved streets, green lawns, school, His-tadrut supermarket . . .
Yotvata	In the Aravah, 120-mile flat rock canyon, the most miserable wilderness of the en-tire Negev . . . an army outpost and tiny experimental farm	Flourishing Kibbutz settlement, with mod-ern apartment buildings and lawns, large cattle herds, chicken flocks.
Eilat	Two huts on the seashore	Booming seaport . . . tourist attraction . . . about 10,000 people working in mines and factories, on docks and fishing boats

NEGEV
ARAVAH

- Arad
- Beer Sheva
- Dimona
- Mizpeh-Ramon
- Yotvata
- Eilat

1967. And still another round in the Six Day War (see Chapter 25).

★ Why were Israeli leaders so eager to get and keep the Negev? (Hint: Look through Chapter 2.)

the nations debated what to do with Palestine, eleven new Jewish settlements went up in the Negev, all in one night. Such bold pioneering impressed the United Nations. In the partition of Pal-estine between Jews and Arabs, the Negev went to the Jews.

But they still had to fight for it. Egypt's army attacked, cut the Negev off from the rest of Israel. From shelters and fox-holes, the Jewish villagers defended themselves. Finally, they drove the in-vaders back, having lost only one village. In 1949, Israel's soldiers swept down through the Negev. They raised their flag, with its Star of David, on the white, coral sand of Eilat, the southernmost tip.

One more round had to be fought to secure the Negev's borders. From Egyptian forts, and with Russian weapons, trained guerrilla fighters slipped across the border into Israel. They slaughtered peo-ple and animals, burned down homes, ruined crops and water-towers. In 1956, Israel struck back. Her hundred-hour Sinai Campaign drove the Egyptians almost to the Suez Canal. One spectacular deed was a 150-mile drive by an Israel column down the eastern side of the Negev, dragging vehicles and big guns over thick sand and sharp mountain ridges. They surprised and captured an Egyptian garrison blocking Israel's ships from the Red Sea.★

Boom Town

Though still unfinished, Beer Sheva is well planned, with five neighborhoods around the heart of the city. An industrial zone produces glassware, plumbing, and pottery from the Negev's own raw materials. Most important are the millions of newly-planted trees—a far cry from Abraham's one small orchard 4,000 years ago!

"Boom town" Beer Sheva is lively and gay. Three-fourths of its people came to Israel after World War II—a cross-section of Israel's "ingathering of exiles." Men from the potash works, phosphate mines, oil wells, road construction camps, add to the noise, color, and excitement. The camel station in the older section contrasts with the new movie and swimming pool. A modern shopping center competes with the bazaars on the old main street. Only two hours by car from Tel Aviv—yet the town has the look of distant frontiers, the feeling of warmth and hospitality, of energy spilling over. The mayor goes around in shirtsleeves, and every one calls him by his first name.

Beer Sheva's proud citizens call it "Capital of the Negev." Some day, they predict, it will be Israel's largest city, after Tel Aviv.

Try This· Read Genesis 21:31-33 and 26:32-33, and the article on Beer Sheva in *The Jewish Encyclopedia*. Write the Hebrew name of the city on the board, and tell the class what you think the name means—and why.

■ **Open-air cafe in Beer Sheva.**

"Lords of the Desert"

On Thursday mornings, the past returns to Beer Sheva—it is market day for the Bedouin nomad tribes of the nearby wilderness. Characters that seem to step right out of the Bible barter noisily over camels and other animals. It might be the Indian trading-post of America's old West—except that here the bargaining is much tougher, and the women are veiled and dressed in black, the men in sweeping, colorful robes and white head-dress.

About 30,000 of these desert nomads roam the Negev's open spaces. They live in goatskin tents and herd their goats, camels, and Arab horses pretty much as their ancestors did all the way back to the time of Abraham. They have resisted many attempts to get them to accept modern government. Each of their five tribes governs itself according to traditional desert laws carried out by a court of "elders." They do not want to stay put anywhere, to exchange tents for houses. Plant a little wheat somewhere, then move on, come back later for the sparse harvest—this is the life they like. It is a never-ending battle against wilderness hardships—the dry spells when sand fills the water-holes, the murderous famines, the diseases that destroy their animals and their children. Reluctantly, when they must, they accept food, water, fodder, and jobs from Israel's government.

Can these restless, primitive "lords of the desert" become farmers and city people? That is the aim of the government. Their tribal feuds and their constant moving about interfere with Israel's plans to develop the Negev. Their herds damage the fields and block the roads. Their smuggling operations take them back and forth across Israel's borders. Fortunately, the Bedouin are friendly and loyal to Israel, and pay little attention to Arab propaganda against her.

Israel brings water to them as well as to Jewish settlers. Fences and green fields are beginning to cover the open spaces, and slowly but surely the wild desert gets tamed. The nomads watch an Israeli tractor doing the work of twenty camel-drawn plows, and they try out the "new-fangled" contraption. Already their crops and flocks have multiplied several times over since 1948.

Mobile health clinics bring them doctors, nurses, medicines, and smallpox and polio injections. Their tuberculosis rate has dropped sharply. When any group settles down, Israel provides schools for the children, who learn new things, new ways. Younger Bedouin from different tribes form Israeli-style cooperatives to farm, buy, and sell together. A few even join the Histadrut, Israel's big labor organization. Their puzzled families try to understand sick funds, workmen's compensation, minimum wages, cost-of-living increases.

Only in Israel

The Bedouin have a magnificent sense of humor. Once a group sent a petition to the government to hold elections once a year instead of every four years.

Puzzled officials sent a representative to ask the Bedouin what they had in mind. With straight faces, they explained they had noticed something strange about the water pipeline coming down from the Yarkon River. It seemed to get extended farther into the Negev only in election years. If elections came four times as often, wouldn't they get water four times as fast?

■ **Market day at Beer Sheva.**

Progressive sheikhs accept the government's offer to lease them land for permanent settlement for only a few cents a year. They forget their tribal feuds and seek justice in Israel courts. More Bedouin traders appear in Beer Sheva wearing shoes. Smugglers no longer slip rifles, camels, and goats to their kinsmen in Jordan and Egypt —now it's shaving cream, wash-and-wear shirts, transistor radios.

Sheikhs have begun buying bicycles and TV sets. The first Bedouin sheikh to build a stone home—near Beer Sheva, in 1962— entertained at his housewarming all the other sheikhs, many Arab leaders, and government officials. That same year, the first Bedouin student enrolled in the Hebrew University—to study medicine and go back to his people in the Negev as the first Bedouin doctor. A year later, a Bedouin tribe, camped near the Dead Sea, started a library with a hundred books donated by the Histadrut Labor Federation.

What a struggle for these picturesque people to give up their old ways! They still won't let girls go to school, and most fathers still want their sons to work rather than study. But Israel's gentle ways, so different from our own country's treatment of the Indians, are hard to resist. Once, the British tried to take a census and were chased off by enraged Bedouin, waving their guns threateningly. A few years ago, in an Israel national election, 2,500 Bedouin came into the towns to vote.

Try This: Look up Indians in a general encyclopedia or an American history book. Report to the class, or design a poster, comparing our treatment of the Indians with Israel's treatment of the Bedouins. Or, pretend you are a Bedouin school boy, learning American history, and make the comparison as if writing a letter to an American pen-pal.

Pioneers—Negev-Style

The Negev's new towns and settlements are prosperous and comfortable today—but their people can recall many early fears, heartaches, failures.

Dimona, for example, twenty miles southeast of Beer Sheva, got off to a bad start. This new town was to provide mountain homes for factory workers at unbearably hot S'dom. Immigrant families from North Africa were also sent to live there and work in the factories. The two groups did not get along. The newcomers especially were appalled by the wild, lonely surroundings. People began to mock the name Dimona, saying it should be changed to Dimyona—"pipe-dream." The whole project nearly collapsed in quarrels and disorder.

But wiser heads took charge, and the government stepped in to help. The people stuck it out. Today, Dimona is peaceful. Its proud citizens confidently expect it to become Israel's leading garment center.

And Israel had learned a valuable lesson. In Arad, twenty-five miles northeast of Dimona, and also a rugged wilderness, immigrants settled in a new town without fear or anger. They found 200 Israelis waiting for them—veteran skilled workers who had given up easy life elsewhere and volunteered to help the newcomers. Friendly guidance made the newcomers feel at home more quickly, and face the future with more faith and patience. Arad soon became an important industrial center for the mineral-rich Dead Sea region.

Not long ago, on trucks piled high with furniture, toys, and pets, seventy young adults left Tel Aviv. Married couples with children, bachelors and single girls, painters, government officials, aircraft mechanics, bus drivers—all bored with routine jobs, city life, an unexciting future. They headed south, past Beer Sheva, to Mitzpeh-Ramon, an empty spot deep in the heart of the Negev. With the help of a government loan, they were going to establish Israel's first cooperative *city*—in contrast to a cooperative farm settlement like the Kibbutz or Moshav. They planned to build homes, and a factory to make parts for TV sets. The idea caught on, and several hundred other young people rushed to join them.

■ Even the Bedouin nomads avoid the wild, desolate Aravah canyon on the eastern Negev border. Yet here seventy young men and women soldiers established Kibbutz Yotvata. In blistering heat, some worked lime into the sand to make soil for crops. Others toiled in the nearby Timna copper mines, or guarded oil and water pipelines. Why is seventy such a popular number with Israeli settlers? Why is it vital for Israel to populate the Aravah?

48

But the idea of a cooperative city did not work out, and Israel had no television as yet. The original group broke up. The government took over, reorganizing the new town along more usual lines. It began to grow and prosper. Bus and car travelers from Tel Aviv to Eilat stop at Mitzpeh-Ramon for lunch, rest, and to enjoy a lively modern town in the midst of wasteland.

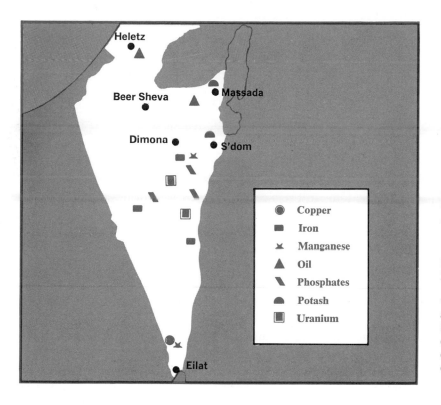

■ Negev resources. Israel is one of the few countries in the world—and the only one between the Dead Sea and Japan—with all the resources for producing phosphates, nitrates, and potash—the three main types of modern chemical fertilizers. The Dead Sea is twenty-five per cent solid matter—the thickest water on earth. When the water evaporates in the great heat, valuable minerals and chemicals are left behind. Israel produces enough potash to supply the whole world for hundreds of years. Europe alone now buys three-fourths of the Dead Sea fertilizers, which are also shipped as far as Japan and South America. Minerals and chemicals make possible large factories producing synthetics, plastics, fertilizers, dyes, explosives, cement, and many other products.

Prospecting in the Negev

In the Negev, the boiling days and freezing nights are so bad that workers need a rest cure somewhere else every six weeks. For centuries "experts" considered the Negev a completely hopeless, empty land—"impossible" to live in, with nothing to work *for*.

But precisely here, especially in and around the Dead Sea, are buried Israel's greatest sources of mineral wealth. Even during the War for Independence, Israelis surveyed the Negev for minerals and chemicals. In 1950, the government and private firms organized exploring expeditions—each a pioneer venture into unknown, dangerous territory.

49

1968. The Heletz oil field now produces about 10 per cent of Israel's oil needs. Israel now has about 40 oil wells.

Only in Israel

Israelis have a way of turning a handicap into an advantage. With the Heletz oil discovery, Israel needed more pipelines. She tried to buy these from Russia and the United States—but was turned down. Apparently, these countries were afraid to antagonize the Arab nations, who own some of the richest oil-producing lands in the world.

Israel built factories, made her own pipelines, and drilled for more oil. Within five years, Russia and the United States were buying pipelines from Israel!

■ **Copper mines at Timna.**

And they paid off, with a long list of discoveries still going on. Around S'dom, the Bible's wicked city that went up in fire and brimstone, flame and smoke climb skyward from modern potash works and chemical plants. Down along the eastern side of the Negev, new mines, refineries, and factories have sprung up.

In 1955 came one of the Negev's most thrilling moments, after seven years of hard searching and huge outlays of money. The whole country went wild at the news—oil had gushed from a mile-deep well at Heletz, just north of the Negev.

Children by the truckloads, and every grown-up who could get away, rushed down to see for themselves, and fill up a souvenir bottle of Israeli oil. Around the gusher itself, excited workers danced, sang, poured oil over their heads. Soon other gushers came in nearby—and still more. When Chanukah arrived that year, a giant menorah at Heletz burned native oil.

Oil—vital for modern machines, vehicles, weapons—is scarce in Israel. The more she gets from her own soil, the less she has to buy from other countries. And so Israelis probe and dig, on land and on the sea-bottom, and rejoice every time a well brings in oil. But even with the best of luck, Israel may still have to buy most of her oil. And so her pioneers of science are exploring other frontiers.

Near Dimona stands a fence with big signs warning against entry or the taking of photographs. In the distance, a round concrete building and some barracks represent Israel's first atomic reactor. Her scientists are seeking ways to get uranium out of phosphates—of which Israel has plenty—and are prospecting for uranium itself. With enough uranium and other radioactive minerals, they can build atomic power stations. These will give plenty of cheap power, without having to depend on coal, gas, or oil. Atomic power has already made Israel the seventh nation in the world to send a research rocket into the skies.

And the desert shall rejoice, and blossom as the rose.

—Isaiah 35:1

"Water Is Life!"*

Once the Negev went four years without rain. The few plants withered away; the desert Bedouin starved. Then, suddenly, it rained—heavy, quick, as if four years of moisture had gathered in the sky for this one burst. When the rain stopped, a thick carpet of flowers appeared suddenly all over the Negev—all kinds, all colors, almost a magical sight. When word of this reached the North, Israelis went to see it. Cars choked the roads, taxis clocked large fares.

The sightseers talked and sang noisily on their way into the Negev. When they left for home, they were quieter, more thoughtful. They had seen with their own eyes a desert blooming.

In many places, Negev soil, dried out for hundreds of years, needs only water to become fertile again. But the scanty rainfall runs off the rocks and down the gullies instead of sinking into the soil. Early towns and settlements had to bring in their water in barrels from Beer Sheva. Since 1955, a pipeline from the Yarkon River in the North has brought life-giving water down into the parched Negev desert. Another pipeline from the Jordan River ties into it. This irrigation has turned thousands of acres of dry land into good soil for many new settlements and farms. But all of Israel's northern water could not supply the whole thirsty Negev.

Israel's men of science found that certain fruits and flowers can live on salt water—if the right amount of potash is added to it. They learned how to grow corn, beets, grapes, and other crops in the desert.

In a pilot plant in Tel Aviv, Israel also pioneers in de-salting ocean water. Many nations, including the United States, suffer from water shortage, and try to get fresh water from the vast seas. Some

*Mayim chayim: מַיִם חַיִּים

■ **This equipment, at the Negev Institute for Arid Zone Research, Beer Sheva, can produce 10,000 gallons of fresh water daily from salt water. Why does Israel "push" this kind of research so hard?**

51

Try This: Make a water map of Israel, showing rivers, lakes, seas. Figure out some way to indicate that she is quite poor in water, but has good untapped resources (what are they?) which scientists are already using to increase her water supply.

experts believe Israel has the best and cheapest de-salting process. Israeli laboratories work hard at it, and Negev households are trying out a new home water de-salter.

Restoring the Negev is no longer a wild dream; some day the Negev will support itself, as in olden times. More water, new settlements, new oil, atomic power, electricity—these turn the land greener each year. Many crops cannot grow in this harsh climate—but certain ones grow better here than anywhere else. From the Negev, Israel keeps getting more wheat, barley, milk, eggs, meat, fruit, cotton, beets, and even flowers. The great Negev heat gives four vegetable crops a year, including Israel's finest peaches. Even Europeans benefit—in their winter season, they enjoy tomatoes, potatoes, and gladiolus plants shipped from the Negev.

■ **Building the Jordan-Negev water pipeline. This is Israel's part of an American engineer's water plan for the whole Middle East, approved by Israel and Arab engineers—but rejected by Arab governments.**

Eilat is a sort of nail in the southernmost part of the map. If this nail is not strong enough, the whole map of the Negev will roll up to Beer Sheva.

—"Yoskl" Levy, Mayor of Eilat, 1962

Window on the Red Sea

Eilat, at the Negev's southernmost tip, is still only a gathering of stone and wooden houses and some larger apartment buildings. The summer heat is almost unbearable; water is scarce and tastes bad. Shops are few, prices high, and life is hard. The scenery is impressive, but most of it belongs to enemy countries. The waterfront, only seven miles wide, is clamped between Egypt and Jordan, with Saudi Arabia just beyond Jordan.

But Eilatis like the mixture of international seaport and majestic desert. In the harbor they see ships from many ports, loading minerals and cement, unloading seeds, hides, and coffee, feeding oil into a pipeline running all the way up to Haifa's refineries. Behind their homes are lofty mountains and desert canyons. They have modern schools, a hospital, a cultural center.

Some are new immigrants assigned by the government. Others have come because wages are higher, and there is no income tax. But many are there as pioneers on Israel's newest frontier—building Israel just as the Chalutzim did farther north in the early days.★

★ Most Israelis, though excited over the Negev, don't want to live there. What holds them back? The government, on the other hand, encourages Negev settlement through lower taxes, higher wages, special loans, prizes for the best lawns. Why?

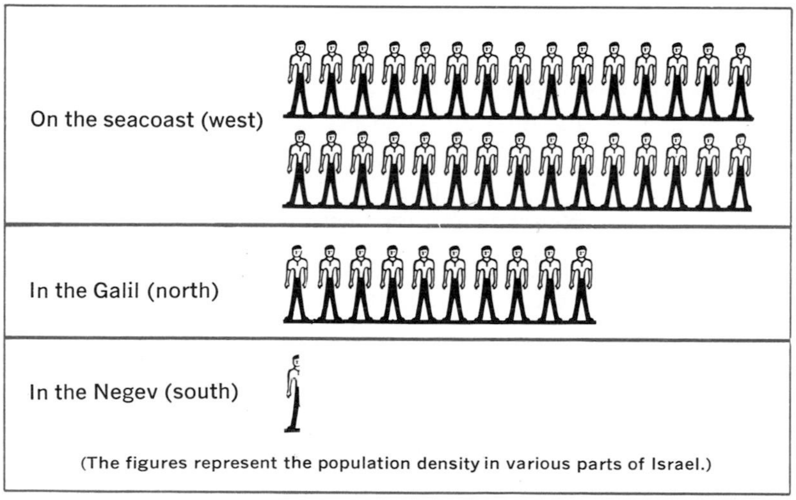

On the seacoast (west)	👤👤👤👤👤👤👤👤👤👤👤👤👤👤👤👤👤👤👤👤👤👤👤👤👤👤👤👤👤👤
In the Galil (north)	👤👤👤👤👤👤👤👤👤
In the Negev (south)	👤

(The figures represent the population density in various parts of Israel.)

■ **Where Israelis live.**

53

■ Haifa, Israel's biggest port and harbor, does fifty times as much business as Eilat, and handles most of the country's visitors, imports, and exports. Eilat's harbor business multiplies five times every year—and may yet catch up to Haifa.

The short strip of land at the tip of the Negev makes Israel a two-ocean state—front door on the Mediterranean Sea and Atlantic Ocean, back door on the Red Sea and Indian Ocean. The back door is vital for Israel's future, surrounded as she is by hostile Arab nations and blocked from the Suez Canal by Egypt. Without an ocean outlet at Eilat, Israel would have to ship her Negev minerals and chemicals to eastern countries by a long, roundabout route. Eilat's harbor means more business, trade, tourists, exchange students with eastern lands. Israel is the only state on the Mediterranean Sea with such a back door, the only one that can ship through both the Atlantic and Indian Oceans without depending on the Suez Canal. Thus, Israel once again becomes a "bridge" between East and West, as she used to be in ancient times.

The pleasant, warm winters attract many tourists and visitors from all over the world. The clear Red Sea waters and the fine beaches are ideal for swimming and sunbathing, for skin-diving and underwater fishing, for viewing brilliant coral and tropical fish through glass-bottomed boats. Eilat has good hotels, and even night clubs—Israeli-style, featuring folk songs and folk dances.

Eilatis are hardy workers, and not easily frightened by their hardships or their Arab neighbors. They work in the nearby mines, on the docks, on the fishing boats, in the factories. They ignore the present and look to the future. And they "imagine big." Their port, they say, is going to be the biggest in that part of the world—maybe some day even as big as Haifa's. They expect to take in 60,000 more people, and attract industries down from the crowded North. They intend to double and redouble Israel's world trade, and to defend Israel, at this dangerous but important spot, with their lives.

The Toughest Battle

Miracles have been accomplished in the Negev. The hot, dry waste-land retreats, green grass creeps southward, homes come, and streets and people—men, women, children, with their fears and hopes, their memories and ambitions. Big new plans are made and tried. Some fail—but most succeed.

Yet there is a long way to go, and time is short. To rebuild the Negev, Israelis admit, is their "toughest" battle yet—and they must win. For here, in the Negev, Israel's future will be decided, as America's was by her western frontier.

YOU'LL ENJOY READING

The Story of Modern Israel, by Dorothy Zeligs

YOU'LL ENJOY SEEING

The Darom and the Negev (filmstrip: Jewish Agency)
South Window (film: National Committee for Labor Israel)
A City Called Eilat (film: United Israel Appeal)

Try This: A committee project: A report or a poster, showing how the Negev *resembles* the American West, and how it *differs*. Think of size, borders, resources in the rest of the nation. In the Negev, what takes the place of Indians, burros and horses, Spanish treasures? Review this chapter *carefully* for other comparisons or contrasts. And be sure to read a fascinating article in *National Geographic* magazine, December, 1958, called "Geographic Twins a World Apart"—about one of our western states *remarkably* like the Negev.

chapter 6

How Zionism Regained a Land

This is the story of Zionism: for almost two thousand years a hopeless dream, until a people scattered among the nations took a new look at their past, present, and future. Then, in less than a century, they won back their land. To make a drug, you need various chemicals; to bake a cake, various ingredients. What do you need to rebuild a people, to establish a new State?

The Leader

First of all, a gifted leader must inspire people, shock and arouse them, put clearly into words the thoughts churning in their minds. In 1898, such a leader predicted a Jewish State within fifty years. In 1948, Israel issued her Declaration of Independence.

This immortal hero of Zionism, Theodor Herzl, worked for his people only seven short years. But he labored so hard that he wore himself out and died at the age of forty-four. He was not the first Zionist, but he was the most brilliant, the most successful.

In 1896, moved by the hatred against his people, Herzl poured out his pain and hope in a pamphlet called *The Jewish State*. But Herzl was more than a writer, more even than a man of deeds. His tremendous personality fired the imagination of millions of Jews. He created the second thing an idea needs to come true: a successful movement or organization.

"If you will it, it is no dream."

Theodor Herzl (Austria, 1860-1904). Founder of modern political Zionism.

■ **(Left, above) Herzl and his associates establishing a Zionist weekly "Die Welt."**

■ **(Below) In 1898, Herzl, leader of the new Zionist Organization, traveled to Palestine, where the young people took him to their hearts. "In fifty years," he told them, "you will be citizens of a Jewish State!"**

57

Political Zionism—Winning the Right

In 1897, Herzl called together 200 Jewish representatives from Europe, North Africa, America, and Palestine—the first Jewish world conference in history, the Zionist Congress. Men and women chosen by their fellow Jews would now meet regularly to consider the problems of their people and act upon them.

The Congress announced a bold program: persuade the world's governments to approve a Jewish homeland in Palestine; set up Zionist organizations in every land; raise funds; make all Jews feel as if they belonged to a living people; settle Jewish farm and factory workers in Palestine.

In the next few years, the new Zionist Organization began to plan ahead for a Jewish state. Excitement rose among Jews everywhere over the first steps forward: A new Jewish national anthem, הַתִּקְוָה—The Hope. A new Jewish flag, blue and white, bearing the star of David on it. The Jewish National Fund—קֶרֶן קַיֶּמֶת לְיִשְׂרָאֵל, to buy land in Palestine in the name of the whole Jewish people. A new Hebrew University. Laws of all kinds to make the Jewish state a model of democracy and social justice.

Try This: Look up the Dreyfus Affair. Present a *brief* report: who-what-where-when-why-result. Then tell, as dramatically as you can, how Herzl *felt* about this affair, and what he decided to *do* about it.

Hatikvah: הַתִּקְוָה   Keren Kayemet Leyisrael: קֶרֶן קַיֶּמֶת לְיִשְׂרָאֵל

Herzl went to see the Sultan of Turkey, the Kaiser of Germany, the Czar's prime minister, the top leaders of England and France. He wanted a charter from Turkey, which owned Palestine, allowing Jews to colonize the land. He wanted the other nations to promise to approve such a charter. Thus, the nations would officially admit Jewish rights to Palestine ("publicly recognized"), and guarantee a Jewish homeland there ("legally secured"). Only then, Herzl felt, could Zionists start large-scale settlement in the land itself.

He did not get public recognition or legal security—but he aroused the whole Jewish people to demand these things, and he forced the governments of the world to consider their situation.★

★ Skim through Chapter 4—especially the Honor Roll. Why were Herzl and other Zionist leaders now able to accomplish so much more than the earlier Zionists?

The Opposition

Some non-Jews approved of the Zionist Organization; most did not. World leaders listened politely to Herzl, promised to "consider," then did nothing. The Sultan of Turkey agreed to a 99-year charter —for twenty million dollars, a fantastic sum for those days. Herzl could not possibly raise this amount—and the Sultan knew it.

Millions of Jews in Eastern Europe, especially the young people, enthusiastically supported Herzl. But in other countries, many well-to-do Jews were satisfied with their comfortable life. Talk about "a Jewish nation" might hurt their chances of being "accepted" by non-Jews. Zionists might be accused of "dual loyalty"—pledging allegiance to two countries at once—and not being truly patriotic. Herzl got no help from such Jews.

Some extremely Orthodox Jews thought it wrong to "rush things." The Jewish exile would end, they said, through God's doing, not ours. Our job was to wait, patient and humble, for God to act. The early Reform Jews considered themselves a religious group, not a nation. Jews, they said, had a "mission"—teaching the nations to accept One God and carry out His principles of good conduct and social justice. For this mission, Jews *had* to live among the other nations. Herzl could not get very far with either of these groups. The Orthodox Jews accepted his goal, but not his methods. The early Reform Jews did not accept his goal *or* his methods.

Jewish socialists and labor leaders thought Zionism too narrow, too selfish. They wanted freedom and equality for all men, not a tiny spot of happiness for one people. Make all governments truly democratic, they said, give every man a decent life, prevent the rich and powerful from hurting the weak and the helpless—and then it wouldn't matter where you lived. Revolutions and social change were more important than regaining a Jewish homeland.

Try This: Look at the Prayer for Israel in Chapter 1 and see who published it—and, of course, this very book on Israel. In *Reform Judaism in the Making,* by Sylvan D. Schwartzman, read about the 1885 Pittsburgh Platform, page 119; the 1937 Guiding Principles, pages 132, 138–139; and comparing the two, page 143. Then present a discussion in which an early Reform leader (1885) discusses Zionism with a Reform leader of today.

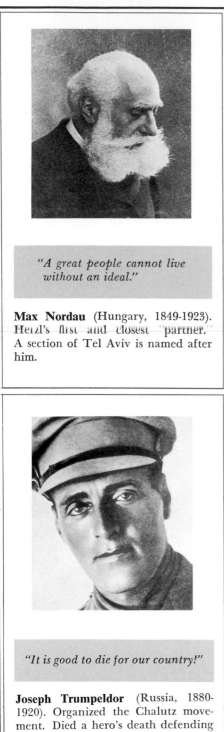

"A great people cannot live without an ideal."

Max Nordau (Hungary, 1849-1923). Herzl's first and closest "partner." A section of Tel Aviv is named after him.

"It is good to die for our country!"

Joseph Trumpeldor (Russia, 1880-1920). Organized the Chalutz movement. Died a hero's death defending the settlement of Tel Hai.

Both the religious and the socialist Jews eventually changed their minds. Socialist-Zionists, religious-Zionists, socialist-religious-Zionists —all helped build the Jewish state, and are governing it today. With a few exceptions, Orthodox and Reform Jews today support Israel as ardently as any others. But in Herzl's frenzied seven years, he found some of his toughest opponents among his own people.

We can smile today at another group of Jews who opposed Zionism—the ones who doubted that history could be changed. A people in exile for two thousand years to create a new state, reclaim a land barren for centuries? Seventy years ago, of course, it did sound ridiculous—as ridiculous as a man orbiting the earth or landing on the moon.

Practical Zionism

An idea, a leader, an organization—and willing workers.

Herzl died in 1904, but the Zionist Organization went on. Other leaders, not as brilliant but just as hard-working, carried on. Zionist groups in Europe, America, and other lands met and talked, raised money, spoke to governments, published books and magazines.

But all this would have come to nothing without Jews actually living and working in Palestine. It takes *people,* human beings in great numbers, to make a new State. Thousands upon thousands of Jews did not wait for charters, recognition, approval. They just went—and worked. If a Jewish homeland in Palestine became "official," well and good. If the nations did not act, then more and more Jews would come and *make* it a Jewish country, with or without "permission." "Political" Zionists, said these Jews, were trying to build a country out of promises and documents. "Practical" Zionists were building it out of houses and farms.

And so עֲלִיָה began—going "up" to the land and settling it. This meant leaving stores and schools, pushcarts and peddlers' packs, and learning to farm a wild, semi-tropical land, or to work for wages in shops and factories. But still they came—from Russia, Poland, Rumania, and other European countries, and from Yemen in Southern Arabia. The United States was open to them, and Canada, and South America—settled, civilized countries. Millions of Jewish refugees, especially from Russia and Poland, went there. But "practical" Zionists still chose the homeland.

A new word arose in Jewish life: חֲלוּצִיּוּת—pioneering, striking out on your own in the Promised Land. The first חֲלוּצִים—pioneers,

---

Aliyah: עֲלִיָה   Chalutziut: חֲלוּצִיּוּת   Chalutzim: חֲלוּצִים

60

were a group of seventeen young Jews, the BILU. Their brave example was followed by others—idealists and dreamers, who came to fight malaria, swamps, hostile Arabs. They did the toughest physical work all day under the broiling sun, then guarded their huts and farms through the long, cold, dangerous nights. They challenged the Jewish plantation owners, who employed poor and ignorant Arabs at low wages. They insisted on speaking their own language—not Russian, or Polish, or Arabic, but Hebrew. They built schools, read and wrote books, played and heard good music, started farm villages, founded new cities.

A nation cannot be created out of merchants and professionals only. The heart of a nation is its workers producing food to eat, clothes to wear, houses to live in, all kinds of tools and equipment. So said the thinkers and the writers. But these Chalutzim practiced what others merely preached. Their worn-out bodies, their stubborn faith, their brilliant ideas, their supreme courage—on these things, too, the State of Israel was built.

The young Jewish community in Palestine called itself the יִשׁוּב —Settlement. By 1914 and the outbreak of World War I, a new Jewish life was steadily growing in Palestine. Jews חוּץ לָאָרֶץ—outside the land, boasted about הָאָרֶץ—the land, and its Chalutzim. The barren country was more fruitful now than it had been for centuries. Such a short time ago, in 1880, only 25,000 Jews lived in Palestine, mainly on charity in four "holy" cities. Now almost twice as many supported themselves. Forty colonies had been built on swamps and sand dunes. Zionism spread, winning many more followers throughout the world.

■ The BILU—named from the first letters of Bet Ya-akov L'chu V'nelchah "O House of Jacob, come and let us go . . ."—started Palestine's first co-operative farm village in 1881. Since 1860, youth clubs in Russia, called Hovevei Tzion (Lovers of Zion) had practiced self-defense, studied Hebrew, and raised money for colonizing Palestine.

Try This: Learn a Chalutz song or dance of this period. Then teach it to your class. Get other pupils who play instruments to accompany you. You can select your material from:

—Jewish Agency publications: *Zemirot: Israeli Folk Songs; Israel Sings*
—Israel Music Foundation recordings: *Land of Israel; Defenders of Israel; Songs of Hope; Israeli Folk Dances*
—*Palestine Dances,* by Corrine Chochem
—*Union Songster,* pages 378–381, 428
—*The Songs We Sing,* by Harry Coopersmith, pages 237–354

Yishuv: יִשׁוּב   Chutz la-aretz: חוּץ לָאָרֶץ   Ha-aretz: הָאָרֶץ

61

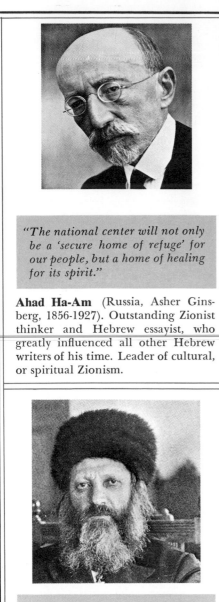

Spiritual Zionism

The coming Jewish state had many eager planners. One group followed the great thinker and Hebrew writer, Ahad Ha-am ("One of the People"), the pen-name of Asher Ginsburg. To him, Palestine was not just a refuge for persecuted Jews, or a place for an independent Jewish state—though both were important. He was just as concerned over Judaism itself. He was afraid the Jewish heritage would disappear from the world if it had no land of its own to live in. Palestine must therefore become the "spiritual center" of the Jewish people. Then it could guide and inspire Jews everywhere.

The new State had to be *Jewish* and *Hebraic* in its culture, ideals, procedures. This kind of thinking wove still another thread in the pattern of Israel. It explains the stress on עִבְרִית—Hebrew, as the everyday language. "Spiritual Zionism" inspired the Hebrew University, a dream that would not come true for another generation. And the idea of farm and factory workers being people of intelligence, and of culture.

"The national center will not only be a 'secure home of refuge' for our people, but a home of healing for its spirit."

Ahad Ha-Am (Russia, Asher Ginsberg, 1856-1927). Outstanding Zionist thinker and Hebrew essayist, who greatly influenced all other Hebrew writers of his time. Leader of cultural, or spiritual Zionism.

Religious Zionism

Many Orthodox Jews accepted Zionism as part of the Jewish religion. For them, Jews were not just a nation, but a *holy* nation. In their homeland they must practice Traditional Judaism, or else lose their special quality and become like other nations. The main purpose of their Zionism was to establish Orthodox Judaism as a complete way of life once more. Only in an independent homeland could Orthodox Jews do this in perfect freedom.

The religious Zionists established their own settlements in Palestine. They gave a religious character to modern Israeli life.

Socialist Zionists

Suffering under the Czar drove many Russian Jews into socialist organizations that hoped to reform the government. But some Jewish socialists were also Zionists. They believed that democratic reform was impossible in Russia. These Jews wanted for their landless people not just a homeland, but a socialist homeland. All over the

"Only in the Holy Land can the spirit of our people develop and become a light for the world."

Abraham Isaac Kook (Lithuania, 1865-1935). Chief Ashkenazic rabbi of Palestine, leader in Mizrachi, a religious Zionist party. Tolerant and understanding, he persuaded religious and non-religious settlers of the Yishuv to work together for their common cause.

HONOR ROLL

Ivrit: עִבְרִית

THE MARCH OF ZIONISM

Important Events

Zionist Movements and Building of Israel

Government anti-Semitism in Russian Empire; Jews impoverished; settlement restricted; pogroms; mass emigration to Western Europe and America. Jews in Western Europe become emancipated, educated and prosper.

Growth of modern anti-Semitism in Germany, Austria, Poland, Hungary.

1830

1836: Rabbi Zvi Hirsch Kalischer urges Jewish colonization of Palestine

1840

1848: Jews granted full civil rights in Austro-Hungarian Empire

1850

1860

1862: Moses Hess urges Jewish Homeland in Palestine

1870

1870: Agricultural School, Mikveh Israel founded in Palestine

1871: Jews granted full civil rights in Germany Odessa pogrom

1878: Petach Tikvah, 1st agricultural settlement

1880

1881: Pogroms in Russia. Mass emigration of Jews to Western Hemisphere

1882: Leo Pinsker appeals for return to Palestine. BILU settlements: Rishon le Tzion, Ness Tzionah, Zikhron Yaakov, Rosh Pinah, Gedera are founded

1890

1894: The Dreyfus Case in France

1896: Herzl publishes "The Jewish State"
1897: 1st Zionist Congress. World Zionist Organization founded in Basle

1900

1901: Jewish National Fund organized

1903: Kishinev pogrom (Rumania)

1909: Tel Aviv, 1st Jewish city founded; Degania, 1st Kibbutz founded

1910

1910: Ben Yehudah publishes 1st Hebrew Thesaurus; the birth of modern Hebrew

1914-1918: World War I, British conquer Palestine from Turks

1917: Balfour Declaration

1920

1920: Haganah succeeds Ha-Shomer. Histadrut is organized

1925: Hebrew University opens

1929: Arab riots in Palestine

1930

1933: Hitler gains control in Germany

1936: Arab riots continue

1937: Proposal for dividing Palestine into Arab and Jewish states

1939-1945: World War II, almost complete destruction of Europe's Jewry by the Nazis
1940: British severely restrict Jewish immigration and land purchase

1940

1947: UN adopts Partition Plan for Palestine

1943: Warsaw Ghetto Revolt
1947: Arab attacks mount; 7 Arab armies invade

1948: Successful War of Independence. Israel becomes an independent state

1950

1949: Israel becomes 59th member of UN

1956: Successful Sinai Campaign. Access gained to Far East through Eilat

1960

Development of Yishuv. Jewish self-government, settlement.

State grows and consolidates.

"Labor alone will heal us."

A. D. Gordon (Russia, 1856-1922). Thinker and writer. His teaching and practice of labor ideals inspired all Chalutzim (pioneers).

"A Chalutz is just a nail, driven wherever the country demands."

Vladimir Jabotinsky (Russia, 1880-1940). Writer, orator. Worked for Jewish self-defense and revival of Hebrew. Organized the Revisionist party in Zionism and the terrorists who attacked and assassinated the British in Palestine.

HONOR ROLL

world, they said, not enough Jews worked on the land or in the factories, and too many of them were professionals or businessmen. Only in a Jewish state could Jews lead a normal, healthy life of many occupations.

And only in a Jewish state, said these Zionists, could Jews develop a community along socialist lines. Here, land, buildings, resources, utilities would not belong to private owners getting rich from profits earned by workers. Instead, the community would own these things. Everyone would work and share equally in the community's wealth and decisions. Thus, Jews would show the world an example of democracy and true social justice.

This socialist Zionist group developed two unique institutions of modern Israel that you will read about later: the Kibbutz farm village and the Histadrut Labor Federation.

The Revisionists

The youngest Zionist group began in 1925. It felt that Palestine was not rebuilding fast enough. The Revisionists (revisers, changers) claimed to be the true followers of Herzl, and accused other Zionists of not fighting strongly enough against British rule in Palestine.

The Revisionists demanded a Jewish State on both sides of the Jordan River, and with a Jewish majority of the population. They did not favor friendly relations with the Arabs, and strongly opposed the labor movement and the socialists. After World War II, before the Jewish State was established, they organized a fanatical "underground" or secret army to drive the British out of the country by bombing and assassination.

The World Agrees

The Jewish State had its basic idea, leaders, organization, and workers. One more thing was needed: world support. And *that* took two World Wars and all the fifty years Herzl had predicted.

In 1917, World War I was going badly for the western Allies. Germany, their enemy, was considering a promise to give Palestine to the Jews if she won. The Allies, too, wanted the support of Jews throughout the world, and especially in America. Zionist leaders had appealed to the nations for years to recognize Jewish claims to Palestine. Finally, Britain issued her famous Balfour Declaration, promising the Jews a homeland.

When the war ended, the League of Nations made an important decision. The older, wealthier nations would help the backward

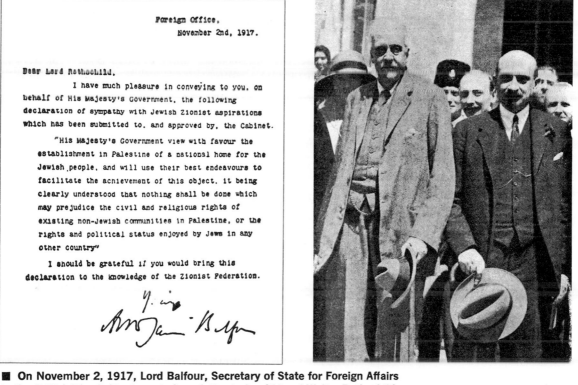

Foreign Office,
November 2nd, 1917.

Dear Lord Rothschild,

I have much pleasure in conveying to you, on behalf of His Majesty's Government, the following declaration of sympathy with Jewish Zionist aspirations which has been submitted to, and approved by, the Cabinet.

"His Majesty's Government view with favour the establishment in Palestine of a national home for the Jewish people, and will use their best endeavours to facilitate the achievement of this object, it being clearly understood that nothing shall be done which may prejudice the civil and religious rights of existing non-Jewish communities in Palestine, or the rights and political status enjoyed by Jews in any other country"

I should be grateful if you would bring this declaration to the knowledge of the Zionist Federation.

■ On November 2, 1917, Lord Balfour, Secretary of State for Foreign Affairs in the British War Cabinet, sent above letter to Lord Lionel Walter Rothschild. (Right) Lord Balfour (left) with Chaim Weizmann, who later became Israel's first President.

regions, formerly owned by Germany or Turkey, to govern themselves. In 1920, Britain received the League of Nations mandate to govern Palestine according to the Balfour Declaration. Two years later, this arrangement was confirmed by thirty-three nations of the world.

All Jews rejoiced over the new milestone in the march of Zionism. This, they thought, was the international charter that Herzl had wanted so badly. But official statements do not make a homeland. Zionists soon found that they had to work and fight harder than ever.

Were the British Fair?

The Balfour Declaration, intentionally or not, contained double talk. It promised *a* national home *for* the Jewish people *in* Palestine. It did not say Palestine would be *the* national home *of* the Jewish people. And it promised that the rights of *non-*Jewish communities in Palestine would not be taken away. Notice the important difference between "a" and "the," between "for" and "of," and how Jews and Arabs could interpret the Balfour Declaration in opposite ways.

65

"Independence is never given to a people, it has to be earned; and having been earned, it has to be defended."

Chaim Weizmann (Russia, 1874-1954). Tried to combine political, spiritual, and practical Zionism. Became the first president of Israel.

HONOR ROLL

Try This: For each man in the Zionist Honor Roll, a committee might write a citation of honor. What did the man accomplish for the Jews of his time? What does Jewish life owe to him today? Display your citations of honor on the bulletin board; or plan an assembly program around a few of the most interesting men, presenting your citations with a musical background.

Perhaps Britain deliberately played the old game of "divide and rule," using each side against the other to keep power for herself. Perhaps British officers personally favored the Arabs and disliked Jews. Whatever the reason, the British in Palestine made unfortunate decisions.

Fanatics stirred up the Arab peasants, using religion and fear to arouse their anger. Agitators spread false stories of Jewish plans to attack Arab holy places. The ignorant Arab peasants, in brutal riots, tore down Jewish property, committed atrocities on innocent Jews. The British could have prevented all this by firmly arresting the few hotheads behind the outbreaks—but they didn't. If not for the secret Jewish defense force, called the הֲגָנָה—self-protection, Arab uprisings in 1921 and 1929 might have destroyed the Yishuv.

The worst Arab outbreak started in 1936 and lasted three years, right up to the beginning of World War II. Arab brigands carried on guerrilla raids of destruction. The 20,000 British troops in Palestine "could not" control them. The Yishuv decided on Havlagah—self-control. Jews vigorously defended their towns and colonies, but carried out no acts of revenge or retaliation.

The British gave the Yishuv no help, and plenty of hindrance. They kept limiting immigration, explaining that the country could not absorb any more immigrants—although it was doing so all the time. They claimed that Jewish land purchases were turning the Arabs into landless beggars. Actually, ordinary Arabs in Palestine were richer and healthier because of Jewish settlement. Arab workers generally got along well with the Jewish settlers. But the British solemnly repeated statements of the Arab leaders condemning practically everything the Jews were doing.

In 1921, the British declared the land east of the Jordan River an independent Arab state. It was three times larger than the western side, but had only 300,000 people, most of them nomads. To the Zionists, Palestine meant *both* parts. They had hoped to colonize this open, empty territory. But the British barred the Jews from it.

In 1930, the British drastically reduced the amount of land that Jews could buy. In 1939, they called the Mandate "unworkable," and claimed they had already carried out the Balfour Declaration. From now on, only a small trickle of Jewish immigrants could come in every year. This meant Jews could not possibly become the majority in the country, or control it. It also closed Palestine at the

---

Haganah: הֲגָנָה

66

The Jews who wish for a state will have it, and they will deserve to have it. . . .
I believe that a wondrous generation of Jews will spring into existence.
The Maccabees will rise again.

—Theodor Herzl

very time when Jews most desperately needed refuge. After 1932, the Nazis began mercilessly destroying the Jews in Germany, and threatened the safety of all European Jews. Some escaped to Canada, the United States, South America. But these countries limited immigration to small numbers. Where could the rest go?

■ **Jewish Border Police on patrol, 1936, members of Haganah (Defense), a secret or "underground" army maintained by the Yishuv from 1920 to 1948. The Haganah took over the work of the Ha-Shomer (The Watchman), guards who had defended the early settlements against Arab raiders. Though severely handicapped by the British, the Haganah, over the years, trained and equipped troops, commandos, police, pioneer settlers, and guides for "illegal" immigrants. They joined the British forces in World War II, then went "underground" again until they became the official Army of Israel in 1948.**

Despite Everything*

The Yishuv stood firm. Lamrot ha-kol (Despite everything!) became their slogan. They persisted—and built.

Between the two World Wars (1918–1939), the Yishuv grew eight times in size. One-third of the population now was Jews.

Over 225,000 German Jews found a refuge there from the Nazi slaughterhouse. Thousands more came from Poland, Hungary, Austria, Rumania, and from other lands of suffering. Jewish farmers produced three times as much as before the British mandate. Palestine became the world's second biggest exporter of oranges. Modern Jewish cities grew up, like Tel Aviv, then the only all-Jewish city in the world. Factories, banks, stores increased. Electric power was drawn from the Jordan River; rich mineral deposits were discovered in the Dead Sea. Railroads came, highways, a new harbor at Haifa.

Hebrew became the accepted language of the Yishuv. A school system was organized, supported mostly by Jewish funds. In Jerusalem, Jews laid the cornerstone of the Hebrew University in 1918, to the sound of nearby Turkish and British cannon fire. In 1925, the university opened its doors to its first few students. Literature, drama, music, art—all created in the Jewish spirit—attracted world-wide notice.

But most important, the Jews made themselves a united community. Coming from fifty countries, speaking many languages, differing sharply in dress, customs, beliefs, they still managed to bind themselves into כְּנֶסֶת יִשְׂרָאֵל—the Community of Israel. They governed themselves in religion and education. They collected their own taxes, organized defense forces, held political campaigns and elections, established hospitals and clinics.★

Try This: With a classmate, write an exchange of letters between an American Jew and his friend in the Yishuv in 1918, 1923, or 1938. Would your letters be gloomy or cheerful over the Balfour Declaration, British and Arab attitudes, Yishuv development?

★ Do you agree with the following quotation? Your reasons?

"Thank Providence we have come to a wasteland, not a ready-made country, or we could have exchanged one exile for another. Only through the trials and tribulations of pioneering can a nation acquire true title to its country."
—Hayyim Nahman Bialik

The Yishuv Fights

World War II broke out in 1939. The Arabs of the Middle East, whom Britain had helped so much, kept neutral or sided with Nazi Germany. The Yishuv had good reasons to feel bitter toward the British—yet four out of five adult Jews immediately registered for war service on the British side. Thirty thousand volunteered for the British army—and two thousand of them died in battle. Jewish paratroopers landed behind enemy lines all over Europe as secret agents, to help the local resistance forces.

---

*Lamrot ha-kol: לַמְרוֹת הַכֹּל   Knesset Yisrael: כְּנֶסֶת יִשְׂרָאֵל

■ When the British tried to keep Jewish immigrants out of Palestine, the Haganah organized "illegal" immigration on a grand scale. The Haganah ship *Exodus 1947* became world famous when it tried to bring in about 4,550 Jewish refugees, but was captured by the British and forced to return to Europe.

A special Jewish brigade fought bravely on the Italian front. Later, this brigade smuggled into Palestine, against British and Arab resistance, thousands of Jews who survived the Nazi concentration camps. On the home front, the Yishuv started workshops to make cloth, metals, machine parts, drugs for the British troops. Allied soldiers on leave found cordial welcome and hospitality in Tel Aviv and other Jewish settlements.

Thus the Jews of Palestine did their part in the war against tyranny, while the Arabs sat by or aided the tyrants. The democratic nations have not always remembered this, unfortunately.

In less than fifty years a leader came, a movement began, pioneers reclaimed the neglected soil of their ancestors. The world showed some kindness and understanding, but supported the venture grudgingly or not at all. Jews regained some of the land, but were still a minority, and not in control. In 1945, again at the end of a World War, Zionist hopes for a Jewish state revived. You will see later how the march of events brought final victory.

Try This: If you and a classmate wrote the letters suggested for the section on "Were the British Fair?" read them over now. What changes would you make?

HAVE YOU WONDERED . . . ?

. . . why Aliyah (going up) means immigration to Israel?

The word comes from עָלֹה —go up. In the synagogue, an Aliyah means "going up" to the pulpit for the honor of a Torah-reading. In Bible days, Jews made an aliyah (pilgrimage) three times each year to the Temple in Jerusalem, on Pesach, Shavuot, Sukkot. The Temple was on a high hill, and the altar for sacrifices was raised above the floor—hence, "going up."

The Bible speaks of our ancestors "going down" to Egypt, and from Egypt, "going up" to the Land of Canaan. This may have meant going southward or northward. But it also may have had a religious meaning. Egypt, to our ancestors, meant slavery, idol worship, persecution, death. The Promised Land meant freedom, worship of One God, justice, and life.

And so, when *Aliyah* is used for "immigration to Israel," we have several things in mind. It is a religious act, like "going up" to "read" from the Torah or traveling to the Temple. It is moving physically, away from an old country towards a new one. And it is a complete change in one's Jewish way of life—from living as a member of a minority in a "strange" land, to living freely as a Jew in a Jewish homeland.

YOU'LL ENJOY READING

Next Year in Jerusalem: the Story of Theodor Herzl, by Nina B. Baker
Chaim Weizmann: Builder of a Nation, by Rachel Baker
Theodor Herzl, by Deborah Pessin
Harvest in the Desert, by Maurice Samuel

YOU'LL ENJOY SEEING

The Nine Years of Theodor Herzl (film: American Zionist Council)
If You Will It—the Life and Work of Theodor Herzl (filmstrip: Jewish Agency)

Aloh: עָלֹה

chapter 7

Two Israels—or One?

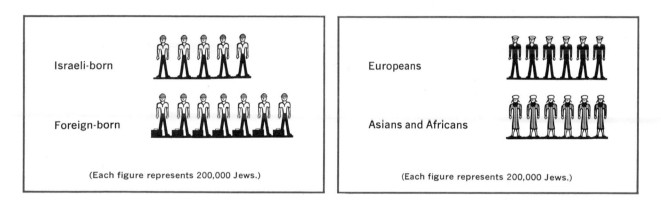

Israeli-born

Foreign-born

(Each figure represents 200,000 Jews.)

Europeans

Asians and Africans

(Each figure represents 200,000 Jews.)

■ Most Israeli Jews are immigrants who retain the ideas and customs of their "home" countries. Jews born in Israel have lived only in an Israeli Jewish culture. Can you think of some reasons why the two groups might not get along with each other?

■ Jews from Western and Eastern (Oriental) lands are almost equal in number—an unusual mixture compared to most countries. Can you think of some differences between the two groups? Some similarities?

The United States is a land of immigrants, blending many different kinds of people into one nation. American Jews, too, came here from many lands. They had the same religion, but their different languages and customs often kept them apart. In time, they forgot most of their conflicts—although, of course, some differences will always remain.

Israel, too, is a "nation of many nations." But there the blending had to work much faster. Americans, and American Jews, had many years to smooth out their differences—Israel, only a few. The United States restricted immigration and Americanized her immigrants slowly, gradually. Israel's immigration never stopped—the newcomers had to be absorbed very quickly.

1968. Since 1948, Israeli-born Jews have increased slightly, from 35% to 40%. But whereas in 1948, 80% of immigrants came from Europe, and 20% from Asia and Africa, today the figures are 50% and 50%.

71

Israel's population has changed greatly since 1948. Many dark-skinned Jews wear Oriental clothes, speak strange languages, and observe Judaism with "strange" rituals and customs. New immigrants from eighty different lands are creating a new Israeli type.

The "First" Israel

In 1948, four out of five Israeli Jews were of European origin. Most of them were self-reliant people, who liked experiments, new ideas. Most of them had a good modern education, and knew Hebrew.

They were mostly young, strong, and ambitious, able to adjust quickly to new ways of life. Many had high ideals of Zionism, socialism, religion. They wanted to live by their ideals, to show the world that Jews could create a successful nation.

THE "FIRST" ISRAEL. These Israelis, or their parents, came from Europe after 1882. These "modern" Western Ashkenazim were mainly responsible for the establishment of Israel.

As modern people, they used machines, factories, mass production. They followed the latest scientific methods in farming, sanitation, medical care, banking, insurance, communication, transportation. They read and produced all sorts of books, magazines, newspapers; they went to movies, plays, and concerts.

They wanted the finest modern schools and the best possible education for every child. Their children did well in school, wanting to be educated like their parents and teachers. Parents could help children with their school work.

Women were considered equal to men, worked alongside them, had the same vote, and the same chance to rise to leadership. Nearly everyone belonged to a trade union and a political party. They conducted their affairs in a modern democratic way. In religion, some were Orthodox, some anti-religious, many were in-between. But they all knew Zionist ideals, history, events, leaders—and what was going on all over the world. They created Israel's farming villages, labor federation, schools, army—everything described in this book.

European Jews coming to Palestine found much that was familiar. They knew a good deal about the place before they got there. They found relatives, old friends, people from their own home towns, people like themselves, talking the same language. Sympathy, understanding, a helping hand came easily to most immigrants. Usually, they adjusted quickly and soon felt at home.

In this backward, undeveloped region, these Jews had nothing in common with their non-Jewish neighbors—neither language, nor culture, nor memories of the past. Their life was modern, Western, democratic, like American life in many ways, or life in a small European state like Switzerland or Belgium. Palestine's Jewish community in 1948 was an island of modern civilization in a sea of backward peoples.

But then came the new State—and new immigrants.

The "Second" Israel

About a third of the new immigrants were from Europe. They had lived through the tortures of Nazi concentration camps. Many were weak, sick, bitter. They did not know Hebrew, and their occupations were already overcrowded in Israel.

And yet, Israel could have managed this group of immigrants fairly well. The other two-thirds were more difficult to deal with. They were from North Africa and the Middle East, from the countries of Yemen, Iraq, Morocco, Kurdistan. These Jews had lived for centuries in Eastern countries. Many were used to primitive houses,

Try This: Talk to your grandparents, or ask your parents about them. They were probably immigrants to this country from Europe. What problems did they face? Who helped them, and how? What part of their "old country" life still exists in your home and synagogue? What part has vanished? With two or three other pupils, hold a panel discussion on these "interviews."

73

THE "SECOND" ISRAEL. These Israelis came mostly after 1948, from backward Afro-Asian lands. They are usually grouped with Spanish Jews who have lived in Israel for 400-500 years, and are called Sefardim ("Spaniards").

furniture, and sanitation, and believed in demons, spells, magic talismans. In religion, they were strictly Orthodox. Religious ideas were part of every moment of life; the name of God was always on their lips. All ancient rituals and customs had to be scrupulously followed—Orientals do not usually like or understand religious change.

These Oriental Jews did not think people could change their lives by their own efforts. In time of trouble, their favorite expression was יְהְיֶה טוֹב—"it'll be o.k." They did not know how to organize and plan and act, as a group, to improve their situation; they simply felt that somehow or other somebody would take care of it.

They knew little of Zionism, Israel's struggles and leaders, Hebrew literature, art, culture, world affairs, and current events. Israel, to them, was a vague, lovely dream, a kind of heaven, where a miracle of God had brought them at last. Not pioneers or rebels, they cared little about social ideals or plans for a new country. They wanted peace and safety, but otherwise to live exactly as they and their ancestors had always done. Israel had few of their families or friends to take them in, explain things to them, smooth their way.

These Jews came from lands where child marriage was permitted, and marriage to more than one wife. Most boys had only a few years of instruction, girls none at all. Most women could not count, tell time, or write their names, and many of the men could not read or write. They had never heard of modern plumbing, typewriters and tableware, trains and telephones. An Israeli newspaperman visiting an Oriental Jewish community could not explain what he did for a living. They insisted he must be a scribe who copied the Torah—they had met no other kind of "writer."

Half the new immigrants were young children, elderly, sick, and/or handicapped. They had never voted in a democratic election. They knew about money-lending, charity, bartering—but not about investing or banking. They took life leisurely, did not try to get more done in less time, go faster to farther places, or get richer every year. Most of them were small merchants and independent craftsmen. They worked at home, with their own families, starting and stopping whenever they felt like it.

Like most Orientals, they were satisfied with few luxuries, but greatly enjoyed the necessities of life. They deeply appreciated art and beauty. They treasured lovely songs and dances, charming tales and legends that were centuries old. They designed intricate jewelry, embroidery, baskets, silver and gold work, leather goods, inlays—all hand-made, with care and pride.

Yih'yeh tov: יְהְיֶה טוֹב

Only in Israel

A veterinary surgeon was called to a village by an excited immigrant from Yemen, to explain the death of his horse. After an autopsy, the vet told the Yemenite: "My dear man, your horse died of starvation."

Incredulously, the farmer replied: "Impossible! When Yemenites don't eat, *they* don't die!"

"Maybe," said the vet. "But this horse was Hungarian."

—Land of the Bible Newsletter

Home life and family feeling were much stronger than in the average modern Western home. Usually, three generations lived together in one household. Old age was deeply respected, with the grandfather as family leader and guide. He, or the father, ruled the family strictly. The home was like a castle where he was king—he felt important, powerful. Yet he helped the mother take care of the children, played with them often. The mother did not work outside the home. Her greatest pride was to have many children and keep busy taking care of them.

The Oriental Jewish family was usually large, with many mouths to feed and a low standard of living by Western ideas. Yet it was superior to the Arab home in intelligence and culture. Even the everyday activities—a meal, conversation with a guest, advice to a child—were carried on with charm and grace, as if they were the greatest pleasures of life. Sabbath, in these homes, was a day not for reading, study, or serious discussion, but for dancing, singing, joking, making merry.

Most of the excitement and drama in their lives took place within their own family circle. On the rare occasions when someone felt bored or lonely, he did not have to go away from home to find fun and relaxation. These people did not hide their feelings or worry about their manners. When they liked something, they said so openly. When they disliked something, they shouted, cursed, argued. They were not ashamed to cry or laugh when they felt like it.

A child in such a home was strongly attached to his family, considered it more important than his own personal life. Independence was not encouraged, or asking questions and showing curiosity. A child was expected to help support the family as early in life as possible, rather than get a higher education.

These were the Oriental Jews—backward in some ways, advanced in others—who fled from misery and persecution to live with their Western brothers in Israel.

Two Israels

From the beginning, the wisest Israelis wanted to break down the barriers between Europeans and Orientals. But prejudiced people in each group had to be taught to live and work with "strangers." Two halves of a country had to join into a single, united nation.

The Israel Army has worked harder than any other agency to integrate the immigrants without weakening their cherished traditions. For instance, all training units are "mixed," so that the Israelis

TWO ISRAELS, OR ONE?

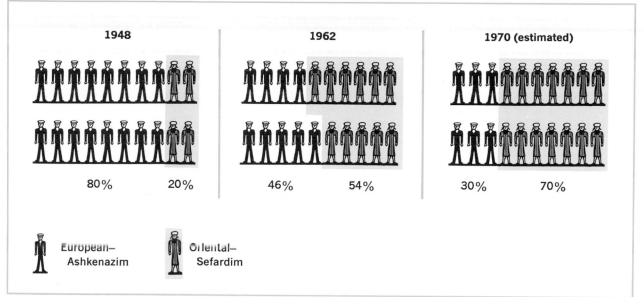

1948	1962	1970 (estimated)
80% 20%	46% 54%	30% 70%

European— Ashkenazim   Oriental— Sefardim

■ After 1948, the proportion of Orientals in Israel's population rose steadily, from about one-quarter to about one-half today. In just a few more years, Easterners and their children will greatly outnumber the Europeans. What do you think has caused this change? (Several answers!) If you belonged to either of these groups, how would you probably feel at seeing this change take place in your lifetime?

of different backgrounds learn to live side by side. Immigrant recruits take courses in Hebrew, trades, history, geography, hygiene, and farming, and soon stop feeling "inferior." Entertainment programs use Oriental music, dance, and humor, which soon become popular with the Israel-born recruits.

After army service, most immigrant youths have more self-control and self-respect, also more respect for authority and government. They are modern young people, but also proud of the old folks' deeper wisdom, humor, culture, love of life and family. Western youths, leaving the Army, usually know and like the Easterners better.

The Israel government has also tackled the problem vigorously. The Prime Minister has a special adviser on immigration and integration. The main political parties, campaigning for the "Oriental" vote, teach the newcomers politics and democracy, listen to their complaints, and try to grant their wishes. Discrimination against race or color has always been illegal in Israeli government and public affairs. Vigorous efforts are also made to eliminate discrimination in private housing and employment. The government encourages

Oriental craftsmen to continue their artistic work. It lends them money and provides materials, advertises their products, helps them find customers in Israel and abroad.

The schools also help to make one Israel out of two. All children learn the same history, songs, dances—and the same basic ideas. The Hebrew language, of course, is a strong binding force. But immigrant children are handicapped in certain ways. They are not used to modern schools. Often they have to study in crowded, noisy homes where parents cannot help them with their homework. And so, in many places, kindergartens take children a year or two younger, schools have a longer day, and classes are smaller than average. Some immigrant communities also have special two-year high schools. High school students from immigrant families receive special grants and loans, extra time to pass their exams, and special tutoring.

For grown-ups, Israel invented a new kind of education. The אוּלְפָּן, or residential Hebrew college, has clever new teaching methods that have spread to adult Hebrew classes in our own country. In a city Ulpan, students live together all day for five or six months, using Hebrew in all their study, work, and play.

These are mainly for professional people, to help them follow their old careers in the new land. In a farming village, students spend six months studying half a day and working the other half to pay for their tuition, board, and lodging. There are also "short" Ulpanim—afternoon or evening courses for twelve to sixteen hours a week, lasting four months. Besides all this, volunteer teachers give private home lessons to immigrants who cannot read or write. Since 1948, half a million newcomers have learned Hebrew through all these special courses.

The government and other organizations send expert advisers among the new settlements. These are trained to show the newcomers better, more modern methods, and to encourage self-confidence and preserve Oriental Jewish arts, music, dance, and customs.

The Histadrut, Israel's giant labor federation, has a special department to train Easterners to be good workers and good union members. Special Histadrut schools and clubs for working youth meet right in the homes, streets, and towns where Easterners live.

Israeli Jews meet one another often at coffee houses, holiday celebrations, dance and music festivals, and the world-famous Bible Quiz—won several times by an Oriental Jew. More Eastern young people are joining youth clubs or youth centers. They sometimes fall in love with the "other" kind of Israeli. Some parents get quite

Try This: Orientals and Europeans were opposites in so many ways that misunderstanding between them was to be expected. What conflicts would arise between them in pairs like these?

—factory workers and their foreman
—farmers and a government farm adviser
—housewives and a government nurse
—customers and a storekeeper
—neighbors living near one another

What conflicts do you think would arise within an Oriental family, between parents and their children going to an Israeli school, youth club, or the Army?

Ulpan: אוּלְפָּן

78

■ **What festival is this Oriental family celebrating?**

upset over this, but the most sensible ones accept it calmly. In recent years, one out of every ten Israeli marriages has brought East and West together.

Such a married couple often combines customs of the East and the West—for instance, to celebrate a holiday. At the family Pesach Seder, Europeans and Easterners take turns reading the Haggadah, each in his own way. The meal includes typical foods of both groups, and each learns the other's songs, legends, and customs.

Israel's writers, actors, musicians do their part, too. They provide literature, entertainment, and music to acquaint each group with the other, to appeal to "mixed" audiences. Newspapers, especially for immigrants, use simpler Hebrew. They feature folk tales of various communities.★

★ Compared to other countries with similar immigrant problems, Israel has done extremely well. In a short time, and despite all their other difficulties, both groups have come a long way towards understanding, accepting, even liking each other. How was Israel able to accomplish this? Think of several specific organizations and characteristics of Israeli life that united the two groups.

Behold, I will take the children of Israel from among the heathen, where they are gone, and will gather them on every side, and bring them into their own land . . . and they shall be no more two nations!

—Ezekiel 37:21-22

1

5

2

FACES OF ISRAEL. Can you guess which country each comes from, or what language each speaks? Match each picture with one of these: Turkey; Yemen; Cuba; India; Czechoslovakia; Poland; Bulgaria; France; Rumania; Yugoslavia; Morocco. Then turn the page to see how many you identified correctly.

4

3

*We will not create in Israel two peoples, one a hewer of wood and drawer of water,
and another—a superior people. We will be one people or we shall not survive
—we must settle the land or we shall lose it.*

—David Ben-Gurion

7

6

8

9

11

10

Behold, how good and how pleasant it is for brethren to dwell together in harmony.

Psalm 133:1

One Israel

And so the two groups draw closer together. Europeans are gradually changing their former ideas about Easterners being ignorant, lazy, noisy. Europeans are less afraid than they used to be about Oriental ideas and customs "taking over" the country. They have gradually realized how much they can learn from the newcomers, and show more respect for Oriental traditions, customs, attitudes. Besides, they want Israel to be strong, prosperous, respected by the world, and true to Jewish ideals. This means they must accept the new immigrants completely.

Meanwhile, the Orientals are getting used to modern life, learning to understand Israel's needs and goals, her problems and opportunities. Their European brothers seem less cold and heartless. They realize how much better off they are than in the countries they left. They see their children healthier, stronger, wanting to learn, studying even harder than the Europeans' children, even winning prizes and honors. They now feel more at home, more important.

They see even more immigrants pouring into the country, and European Israelis moving heaven and earth to take care of them properly. They understand that immigrants from an undeveloped country usually start at the "bottom." But they have complete equality, the right to vote and live as they please, with all higher schools and careers open to them as soon as they qualify.★

★ Israelis had to learn to understand the newcomers, and change them without destroying their pride and other good qualities. Did Israelis benefit in any way from having to deal with this problem? Any benefit to the whole world if they solve this problem successfully?

The Israel to Be

Fashioning a new Israel is a difficult task and cannot be hurried or forced. Conflicts and unpleasant "incidents" continue. A European family keeps its children from playing with newcomers, or even from going to the same school. A restaurant owner refuses to serve "blacks." An immigrant sues an apartment house owner for not letting him live there. Orientals complain of crowded schools, of being "segregated" in the Negev. Westerners accuse the government of "coddling" Orientals, giving them favored treatment over other Israelis.

FACES OF ISRAEL.

1. Czechoslovakia
2. Morocco
3. Yemen
4. Bulgaria
5. Turkey
6. Rumania
7. Poland
8. Yugoslavia
9. India
10. France
11. Cuba

ONE ISRAEL. In a settlement near the Jordan border, this "sabra" (native Israeli) teaches sixty kindergarten children whose parents come from Tunisia, Syria, Rumania, Bulgaria. What story might she be telling them to prove that "all Israelis are brothers" despite their differences? Can you suggest a follow-up song?

The average Oriental immigrant family had twice as many children as the average European family. Within twelve years, Oriental Jews were more than half the total population, and growing. Top government leaders, managers, army officers, businessmen, high school and college graduates, professionals—they were nearly all Europeans. Laborers, in the heaviest and dirtiest jobs, temporary workers, the unemployed—they were nearly all Orientals.

83

Sometimes, strong feelings break out. In 1959, North African Jews in Haifa rioted against the older settlers to protest "discrimination" and "unfair treatment." In 1962, a secret organization spread posters all over Jerusalem demanding an end to "discrimination" against Oriental Israelis.

Both sides have made mistakes—misunderstanding will continue for some time. But slowly and surely the two groups are merging into one. In another generation, or perhaps two, Israeli Jews will have a darker complexion than most Europeans, but lighter than most Orientals. Israel will still be a land of modern education, medical care, farm and factory methods, social security, democracy, freedom. But it will also be a land with an Oriental flavor—in family life, food, clothing, home decorations, arts, music, religion.

Caring for so many newcomers and absorbing such different people has severely tested Israel's ideas and character—but she "passed." To help these people, Israel pioneered in the Negev, solved new problems in social welfare and education, developed a new kind of Army. European Israelis needed tact, patience, love. They had to forget their own hardships and provide for people far worse off than themselves. Israel became a "social laboratory"—one of the few places in the world where Easterners and Westerners can meet as equals. This could be a valuable lesson for both the dark-skinned peoples of Asia and Africa, and the whites of Europe and America.

Try This: You are an Oriental child, and the rest of the class are Westerners. You ask questions about Israel, which the group answers. They teach you one of their songs or dances; you teach them one of yours. They try to teach you a little Hebrew conversation. See if you and the class can act shy and nervous at first, but gradually "warm up" and end completely at ease.

HAVE YOU WONDERED . . . ?

. . . about the term "Ashkenazim" and "Sefardim"?

The Jews began their long exile from Palestine about 200 C.E., and eventually became established in three parts of the world:

1. Many Jews remained in the Middle East, as Oriental communities. Some of these spread as far east as India and China.

2. Other Jews moved into North Africa and Spain, as communities in Moslem lands. The Christians conquered Spain, and in 1492 drove out the Spanish Jews. Some settled in Holland and England. The vast majority spread around the Mediterranean Sea, and into Turkey and Asia Minor. These were the Sefardim ("Sefarad" means Spain), or Sefardic Jews. They spoke Ladino, a mixture of Spanish and Hebrew.

3. Still other Jews, who settled in Germany, were called Ashkenazim ("Ashkenaz" means Germany), or Ashkenazic Jews. In the Fifteenth and Sixteenth Centuries, many of them moved to Russia and Poland. Here they developed a strong community, speaking Yiddish, a mixture of German and Hebrew. Most American Jews today are de-

scendants of these Ashkenazic Jews. They produced important new religious and cultural ideas, developed Zionism, and founded the Jewish state.

"Sefardic" and "Ashkenazic" originally referred to differences in prayers and prayer books used in synagogue. The two groups also developed different kinds of music and ceremonies—and different Hebrew pronunciation. Israelis today use the Sefardic pronunciation. Many Jews elsewhere in the world use Ashkenazic pronunciation. Which pronunciation is used in *your* school and synagogue? See if you can also find out *why*.

YOU'LL ENJOY READING

The Bar Mitzvah Treasury, by Azriel Eisenberg, pages 181–216.

YOU'LL ENJOY SEEING

The Desert Shall Rejoice (film: Jewish National Fund)
Home at Last (film: Israel Office of Information)
The Key (film: United Jewish Appeal)
Man on a Bus (film: United Jewish Appeal)

chapter 8

The Arabs in Israel

The Testing of Israel

For almost 2,000 years, Jews lived in Moslem or Christian countries, usually as strangers without rights, who could be persecuted or expelled. Now, in Israel, the tables are turned: Jews are the all-powerful majority, outnumbering Arabs nine to one. How does Israel treat her Arab minority? ★

Israel's Arabs

About one-fourth of Israel's Arabs live in cities and towns, working along with Jews in factories and offices. You can hardly tell them apart from other Israelis, except when they wear their national head-dress on ceremonial occasions. Most Arabs are farmers who have long followed primitive methods of tilling the soil. Until the Jewish State, they had very low incomes and little health care, education, or self-government.

The Arab population is mainly concentrated in three regions, which worries the Israel government and army chiefs. A careful look at the chart (see page 93) will show you why.

Farmers and Workers

In Israel, four out of five Arab farmers own their own land, and the fifth leases his land from the government. Either way, they own all that their land produces. In Arab countries, most of the land belongs to rich landlords, and the average farmer keeps for himself only one-third of his produce.

★ Here is one of the Bible's best known verses:

"If a stranger lives with you in your land, do not wrong him. The stranger living with you shall be as one of your own countrymen, and you shall love him as yourself; for you were strangers in the land of Egypt: I am the Lord your God."

—Leviticus 19:33-34

Can you think of examples in the history of any people when these verses were carried out? Were not carried out? Would Israeli Jews find them easy or hard to obey?

HOW ISRAEL'S ARABS BECAME A MINORITY

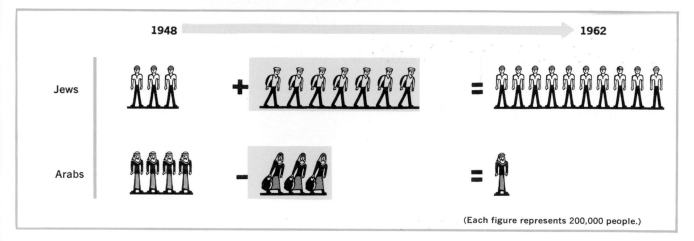

(Each figure represents 200,000 people.)

■ **Up to 1947, Arabs outnumbered Jews three to one. Soon after the War for Independence began, most Arabs fled. Jewish population has tripled, mainly through immigration. Now, Jews outnumber Arabs nine to one.**

1967. The average yearly income of an average Arab family in the town of Nazareth was 7,000 Israeli pounds; of a Jewish family, 7,360 pounds.

Israeli Arabs now use tractors and other farm machinery. Cattle and poultry are healthier; villages are cleaner and have new roads and buildings. Homes are larger, with electricity and running water instead of oil lamps and a well perhaps many miles away. Families raise many crops instead of depending only on a few "staples." Arab farm produce is now worth six times as much as in 1948. Fifteen times as much Arab land is irrigated. Water flows through irrigation pipes to each farm, at a reasonable price. Government loans are easy to get, and the average Arab farm family even has extra money for small luxuries. Most Arab farmers displaced during the War for Independence have been repaid for lost property, or given new homes and farms.

Arab workers are covered by Israel's labor laws regulating working hours, the weekly day off, and paid holidays. Every Arab is also covered by the insurance laws on death and injury benefits, help for expectant mothers, allowances for large families, and old-age benefits. Arab mothers, working women, and children are fully protected by law the same as Jews. All these labor benefits are completely new in Arab life anywhere in the whole Middle East.

Over 30,000 Arab workers have joined the Histadrut, Israel's labor federation. A special Histadrut Arab Department, along with the government and other agencies, organizes Arab workers into unions to defend their rights. The four out of five Arab workers who are unskilled learn new trades at vocational centers. Arab cooperatives, from bakeries to banks, have grown up in cities. There is even an Arab Kibbutz called "Achvah"—"brotherhood"—outside the town of Lod. The Histadrut also sponsors an Arabic publishing firm.

I am certain that the world will judge the Jewish State by what it will do with the Arabs, just as the Jewish people at large will be judged by what we do or fail to do in this State where we have been given such a wonderful opportunity after thousands of years of wandering and suffering.

—Chaim Weizmann

In 1947, the average Jewish worker's daily pay was five times larger than the Arab's. Today, Arabs and Jews are paid alike in all government jobs and public institutions, companies owned or part-owned by the Histadrut, Jewish farm settlements, and Jewish firms employing Histadrut members. But Arab pay is still too low in Arab-owned firms and in small non-union Jewish companies. Nevertheless, average pay for Israeli Arabs is the highest in the Middle East —three times higher than in Egypt, twice as high as in Iraq.

Self-Government

Israel wants her Arabs to be self-supporting citizens, not charity cases. But they often resist improvements and do not make full use of new opportunities. Many cannot overcome centuries of backward habits and fixed attitudes. They are not interested in new ideas, suspecting every change as some kind of trick. Especially in local self-government, Arabs sometimes have to be encouraged or even forced to help themselves.

For four centuries under the Turks and for thirty years under the British, most Arabs relied on a central government to set their taxes and provide for their needs. By 1947, Palestine's Jews had local self-government everywhere; the Arabs had just one local village council. In 1948, Arabs became citizens of a democracy, with new privileges—and new responsibilities. Now they were expected to govern themselves in their own villages. But only the city dwellers had any experience in self-government.

Many Arab villagers still expect the authorities in Jerusalem to solve all their local problems, such as education and sanitation. Villages are often divided by family feuds, as Arabs are generally more family-minded than community-minded. The well-to-do are not eager to start paying their share of local taxes. As a result, only half the Arabs now have self-government, in two all-Arab towns and twenty-six local village councils. Three out of four Arab villages have not even made a beginning.

Only in Israel

Negev Bedouins have about 10,000 camels. In 1962, the government began marking each camel with its own ear-tag and lip-brand, and listing it in a special book.

Officials explain this is to stop the smuggling of camels and to locate diseased animals that may be spreading infection. Bedouin say it's a long overdue recognition that in desert country a camel's as good as a car—both have to get a "license."

1968. Except for the Bedouins, 80 per cent of Israel's Arabs live under their own local government.

89

HEALTHIER ARABS. Israel goes all-out for Arab health, as at this Government Health Station in an Arab village. One result: Arabs live longer than they used to, and longer than people in Arab lands. Why do you think Israel's Arabs do not live as long as her Jews?

LIFE EXPECTANCY

Israeli Jews	70 years
Israeli Arabs	50 years
Egyptians	34 years
Iraqis	27 years
Americans	67 years

1967. After the Six Day War (see Chapter 25), the government encouraged more high schools to teach Middle Eastern, Arabic and Moslem cultures. Two Tel Aviv high schools made Arabic a compulsory subject for all students. Intensive "Ulpanim" teach Arabic to Jewish adults.

But progress, though slow, is steady. The Israel government encourages village councils by offering to help pay for roads and water, electricity and sewers, for teachers and hospitals, clinics, social services, religious needs. To get this help, Arabs are gradually learning to plan their own community improvement projects, tax themselves, and be more responsible for their own welfare.

Health

All Israeli hospitals and clinics are, of course, open to Arabs. But most of them live in remote villages, so visiting nurses and mobile medical units come to them. In their most populated region, Arabs now have their own tuberculosis hospital, medical centers, and a special network of mother-and-child clinics. Most Arab women still prefer to have their babies at home instead of in a modern hospital. For this reason, the death rate of Arab infants is still high compared with the Jewish. But it has dropped sharply, to just half the 1948 figure—the lowest Arab infant death rate in the Middle East.

All Israeli rules of public health apply equally to Arabs and Jews. The fight against malaria, once so frequent among Arabs, has been won. Tuberculosis and the dread eye disease, trachoma, both once wide-spread among Arabs, have been greatly reduced. The cleanliness of the water supply, of food shops and factories, is rigidly inspected. Arabs are encouraged to give more care to their poor people, orphans, aged, delinquent youth. Israel has Arab social workers and public health officers—something unknown until now among Arab nations.

Education

Before 1948, the British government managed Arab schools and the Jews took care of their own. Only two out of ten Moslem children learned the "3 R's" as compared with nine out of ten Jewish and Christian children. In Arab villages, five different grades usually met with only one or two teachers. Girls rarely went beyond second or third grade.

Today, elementary education is provided by the State of Israel. In Arab schools, instruction is in Arabic, but Hebrew is also taught. Over eighty per cent of all Arab children between the ages of five and fourteen, including practically every boy, attend school regularly. In Arab lands, school attendance still runs as low as one-fourth of the children in Jordan, or two-fifths in Iraq. Israel, in contrast, will eventually have the first Arab community in the world where almost everyone can read and write.

Arab school children now have kindergartens for the first time in history. Arab schools no longer teach the ancient Arabic language of the Koran, the Moslem sacred scriptures, but the language used in everyday life. Many Arab boys and girls study together in the same classrooms—something utterly unheard of in most of the Moslem world, and still resisted by some villages and the Bedouin tribes of the Negev.

For complete equality with Jews, Israeli Arabs must have a good modern education. They are just beginning to appreciate the need for advanced schooling. Six out of ten Arab high school students get scholarships or lower fees, compared with three out of ten Jewish students—a sign of Arab unwillingness to pay for higher education, as compared with Jews. But time is on the side of progress. In a recent three-year period, the number of Arab high school pupils doubled. In 1949, just *one* Arab attended college. Now, over one hundred Arab young people attend the Hebrew University or the Haifa Technion, studying medicine, law, and other professions.

The New and the Old

Israel encourages Arabs to drop traditions that prevent them from enjoying modern life. For example, a quiet revolution has been going on, in the new Israel, for Arab women and girls. They used to stay hidden behind shuttered doors and black veils, as the outright "property" of father or husband. Now, they attend classes in housekeeping, sewing, bookkeeping. They work in factories, earn their own living, may even vote or be elected to office. These are all "firsts" for Arab women anywhere in the Middle East. But even as

1967. After the Six Day War (see Chapter 25), 35 Arabs from East Jerusalem applied for admission to the Hebrew University—and were accepted. About 400 Arab students attend the Hebrew University and the Haifa Technion.

ARAB EDUCATION. Elementary education is free and compulsory for Arabs as well as Jews. A larger percentage of Arab population attends school than of Jewish population, because of higher Arab birthrate and larger Arab families.

Arabs begin to catch up with their Jewish fellow-citizens, many still insist on the old ways. Israel tries to deal gently with such people. For instance, the government does not prosecute Arab parents who refuse to send girls to school. The march of events will take care of these "old-timers."

On the other hand, Israel encourages Arabs to preserve traditions that give beauty and character to life.

Arabs may use their own language in the Knesset (Parliament), the law courts, and in letters to the authorities. Israeli stamps, coins, and currency use Arabic along with Hebrew. The government prints its official news bulletin, and publishes Supreme Court decisions, in both Arabic and Hebrew. It sponsors and helps pay for Arab club-houses, lectures, music lessons, orchestras, choirs, art exhibits, libraries, athletic teams. Israel has an Arabic daily newspaper and seven Arabic weekly papers. The Israel radio broadcasts regular Arabic programs several hours a day, including frequent readings from the Koran and Christian worship services.

In recent national elections, almost ninety per cent of Israeli Arabs voted—a higher proportion than the Jews! Several Arab members sit in Israel's Knesset, most of them representing Arab communities, the others elected by mixed communities. Israeli Arabs have more to say in the government than most "citizens" do in the Arab countries. They have full freedom of speech, assembly, worship. They may vote at eighteen, and run for office at twenty-one, like all Israeli citizens. They may—and do—criticize the government freely.

Israel does not wish to separate her Arabs as a backward minority, or destroy their culture and assimilate them into the Jewish majority. She wants them to be loyal citizens and at the same time follow their own culture with pride and love.★

★ 1. One government aim is to make Arabs completely equal to Jews. How well has Israel succeeded in this aim?

2. Why did leaders of surrounding Arab nations resist Jewish settlement in Palestine, and why do they now oppose the State of Israel? (Hint: Suppose Arabs in other lands start comparing themselves with Israeli Arabs?)

Second-Class Citizens?

In three border regions in the Galil, Israel's Defense Forces at first put certain controls on the people. They could not move freely in these territories, or go in and out of them, even for short journeys, without a special permit. Arabs there had special identity cards. A curfew required farmers to return to their village homes by a certain hour each evening.

Many Israeli Jews opposed these restrictions as strongly as the Arabs themselves. Arabs, they said, felt set apart from the rest of the population, not trusted as citizens—and therefore more willing to side with the enemy in case of an invasion. The restrictions also kept alive the resentment of many Arabs over certain military

In the midst of wanton aggression, we yet call upon the Arab inhabitants of the State of Israel to return to the ways of peace and play their part in the development of the State, with full and equal citizenship and due representation in all its bodies and institutions. . . .

—Israel Declaration of Independence, May 14, 1948

actions by Israel during the War for Independence—seizure of some Arab property, moving the population of a few villages to new locations and destroying the old ones.

The government's answer was simply to point to the map. Four out of five Arabs live close to the borders between Israel and Arab nations. At one place, foreign territory touches Israel's narrowest point, where invaders could most easily cut the country in half. Israeli Arabs are within easy reach of Israel's enemies on the other side of a single strand of barbed wire. Sometimes the border cuts a village in half, separating Israeli Arabs from Israel's enemies by only a narrow street.

These border zones are dangerous for Israel. The enemy would naturally use them as springboards into the country, counting on support and protection—or at least non-resistance—from Arabs living there. Some Israeli Arabs illegally cross the border to "visit" relatives and friends, meanwhile doing a little smuggling or coming back trained as spies and troublemakers. In 1962, the evening curfew in existence since 1949 was abolished for an eighty-mile strip along the Jordan border. Within two days, seven Israeli Arabs were arrested for hiding Syrian agents planning to blow up Israel's water pipeline to the Negev.

Israel's restrictions were not imposed because the Arabs are of different race or religion. The restrictions applied to *Jews* also, and only to the *movement* of people in the three danger zones. Israel's Army had no say whatever in the politics, business, religion, or culture of the villages concerned. The restrictions did not apply to Arabs anywhere else in Israel.

The rules, strict at first, were gradually relaxed, and many districts gradually got complete freedom of movement. The government tried to make life in the danger zones more tolerable as time went on. In 1963, all restrictions on travel in this region were lifted, except in five borderline villages, and except for several hundred individual Israeli Arabs under suspicion.

The restrictions were frequently debated in the Knesset. Israel understands the mixed feelings of Israeli Arabs—religion and nationality tie them to kinsmen in Arab lands, yet they want to live and work peacefully in Israel. To prevent more tension, Israel does not require Arabs to serve in her Army, but they may volunteer.★

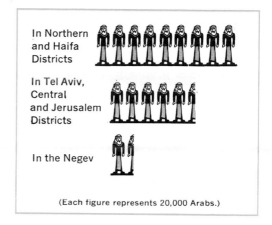

In Northern and Haifa Districts

In Tel Aviv, Central and Jerusalem Districts

In the Negev

(Each figure represents 20,000 Arabs.)

WHERE ARABS LIVE. Arabs in the Galil and the Negev, compared to the city Arabs, are a special problem for Israel. Why? (Several answers—consider the size, location, and kind of life of each group.)

1966. Another step toward complete integration of Israel's Arab citizens: abolition of military government in border areas.

★ Why has Israel been able to abolish nearly all border restrictions? (Two or three answers.)

"The State of Israel . . . will uphold the absolute equality of rights, social and political, of all its citizens without distinction of religion, conscience, language, education and culture. . . ."

—Israel Declaration of Independence, 1948

Jews and Arabs—Israelis All

1964. Haifa established a community center as an Arab-Jewish meeting place for social and cultural activities by young people. Some Arab parents, at first, were suspicious, fearing "assimilation" of their young people. Within a few years, the center was so popular and successful that several other towns with mixed populations have established similar centers.

In Haifa, Jews and Arabs mingle easily and pleasantly in business, cultural, and community activities. In Tel Aviv, thousands of Arab workers come from poor villages where they cannot earn a living. For six days a week, they work among Jews, but keep to themselves. On the seventh day, they return to their own homes and families.

Most of Israel's Jews and Arabs do not come in close contact with one another. Unpleasant feelings, suspicions, exist on both sides. The middle-aged and older people, Jews and Arabs alike, cannot shake off the harrowing memories of the war years.

What do Israeli Arabs really think about Arab countries that keep promising "a second round," this time to "drive the Jews into the sea"? It is hard to know for sure. Foreign radio and television programs are freely heard and discussed among Israeli Arabs. Who knows how many of them are swayed by the unceasing anti-Israel propaganda from Egypt and other lands? Arab youth, if ignorant and uneducated, easily fall into hatred of the Jewish state. Educated young Arabs sometimes find themselves accepted neither by their own people nor by the Jews. Many injustices to Israeli Arabs still

HIS BROTHER'S KEEPER. Jewish expert, teaching Arab farmer how to use modern machinery, makes a point about care of the soil. Why is the Arab so pleased?

wait to be straightened out. Israel has allowed thousands of Arab refugees to return from Arab countries and rejoin their families. Thousands more want to come back, but Israel hesitates to accept them. The claims of Arab farmers for land taken away from them during the war have not yet all been settled.

Some Israelis believe that Jewish-Arab tension will be almost impossible to change. But signs of progress are growing. The first joint Arab-Jewish factory was opened in 1959 to can vegetables and fruit. A number of Arabs have volunteered for Israel's Defense Forces. In Haifa, recently, a Jewish-Arab Youth and Community Center opened. Non-Jewish residents are beginning to understand that equal rights means equal duties. More Arabs call themselves "Israelis" instead of "Palestinians." Arabs and Jews influence each other more, in food, music, dance, language, literature.

Several groups work hard to bind Israeli Jews and Arabs into a more united nation. The "Ichud" ("Unity"), organized many years before the Jewish State, stresses the ethical ideals of Judaism in dealing with Arabs. It has urged the removal of the military restrictions, help for Arab refugees on the other side of the border, and more Arabs in the higher government posts.

The Jewish-Arab Association, organized eight years after the Jewish State, provides free lawyers for Arabs claiming unfair treatment. It worked for the end of military controls, and tries to present all sides of every Jewish-Arab controversy. The Arab-Jewish Association of Poets holds an annual poetry festival, with awards for the best poems in Arabic written by either Arabs or Jews.

To harmonize relations between Jews and Arabs will be mainly the job of the younger generation—the children who did not suffer the tragic war experiences, who freely play and study together. The olive, the Arab farmer's favorite tree, takes forty years to bear good fruit. An Arab farmer will tell you he plants this tree not for himself, but for his children to enjoy. Maybe Jews will have to show the same kind of patience and understanding toward their Arab brothers.

Only in Israel

In 1962, an Arab and a Jewish student, both graduates in architecture at the Technion, Israel's Institute of Technology, did a joint research project on the problem of displaced Arabs. One was the son of a Moslem farmer, the other the son of a Jewish lawyer. They submitted their work, including a plan for a model Arab village, for a master's degree in architecture.

1966. A joint summer camp opened in Akko, north of Haifa, to foster Jewish and Arab youth contacts. Haifa itself has a Jewish-Arab school and a large joint community center.

95

1966. About 140 kibbutzim "adopted" nearby Arab and Druse villages, arranging joint outings and exchange visits of children to provide closer contacts between Jews and Arabs.

★ The government's first aim for Arabs: to make them fully equal to Jews. The second aim: to provide military protection for the dangerous border zones. What is the third aim? How well is it being accomplished?

Israel's Jews wonder how Israeli Arabs will act if Arab nations attack the country. Israel's Arabs wonder about themselves as a small minority in a country where once they outnumbered the Jews so greatly. Perhaps peace will have to come to the whole Middle East before Israeli Jews and Arabs can break down the wall between them. Perhaps if they break down this wall first, by themselves, they will help bring about such a peace.★

YOU'LL ENJOY READING

Israel Without Tears, by Ruth Gruber

YOU'LL ENJOY SEEING

To Win the Peace (filmstrip: Women's Labor Zionist Organization)

THE NEW AND THE OLD. Combines and other modern farm machinery, given to the Negev Bedouins by the Government, puzzle the camels—but please the Bedouins.

chapter 9

Israel's Youth at Work and Play

Israel's Schools

Education in Israel is free and compulsory in the first eight grades, for children from five to fourteen years old. An Israeli family has a choice between two different types of free public school. The "State Schools" do not stress religion. The "Religious State Schools" teach Orthodox Judaism, prayers, ceremonies, and more detailed courses in Bible and Talmud. These schools employ only Orthodox teachers, principals, and supervisors, and use specially prepared textbooks. All schools must cover the same basic subjects, employ qualified teachers, use approved texts, and have safe, sanitary buildings.

Israeli schools lack funds, teachers, and buildings. The tremendous rise in population after 1948 has been hard to keep up with. The government has trouble planning standard courses, textbooks, or even methods, because of the great variety among Israel's people. Although schools are in session six days a week, the school year is short, with long holidays. In some places, the extremely hot climate prevents concentration on books and homework.

And yet, the educational level is quite high. The United Nations, in a recent study of the schools of all nations, found Israel doing as good a job as some of the most advanced European countries. Israeli teachers are generally well-trained, and use the latest methods and devices. Most pupils are eager to learn and advance themselves.

TOUGH BUT TENDER. The sabra (cactus pear) is thorny outside, but sweet inside. Early Chalutzim called their children "sabras." They too had to be tough, against the hard life and many dangers—yet gentle to one another and with high ideals, for a new, better way of life.

Sabras at School

In the first six grades, pupils get little homework and few tests, and promotion is almost automatic. The Bible is stressed in all subjects, and in all grades, especially the Prophets and their ideals of righteousness and justice. Farming, physical work, and home economics

■ Israeli pupils, when not playing or gardening, study much the same subjects you do, but in Hebrew, of course. They read many of your "classics"—Poe's tales, *Tom Sawyer*, *Gulliver's Travels*, *Moby Dick*. Most schools are co-ed. Nearly 700,000 children attend school—about a third of the whole population—including many thousands of immigrant and Arab children who need special education.

are also emphasized. Most schools have their own piece of farmland, their own wood and metal shops. Boys and girls often take turns cooking a warm lunch for the rest of the school. Teachers also emphasize safety, hygiene, good health. Sometimes they even check lunches brought from home, to make sure there's enough food and a well-balanced diet.

These grades also provide a great deal of sports, artcrafts, singing, dancing, and social life. The "big moment" each week is the Friday afternoon party when the whole school welcomes Shabbat together —not as teachers and pupils, but as older and younger fellow Jews.

High School

In Grades 7 and 8, pupils suddenly get long homework assignments, holiday and summer vacation tasks, stiff tests, strict marking. Parents begin "pressuring" both children and teachers for higher marks.

Israeli high schools are neither free nor compulsory. They do not automatically accept elementary school graduates, and require superior marks. They also charge tuition, up to $250 a year. This, plus the cost of books and other expenses, creates a hardship for poorer families. The national and city governments give scholarships to the better students, the amount depending on family income, number of children, length of time in the country, and marks in class work and special examinations.

Jewish organizations, both in Israel and in our own country, also provide scholarship aid. Yet only one out of four children between fourteen and seventeen enters high school. Out of every two pupils admitted to high school, only one goes on to graduation. There are not enough high schools, and they are not spread evenly over the country. City high schools are cheaper, but harder to enter. Only a third of all high school pupils attend a full day, the rest going part-time to schools with double shifts. Many high schools are private institutions, some owned by teachers and parents, others run as a business for profit.

Much tension may develop in Grades 7 and 8, over whether or not a youngster can go on to high school. Some families start saving up for high school tuition when a child begins the first grade—or even take out an insurance policy. You can see why few high school pupils come from Arab or immigrant families, and why Israelis and their government are concerned. Israel is a small country with many problems. The only way she can succeed is to have well-educated citizens. Everyone must work at his best; no one should remain

1965-1970. The government plans to build 55 new high schools, in new towns and others with large immigrant populations.

THE BIG QUESTION. As students enter a high school in Jerusalem, the two younger children may be wondering if they too will "make it" some day, scholastically and financially.

1967. About ¾ million young people attended schools and colleges. Education was the second largest item in Israel's budget, after defense. Almost half of all high school students received their schooling free, the rest paying tuition according to their family's finances. Plans were under way to raise the minimum age for leaving school from fourteen to fifteen.

ignorant or untrained. And yet—she cannot afford free education beyond the age of fourteen.

Each year, more young people attend high school, more schools are built, the government can afford more scholarship help, and tuition fees decrease. But a completely free high school education for everyone is still some years away. Meanwhile, one out of three pupils who can't go to high school attends a vocational or farm school. Some attend evening classes after their day's work.

Besides language, math, and science, high school students devote much time to Bible, Talmud, Hebrew literature, Jewish history. Arabic is taught in over a hundred Jewish high schools as well as in Arab schools. For their foreign language, most Israeli youngsters choose English—spoken with a British accent!—or French.

In the last two grades, a student may specialize in a particular field of studies. High schools also emphasize dramatics, music, folk-dancing—and service to the country. Students are expected to assist with immigrants, help in agricultural pioneering, and work on farms, especially in times of emergency.

The big event of the high school year is the annual class trip in the spring. The class chooses its own destination—city youth generally selecting a farm village, and the other way round. Before such a trip, students spend several days studying maps, reading up on the region, planning activities, and packing their knapsacks, sleeping bags, canteens, and food. Then off they go in a hired truck, for three or four days of exciting adventure and new experiences.

Graduation requires passing marks in eight different written tests: Hebrew literature, language, grammar, English, math, Bible, and two subjects chosen by the student from Talmud, Jewish thought, history, chemistry, biology, French, Arabic. This is about as much as a college freshman or sophomore is expected to know in our own country—and there's plenty of private tutoring! But a successful high school graduate is automatically admitted, after his army service, into college.

Try This: How does Israeli school life resemble our own? How does it differ? List the answers to both questions on a bulletin board poster. Indicate clearly what you consider to be the strong and the weak points of Israeli education.

Sabras at Play

Sabras, like most Israeli adults, are sports-minded. Everywhere, in the smallest village and the largest city, in Kibbutz schools and universities, they engage in athletics or cheer other players on to victory. Many of them dream of becoming star athletes. They worship the country's champions, and will often mob a star soccer player for his autograph.

School children with a few minutes to spare kick around any kind of ball, even a small one—just as you would "have a catch." After soccer, basketball is their most popular game. Sabras learn to swim almost from infancy, and go in for every other sport you do—except perhaps football and baseball.

Besides two hours of physical training a week, Israeli schools give all pupils a planned sports program from kindergarten to university. But as a new, struggling country, Israel hasn't much extra money to spend on school sports and athletic equipment. Qualified coaches and gym teachers are in short supply. Many a gym teacher dashes from one school to another for ten hours a day.

The school system also has hundreds of playgrounds, summer camps, day camps, youth centers, and hikers' rest-houses—many of them located in the newer immigrant centers. There are also libraries, free concerts both recorded and "live," film showings, and art classes. Individual hobbies include everything from collecting napkins to archeology.

A SPORTS-MINDED COUNTRY. Women's class at the Wingate Institute of Physical Culture. Find out for whom this school is named. (Opposite page) "Football" (or soccer, as we call it) is Israel's most popular sport. There are no professional athletes in Israel—all are amateurs.

101

★ Why do Israeli youth favor instruments like the flute, accordion, harmonica, drum? Why do most of them prefer accompanying themselves rather than recorded music?

Teen-age Sabras love to sing and dance, especially folk and group styles. Many prefer to accompany themselves on the chalil (flute), accordion, drum, or harmonica, rather than use records or a jukebox. In the cities, there is social dancing, "dating," and going to the movies.★

In summer vacation, Sabras may sleep late, read, work, go swimming, or do their school summer assignments. But best of all, they love to travel up and down the land. They have a deep love for Israel's streets and countryside. They'll go on a טִיוּל—a hike, at the slightest excuse—when spring flowers come out, to look at a new building, to watch an archeological "dig," to help a nearby village harvest crops, or to honor the grave of an Israeli hero.

Israel's Youth Clubs

A tourist in Israel often meets such a group of Sabras, getting together at a bus station, or marching briskly along a city street or country road—and usually singing at the top of their voices. He may notice some מַדְרִיכִים—teachers or counselors, among them, only a few years older, but obviously their leaders. These Sabras belong to one of Israel's nine youth groups.

Tiyul: טִיוּל   Madrichim: מַדְרִיכִים

Such groups provide recreational and social affairs, courses, and discussions. They are sponsored by some adult organization eager to train leaders, and to guide young people to live according to its own ideas. All but two religious groups are co-ed.

The Histadrut, Israel's labor federation, supports the only youth group of its kind in the world. It finds jobs for members, trains them for new jobs, protects them in disputes with employers, and stresses socialist Zionism as the best way of life—a sort of junior trade union. Other youth groups are sponsored by political or religious parties. There is an Arab youth organization, and several for Oriental youth. Two youth groups are sponsored by the Army and one jointly by the government and the schools. Each group has its own uniforms and insignia. About 100,000 boys and girls between ten and eighteen are youth group members.

An Israeli youth group takes a major part of a member's time and interest, and influences his politics, career, attitudes. A Sabra's close friends are usually his comrades in a youth group, rather than kids living on the same block or schoolmates. He is closely connected with an adult group trying to influence the whole country. Even more than his home or school, a youth group shapes a youngster's whole life.

Try This: Find out about the Reform movement's NFTY (National Federation of Temple Youth), the Conservative movement's LTF (Leadership Training Fellowship); also the Young Judaea, BBYO (B'nai B'rith Youth Organization), Junior Hadassah, and other American Jewish youth groups. How are they like and unlike Israel's?

Scouting in Israel

The largest youth organization, the Scouts, tries to be "non-political"—to stress general values for all Israeli youth, not the ideas of one particular party or organization. A "religious section" of Orthodox scouts conducts its own program, but often joins other scouts for combined activities. In this way, Israeli youth meet one another, and learn to respect differences.

Israeli scouting has special ties with American Jewish Youth. Young Judaea, a youth group sponsored by Zionist organizations in the United States, works closely with Israeli scouts, who are of the same age. שְׁלִיחִים—delegates from Israeli scout troops, come to this country to lead Young Judaea clubs and serve as junior counselors in Young Judaea camps. Young Judaeans raise money for a "farm" in Israel where Israeli scouts get leadership training. Young Judaeans take summer courses in the Kibbutzim built by Israeli scouts.

In 1967 the Israel Scout Federation had over 27,500 scouts—Jewish, Christian and Moslem—grouped into 6 federations. They have

Shlichim: שְׁלִיחִים

SHOMRIAH (Scout "Jamboree"). Israel is the only country with co-ed scout troops, beginning at age fifteen. (Several reasons—what are they?) A troop meeting opens with reciting the Scout Law. Then the Scoutmaster asks: "Tzofim (Scouts), what does God require of you?" The troop answers: "To do justice, love mercy, and walk humbly with God!" (Where are these words taken from?) High point at a scout campfire is the solemn "dedication" of a log to the fire in honor of scouts who died in the War for Independence.

common national and district headquarters. Israeli scouts of all faiths have attended International Scout Jamborees since 1955.

The Jewish scouts are called צוֹפִים. Their mottoes are הֱיֵה נָכוֹן —"Be Prepared," and חֲזַק וֶאֱמָץ—"Be Strong and Brave." They are organized into שְׁבָטִים—tribes, גְדוּדִים—troops, and קְבוּצוֹת— groups or patrols, in three different age levels of 10-13, 13-15, 15-18. Scouts take the usual tenderfoot, second class, and first class tests, and have junior and senior leaders. Scouting emphasizes good citizenship, honesty, responsibility, helpfulness, respect for others, democratic ideals. Scouts hike, camp out, sing, dance, hold discussions, help in fund drives and community projects. Younger scouts study Zionist heroes and history, and discuss problems of rebuilding the homeland and the importance of labor. Older scouts do actual work in new settlements, immigrant camps, and army posts. In addition, they study Israeli politics, the United Nations, and international problems. Scout troops often join the Army as a group, and volunteer to help out a new settlement short in manpower, or start one of their own.

Senior scout leaders are generally teachers. In fact, teachers founded the Israeli scout movement in the high schools of Tel Aviv and Haifa between 1900 and 1910. Often scouts build their club house on their school grounds, and use their school's playground and other equipment. They gather for meetings and activities two afternoons a week. On Shabbat, they meet in the middle of the afternoon, and spend the rest of the day and evening together.

Tzofim: צוֹפִים He-yay nachon: הֱיֵה נָכוֹן Chazak ve-ematz: חֲזַק וֶאֱמָץ

Shevatim: שְׁבָטִים Gedudim: גְדוּדִים Kevutzot: קְבוּצוֹת

104

As Sabras Grow Up

Israelis adore their Sabras and at the same time criticize them bitterly—like an older generation anywhere else.

Sabras can be unpleasant youngsters—tough and unmannerly. Some are interested only in dating, dancing, new clothes, and cheap paperback fiction. They don't seem to realize that the border is barely ten miles from Tel Aviv, or that Israel has serious immigrant problems. Even in such an exciting country where there is so much to do, some young people manage to be bored or become juvenile delinquents.

But there are other Sabras, too. One out of every ten boys and girls going to high school works his way through school by baby-sitting, doing housework, or clerking. A Tel Aviv high school class decided, for its spring trip, to visit a new border village—to get better acquainted with Israel's immigrants. Four out of five Hebrew University students put in forty hours a week in class, then work nights to pay their tuition, and use their vacations to get in some of their army service or to catch up on their required reading. Scouts and other youth group members toil for the nation in the summers, volunteer while in the Army to guard a border village and share in its work.

Sabras have fought in the Haganah, the "underground" volunteer defense forces, against the British and the Arabs; in the War for Independence; in the Sinai Campaign. Right now, as you read this, Sabras are studying in school, working in a factory or on a farm, relaxing between sessions of hard labor. Still others are manning border villages, turning the Negev wasteland into farms and towns, helping in immigrant camps, or building roads.

Understanding the Sabras

American teen-agers, on first meeting Sabras, find them a bit "cold." Sabras do not make friends as quickly as Americans—they have to meet you many times, get to know you well. But they have something that American teen-agers envy. They are treated with greater respect, as though already adults, and have more responsibility.

In appearance, Sabras are well-built, stronger, healthier, and usually taller than their parents. They carry themselves with confidence—head high, shoulders back, muscles flexed. Their outlook is different, too. They grew up in Israel, feel completely at home there. They've known no other life than that of free Jews enjoying their own land. They are naturally proud and independent.

Only in Israel

When Sabras haven't got what they need or want, they "make do" in clever ways. It's fearfully hot in Eilat, but its marine museum is quite comfortable.

In front of the door, and facing the main winds, is a screen of chicken wire, plaited with strips of seaweed. A garden hose hanging over it keeps dripping water. The wind blows, the wet seaweed evaporates its water, and the interior stays cool. With straight faces, Eilat's people tell visitors it's "desert air-conditioning."

What's more, they add, it can't be really that hot—East African sailors, who get an "Arctic bonus" on voyages to cold climates, ask for it at Eilat too—and get it.

Sabras may behave as though they personally started a new chapter in Jewish history. They study the biblical past and are thrilled with it. But they don't know or care very much about the long story of the Jewish people since then. They think of themselves as descending directly from Bible heroes. There are good reasons for such an attitude. Jewish life in modern Israel is quite different from that of their parents in other lands and bygone days. Sabras do not share the emotional ties of their parents with the vanished life of European communities.

These young Israelis sometimes tend to look down on Jews who live elsewhere. They can't understand why American Jews don't rush to become Israelis like themselves, or how a Jew can be a "Zionist" and still want to live outside of Israel. They have had little contact with other Jews. They think Jewish life in America resembles that of their parents and grandparents in Europe—a life of persecution. They are ashamed and scornful of Jews who, they think, let themselves be beaten and murdered. Sabras have never let themselves be pushed around—they believe in fighting back.

Sabras are often confused about religion. They will drop everything to listen to the broadcast of the Bible Quiz, sometimes for hours. They celebrate the festivals enthusiastically, often creating new customs. But some say they do not "need" Judaism or its traditional practices connected with "life in the exile."

Other Sabras earnestly seek answers to religious questions, and look for religious meaning in life. They organize discussion "circles," and join new Reform and Conservative congregations just starting up in Israel. Such Sabras, in 1960 and again in 1963, called world conventions of Jewish youth. Over two hundred young people from thirty-five countries joined almost a hundred Sabras for discussion on how to get young Jews the world over to live a more Jewish life.★

★ Consider all you have learned about Sabras at school, at play, in their youth groups, their character and personality. Do they deserve their nickname? Are they like the tzabar (pear)—tough and thorny on the outside, but fine and noble inside? Try to give specific reasons and examples to prove your answer.

HAVE YOU WONDERED . . . ?

. . . about college education in Israel?

Israel has several fine universities and colleges. The oldest is the Technion, or Institute of Technology, in Haifa. It offers courses in many branches of science and technical skills, as well as academic subjects, and conducts hundreds of valuable research projects. Technion graduates—half of Israel's engineers—have supervised the building of many roads, bridges, factories, and other buildings.

The Hebrew University, in Jerusalem, is the Middle East's finest institution of higher learning. It includes colleges of law, medicine,

At school assemblies, rallies, etc., no more than three speeches may be delivered, and at least one of them must be by a pupil.

—Government Order to School Principals, 1962

science, social work, and so on. Many professors are former graduates. They too carry on hundreds of research projects and experiments in science, agriculture, archeology, and other fields. They have helped educate many of the country's leaders, and have directed development in the Negev and other places. Recently, with aid from the National Council of Jewish Women of America, the Hebrew University opened a model high school.

The Bar-Ilan University, at Ramat Gan near Tel Aviv, includes Orthodox religious courses in Bible, Hebrew literature, Talmud. The Tel Aviv University stresses science, Jewish subjects, and music. Over thirty colleges train teachers for kindergarten and elementary grades, art, music, and physical education. Almost twenty conservatories train both musicians and music teachers. The Weizmann Institute, in Rehovot, is a world-famous graduate institution for advanced research in all branches of science.

Israeli higher education seems to stress what two things? Can you figure out why?

1968. American College, a new institution, opened in Israel, for non-Israeli students. Purpose: to foster Jewish and Hebrew culture in English-speaking countries (not American culture in Israel). All courses are taught in English, but Hebrew study is required.

1965. Beer Sheva University opened its first building. Why is it important for Israel to have universities, colleges and high schools in the Negev?

YOU'LL ENJOY READING

Children of Freedom, by Libbie Braverman
The World Over Story Book, by Norton Belth, pages 113, 373, 385, 401, 411, 467, 479

YOU'LL ENJOY SEEING

Deadline for Danny (film: United Israel Appeal)
House on the Hill (film: American Friends of the Hebrew University)
A Letter from Ronny (film: Israel Office of Information)

chapter 10

Israel's "Mixed" Economy

The United States is a capitalist society. The government does not control the way people earn a living. A man may work for the government, or a non-profit organization, or an employer who runs a business for profit—or he may have his own business. In communist Russia, the government owns all farms, factories, and shops, and controls the way people earn their living—everyone works for the government. The United States is a democracy—the people control the government, and make up their own minds about politics, religion, art, literature. Russia is a dictatorship—a small Communist Party rules the people and guides their opinions on almost every subject.

Israel is a democracy like the United States. She has borrowed much from capitalism, but also uses some socialist ideas, to develop an unusual society of her own.

PARTNERS ALL. Recently, the J. N. F. bought the wild, hazardous Adullam border region, and paid settlers of seventeen different villages to remove stones, lay roads, drain marshes. The Keren Hayesod installed water and electricity, built houses and fences. The 800 families here took two to four years to become self-supporting. Border Police gave day-and-night protection. Government, Israelis, Jews of the world, including you—all partners! (Opposite page)

The Moshavah—Private Ownership

The First Aliyah settlers (1882–1904) were capitalists. They lived together in a village and cooperated on common problems. But each owned his house and equipment, and his piece of land outside the village. He made his own decisions, kept his profits, paid for his losses—like a businessman in this country.

These settlers soon found they were not experienced or strong enough to do field labor. They hired Arab workers and guards at low wages, and supervised them as plantation owners or "gentlemen farmers." They had many difficulties. Their attempts would have ended in complete failure except for the help of an unusual Jew, the

French nobleman, Baron Edmond de Rothschild. He donated millions of dollars to build houses for them, plant vineyards, erect large modern wine-presses. He also sent agents to show them how to run farms.

They called their type of village a מוֹשָׁבָה—Colony, Privately-owned Village. Many Moshavot raised fruits, like oranges and lemons. These became a major crop in Palestine, and today are still a major export of Israel. Plantation companies, organized by Jews abroad, bought land for new colonies. Over the years, Moshavot continued to prosper, and some, like Petach Tikvah, Rosh Pinah, Rishon Letzion, and Zichron Yaakov, have grown into large towns.

The K'vutzah—Group Ownership

The Second Aliyah (1902–1914) brought Zionists who wanted a socialist Jewish homeland. Bitter conflict raged between the two groups. The new settlers demanded jobs on the plantations in place of Arab workers, and at decent wages. They announced they were going to change the whole farming system of Palestine. They would build a society where no man would profit from another man's labor. The older settlers preferred Arab workers who accepted low pay and had no "dangerous" socialist ideas.

The new settlers soon decided to establish their own villages to carry out their ideas. Here the whole group owned and controlled everything. Everyone worked with his own hands instead of employing others; all shared equally in the group's gains and losses. They did not even have separate houses, or live as separate families. They worked, ate, brought up their children as a group. They called this kind of village a קְבוּצָה—Group, Gathering.

■ This group was photographed in 1912 in Deganiah, Israel's oldest collective village (founded in 1909). How did a K'vutzah like this resemble a Moshavah? How did it differ?

Moshavah: מוֹשָׁבָה   Kevutzah: קְבוּצָה

110

Socialism and group living were more than ideals. They were the only practical answer to the hardships, poverty, Arab enmity, and lack of water, soil, and equipment. An individual Jewish settler could not battle all these single-handed. The settlers had to cooperate or perish. They too were helped by Jews and Jewish organizations of other lands.

Their devotion, unselfishness, and intelligence enabled them to conquer the most difficult obstacles. They developed new farming practices. They proved that a group of Jewish workers, sharing alike in all duties and decisions, could produce more and better crops than the hired labor of Arab peasants. To defend themselves against hostile Arabs, they organized an armed and mounted guard force, הַשׁוֹמֵר—The Watchman, which eventually developed into the modern Israel Army.

The socialist villages spread and became a permanent part of the Jewish homeland, to this day. The early K'vutzot became models for all later farm settlements.

Try This: The Second Aliyah settlers made up a lively song about their goal: "We have come to the land, To build and be rebuilt in it! . . . To redeem it and be redeemed in it." Hold a discussion to explain the terms "build" and "be rebuilt." Then ask your music teacher to teach you how to sing this song—in Hebrew, of course!

Back to the Soil

In the early days of Zionism, Palestine's Jews depended for their food mostly on Arab farmers and imports from abroad. Today, Israel's farmers produce three-fourths of the country's food—all it needs except cereals, grain fodder, and fats—and they export food to other countries. The foundations for this success were laid by the trailblazers of the first two Aliyot, and especially of the Second Aliyah.

Both Aliyot—the capitalist and the socialist—agreed on three things. Palestine must become a Jewish homeland, its Jews must become self-supporting, and its Jewish life must be solidly based on farming. A successful nation must, above all, be able to produce its own food, clothing, shelter.

These settlers started a "back-to-the-soil" movement such as the Jewish people had not seen for almost 2,000 years. They turned swamp and desert into fertile soil. They changed themselves from merchants, peddlers, students, office workers into a strong, tough people of the land.

The first problem was to *get* the land. It belonged mostly to rich Arab landlords, who did not welcome Jewish settlers or a Jewish homeland. They demanded fabulous prices. Once land was bought, settlers needed more huge sums to drain swamps, clear away rocks,

Hashomer: הַשׁוֹמֵר

111

The land must not be sold permanently, for it is mine—you are only strangers and settlers with me. . . . You must provide for the redemption of all land.

plant trees, buy tools, seed, buildings, animals, machinery for modern scientific farming. They needed training schools. They had to improve the soil, find better seed, breed better livestock, try out new crops, fight plant and animal diseases.

The Jewish National Fund*

The J.N.F. was established in 1901 by the World Zionist Organization, to buy land in Palestine and help settlers develop productive farms. It collected money, mainly in coins and small sums, from Jews in every country. The land thus became the property of the Jewish people as a whole. It could never be sold—only rented at low rates—to settlers starting a new colony, workers building houses for themselves, or cultural institutions.

This remarkable organization helped the early K'vutzot get started, providing land, tools, seed, and animals. Since then, it has also installed water supply systems, drained vast quantities of swampy land. It has planted millions of trees to hold moisture in the earth, prevent floods, and provide shade, beauty, and fruit.

After 1948, the J.N.F. worked with the government to plant forests, reclaim deserts, supply land for new settlements and towns, train youth for farming, and build new roads. J.N.F. leaders estimate another twenty years of important work to be done for the country.

Today, only about ten per cent of the farm land of Israel belongs to private individuals. The rest is equally divided between the J.N.F. and the government. The government adopted the basic J.N.F. principles. This means no one in Israel can get rich by buying and selling farm land.

The J.N.F. is probably the only large-scale project in history to colonize a country through legal purchase rather than conquest.★

RECLAMATION. (Across left) In 1949, Israel began draining the Huleh swampland in eastern Galilee. (Below left) The Huleh region today—Israel's best farmland. Thirty years earlier, the Jewish National Fund bought a huge swampland running east-west across northern Palestine. Within ten years, Chalutzim (pioneers) had turned the *Emek* ("Valley") into rich, fertile farmland—as it had been once before in Bible days.

1968. The J. N. F. had reclaimed over 100,000 acres of land, planted over 85 million trees, and rebuilt over 1,100 miles of roads. In 1968, the Union of American Hebrew Congregations completed its Bar Kochba Forest project and began on a new one, the UAHC Victory Forest in Jerusalem Restored. Write to 838 Fifth Avenue, New York, N. Y. 10021, for information.

★ The J.N.F. is an example of a "public" organization. Is it a capitalist or socialist enterprise? Neither? Both?

---

*Keren Kayemet Leyisrael: קֶרֶן קַיֶמֶת לְיִשְׂרָאֵל

113

The Pioneers*

"A Chalutz, Chalutz is what I am, a Chalutz, do or die!
Without a coat or pair of shoes, or even a necktie!"

This was a favorite song of the Third Aliyah settlers (1918–1925). They took the name "Chalutz" from the Bible word for a front-line soldier, or "pioneer"—someone who prepared the way for others.

The new settlers accepted the ideals of the Second Aliyah: socialism, group living, labor on the soil, self-defense, use of Hebrew, striving for a homeland based on social justice. But they also had ideas of their own. For example, they started an international organization of training camps in various lands. Here, while still living at home, young Jews could study Hebrew and farming, and prepare themselves physically and spiritually to join a settlement in Palestine.

These settlers organized the first קִבּוּץ —Gathering, a new type of farm village. It was much like a K'vutzah, but accepted more members, allowed a larger village, and employed outside workers for wages when necessary. Kibbutzim not only farmed the soil and raised animals, like the K'vutzot; they also went into factory work and large-scale enterprises and organized national federations of Kibbutz villages. They felt that with these changes they could do a better job of carrying out their ideals.

K'vutzot and Kibbutzim grew more like each other as the years went by. Today, we usually call both types of villages a Kibbutz. Later you will explore the unique Kibbutz-K'vutzah types in more detail.

Others of the Third Aliyah developed still another type of village, the מוֹשַׁב עוֹבְדִים —Workers' Settlement. They wanted to build a cooperative society, yet have more individual freedom than in a Kibbutz.

The Moshav Ovdim is halfway between the capitalist Moshavah and the socialist Kibbutz. Each family owns and manages its land as it pleases, but may not employ outside labor. All contribute to a special fund to aid anyone who gets sick or suffers farm damage. The land of a sick farmer is worked for him by his neighbors. Business is organized in cooperatives: the members buy and sell as a group, and jointly maintain chicken incubators, cold storage rooms, and so on.★

★ Settlers now had three different types of socialist villages to go to, also the capitalistic Moshavah, and private business in the cities. Suppose you were settling in Palestine at that time, and had your choice. Which would it be, and why? Your second and third choices, and why?

---

*Chalutzim: חֲלוּצִים   Kibbutz: קִבּוּץ.   Moshav Ovdim: מוֹשַׁב עוֹבְדִים

114

The difference between a refugee and a pioneer is a difference of prepositions.
A pioneer goes to, *and a refugee comes* from.

—Maurice Samuel

Labor Israel

In the 1880's, industry in Palestine consisted of a few soap factories and flour mills. A few hundred Arab and Jewish craftsmen made tourist souvenirs out of beads, mother-of-pearl, and olive-wood. Forty years later, after World War I, Jews still had no factories and few factory workers. Looking ahead, they realized that a successful homeland needed industry as well as agriculture. Only thus could they take in large numbers of immigrants, manufacture the necessities and conveniences of modern living, and reach the standards of a modern nation.

But creating new industries was difficult. A few private owners wanted to start factories but could not get trained workers, raw material, cheap power to run their machines, or loans to buy supplies. Businessmen and investors in other lands could not be sure of a worthwhile return on money put into Palestine ventures.

Arab leaders, of course, bitterly opposed Jewish growth in the country, and obstructed it in every possible way—from charging astronomical prices for land to outright bloodshed. England did not care for Zionist projects either. She was more interested in maintaining her own power in countries around the Suez Canal and in getting along with Arab leaders who controlled rich oil lands. A "colony" was not supposed to develop its own industry, but to buy everything it needed from the "mother country." Big changes in an undeveloped country usually create problems and disturbances, which England wished to avoid.

And so, in 1920, the 4,500 Jewish workers of Palestine—hardly one out of twenty of all Jews there—set out to do the "impossible" by themselves. From the little they could spare out of their earnings, they collected a small treasury and organized a labor union. Like any union, they planned to fight for decent wages and working conditions, resist unfair employers, and provide for their own insurance, health, welfare, education. But they planned to do far more besides. They would bring in more Jewish immigrants, and train them to be farm and factory workers instead of scholars and storekeepers. On J.N.F. land, they would start new settlements, build factories, try new business ventures. They would build a whole country belonging to workers rather than employers.

Only in Israel

In 1962, the salary of Israel's second president, Yitzhak Ben-Zvi, was $1,500, about what his chauffeur earned, and less than many government workers. His extra expense allowance of $5,000, he donated to charities.

The Knesset decided he ought to have a bigger salary—four times bigger, in fact, or $6,000.

Ben-Zvi objected. He didn't need or want the increase, considered it a bad idea. The Knesset insisted, so he accepted it—against his will. Then he donated half his new salary to a fund for publishing historical documents.

115

From small streams of money, from savings and sacrifices and grand dreams, grew the Histadrut—the most unusual and powerful labor union, for its size, in the world. It owns and controls two-thirds of Israel's agriculture, half her industry, one-fourth of her factories, and most of her transport—and earns one-fourth of the country's entire income. Since it began before Palestine had any modern factories, the Histadrut greatly influenced new trade and industry. It could set high wages and control working conditions for private companies as well as for its own. It could establish the principle that no man or group of men should be allowed to get rich and powerful while others remained poor and weak. It could start farms and factories not profitable for a private company, but necessary for the country—so that some day private businessmen *would* want to invest their money in it.

Try This: Make a list of all the similarities and differences you can think of between the Histadrut and the usual American labor union. Arrange your list in two columns for display on the blackboard or bulletin board.

Cooperative Israel

Probably no other country in the world has as much cooperative enterprise for its population as Israel, and many newer nations closely study this part of Israel's pattern. Thousands of "co-ops" with hundreds of thousands of members handle most of the country's farming, practically all of its bus lines, many wholesale and retail stores, housing projects, and credit unions for lending money.

To join a co-op, a person must buy at least one "share" of its stock, the price of which rises or falls with the value of the co-op's profits. In some co-ops, owners, workers, suppliers, and customers are all the same group of people. Others employ for wages workers who are not members. Such outside employees may sometimes buy a co-op share out of their wages, and eventually become full members. Then they, too, have a vote in co-op affairs and share in its benefits or dividends.

In 1968 Israel had about 2,000 cooperatives.

Try This: Look up "Cooperative" in an encyclopedia, and read the "Rochdale" principles behind this kind of enterprise. Which of these principles are followed in Israel's cooperatives? What other ideas seem to be behind Israel's group? What do you know about cooperatives in the United States? Canada?

The Foundation Fund*

The Keren Hayesod is another fund by which Jews of the world helped Jews of Palestine. The World Zionist Organization established it to provide for all Yishuv needs except buying and improving land, which is the task of the J.N.F. It still collects money in seventy different countries, through the United Israel Appeal campaigns.

Try This: In the latest *American Jewish Year Book,* look over the list in the section on "National Jewish Organizations," under the heading, "Zionist and Pro-Israel." Choose one organization that interests you, and write a letter asking for pamphlets and magazines. When they arrive, make a bulletin board or table display.

*Keren Hayesod Leyisrael: קֶרֶן הַיְסוֹד לְיִשְׂרָאֵל.

116

Until the establishment of Israel, the Keren Hayesod helped pay for transporting and training immigrants, new houses and villages and towns, public health and social welfare projects, new industry and business, schools and cultural institutions, and the defense forces. When the government took over many of these tasks, the Keren Hayesod concentrated on immigration and settlement. It pays for travel, seeds, fertilizer, machinery, irrigation, and houses for the new immigrants. It sends expert advisers to help new settlers, and supports them financially until they can pay their own way.

Other agencies were started throughout the Jewish world, most of them developed by the World Zionist Organization. Some provided funds and advice. Others organized business ventures, lent or invested money for profit. The Haifa Bay area, the Palestine Potash Company, and the King David Hotel were some early enterprises financed in this way.

1968. Since 1948, the Keren Hayesod has spent over \$2 billion. In 1966-67, it spent \$120 million. The largest expenditures are for immigration and farming settlements, but it also contributes to Youth Aliyah, and to education and information in lands outside of Israel.

A GREATER PARTNERSHIP. In 1929, the Jewish Agency was organized, to include non-Zionists who wanted to support a Jewish Palestine though not necessarily as a Jewish State. Until 1948, the Jewish Agency worked closely with British authorities, the Yishuv, and the Zionist Organization in politics, business, education, and all other problems of the Jewish community. It sponsored and supervised large-scale farm settlements, started agricultural experimental stations and technical schools, maintained immigration offices in European countries. After 1948, the Jewish Agency remained the official international Jewish organization recognized by both the State of Israel and the Zionist Organization. It has headquarters in Jerusalem, New York, London, and Paris, and many different departments. These work on immigration, settlement, obtaining investments, training-farms outside of Israel, educational and cultural projects, and helping professionals find jobs in Israel. The picture shows the Jewish Agency Building in New York City.

Hermann Tzevi Schapira (1840-1898). Rabbi, mathematician. First suggested the Jewish National Fund and the Hebrew University.

Berl Katznelson (1887-1944). Labor leader, journalist, editor.

Private Enterprise in Palestine

The last two Aliyot increased still more the role of private enterprise. The Fourth Aliyah (1925–1928) consisted mostly of tradesmen and manufacturers, mainly from Poland. Most of them settled in Tel Aviv and invested their money in business and real estate. But too much money was being invested too fast, and in the wrong enterprises. The country was not yet ready to support that much capitalist growth. The get-rich-quick attitude of some immigrants soon led to a depression, in which they lost their money and many workers lost their jobs.

The Fifth Aliyah (1933–1939) of experienced business and professional people from Germany, brought many millions of dollars into the country, as well as new ideas and skills. These were years of prosperity. New factories opened, jobs increased, Jewish population jumped, cities swelled. Legally or illegally, immigrants poured in, new colonies and settlements sprang up. Even Arabs outside the country slipped across the border to take advantage of new opportunities in Jewish Palestine.

England needed much war material in World War II, and encouraged Palestine industry for the first time. The Yishuv, despite British unfairness over the years, rallied to the cause of freedom. It supplied the Allied armies with leather and metal goods, textiles, chemicals, machines, weapons. But this was an emergency war situation and would not make Jewish Palestine a self-supporting industrial country. Jews had to import all their materials, turn over their products to the British, and buy most of their own needs from other countries.

A new type of farm village was started in 1936, mostly by former Kibbutz members, a מוֹשָׁב שִׁיתּוּפִי—Cooperative Settlement, a combination of Kibbutz and Moshav Ovdim. Each family lives by itself in its own cottage. But all work, income, expense, profit, or loss is controlled by the group. This represents still another combination of capitalism and socialism in Israel.

Israel's Unusual Society

By 1948, the Five Aliyot had developed a united nation eager and ready for an economic life of its own. From people living mostly on charity, not interested in supporting themselves, the Jews of Palestine had become a self-reliant community in just fifty-six years. They knew what they wanted and were determined to have their way.

Moshav Shitufi: מוֹשָׁב שִׁיתּוּפִי

118

Geographically, Israel is an Asian country, part of the Middle East. Her scenery, soil, and neighbors are all Asian, along with over half her population. But investment money and mechanical know-how come mainly from the United States—also the books stacked high in the bookstores. Ways of thinking, behaving, governing—these are from Europe. Social ideals are partly borrowed from the British labor movement and European socialism. Israel's style of life, her ways of earning a living and doing business, are Western in their high standards and high hopes for the future.

Out of all this has come Israel's unusual society—a mixture of many things, but especially of age-old Jewish ideals of social justice and modern principles of democracy.

The government owns Israel's radio, telephone, and telegraph systems, airlines, ports, electric power, railroads, and mineral resources. Yet there is less government ownership in Israel than in France, Italy, or England. The leading party in control of the government is socialist, but encourages private business and investment, with special laws permitting high profits. Several hundred new private enterprises start every year.

Israel has plenty of capitalist business, from the barber or small café owner to the big Israeli-owned iron works. Private capitalists pioneered in growing citrus fruits, manufacturing electric power and chemicals, and developing other trade and industry. Among the big American firms with branches in Israel are General Tire Company, Studebaker-Packard, Fairbanks Whitney, Willys Overland, and Sheraton Hotels. The Tel Aviv Stock Exchange lists many local and foreign firms owning much property in Israel and elsewhere. Recently, a new stock was issued with low-priced shares and limited to three per customer. Fifteen thousand people immediately bought these shares, and nearly four hundred thousand others—twenty-seven times as many—applied too late.

Almost two-thirds of Israel's workers are employed by government agencies, the Histadrut labor union, or other public institutions. Yet about two-thirds of her factories and workshops are privately owned. The Israel Manufacturers Association plays an important role in helping to build a balanced economy.

Zionism and the labor movement developed various kinds of farm settlements and business ventures. Israel has both capitalist and socialist villages, and several in-between combinations. The labor movement owns many large and important companies, and is the country's biggest employer.

Much private money has been invested in the industries of Kibbutzim and cooperatives. Big industrial enterprises are financed through a partnership of private and cooperative funds. Public or-

Try This: Skim through Chapters 6 and 10, noting the dates and main facts about each of the five Aliyot. Then draw up a list of the events and causes that led to each group leaving its country and going to Palestine. Add a Sixth Aliyah after skimming through Chapters 18 and 24.

Only in Israel

A Tel Aviv family owned a profitable ironworks and lived an easy life. But then Prime Minister Ben-Gurion called on Israelis to move to the Negev and make it livable. Many thought the immigrants should have this task. Others agreed to go when offered higher wages and lower taxes. The members of the ironworks family sold their plant in Tel Aviv and invested their money in opening a similar plant at Beer Sheva. The government lent them additional money, and the J.N.F. leased them the land.

This family works long, hard hours. They have many problems—meeting the requirements of the Histadrut labor federation, training unskilled immigrants to handle delicate machinery, competing with foreign firms and with their own former firm in Tel Aviv. But they're quite happy. Israel's future, they explain, depends on the Negev, and they're doing their part to build and preserve Israel.

David Ben-Gurion (Poland, 1886-   ). Chalutz (pioneer), leader of Histadrut Labor Federation, and Israel's first Prime Minister.

Yitzhak Ben-Zvi (1884-1963). Labor leader, historian, statesman, Israel's second president.

Meir Dizengoff (1861-1936). Industrialist, a founder and first mayor of Tel Aviv.

HONOR ROLL

ganizations representing Jews of other lands operate hospitals and schools, lend money, buy land, bring in immigrants, build houses, and establish towns.

Israel has all sorts of ownership combinations: government and labor, labor and private business, government and businessmen, and so on—even to *three*-way partnerships. She is a unique mixture of every kind of society—except dictatorship.

How Israel Differs

Israel, one of the world's newest countries, is more advanced than many of them. In most new countries, farming develops first, then manufacturing, and finally service and professional jobs. Israel has tried to develop soil, factories, and science all at the same time.

Most of Israel's co-ops are affiliated with the Histadrut labor union, and are more socialistic than co-ops elsewhere. Yet co-ops have invested in private business enterprises, and private businessmen have also invested in co-ops. The co-ops were helped by money from American capitalists—otherwise they could not have supported themselves. They rented their land from the J.N.F., got their tools and livestock from the Keren Hayesod, and often had to make up their losses by loans and gifts from Jews abroad. The givers were capitalists, the receivers were socialists. But both were pioneering—establishing a country where the social ideals of the Bible prophets would be carried out. The help of the "outside" capitalist Jews made the socialists less radical and revolutionary, willing to move more slowly, and accept the good in capitalism instead of rejecting it completely. Israel's socialism thus became different from most other forms of socialism. Her cooperative society is watched carefully by many other undeveloped countries, who may some day try to copy it.

Israel has unusual social and economic equality, perhaps more than any other modern industrial society. In our own country, great differences still exist between rich and poor. Even in Russia, a high official can make thirty times as much money as a factory worker. In Israel, the Prime Minister's salary is only four times as high as the lowest paid government worker. Middle class city people do not live much better than members of farming co-ops; professionals do not live much better than factory workers. The differences between groups are not so great as in other lands. This equality gives a special charm to Israeli life. Most people respect not the money-makers but the Chalutzim, those who lead the rest in building the country's future.

PINHAS RUTENBERG, an imaginative engineer, tried to persuade America's General Electric Corporation to build a water-power electric plant on the Jordan River. They laughed at him. His plans, they said, would not work—and even if they did, Palestine would never have enough people to use the electricity. Rutenberg raised the money himself, persuaded the British government to grant him a concession, designed and erected his own plant in 1926. Partition of Palestine in 1947 left this power plant in Arab territory, still rusting away today because Jordan will neither use it herself nor let Israel use it. But Rutenberg's company still supplies electricity for the State of Israel.

MOSES NOVOMEYSKY struggled many years to get mineral rights from the British, and to raise money for a chemical plant at the Dead Sea. Few people saw any future in a "dead" sea, a "dead" country. But in World War II the whole British Empire depended on Novomeysky's plant for vital chemicals like potash, bromide, magnesium, and it now leads the world in potash production. The "dead" region turns out to be the world's only spot where a dozen all-important chemicals can be found together, and Israel has a major mineral-chemical center there. Capitalists and businessmen like Novomeysky and Rutenberg gave their strength and wealth to establish basic industries of modern Israel.

Most Israelis believe their "mixed" economy is better than total capitalism or socialism. Their strong labor union, which owns factories and co-ops, competes with capitalist owners who must make better and cheaper products. On the other hand, private business competes with the socialist enterprises of the co-ops, and forces them to do a better job. For example, a Canadian-American firm opened a modern supermarket, over strong opposition from Israeli co-ops and small store-owners. Soon the Israelis were modernizing their stores, lowering prices, and opening their own supermarkets.

Of course, Israel is far from a perfect society. There are disagreements, conflicts, strikes, complaints, failures. But Israelis are creative people, not too much tied down by past traditions or afraid to try new ideas. Out of their problems past and present, Israelis are developing an economic style of their own.★

★ Israel's "mixed" economy includes many conflicting groups and patterns. What enables the Israelis to cooperate and keep the country unified, instead of fighting so hard among themselves that the country is weakened?

121

Try This: Prepare a citation of honor for one or more of the Zionist leaders mentioned in this or other chapters. Or write your citation for an organization mentioned in this chapter or selected from the list in the *American Jewish Year Book,* under "National Jewish Organizations—Zionist and Pro-Israel."

YOU'LL ENJOY READING

Picture Story of the Middle East, by Susan R. Nevil (section on Israel)
The Second Aliyah (published by Zionist Youth Council)

YOU'LL ENJOY SEEING

Dunam Po V'Dunam Sham (film: Center for Mass Communications)
Golden Harvest (film: National Committee for Labor Israel)
Through the Eyes of Children (filmstrip: Jewish National Fund)
The Voice of the Land (film: Jewish National Fund)

chapter 11

Building a Nation

How Israel Grew

In 1948 you could not buy an Israeli clock, air conditioner, radio, fountain pen, refrigerator, tire, electric light bulb, or anything made of plastics. These, and many other modern products, had to be imported from other countries. Food was so scarce that American Jews sent parcels of canned goods to their Israeli relatives.

Within ten years, Israel was making all these things herself—enough for her own people and for customers in seventeen other countries besides. Israeli farmers had so many extra eggs, chickens, and vegetables that they couldn't find enough customers, at home or abroad.

Israelis have certainly come a long way since 1948. Their living standards are the highest of all new states created since World War II, according to a United Nations survey. They earn more money and live better than the neighboring Arab peoples. They equal and even surpass some modern Western countries in health standards, industrial products, scientific research, and cultural life.

"WHAT ISRAEL MAKES, MAKES ISRAEL." In 1962, Israel began holding an annual Near East Fair in Tel Aviv, to display new products of many countries along with her own. The newest Israeli offerings included canned vegetables, dehydrated soups, juices, spaghetti-in-sauce, roasted peanuts, cocoa powder, and instant coffee. Unique Israeli specialties included fruit soup and dehydrated felafel—an oriental combination of pizza pie and hot sandwich. A thousand firms from thirty-three countries—including ten in Africa—took part, and over half-a-million visitors attended.

1967. Israel's yearly rise in production was proportionately greater than that of West Germany, Holland, and the United States. In average income per person, Israel ranks among the world's top 15 countries.

ISRAEL'S GROWTH AT A GLANCE

	1948-49	1967	Approximate Times Increased
POPULATION			
Jewish	650,000	2,344,900	
Non-Jewish	140,000	312,500	
Total	790,000	2,657,400	
INDUSTRY			
Production	Almost none	$2,280,000,000	
Electricity	73,000 Kilowatts	874,000	
AGRICULTURE			
Villages	300	800	
Farm Land	400,000 acres	1,110,500	
Production	$54,000,000	$380,000,000	
Irrigation	75,000 acres	380,000	
Tree Planting	13,000 acres	98,000	

124

	1948-49	1960	Approximate Times Increased
HOUSING			
Homes	750,000 sq. meters	2,000,000	🏠 🏠 🏠
Public Buildings	28,000 sq. meters	230,000	
Industrial Buildings	40,000 sq. meters	310,000	
Commercial Buildings	26,000 sq. meters	87,000	
Hotels, etc.	Almost none	9,000 sq. meters	? ?

		1966	
TRANSPORTATION COMMUNICATION			
Ships	4	101	
Ports	1	7	
Railroads	100 miles	455	
Telephones	18,000	216,000	

ISRAEL'S GROWTH AT A GLANCE

	1948-49	1966	Approximate Times Increased
EDUCATION			
Elementary School Attendance	130,000	740,000	
Arab School Attendance	6,700	72,000	
Teachers	6,000	38,000	
Hebrew University Students	1,000	12,000	
Technion Students	680	5,000	
HEALTH			
Hospitals	63	135	
Beds	47,000	120,000	
TRADE			
Exports (Income)	$30,000,000	$818,000,000	
Imports (Expense)	$250,000,000	$475,000,000	

■ Since 1948, Israel's population and total production have tripled. Most aspects of her economy have increased even faster—from four to thirty-two times. The last two figures show how Israel, though rapidly becoming more self-supporting, still needs investments, loans, and contributions to help her meet her expenses.

Why Israel Needs Help

But compared to the most advanced nations, Israel is still poor and struggling. Nearly every home has a radio, but very few homes have a TV set. Out of every ten families, only three have electric refrigeration, five use ice-boxes, and two have nothing. Only two out of ten own a gas range or a bicycle, only one out of ten a washing machine or a record player, and only one out of fifty a car or a piano. The Israeli family eats about as much all together as the American family—but less meat, and more cereals and fats.

Israel started out with a land three-fifths desert, poor in natural resources and power. Her oil and other minerals will take years of hard work and much money to develop. In addition, Israel had to defend herself against Arab wars and raids. She now spends one-fourth of her entire income on weapons, stockpiles of food and ammunition, military training. She has taken in a million immigrants—and they are still coming—who could not support themselves. She spends huge sums on them—for houses, food, clothes, teachers, books, doctors, nurses, medicines. Taming the Negev, the water projects, the new mines, roads, villages—all these take more money. In time, these immigrants and projects will pay for themselves, but meanwhile, for many years, they drain away millions of dollars.

Israel's problem is not just a matter of dollars-and-cents. Israel doesn't ask how much she can afford, and then hold expenses down to that amount. She starts with certain *ideals*: to develop a country superior in social justice, science, industry, farming, education, health—and a home for all Jews who want to come. Then she spends whatever this requires, whether she has the money or not. Israel does not permit child labor, as many backward countries do: a child's "job" is getting the best possible education, as in our own country. And there are no masses of cheap labor, as in some of the new Asian and African nations.

1968. The average Israeli earns $1,600 a year; the average American, $4,000, or almost 3 times as much. Israel produces about $4 billion worth of goods a year; the United States, about $800 billion, also about 3 times as much proportionately to population.

Israel has 22,000 TV sets; the United States, over 77 million, or about 6 times as many proportionately to population.

Try This: Israel's growth after 1948 was not even—some items increased much faster than others. Study the growth chart for examples of uneven growth where Israel has to "catch up." (For instance, industry and electric power.) Use your answers in a poster entitled "Israel Needs . . . Because . . ."

Troubles Galore

The 500 new farming villages since 1948 were set up in a hurry. Israel could not afford the time for careful, gradual development, because of the immigrants and the Arab threats. She needed homes immediately, and extra food reserves in case of war. Some new settlements had to go up at the wrong times and places. People, farms, factories had to be located where they could help the Israel army

TRANSPORTATION. Israel's modern transportation system was built up after 1948 from almost nothing. Equipment, efficiency, safety, and service are the best in the Middle East, respected by travelers. (Opposite page, top) Haifa's railway station. Israel has complete north-south road, rail, and air transportation. She is also building many east-west rail lines and highways, like the new Beer Sheva—Sdom Road (below). The "Carmelit" subway (opposite page, bottom) climbs from Haifa's harbor to the top of Mt. Carmel, one mile up. Because Israel is land-locked by hostile neighbors, she has stressed sea and air transportation, and considers "conquering" the sea as vital as "conquering" the Negev. Her two water outlets to the world—The Mediterranean Sea and the Red Sea—make Israel an important commercial link between the eastern and western halves of the world.

In 1965, a railroad line was extended from Beer Sheva to Dimona. Check map at front of book to see if this is a north-south or an east-west line.

and hinder Arab invaders. Many new settlers lack water and other necessities, are without many comforts and conveniences, and have low incomes.

New housing puts a big strain on Israel's "pocketbook." Since 1948, new homes have almost caught up with Israel's exploding population, but not quite. Everyone has a place to live, but not always as roomy or comfortable as it should be. Sometimes plasterers and painters are still working on new houses as busloads of newcomers drive up. The newcomers have top priority in new housing—something unheard of in other countries.

One-third of Israel's population lives in a narrow strip along the coast, consisting of Tel Aviv and nine other cities and towns. Settlers tend to stay in the part of the country where they first arrive. The older, established communities have more and better schools, libraries, theaters, museums—and a more comfortable life. But it is not wise to overcrowd one small region, and leave many open, empty spaces—especially near the borders.

Israel has a serious manpower shortage. The government's employment service gets 2,000 requests a month for workers—but can't fill them. The country's uneven growth pushed industry, shipping, and hotels far ahead of the rest of the economy. Almost half the officers on the merchant ships are foreigners, and hotel workers from maids to managers are almost impossible to find. The country badly needs skilled workers and expert mechanics for all kinds of factories

and machines, also unskilled workers for hard physical jobs. But the unemployed people looking for work are mainly storekeepers, real estate agents, and salesmen. The Oriental immigrants are mostly untrained, and too old or too young to work. The European immigrants, mostly well-off and well-educated, are not interested in heavy labor or factory jobs.

Israel needs over a thousand new skilled workers every year, but her vocational schools graduate less than half this number. Thousands of workers need re-training. Her average worker, in the same time and with the same tools and materials, produces only about one-fifth as much as the average American worker, and only about half as much as the average European.

Israel has thousands of small companies. The typical owner is not an expert in modern business management. His few employees work in an old-fashioned shop, poorly equipped, cramped, inefficient. He cannot afford to buy supplies in large quantities, and so has to pay higher prices. He makes just one or two items, producing so many of them that he has to keep lowering his selling price in order to dispose of them. He cannot handle big orders, and loses much profitable business.

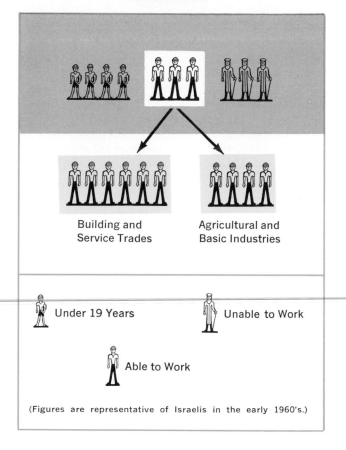

MANPOWER

Building and
Service Trades

Agricultural and
Basic Industries

Under 19 Years

Unable to Work

Able to Work

(Figures are representative of Israelis in the early 1960's.)

■ Compared to western countries, a smaller proportion of Israel's population (three out of ten) works. Out of every ten workers, only four are in agriculture and industry, producing things for the rest of the population. The other six work in trade, building, transportation, offices, and so on—consuming rather than producing. Israel thus has too many professionals, civil service and office workers, and not enough farm and factory workers. This is mainly because Arab and British attitudes before 1948 held back Jewish farming and industry. Out of every three Israelis, one is too young to work, one is too old or sick and usually cannot read or write—and only one is able to work. One out of every four Israeli employees works part-time or only in certain seasons. Israel's manpower is both insufficient and unbalanced.

How Israel Gets Help

It takes huge sums of money to pay for defense, immigrant care, new towns and industries, and Israel is helped a great deal by others.

The United States government, for example, has given her generous grants for research, experiments, and improvement projects. Our country has also lent Israel many millions of dollars, at low interest, and with many years to pay the loan back.

In 1952, West Germany agreed to pay Israel 750 million dollars over a period of years up to 1966—"reparations" for Jewish homes, factories, and stores confiscated by the Nazis. The money helped Israel to care for immigrants and develop new land and industry.

Jews the world over send money to Israel through the yearly campaigns and emergency drives of the United Jewish Appeal. As the world's largest and richest Jewish community, American Jewry contributes the biggest share. We also donate large sums to many organizations supporting special projects in Israel: Hadassah, Zionist Organization of America, Pioneer Women, Labor Zionist Organization, Mizrachi, Jewish National Fund, Friends of the Hebrew University, American Technion Society, and others. Some Israeli institutions conduct their own campaigns in our country.

Since 1951, Israel has sold bonds, just as the United States and other countries do, even the United Nations. Buying a bond is an investment that earns or loses money depending on the country's progress. You give the Israel government $100.00 or some larger amount, and in twelve or fifteen years (depending on the terms of the bond) Israel pays it back with interest. In 1963, Israel began to pay back the first bonds issued in 1951. Not many new countries have been able to meet their obligations so promptly. Israel's credit rating with most governments and investors is quite high.

Investors in many lands also put money directly into Israeli enterprises. They may become partners in an Israeli business, or buy stock in it, or lend it money. For example, Haifa's subway from the harbor up Mount Carmel was built by a French company, with money from non-Jewish investors.

Loans, gifts, and investments show that people *believe* in Israel. Both Jews and non-Jews feel sure that Israel will some day be able to support herself without too much outside assistance.

Try This: Ask your parents to what organizations they contribute money for Israel's benefit. Why did they choose them? Do your parents own Israeli bonds? Why, or why not? Find out about the United Jewish Appeal campaign in your community. Who conducts it? When? How much is raised? How much goes to Israel? What is the rest of the money used for?

HARNESSING THE SUN. At a solar energy plant at the Hebrew University, Jerusalem, scientists try to turn sunlight into energy to power machines and provide electricity. The Negev has little water but plenty of hot sunlight for sun-powered engines. Israeli experiments may some day revolutionize life in Israel and in other developing countries—and even in the advanced western countries.

How Israel Does Her Share

The money Israel gets from other countries and from other Jewish communities is not spent on luxuries—or even on things the people need immediately. It pays for a "Development Program" of projects in irrigation, farming, mining, housing, transportation, communication, education, health, research, experiments. Four-fifths of the program is paid for by foreign help, and Israel herself pays for the other fifth, out of taxes. These are higher, for the average person, than they are in our country.

For greater efficiency, a number of firms in the same general field have joined together in an "industrial estate." The first of these, in Tel Aviv, has thirty separate companies making metal tools and products. With government help, they built separate factories, but with central offices, tool shops, and warehouses. One laboratory does all the testing, one department keeps all the records, another seeks customers and makes sales for all. Each small plant operates independently, but all work together to gain the advantages of a single big firm—a sort of cooperative industry set-up, like Israel's cooperative farms and stores.

1968. An Israeli worker earning $4,000 a year pays as much as *half* of it to the government in taxes.

BUILDING AN INDUSTRIAL COUNTRY. Israel's industries have grown faster than in most new countries. She has some of the world's largest drug and chemical factories (below, left), and rapidly growing industries in building materials (below, right), food (opposite page, top) clothing, furniture, machinery, tools, and many other products. A well-known American jeep is manufactured in Israel (opposite, bottom).

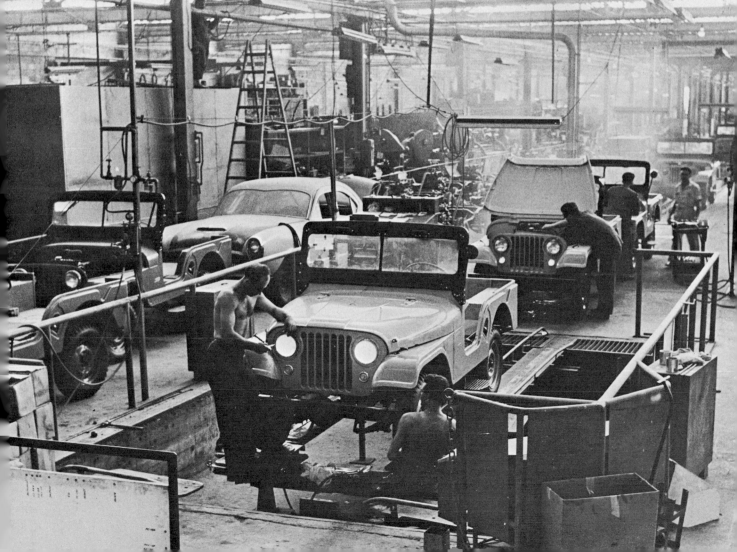

FOR MORE SKILLED WORKERS. An agricultural school (above) is a major institution in this Youth Aliyah village near Ashkelon, for teen-age immigrants. In the Haifa Technion (opposite page, top), budding architects learn their trade. An ORT school in Tel Aviv (opposite page, bottom) prepares technical draftsmen.

The government selects certain places for "development," and encourages new immigrants and other citizens to move there to start new settlements. It gives them low-rent houses, reduces their taxes, and guarantees higher wages. This makes up for the rougher life, higher cost of living, and harder work. Businessmen willing to start companies and factories in "Development Areas" get larger government loans, lower tax rates, and government-built houses, equipment, roads, water, electricity. In time, this program will relieve the cities and larger towns of their overcrowded population. It will also help Israel earn more money and be able to pay more of her expenses.

With the Hebrew University, the government has opened research laboratories, experimental and training farms. It spends even more on agriculture than on housing or industry. Many scientists, engineers, and farm experts are sent abroad to study advanced methods; many are brought from Europe and America to advise Israelis. Pest control, fertilizers, irrigation, machinery, packing, and shipping have all greatly improved. Farmers are required by law to use terraces and contour plowing on hills, to prevent water from running off and carrying away the soil.

134

Labor unions and business firms, along with the government, organize courses in labor-saving devices and modern business methods. These are attended by both managers and workers, by scientists and foremen, from both farm settlements and factories. Groups have also been sent to the United States to study business and industrial procedures. The "efficiency expert" is a familiar figure in farm villages and industrial towns.

Israel stresses vocational education. Pupils who cannot go to high school get special job training in the eighth grade. Labor organizations and American Jewish groups like Hadassah, ORT, and Mizrachi Women, help the government maintain farm schools, vocational high schools, evening schools for working youth, and adult training centers. "Crash" programs of six-to-twelve months are free until the student finds work and can pay the tuition back in installments. A wide-spread apprenticeship program enables young people to work at their jobs while learning. In the "Training Workshop" program, lessons are taught as part of the job itself. In the "Sandwich Scheme" a pair of apprentices switch places between school and a job every three months. Special programs train nurses, retrain the handicapped, give vocational guidance to young people. A special college trains vocational teachers.

To encourage more Israelis to take up farming, the government offers assistance of all kinds to new farmers. To get more Israelis to become sailors and officers in merchant ships, the government raises wages, finds ways to make ship life easier and more interesting, and speeds up courses at its two naval training schools.

From Aid to Trade

1967. Israel took part in 28 international fairs and held special "Israel Weeks" in thousands of shops in several countries. In 1968, Israel exhibited her products on five continents.

1968. Israel now overflows with milk and honey, producing more than she can use. So, Israelis export the extra honey and turn the extra milk into powdered form instead of importing powdered milk. Special attention to cattle breeding has produced four times as much milk and an average yield among the highest in the world. Israel now produces all her own eggs and vegetables, 90 per cent and over of her own potatoes, fruits, fish, meat, and dairy products; but only 23 per cent of her own oils and fats and 16 per cent of her own cereals.

Only in Israel

In 1939, some Kibbutzniks became homesick for the taste of "gefilte fish," their favorite delicacy of old East European days. They sent a delegate back to Yugoslavia, to learn how to breed and raise carp. He came back with the information—and six live carp. Today, carp-raising accounts for two-thirds of Israel's profitable fishing industry. The Kibbutznik carp expert has been sent to Haiti by the United Nations to set up carp ponds, and from there the idea has spread to other South American countries. Israel now produces much more carp than Yugoslavia, with only half as many acres of fish ponds. And so, the original "carp" Kibbutz recently sent *its* expert to show Yugoslavia how to do it —and repay its "debt."

Israel hopes to become the central trading country between the young nations of the East and the advanced nations of the West. She holds an annual international trade fair in Tel Aviv, has many displays at fairs in other lands, and has signed trade agreements with about thirty countries. Food and department stores in various lands often hold an "Israel Week" to advertise, display, and sell her products. Hundreds of farmers and farm experts from over thirty countries come to her annual Farmers' Convention to see what's new in farming and take the information back home. Israel's International Stamp Exhibit is another popular annual attraction.

England and the United States buy about one-third of Israel's exports, and another third goes to Germany, Switzerland, Belgium, Holland, and Turkey. Biggest items are diamonds, citrus fruits, textiles and clothes, fruit preserves and juices, eggs, tires and tubes, phosphates and fertilizers, motor vehicles, plywood, cement, oils for cooking and eating, drugs, peanuts, postage stamps, books, glass, and handcrafts. You can find תּוֹצֶרֶת הָאָרֶץ—goods with a "Made in Israel" label, in the Judaica Shop of your synagogue, and in larger cities, in gift shops, department stores, food and "package" stores.

For Jews, the "Made in Israel" label has a special appeal in objects like Chanukah menorahs, Passover wines and matzah, or artistic editions of the Bible. Among the Oriental immigrants are families in which the craft of making Tefillin (phylacteries) and artistic designs for the Talit (prayershawl) has been handed down from father to son for centuries. The government encourages such experts to continue their work in Israel. It makes sure they get materials and customers, lends them money, advertises their work. For customers, the government certifies that the products are of highest quality and meet all requirements of Orthodox Jewish law. Such products used to come from Eastern Europe. Now, Israel is the world's center for sacred Jewish symbols, Torah scrolls, shofarot (ram's horns for the High Holy Days). Seventy out of every hundred Chanukah candles sold in the United States come from Israel.

Israeli stamps are sold in great numbers, especially in America. Beginning with the first one issued two days after independence, Israel's stamps have featured holidays and religious ideas, Israel's progress in agriculture and industry, and her great heroes past and present. Stamp sales are quite profitable, and increase year by year. Israeli coins and medals, minted every year on anniversaries and holidays, also find many interested collectors.

Totzeret Ha-aretz: תּוֹצֶרֶת הָאָרֶץ

TOWARD COMPLETE SELF-SUFFICIENCY

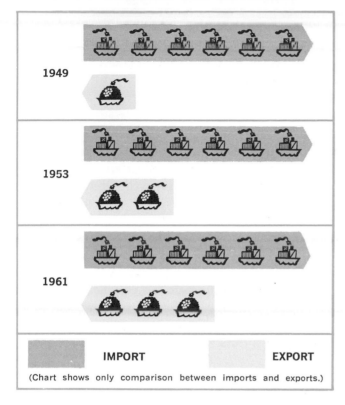

1949

1953

1961

IMPORT EXPORT

(Chart shows only comparison between imports and exports.)

■ Israel raises practically all her own food, but does not yet produce all the other things she needs, spending two dollars abroad for every dollar she earns. She hopes by 1970 to increase exports over imports and support herself without outside help. She tries to make, and sell abroad, better and cheaper products—from the world's only compact car with a fiberglass body (above) to uniquely beautiful jars and pitchers (below).

Not satisfied with sales due only to sentiment or religion, Israel tries to make every export product superior in price and quality. The country was always famous for citrus fruits and wines, even in ancient times. Many Jewish diamond workers, driven from Belgium and Holland during World War II, settled in Palestine and made Israel a world leader in cutting and polishing jewels. Israel also has a high reputation for clothing, especially handmade articles designed and made by European immigrants. Israeli raincoats are so good that they rank third in world sales. While Israel is not a world fashion center, her clothing earns much praise and is sold widely, especially knitted goods and Eastern designs with "desert" colors.

Israel searches hard for new products, especially those that Israeli workmen can produce faster, cheaper, or better. For example, Israel became a popular source of furs by raising baby broadtail, a little-known type. She tries to give her chocolates and other candies a distinctive taste. The unique designs of Israeli silver and embroidery by Oriental immigrants are appreciated everywhere. Israel recently began to win attention for decorated tiles done by Armenian Jewish immigrants, and "character" dolls by Viennese Jews.

1968. In 1949, Israel's income from exports was only about one-tenth of her payments for imports. This "trade gap" had to be made up by taxes, loans, contributions. In 1965, export income was just half the import payments, and in 1968 almost three-fifths. The "trade gap" is slowly but steadily closing, so that Israel is becoming more self-supporting all the time. When the two figures equal one another, she will "break even." And when exports exceed imports, she will be making a profit.

137

Travelers' Paradise

1967. Over 300,000 visitors came to Israel that year; about one-third of them were Christians.

Tourists are vital to Israel. They bring a good deal of money into the country and provide work for many people. They get to know Israel and her people. When they return home, they encourage business and cultural contacts with her, and expose false Arab propaganda against her.

Israel's people are friendly and hospitable to strangers. The government tries hard to provide hospitality, inspiration, and fun. Special roads take visitors to out-of-the-way spots, and signposts describe the ancient events that took place at certain sites. The holy places of all religions are protected and preserved. Observation posts overlook scenes of special beauty or historical interest. Israel has modern tourist buses and drive-yourself cars, all kinds of hotels and every conceivable kind of sport to play or watch. Visitors find modern shops, movies, plays, night clubs, opera, symphony and dance performances. Trained guides take them to many special events and festivals. They can even arrange to spend an evening in an Israeli home, sharing the family's meal, conversation, pastimes, and problems. Israel has motels, youth hostels for hikers and bicyclers, a golf course, and even a country club.

■ Israelis work hard, pay high taxes, do without many luxuries. But they enjoy life, know how to relax and play. Vacationers and tourists of all ages flock to cities, farms, mountains, deserts, and the seashore—as at this hotel at Beer Sheva.

About 200,000 visitors come each year, and the number constantly rises. International organizations, Jewish and non-Jewish, often hold their meetings in Israel. American synagogues and other Jewish organizations—and even mail order firms like Sears Roebuck and Montgomery Ward—arrange group tours to Israel. Several guidebooks have been published, and a variety of booklets and pamphlets answer the tourist's questions in advance.

Many Jews now make a "pilgrimage" to Israel every few years. Families who can afford it give such a trip as a Bar Mitzvah or Confirmation present. Jewish youngsters visit Israel on full or partial scholarships given by various organizations. Scholars, teachers, young people, rabbis, businessmen, scientists—all are drawn to this bright new country with its age-old history.

Israel's Balance Sheet

Israel will be walking a financial tightrope for many years.

Some income will decrease in the years ahead—as German reparations stop and some money from new loans and bonds goes to pay back current ones. Trade competition from other countries is growing. Expenses, on the other hand, will increase. Thousands of new immigrants a year must be settled—at a cost of about $2,000 each. Whenever trouble breaks out for Jews in any country, immigration figures suddenly jump. Defense costs, too, are rising.

Of course, Israel can count on the United Jewish Appeal and other organizations to help. But that is not the same as being self-supporting. Israelis are used to walking all sorts of tightropes, and surprising everyone who expects them to fall off. Nearly everything they have accomplished since 1880 was called "impossible" until they did it. They have friends, and do not stand alone. Time is in their favor; they are confident and cheerful about the future.

YOU'LL ENJOY READING

Ingathering, by Robert Gamzey

YOU'LL ENJOY SEEING

Happy Valley (film: Jewish National Fund)
Hope from the Huleh (film: Jewish National Fund)
Israel Today (film: Israel Office of Information)

Try This: Write to Israel Office of Information, 11 East 70th Street, New York, N.Y. 10021, for tourist information—pamphlets, calendar of events, and so on. Also ask for names of specific American organizations which sponsor tours or scholarships. Write to these also. Display all your "returns" on a table or the bulletin board.

Try This: Start a class project to help Israel. You might:

—buy Totzeret Ha-aretz (Products of Israel) as gifts for your school;
—buy a tree-planting certificate from the Jewish National Fund in honor of your rabbi, principal, or teacher;
—send to a new settlement in Israel a package of school supplies, books, recordings, maps.

1965-66. Israel had a "depression" in this period — increasing unemployment, decreasing money value, and so on. In 1967, the Six Day War brought Israel heavy losses and new expenses, but also new contributions from world Jewry, new income from occupied territory, more exports, more new business ventures. As this is written (May, 1968), it is too early to draw up an accurate balance sheet for the victory. See Chapter 25 for a further discussion.

Young Kibbutzniks get acquainted with a new herd.

chapter 12

The Kibbutz Way

How would you like to have *two* homes? You would be in your parents' house or apartment evenings, week-ends, on holidays and other special occasions. Your other home would be around the corner, in a dormitory where you'd eat, sleep, study, and play with boys and girls your own age.

That's how children live in an Israeli קִבּוּץ—Group Settlement, one of Israel's several types of farming village. The Kibbutzim (plural of Kibbutz), though a small part of the country, are world-famous as a unique social experiment.

How a Kibbutz Works

Everything in a Kibbutz belongs to the whole village. Land is rented from the Jewish National Fund, or the government. Buildings are often erected and owned by the Histadrut. A Kibbutz cannot acquire more land. If the members want to improve their life, they have to work harder and use better methods.

All Kibbutzim have farms, on which they raise crops and animals. Many also have industries. A Kibbutz may operate a small factory or fishpond, a hotel for tourists or vacationers, a printing shop, or even a supermarket. Several Kibbutzim may jointly run larger factories, truck and bus lines, banks, wholesale and retail stores, schools, health centers.

All the money earned by a Kibbutz or its members goes into a common treasury. Kibbutzniks (members of a Kibbutz) get no wages, have no income or expenses of their own. Everything is paid

A TYPICAL KIBBUTZ. After reading this chapter, see if you can trace the daily route of a Kibbutz parent and a Kibbutz child.

1. Water tower
2. Dining hall
3. School
4. Children's quarters
5. Cultural and religious center
6. Administration and notice-board
7. Medical center
8. Laundry
9. Toolshed and workshop
10. Sheep run
11. Chicken coops
12. Fields
13. Cowshed and stables
14. Shoemaker, carpenter, distribution center for personal articles
15. Bakery
16. Living quarters
17. Orchard

Kibbutz: קִבּוּץ.

141

1968. About half of Israel's 240 kibbutzim operated factories and hotels, employing about 6,000 people, half of them "hired hands" from outside the kibbutz. Think of reasons why so many kibbutzim break the rule of "no outside employees."

★Kibbutzniks might disagree over many things—for instance, the best size for their community. Too few people—not enough work gets done. Too many people—not enough self-government. What other arguments might develop in a Kibbutz?

for by the community. There are no employers or employees, no rich or poor. The Kibbutz as a whole may be poor or well-off, but all members enjoy the same standard of living.

Each member gets his own apartment and furniture, and an allotment of clothing, which is washed, ironed, and mended for him by the Kibbutz laundry. The Kibbutz treasury provides for all medical care and all expenses of a sick member no matter how long it takes him to get well.

Kibbutzniks get a week or two of vacation each year in addition to holidays. Every family gets pocket-money for vacations and extra trips. Everything is supplied by the Kibbutz: soap, haircuts, toothpaste, razor blades, postage, concert and drama tickets, movies, wedding and honeymoon arrangements, support of needy parents. A Kibbutznik has all the necessities and complete "social security," from cradle to grave, plus his share of whatever "extras" the Kibbutz can afford.★

Managing a Kibbutz

The entire Kibbutz meets every week in a General Assembly, where every member votes on all questions raised, and the majority decision is binding on all. Once a year, Kibbutzniks elect an Executive Committee consisting of a General Secretary, Treasurer, Market Agent, Work Manager, and Production Manager. Each officer heads a committee, and other committees supervise culture, education, health, housing, parents, and so on. Kibbutz officers and committee members receive no pay or special privileges, and do their full share of Kibbutz work. They serve only because it is their duty.

Kibbutzniks may work on a farm, or in a kitchen, factory, school, or office. They may operate machinery, or supervise other workers. Some may be elsewhere in the country, helping other Kibbutzim or working for a political party.

Kibbutz officials assign jobs to all members, according to a סִדוּר עֲבוֹדָה—Work Plan. A job may be permanent, or different members may take turns at it, especially if it is something like dishwashing or cleaning the shower rooms. Veteran Kibbutzniks may be "specialists" in their own trade or profession. Newcomers are often "corks"—assigned each morning to "fill in" wherever needed. Sometimes a Kibbutznik is on the Executive Committee one year,

Only in Israel

A visitor to a Kibbutz is sometimes surprised to recognize a member of the Knesset (Israel's Parliament) waiting on him in the dining room. Or to see the dishwasher tear off his apron and rush to conduct a meeting of the "Executive" —he is the *Mazkir,* General Secretary or "Mayor" of the whole Kibbutz.

Sidur avodah: סִדוּר עֲבוֹדָה

142

and a kitchen worker the next. In slack seasons, some members work "outside" for wages, which go into the Kibbutz treasury. In rush seasons—planting or harvest time—all assignments may be cancelled and every member sent to the fields.

A Kibbutz woman does not depend on a husband to support her. Her children and the housekeeping chores are looked after by the Kibbutz, and she gets her own work assignment the same as a man. She might work in the kitchen or laundry, if she wants to, or if it is her turn. Or, she might herd cows, drive a truck, keep records, be an official, stand guard, or mend shoes.

Members of a Kibbutz run it as they see fit. Some Kibbutzim are more socialistic than others. In religious Kibbutzim, members practice Orthodox Judaism along with socialism. In other Kibbutzim, each member may be as Orthodox as he wishes—he may fast on Yom Kippur, for instance, or have kosher food specially prepared for him, just as if he were on a medical diet. Quite a few Kibbutzim have no synagogue, give the children no formal religious education, have no religious ceremonies other than marriage and circumcision. Some of these provide a small hut or room as a synagogue, and sometimes a separate kosher kitchen, for elderly parents who are Orthodox.

Kibbutzim differ among themselves on whether to stress farming or industry, limit themselves to a certain size, and employ outside labor. All Kibbutzniks are automatically members of the Histadrut Labor Federation and the World Zionist Organization, but their views on politics, socialism, and religion are entirely up to them. In some Kibbutzim, all members must belong to the same political party; in others, various political parties are represented.

The Kibbutzim are grouped into five federations. Each of these supports a particular political party, deals with the government and other organizations, and tackles large enterprises. Each Federation has its own teacher-training and vocational schools, and publishes newspapers, magazines, and books. It operates a central bank, and has a staff of experts on every Kibbutz problem. The Federation buys and sells for all its members, getting better prices because it deals in large quantities. It holds frequent meetings to discuss common problems and exchange ideas.

Kibbutzim must obey government rules for "cooperative societies." They have no formal constitution, but certain practices have been established over the years. No police enforce these rules. To stay in a Kibbutz, you have to get along with the group. If you cause trouble, the Kibbutz may expel you. The whole community decides whether to accept or reject a new member. A person may join or leave at any time.★

KIBBUTZ PRINCIPLES

Collectivism. Group responsibility for work, child care, earning a living, meeting expenses.

Socialism. Group ownership of land, buildings, equipment, supplies, products, money.

Zionism. Development and growth of a Jewish Commonwealth.

Cooperatives. Group management of all business activities — buying, selling, renting, banking, building.

Equality. Equality among all members regardless of sex and what or how much work each member does.

Dignity of Labor. All labor done by members is worthwhile and all types of work are equally valuable and honorable.

Mutual Aid. Complete "social security" for members to meet all needs.

Democracy. Self-government, with participation in all decisions by all members.

Self-Labor. All work must be done by members; no outsiders to be employed for wages.

1966. The non-religious kibbutz of Ein Harod applied to the government for help in building a synagogue. Since these kibbutzniks claimed to be "non-religious," why do you suppose they wanted a synagogue?

★ What similarities can you see between a Kibbutz and an American voluntary organization like a synagogue, a charity organization, or a children's club? What differences?

Moshe, a younger member in his thirties, foreman of the Kibbutz factory, complains about the "outside" wage-workers they've employed: lazy, inefficient, not interested, always demanding higher wages, and leaving extra work for him.

Aharon, older Kibbutz veteran, recalls original Kibbutz ideals and purposes, criticizes both Moshe (for objecting to the extra work) and the idea of employing outside labor (which violates an original Kibbutz principle).

Dvorah, of the Housing Committee, objects to waste of water by people with lawns, reminds members about Kibbutz principle of self-discipline.

Yehezkel, secretary, reads a letter from Mordecai, who quit the Kibbutz a year ago, and now wants to rejoin. Big discussion of how good a Kibbutznik he was, and how likely he is to stay put this time. Final decision is left to the "Executive."

Eliezer, a bit embarrassed, says he and his wife are not completely happy, and he knows several other Kibbutzniks feel the same way. He wants the Kibbutz to consider changing itself into a Moshav, with separate family life and more privacy. Big discussion -- no decision.

Miriam has been offered money by the government of West Germany to pay for property that the Nazis destroyed. Does it all go into the treasury, or is she entitled to some of it for herself? And what should the Kibbutz use this "windfall" money for? General expenses, or some luxury like a swimming pool or air conditioners? Heated discussion -- vote postponed until next meeting.

Uri, in charge of the dining room, complains of food waste and broken dishes. He reminds them all that each Kibbutznik is personally responsible for group property.

Kibbutz Life

Kibbutzim range in size from 60 to 2,000 members. Besides the חֲבֵרִים and חֲבֵרוֹת—men and women members, and their children, a larger Kibbutz has candidates on probation for a year, students on a work-study program, visitors and guests, grandparents. Newer Kibbutzim are made up of young immigrants and city youth groups. In a border Kibbutz, an Army unit of young men and women share in the work and also guard the village. Members of a Kibbutz usually come from different countries and from various social backgrounds.

The older Kibbutzim are generally well off, with fine buildings, good land, the latest equipment, efficient factories. Members live in modern cottages or apartments, and enjoy their own radios, electric shavers, record players, private bathrooms. Often, the Kibbutz has both older and newer living quarters. Naturally, everyone prefers the latter, but the oldest members have first choice.

Young, struggling Kibbutzim are much like those of fifty or sixty years ago. Housing is crude, and several couples may share the same washroom facilities. Furniture and clothing are plain, often homemade. Food consists of vegetables and dairy products, with meat and desserts only on Sabbaths, holidays, and special occasions. The land is poor and rocky, the work extremely hard.

Old or new, a Kibbutz is a lively, exciting place. Something is always going on, and there is little privacy. Meals, prepared in a common kitchen, are eaten in a common dining room which is usually also the village social center. Nobody ever dresses up, except on Shabbat and holidays. Everyone uses first names or official Kibbutz titles, like מַזְכִּיר—Secretary, or גִּזְבָּר—Treasurer. Most of the day is spent outdoors, close to nature, in a carefully planned program of work, meals, rest, and recreation. The "walks" between one place and another are narrow, so that Kibbutzniks on the move constantly meet and chat with one another.

Often, a Kibbutz has a "personality" of its own, attracting certain kinds of people and developing its own "special" atmosphere. One Kibbutz may be known for its quiet dignity, another for its loud and fun-loving people, still others for musical programs or inventions and experiments.

Kibbutzniks work six days a week, up to ten or twelve hours a day, especially at harvest time. After work, they shower, clean house, tend to gardens, letter writing, hobbies, and personal matters, then

A KIBBUTZ "SICHAH" (opposite page). These "minutes," based on an actual Kibbutz discussion meeting, give you some of the "flavor" of Kibbutz life. Of course, a "sichah" isn't all argument. Here the Treasurer, for instance, had a good report on profit-and-loss from each "Anaf" (Branch) of Kibbutz operations. Only the factory was not earning enough for the money and work put into it. The Treasurer wanted the Kibbutz to borrow money for new labor-saving equipment, and make new products for more sales, more profits. No argument this time—the loan was unanimously approved.

Chaverim: חֲבֵרִים   Chaverot: חֲבֵרוֹת   Mazkir: מַזְכִּיר   Gizbar: גִּזְבָּר

MOTHER AND CHILD—statue by Hannah Orlof at Kibbutz Ein-Gev—is an example of the vigorous artistic and cultural activities of Kibbutz life. Can you interpret the sculptor's purpose—her feelings and ideas? Don't overlook the base, or the view—eastward across Yam Kinneret (Sea of Galilee) toward the hills of northern Israel.

spend a few hours with their children. Kibbutz life begins all over again at nine o'clock at night, with committee meetings, emergency tasks, military training, guard duty. There's always a Kumzits (German for "Come sit," or gathering) to attend in someone's rooms, and two nights a week are taken up with a community meeting and a movie.

Most Kibbutzim have soccer and basketball teams, and ardently "root" for them in Kibbutz league games. Volley ball is gaining in many Kibbutzim because it requires little space and can be played almost anywhere. Archeology and hiking are two other favorite Kibbutz hobbies.

These farmers and workers are intensely interested in all forms of culture. A special committee arranges lectures and study groups,

146

especially during the winter months, in Hebrew, English, literature (especially the Bible, of course), music, and art. And no outside teachers—they use "local talent." This committee also publishes a weekly paper and maintains a reading room and library. It may also provide a record collection or an archeological museum, or sometimes even an art museum. In one Kibbutz, so poor it can afford only one cup of Kiddush wine for the whole group on Erev Shabbat, every member has his own personal collection of books.

Nearly every Kibbutz has its own dance group and choir, and many have a drama חוג—circle, as well. They'll arrange a מְסִבָּה —party, of brief sketches, readings, playlets, on the slightest pretext —an anniversary, inauguration of officers, some Kibbutz achievement. A Kibbutz in the Negev, for example, reached a record milk production one day. The milkers wrote and presented a skit that very evening entitled "Oh, for the Life of a Dairyman!" On holidays, especially Purim, a Kibbutz may stage a complete play, also home-made, or even an elaborate pageant. Some Kibbutzim have become famous, both in Israel and abroad, for their ways of celebrating or interpreting a specific holiday. Some have even written new passages for the Pesach Haggadah, about the troubles and triumphs of their own lives.

Several Kibbutzim often join together for bigger cultural activities, such as the Kibbutz Symphony Orchestra. Kibbutz actors, singers, musicians, conductors, dancers, composers, writers, and painters do not worry about making a living, or the commercial success of their work. The Kibbutz helps them develop their talents in childhood, and sometimes sends them abroad to study. Artists do their share of Kibbutz work like everyone else, though the Work Committee tries to give them as much free time as possible. They contribute greatly to the whole nation's cultural life as well as to their own communities.

Folk dancing is especially popular. Crowds of Kibbutzniks, along with many other Israelis and visiting tourists, attend the annual dance festival of Kibbutz Dalia, the annual Passover music festival at Ein Gev, and the annual Sukkot pageant at the religious Kibbutz of Yavneh.

City theater companies and symphony orchestras make annual tours through Israel's countryside to perform in the Kibbutzim. Great concert artists from all over the world, after playing for a Kibbutz audience, speak with admiration of their unusually friendly and intelligent reception.★

★ What similarities can you see between a Kibbutz and the American family, a summer camp, or a resort? What differences?

Chug: חוג   Mesibah: מְסִבָּה

Children—Most Important of All

Kibbutz children usually live away from their parents, in a separate house with sixteen to twenty children of the same age. In their own bedrooms, classrooms, playrooms, kitchen and dining room, and outside grounds, they spend most of the day.

Ordinarily the Kibbutz work day ends before five o'clock, usually with a four o'clock snack. Then parents and children get together for a few hours. Families talk and walk together, play, visit grandparents or other families, go swimming, or just "sit around." At bedtime, children return to their own quarters for the night. Families are also together on Shabbat, festivals, vacations, social affairs.

As children grow older, they move to a house especially designed for their new age-group. They are trained to become farm and factory workers—but of a special kind. They learn the most modern methods and the use of the most modern machinery, and also get a first-class general education in languages, history, mathematics, science. From babyhood on, they are also taught to be good Kibbutzniks—to work for the benefit of their group, yet to develop their individual personalities and talents. Every group of children has its own small farm, looks after its quarters, selects its form of self-government, punishes its wrongdoers.

Most of their מַדְרִיכִים—teachers, or counselors, are also Kibbutz members. They do their best to help children understand, love, and live by Kibbutz principles. As part of the national educational system, Kibbutz schools follow government courses for about three-fourths of the studies. The main subjects are mathematics, Bible, history, language, science, geography, music, art. As pupils advance, they spend less time on academic subjects and more on farm work and agricultural sciences, such as botany, biology, and chemistry.

For the upper elementary grades and מוֹסָד—institute or high school, students go to a regional "Gymnasia" (high school) supported by several Kibbutzim—often biking or using buses, as the distance can be considerable. Some Gymnasia are boarding schools. The Kibbutz high school system takes a youngster through the age of sixteen or seventeen, and if he wishes, to eighteen. This means he can get an education equivalent to that of an American high school student, plus one year of college. Outside the Kibbutz, free public education is available only up to the age of fourteen. A Kibbutz graduate is thus among the best educated youth in Israel.

Madrichim: מַדְרִיכִים   Mosad: מוֹסָד

The Kibbutzim will send a talented student to a special art or music school, or even to the university. However, they want their youth to remain Kibbutzniks. They feel that they have "invested" a great deal in their children's education, and that a college degree, besides being expensive, is not always essential. They sometimes insist that their college students major in courses that will make them most useful to a Kibbutz.

The Kibbutz schools have a world-wide reputation. The teachers are highly trained and use the most up-to-date teaching tools and methods. Kibbutzim spend a far larger proportion of their income on education than most American communities do.

In spite of the separate living arrangements, members of a Kibbutz family do not become strangers to one another. Families are just as close and loving as anywhere else. Kibbutz parents spend a great deal of their free time with their children. They have less on their minds when they are with the children—no shopping to do, no preparing meals, cleaning up after the children, waking them in time for school, stopping their quarrels. Free from daily irritations, parents and children enjoy each other all the more when they meet just for fun and companionship. Kibbutzniks take good care of their elderly parents, too. There is less friction among Kibbutz grandparents, parents, and children than in American life. There is less divorce, and fewer marriage problems.

■ Children's House, Kfar Hanasi, a Kibbutz in Upper Galilee. From what you have read about Kibbutz children, what kind of relationship do you think exists among brothers, sisters, and cousins of different ages—especially as compared with such relationships in our own type of life?

Visiting educators say that Kibbutz children are somewhat over-protected, perhaps even spoiled. Perhaps *too* much care and attention—and money—are lavished on them. But they are usually more alert and better educated than the average worker's children in other places, or even those from middle-class homes. They generally turn out to be good, resourceful workers, with independent minds and a cooperative spirit, ready to take on full adult responsibilities at the age of eighteen. They advance rapidly in the armed services, where they are respected for their self-reliance, ability to get things done, and readiness to go the limit for their comrades and their nation.★

★ Why do nine out of ten Kibbutz children remain in a Kibbutz when they grow up, instead of moving to a town or another kind of village? Think of more than one answer. What difference does this fact make for the welfare of the whole country?

What We Owe to the Kibbutz

When Jews began settling in Palestine in 1882, only one Jew out of fifty was a farmer. Today, two generations later, one out of every *four* Jews works in one of the 800 farming villages that dot Israel's landscape. The Kibbutzniks were among the leaders in this Jewish conquest of the soil.

They also helped to develop respect for labor, social justice, and democracy. They made possible Israel's labor federation, the Histadrut. They volunteered for every Jewish project, played a major role in all Zionist affairs of the Yishuv—and still help new Kibbutzim get started.

These villages organized the first Jewish defense forces, the שׁוֹמְרִים—Watchmen, against Arab raiders in the early days. From these *shomrim* developed the הֲגָנָה—Defense, the highly trained secret Jewish army that defended Jewish settlements and brought in "illegal" Jewish immigrants in the days of British rule. Beginning in 1933, the Kibbutzim took in thousands of homeless, orphaned Jewish children—the famous Youth Aliyah—from Germany and Poland. These children needed food, clothing, shelter, education—and something more. The Kibbutzim gave them love, happiness, hope. During World War II, Kibbutz agents were smuggled into European countries to help persecuted Jews. They organized an "Underground Railroad" which secretly transported thousands of Jewish refugees to Israel, despite the British blockade. Kibbutzniks led expeditions to set up new settlements along Israel's borders, went into the towns to lead workers' organizations, volunteered for some of Israel's most important archeological investigations. They fought in the War of Independence against Arab invaders—farming in the daytime and standing off attacks at night.

Only in Israel

The Kibbutz of Ein Hashofet, when it started about thirty years ago, sent samples of its soil to Washington, D. C., for analysis and advice. The answer: "Substandard soil. Don't try to grow anything in it."

The Kibbutzniks decided to become their own soil experts and learn how to make good earth out of bad. Today, after many heartaches and failures, Ein Hashofet produces top-quality fruits and fruit juices of all kinds.

Shomrim: שׁוֹמְרִים   Haganah: הֲגָנָה

150

BIG FOR ITS SIZE

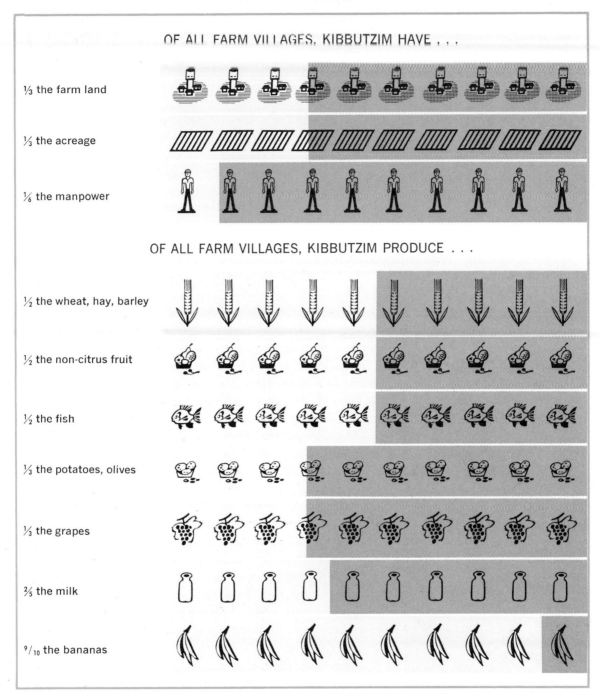

OF ALL FARM VILLAGES, KIBBUTZIM HAVE . . .

⅓ the farm land

⅓ the acreage

⅙ the manpower

OF ALL FARM VILLAGES, KIBBUTZIM PRODUCE . . .

½ the wheat, hay, barley

½ the non-citrus fruit

½ the fish

⅓ the potatoes, olives

⅓ the grapes

⅖ the milk

⁹/₁₀ the bananas

■ The Kibbutzim achieve these remarkable results through scientific farming, hard work, and the devotion of each member to the Kibbutz principles on page 143.

151

Hundreds of Jews of all ages, rescued from lives of misery in Europe and Africa, have found homes, jobs, friends, in the Kibbutzim. Kibbutz teachers, social workers, and managers, "on loan" to the government, help out in temporary camps and new immigrant settlements. Kibbutzniks have gone to Persia and Morocco, and as far as South America, to help guide Zionist youth movements.

Perhaps the finest Kibbutz gift to American Jewish life is modern Hebrew. Early Kibbutzniks insisted on speaking and writing only in this language. The Hebrew you study today, the Hebrew magazines and clubs in our country, the many public school and college Hebrew courses—these are all partly a heritage of Israel's Kibbutzim. No other Israeli group did so much to make Hebrew a modern everyday language instead of one used only for prayer and study.

Are the Kibbutzim Changing?

1

2

As life becomes easier for them, Kibbutzniks want more personal possessions, modern comforts, privacy. Some basic Kibbutz principles seem to be weakening under the new pressures.

After 1948, hundreds of thousands of jobless, untrained immigrants had to be cared for. The Kibbutzim employed as many as they could—a temporary measure and done for good cause, but still a violation of the Kibbutz principle of "no hired hands." Kibbutzniks profited from the labor of others, from people not interested in their ideals or even opposed to them.

Many women, supposed to share equally in Kibbutz work, find themselves still at the same old housekeeping chores. Also, they miss the pleasure of caring for their own children, baking their own cakes, sewing their own curtains. They are not so sure now that they really want to be "equal" to men. Or that living apart from their children is always best for them or their families.

Some Kibbutzim have made living quarters larger and more comfortable, or even have family living quarters. Kibbutzniks are discovering that many children, especially the younger ones, need more family life in order to feel loved and secure, to grow up with healthy emotions.

When German reparation money is offered to a Kibbutznik, some Kibbutzim let him keep a fifth or a quarter of the money for himself. They may then use the rest to build a swimming pool, library, or theater, to buy new furniture, or allow more spending money for vacations. All sorts of new luxuries have appeared in some Kibbutzim—weekly pocket money for each member to spend as he wishes, personal tape recorders, or electric refrigerators. Recently, a Kibbutz or two have built a city-style "coffee house," with counterman, Espresso machine, round tables, chairs—for sitting around, chatting, reading magazines, playing chess or dominoes. Older Kibbutzniks take one look, and wonder what the world is coming to.

Kibbutzniks differ politically, and sometimes cannot agree as socialists or Zionists either. The Kibbutz federations disagree over which side to favor in the "cold war" between Russia and the United States—or whether to stay neutral altogether.

All this means arguments, unpopular decisions, hurt feelings. Sometimes, a Kibbutz even changes itself into a *Moshav*. Violent quarrels, departures, and expulsions sometimes destroy the unity necessary for group life.

3

5

4

A DAY IN A KIBBUTZ. (1) Checking in at the notice-board. "What's for me today?" (2) Off to work—the fields will be hot and thirsty, but better than the stables or the kitchen. (3) Harvesting the crop—hard labor, but pleasant, too. (4) Dinner time, with the day a memory and plans for the evening. (5) No committee meetings tonight—so let's dance!

Has the Kibbutz Movement a Future?

Try This: You are going to visit a Kibbutz in Israel, but will not have time to learn all about it. Pick out a few Kibbutz features mentioned in this chapter that you would observe in your limited time. Arrange them in order, with the most interesting or most important first. Explain your preferences.

Despite all these changes and problems, most Kibbutzniks are still confident that the Kibbutz way of life is best for them. A Kibbutz appeals to many Israelis concerned for their children's education, because Kibbutz children get special attention, superior teachers, and a costly education up to the age of eighteen. A Kibbutz gives members a sense of purpose, of building something big for the future. Many people like to live in a small, intimate community and lead a quiet outdoor life.

Hopeful Kibbutzniks point out that Kibbutzim produce a big share of the nation's food. Kibbutz methods, they say, are still best, as in the early days, for rebuilding ruined land, training workers and leaders, strengthening the country's border defenses. Kibbutzniks team up with Israel's Army to start new settlements, and join older settlements needing "new blood." Many foreign experts visit Israel's Kibbutzim to observe and work there. The Kibbutzim have been imitated by several new countries in Asia and Africa. Thus they spread the democratic and cooperative idea, and win more friendship for Israel.

The Kibbutz movement still has plenty of drive, and will probably continue for a long time. But will the Kibbutzim make so many changes, in order to survive, that their old principles will disappear? Or will they continue to teach new ideas to the world? Were they good only for the pioneer days of the country, or can they still attract people under more settled conditions?

Try This: Have a debate. Topic: Why I would (or would not) like to live in a Kibbutz.

Nobody can definitely answer these questions at this time. But one thing is certain: in her Kibbutzim, Israel is blessed with the most educated, cultured, progressive farmers in the world. Their achievements are already part of history.

YOU'LL ENJOY READING

Israel: New People in an Old Land, by Lily Edelman
The Stone of Peace, by Sarah Feder-Tal

YOU'LL ENJOY SEEING

A Boy Named Ami (film: Hadassah Film Library)

chapter 13

A Most Unusual Organization

Try to imagine a *labor union* that:

— *owns* the country's largest factories, construction firm, bank, newspapers, medical organization, insurance company, bus and truck lines;

— is *part-owner* of the country's biggest airline, merchant fleet, oil company, quarry, tire factory, plastic factory;

— represents eight out of ten workers in the country, including doctors, lawyers, engineers, farmers, and even housewives along with factory and mine workers;

— gives medical care, hospitalization, unemployment insurance, and social security to two-thirds of the entire nation, spends twice as much as the government on health care, runs the country's biggest sports organization and a good deal of its cultural life;

— pioneers new villages and towns in dangerous territory;

— is the country's biggest *employer* and *landlord*.

MEDICAL CENTER OF THE NEGEV. This hospital in Beer Sheva is operated by the Histadrut—Israel's unusual labor union which is also the country's largest health, education, and welfare agency.

That's the הִסְתַּדְרוּת הָעוֹבְדִים—Israel's General Federation of Labor, the Histadrut. It does everything expected of an ordinary labor union. It bargains with employers for higher wages, shorter hours, better working conditions. It sponsors recreational activities for its members, and college scholarships for their children. It campaigns for better labor laws, and supports candidates for government office. But the Histadrut is also a huge health, education, and welfare agency, a giant business corporation, and pioneering organization.

Histadrut ha-ovdim: הִסְתַּדְרוּת הָעוֹבְדִים

Trade Union Activities

Workers committees in places of employment

Executive Council and local labor councils

National trade unions

Workers cooperatives

Working Women's Council and Working Youth Organization

Department of Arab Affairs

Agricultural Workers Center

Wage agreements with employers

Promotion of labor laws and labor candidates

Labor exchanges (employment offices)★

General Cooperative Association
(Business Enterprises)

T'nuvah — agricultural marketing cooperative

Hamashbir Hamerkazi — cooperative wholesale society

Solel Boneh — construction company; factories; harbor services and foreign building

Koor — industries, factories

Banks, buses and trucks, hotels, movies, diamond exports

Housing cooperatives

Credit societies

Kibbutzim, Moshavim — collective and cooperative farm villages

HISTADRUT
General Federation of Labor

Welfare Services

Kupat Cholim — sick fund (clinics, hospitals, physicians, nurses)

Pension and retirement funds, fund for elderly workers, and unemployment benefits

Correspondence courses, vocational schools, evening classes

Daily and weekly newspapers and publishing firm

Theatres, libraries, lectures, concerts, discussion groups, and sports organization (Hapoel)

School systems★

Defense forces — Haganah, Palmach★

Sanitation, preventive health services★

Fund to help employers

Partnerships

(with government, cities, JNF, private investors, foreign firms, etc.)

Mekorot — water and prospecting

Zim — shipping

Employment offices

Nesher — cement works

Delek — oil

El Al airline

Factories: tire, glass, steel, pipe, plastics

Quarries

Egged, Dan, and Hamekasher—city bus lines

Private cooperatives

THE BIG "H". The left-hand side of the "H" shows how the Histadrut is a complete labor union, like any other—though with some differences. (Can you find them?) The starred activities were transferred to the government after 1948. The right-hand side of the "H" lists the business activities that make the Histadrut Israel's biggest employer, landlord, and "capitalist."

Our job is not to divide the cake equally, but first of all to see that there is a cake to divide.

—Histadrut leader

The Unique Histadrut

Farmers want higher prices and city storekeepers don't. Bus drivers want higher fares and company officers don't. Factory workers strike for better wages and the managers bargain with them. *All* are fellow members of the same labor federation, pay the same dues, have the same voting power, and share alike in all benefits. They all "own" the farms, bus lines, and factories of the Histadrut. In its own companies, the Histadrut actually bargains with itself, goes on strike against itself, and comes to an agreement with itself.

The Histadrut is also part-owner of many Israeli firms. Its representatives sit on the boards of directors of these companies, and have a voice in their policies. Israeli *customers* of these companies are mostly Histadrut members, too—workers-employers-customers all in one.

Most unions start *after* a country has been industrialized and already has a government to settle labor conflicts. Most unions oppose the immigration of foreign labor that will compete for jobs with their own members. In most countries individual trade unions are established first, and then these combine to form a larger federation. But the Histadrut is almost thirty years *older* than the State of Israel. Two whole generations of people lived by Histadrut policies before there was an Israel government. Histadrut leaders became important government figures—a prime minister like Ben-Gurion, a president like Ben-Zvi. The Histadrut always *wanted* immigrants, and still helps to settle them. The general labor federation organized the individual trade unions, instead of the other way round.

The families of Histadrut members today include about 60 per cent of Israel's Jewish population. Two other labor organization workers use the Histadrut's Sick Fund, marketing and wholesale cooperatives, and trade union section. The Histadrut thus serves about 90 per cent of all Jewish workers and their families in Israel.

Histadrut members belong to several different political parties—including religious and communist, socialist and capitalist. A Histadrut election is also a political campaign—each party puts up its own candidates and tries to win votes for them. At a Histadrut meeting, delegates speak as representatives of their political parties. The three strongest parties in the Histadrut are also the most powerful in the government.★

Try This: Look through Chapters 6 and 10. Then explain why a labor federation should engage in so many unusual activities.

★ Where would government and Histadrut leaders be most likely to cooperate? To be in conflict? Who in Israel would tend to be against *both* of them?

157

What the Histadrut Accomplished

In its first thirty years, the Histadrut was the major organization in Palestine to set up cooperatives in every conceivable business, from bus lines to shoemaking. It set standards for the country in wages and hours of work, in education and socialized medicine, in settling more immigrants in defiance of England and the Arabs. The Histadrut also created the kind of settlement that includes farm and factory, agriculture and industry. This combination allowed the settlers to shift from one to the other in different seasons, and to manufacture food products right on their farms. It also helped to spread industries more widely over the country.

The Histadrut fought strongly against child labor, insisting that children belong in school. It refused to let women engage in hard physical labor. Israel's progressive labor laws today are a result of the Histadrut's years of struggle. These laws include an eight-hour day, a forty-seven-hour week, with thirty-six continuous hours of rest, and at least twelve days of paid vacation each year. Special rules protect young people and women. Employers pay penalties for delaying wages, and the government inspects all places of work for health and safety.

HOW THE HISTADRUT HELPED TO BUILD ISRAEL

■ Many organizations, between 1920 and 1948, helped to create the Jewish homeland. But as you see from the diagram, the Histadrut was one of the most important. Which of its contributions represent mainly benefits for its own members? Which represent service to the whole country, not usually done by labor unions elsewhere? Which represent *both* kinds of activity? Because of the Histadrut, the new government after 1948 found its work both easier and harder—can you see why?

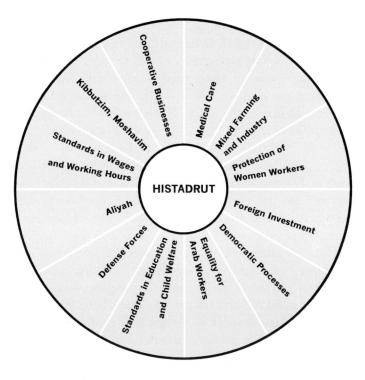

The Histadrut also fought hard for Arab workers. In 1920, they were poorly paid, ignorant, without hope or ambition. The Histadrut, of course, stood for just the opposite: well-paid workers, educated, with high goals. As long as Arabs accepted low pay and poor treatment, Jewish workers could not get far with their demands. So, from the start, the Histadrut tried to get Arab workers to organize and fight their own battle. In 1927, an Arab trade union was formed, which the Histadrut helped and encouraged. For example, its members received the Histadrut medical benefits in return for a small fee.

After 1948, the Histadrut worked closely with the government to help Arabs achieve full equality with Jewish workers. The rapid advance of Arab workers in the State of Israel shows how the Histadrut has answered the age-old question, "Am I my brother's keeper?"

The Histadrut helped to build up Israel to a point where nations and investors were willing to do business with the new country. The Histadrut had taken some of the biggest risks, in the most dangerous and undeveloped parts of the country. It had poured money and manpower for new settlements, schools, factories, stores, banks, hospitals, cultural institutions. The remarkable success of Israel's bonds and investment program during her first fifteen years was partly due to the heroic pioneering of the Histadrut.

The Histadrut also succeeded in its other aim—molding the Jewish community into a democratic, partly-socialist country. From its beginnings, the Histadrut stressed democracy—everyone taking part, sharing in decisions and responsibilities. This was the natural way of life in the Kibbutz and the trade union. Since most workers were Histadrut members, the Histadrut influenced the way of life of the entire country. So, too, it helped to make Israel a country of unusually well-educated workers.★

The Histadrut, along with other organizations, was of great help to the new state. For example, with the very first wave of immigration in 1947–48, the Histadrut opened a new steel mill, a pipe factory, a cement plant, and other firms in towns and territories with little Jewish population. Thus, at one stroke, the Histadrut helped to take in Jewish immigrants, make them self-supporting, distribute them over the country, improve neglected land, increase export products, and strengthen the country's defenses.

The new government's job was much easier because of organizations like the Histadrut. In other lands of Asia and Africa, new governments often had great trouble getting started. They suffered from civil wars, bitter quarrels among different groups, and even intervention by the U.N. In Israel the new government needed no outside help to strengthen its authority. It quickly solved the usual

Only in Israel

A few years ago, twelve teachers and nurses asked to join the Histadrut. They did not want higher salaries or shorter hours, or health insurance, hospitalization, old-age pension. They were Christian Arab nuns, with special permission from their convents to associate themselves with Israel's workers. Their purpose: to show appreciation for the Histadrut's services to Arab women in Israel. The Histadrut accepted them, but as they received no pay for their work, charged them only "token" dues.

★ Once a year, Haifa's workers gather at their lunch hour to hear lectures by outstanding writers and hold discussions on Israeli literature. During this "Book and Author Week," the Histadrut brings in up to fifty authors. In groups, they deliver addresses in various meeting halls. Each writer also talks directly to people at schools, clubs, factories, garages—even the post office. What is the purpose of this project? (Several answers.)

If I am not for myself, who will be for me? And if I am for myself only, what am I? And if not now, when?

—Hillel

Try This: Look back at Chapters 6 and 10. What were some other organizations that helped to prepare the country for self-government? How do they differ from the Histadrut?

Only in Israel

A cement works, part-owned by the Histadrut, got a big profitable contract from a foreign construction company because it was able to charge an unusually low price. Reason: an Israeli shipping firm, also part-owned by the Histadrut, gave the cement works a special low rate for transporting the cement.

And yet—the Histadrut itself owns the biggest construction company in Israel and the whole Middle East. This "deal" helped a foreign competitor—but it also helped Israel.

---

problems of a new regime—and some unusual ones besides, like the War for Independence and the vast immigration. Israelis had differences among themselves, but they were able to handle them in a peaceful, democratic manner, and to work together as a united nation. This, too, was partly due to thirty years of practical experience in self-government in the Histadrut and other organizations.

Histadrut—Partner of Government

The Histadrut, after 1948, gradually turned over to the government its sanitation services, four elementary school systems, and employment offices. It invited the government to become a partner in *Mekorot,* its water company. In Zim, its shipping company, the Histadrut not only made the government a partner, but gave it veto power on any matter of foreign policy or defense.

On the other hand, the Histadrut has retained control of קוּפַּת חוֹלִים—the Sick Fund. Histadrut leaders believe that medical care is best handled by an independent public agency representing the people concerned. Yet the Histadrut supported government laws for compulsory health insurance, even though its own members do not need such a law.

Recently, the Histadrut voted to give up part of its control over the transport cooperatives that run buses and trucks. This industry has been much criticized for poor service, too much power in the hands of a few officials, and so on. The Histadrut wanted to make motor transport a public company, managed by both Histadrut and government representatives. But the drivers themselves refused to allow government partnership, insisting on full control of their co-ops.

The Histadrut helps the government to encourage private business. It goes into partnership with many private investors. Its Employment Fund lends businessmen money to start new firms, or to keep their firms going when business is bad. Histadrut representatives help private employers to increase the efficiency of their workers

---

Kupat cholim: קוּפַּת חוֹלִים

■ Israel's newest ship, the "Shalom." Largest and most beautiful passenger ship of the Zim Israel Navigation Company (named from the initials of Zi Mischari, "Merchant Fleet"). Zim is a partnership of the Histadrut, the Israel Government, and the Jewish Agency (representing Jews of the world).

■ The Histadrut's Bank Hapoalim stands on Ahad Ha-am Street in Tel Aviv. This bank serves Histadrut business firms and union members. It also lends money to businessmen who may be Histadrut partners or competitors, employers of Histadrut members, or foreign investors. What are Histadrut's two goals?

and so produce more goods. For example, the Histadrut offers a bonus to workers in private firms who increase their output—actually helping its competitors!

The Histadrut is not, like the ordinary labor union, mainly concerned with fighting employers. Its leaders have often *opposed* their own members who wanted an improvement for themselves as against the welfare of the whole country—such as wage increases that raise prices and reduce sales. The Histadrut believes in strengthening the new state and improving the whole country, so that *everyone* is better off.★

★ The Histadrut and the government run some enterprises together, some separately. Each runs some enterprises alone, some with other organizations, some with foreign firms and investors. Why has this flexible or "mixed" approach helped the country to improve so much in such a short time?

Histadrut Problems

A unique Israeli creation, the Histadrut has impressed the labor movement in other lands. New nations especially have studied its role in building up a successful country from almost nothing, and against great obstacles. Some have already taken the Histadrut as a model for their own workers' organizations.

But the existence of the State of Israel raises questions about several of the Histadrut's original labor policies. Three principles especially are challenged by some Israelis, including Histadrut members themselves:

Seniority. According to this Histadrut rule, a business that does not need all its workers must fire the newest employees first, and the oldest employees last. A worker's ability, the size of his family, his wages, the kind of work he does—these do not matter. It is simply a question of the date he was hired—last in, first out.

High wages. The Histadrut has generally insisted on the highest possible wages, and usually refuses to accept wage reductions. The average Israeli worker earns about one-fourth of the average American worker's pay, but only slightly less than the average European worker, and far more than the average worker in Arab countries or the underdeveloped lands of Asia and Africa. But then, Israel's high income taxes drain off much more of a worker's income than in the United States and many other countries.

Equal pay. This means that *all* workers are paid on the same scale—a doctor or engineer the same as a farm or factory hand. In recent years, professionals have demanded higher pay than ordinary workers, and high school teachers have requested more than elementary school teachers. In 1955, and again in 1962, thousands of Israeli professionals went on strike. Some even left the country to work in the United States, where most professionals earn more than factory workers. In other lands, ordinary workers usually have to fight for equality with businessmen and professionals. In Israel, it is the other way round: professionals consider themselves the "underdogs," and fight for better treatment than the "working class."

None of these problems has yet been settled to everyone's satisfaction. They represent a struggle between the ideal of complete economic equality and two other strong factors: the best way to run a profitable business, and the desire of every group to better itself. Every democratic nation has this conflict. Perhaps if Israel learns how to handle it, she could make another new contribution to world betterment.

YOU'LL ENJOY SEEING

Design for Israel (film: National Committee for Labor Israel)
Faces of Israel (film: National Committee for Labor Israel)

Only in Israel

A household helper in Haifa sued her employer for not giving her an annual paid vacation. The housewife argued that the girl came in only twice a week to do the scrubbing, for only ten hours a week—surely not the same as a permanent employee! "Makes no difference," answered the judge. "She's a worker, workers get vacation with pay, *she* gets vacation with pay."

Try This: For class discussion: Why did the Histadrut set up each of the three principles? Why is each one, in a way, fair, logical, helpful to the country? On the other hand, what is wrong with each one—how does it weaken the country? How would you vote on each rule —and why?—if you were a Histadrut member? If you were a non-member?

chapter 14

A Language of Their Own

The Fight for Hebrew

In 1913, the Jewish schools of Palestine went "on strike." Teachers and pupils "walked out" of classrooms and held their lessons on the sidewalks or in the fields. "Sympathizers" milled about on the city streets, threatening and demanding.

And all over Hebrew! A new Institute of Technology, the Technion, was being organized in Haifa. The directors had announced that the Bible and other Jewish subjects would be taught in Hebrew, and the sciences and technical subjects—in German. This seemed logical. German Jews were starting the Technion, German was the world's foremost scientific language. Top scientists and engineers didn't know Hebrew; Hebrew-speaking teachers couldn't teach college math and science. Hebrew also lacked a modern scientific vocabulary, and was the official language of no country in the world. Students trained in German would be accepted in any scientific institution in the world, but students trained in Hebrew . . . ?

But the objectors didn't care about "logic." They wanted all-Hebrew instruction, and created such a fuss that the Technion directors had to give in.

The Holy Tongue*

Our ancestors spoke Hebrew in ancient times for about 1,400 years. In this language, they produced the Bible, the Mishnah, and other great works of literature and religion. As conquests and exile scattered Jews among other lands, they began speaking other languages

---

*Leshon Ha-kodesh: לְשׁוֹן הַקֹּדֶשׁ

HONOR ROLL

"God will raise up the tabernacle of David from the dust. . . . Then he will also send His spirit into our sacred language, to revive it, to put it back upon the pedestal on which it once stood."

Moses Mendelssohn (1729-1786). Began the movement of "Enlightenment" to win citizenship and equality for Jews, and to persuade Jews to study modern European subjects. He and his followers tried to use Hebrew for writing on modern subjects.

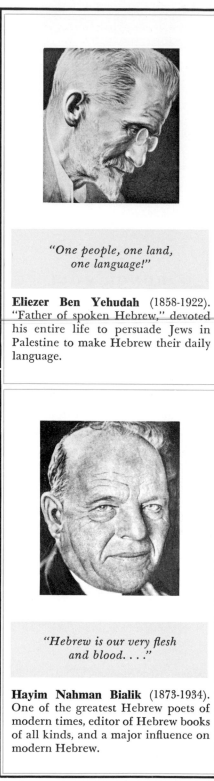

"One people, one land, one language!"

Eliezer Ben Yehudah (1858-1922). "Father of spoken Hebrew," devoted his entire life to persuade Jews in Palestine to make Hebrew their daily language.

"Hebrew is our very flesh and blood. . . ."

Hayim Nahman Bialik (1873-1934). One of the greatest Hebrew poets of modern times, editor of Hebrew books of all kinds, and a major influence on modern Hebrew.

HONOR ROLL

too—Aramaic, Greek, Arabic, the European languages. Sometimes they blended Hebrew and other languages to create an entirely new one, like Yiddish (Hebrew and German, plus several other European languages), or Ladino (Hebrew and Spanish languages).

Every Jew knew Hebrew and used it—in reading from the Bible and the prayer book, celebrating Sabbath and festivals, and observing ceremonies of birth, Bar Mitzvah, marriage, and death. In every generation, poets composed hymns, historians wrote chronicles, scholars wrote commentaries, learned men wrote letters, diaries, business records, and wills—in Hebrew. Jews in different lands corresponded with one another in Hebrew. Jewish travelers in a strange country always headed for a synagogue, where they could make friends and feel at home because of the common language. Since Jews did not use it regularly for everyday life, Hebrew lacked a great many ordinary words. It was a "holy tongue," a "special language"—but never a "dead" one.

Then a change came, about a hundred years ago. Some Jewish writers in Europe began to publish Hebrew novels, poems, essays, plays, newspapers, and magazines. They used the ancient language for modern types of literature and to discuss modern problems.

Zionism was closely connected with the love of Hebrew and the desire to "bring it back to life." A "living" people needs a language of its own not merely for religious purposes, but for all activities of daily life. Zionists started Hebrew-speaking clubs, and pioneers preparing for Palestine began practicing Hebrew conversation.

Only Hebrew*

Several of the early pioneers set out to make the Jews of Palestine a Hebrew-speaking community. They forced themselves to speak and think in Hebrew—a language not suited at first for modern everyday living. They also had to convince the other settlers, who resisted the idea fiercely.

For most of the settlers, Hebrew was a "holy tongue," and its use in everyday life a "sin." New immigrants naturally preferred their native language. Many settlers thought a revival of spoken Hebrew was impossible—other nations had tried to restore an ancient language, and had failed. But the Hebrew-speaking groups persisted. They wrote pamphlets, books, and dictionaries, invented new Hebrew words, published newspapers and magazines, talked, argued—and always in Hebrew.

---

*Rak Ivrit: רַק עִבְרִית

Teachers in the Jewish schools helped greatly to turn the tide. In 1893, they voted unanimously to refuse to teach in any language but Hebrew. They had to write their own textbooks and invent new Hebrew words for subjects like algebra, chemistry, and physics. Their students made up Hebrew slang and common everyday expressions. Gradually, more Jewish families joined the battle for Hebrew. Immigrants heard their children speak the Hebrew they learned in school, and began to imitate them. By 1913, when Hebrew-speaking settlers won "the language struggle" with Technion's directors, almost half the Jews of Palestine could speak Hebrew fluently.★

★ Why were the early settlers so set on Hebrew and only Hebrew? What difference does it make which language, or how many languages, a people speaks?

The Last Round

In 1921, the Zionist leaders, after much argument and debate, persuaded the League of Nations to make Hebrew an official language of Palestine along with English and Arabic. Now the settlers set out to win the final round. They were already using only Hebrew in Jewish institutions, newspapers, books, theaters. Now they insisted that the British government use Hebrew, along with English and Arabic, on coins, stamps and railroad tickets, in all documents, records, and publications, in all law courts and post offices. Audiences in those days often had to sit through the same speech three times, in English, Arabic, and Hebrew. But it was worth the trouble. Hebrew was strengthened in the country. New immigrants gave up their own language more readily. Use in official situations helped to expand and modernize the Hebrew vocabulary.

There were other victories, like the opening of the Hebrew University in 1925. Now the Yishuv had a complete educational system, from kindergarten through college, all in Hebrew. In 1948, with the new Jewish State, Hebrew came into its own at last. After nearly 2,000 years, Hebrew was again the official language of an independent Jewish country.

Now, "the language struggle" took on a different form. A huge immigration of a million people had to be taught modern Hebrew—and fast. Israel developed the אוּלְפָּן*—the Hebrew study-and-living program. In a city Ulpan, students live together for five or six

Only in Israel

Eliezer ben Yehudah, a penniless crusader for "Hebrew only," once received a money order for $100 from relatives in Europe. It was made out to his Russian name, Perelman, and he had to sign the post office receipt that way. Ben Yehudah, according to his principles, refused to sign anything but his Hebrew name, and did not claim the money. Poor as he was, Hebrew was more important to him than $100.

---

*Ulpan: אוּלְפָּן

In 1910, for the first time, I tried to make a speech in Hebrew at a meeting, because I couldn't speak Yiddish. Almost everyone left the room because they could not understand Hebrew—except three people: Yitzhak Ben-Zvi, his wife, and his brother. He didn't think then that he was going to be a President, and I didn't think I was going to be a Prime Minister. Later, I had to make another speech at a conference in America, and again I had to do it in Hebrew. That time nobody left.

—David Ben-Gurion

Try This: Write to Histadruth Ivrith of America, 120 West 16th Street, New York, N.Y. 10011, for information about Hebrew Month and other ways in which this organization promotes Hebrew language, arts, and culture in our own country.

Only in Israel

Israel is the only country that has revived an ancient language for everyday speech.

In 1952, De Valera, head of the Irish State, visited Jerusalem. Prime Minister Ben-Gurion said to him: "You have been independent for forty years, and trying to revive Gaelic, your ancient Irish language. Have you succeeded?"

De Valera replied, sadly: "Learning Gaelic is compulsory in our schools and Parliament. But in the homes, in the streets—the people still speak English."

Ten years later, De Valera sent this message to Ben-Gurion: "Reviving Gaelic is still a complete failure. Perhaps what Ireland needs is some Zionists!"

months, using Hebrew in their studies and activities. These are mainly for professional people, to help them follow their old careers in the new land. In a farming village, students spend six months, studying half a day and working the other half to pay for their tuition, board, and lodging. There are also "short" Ulpanim—afternoon or evening courses for twelve-to-sixteen hours a week, lasting four months.

New methods were developed for teaching "basic" Hebrew to large numbers of people. A list of one thousand most useful Hebrew words was worked out, then one of five hundred. Volunteers went into immigrant homes, to teach the whole family at once. The government, and many organizations, set up all sorts of classes. Radio, newspapers, schools—all gave special attention to the task. The immigrants responded—eagerly and industriously. "Operation Hebrew" marked up another victory for the language that never died.

Hebrew Up-to-Date

The Bible uses only about 7,700 different Hebrew words. A modern unabridged Israeli dictionary has about 30,000 words, about one-third of them invented during the last fifty years. In addition, modern Hebrew has over 30,000 new technical terms for the various sciences and occupations of today.

The new words were created by a council of scholars which began in 1890 to consider questions of modern Hebrew grammar, spelling, and vocabulary. Today, decisions of the Hebrew Language Academy, located at the Hebrew University, are compulsory for all schools and government departments.

One of the most important language decisions in the early years was to use the Sefardic pronunciation of Hebrew. This was the pronunciation of Hebrew thousands of years ago. In the Middle Ages

166

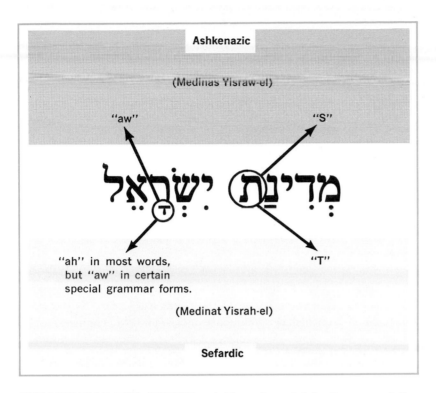

Ashkenazic

(Medinas Yisraw-el)

"aw"   "s"

מְדִינַת יִשְׂרָאֵל

"ah" in most words,
but "aw" in certain
special grammar forms.

"T"

(Medinat Yisrah-el)

Sefardic

ONE LANGUAGE, TWO ACCENTS. Ashkenazic and Sefardic pronunciation differ in several ways, but these are the two most important.

the Ashkenazic pronunciation was developed in Europe, but Jews in Oriental and Mediterranean countries continued to use Sefardic.

Sabras have an accent all their own. They talk extremely fast, slurring syllables carelessly, skipping certain sounds, in much the same way that some American-born youngsters speak English. Perhaps the most beautiful Hebrew is spoken by the educated Oriental Jews.

Modern Hebrew is a lively, vigorous language. It is much like Bible Hebrew, but uses many words and expressions from all periods of Jewish history. For this reason, there are often several different expressions for the same idea, each with its own "flavor" from the past.

A good deal of Arabic is spoken and written in Israel. English, the most popular foreign language, is studied widely in schools and universities. French is also quite popular—in fact, it seems to be giving English a close race. Yiddish used to be scorned in Palestine, as a symbol of exile and ghetto days, but recently it has become more common. It is taught at the Hebrew University, and Yiddish plays and concerts are often presented in theaters.

■ The official Israeli school style of writing the Hebrew letters. Israeli printers have also designed new, clearer styles for the printed letters.

167

Hebrew has proved to be a strong binding force. It has brought together different immigrant groups coming from eighty different lands. It has linked Israelis with many American Jews. And it has tied the modern Jewish state to all of the Jewish past.

HAVE YOU WONDERED . . . ?

. . . how new words are formed?

One method of forming new words is to use a basic Hebrew root in a new way. For "movies," for example, רָאִי—see, was joined to נוֹעַ —motion, to make רָאִינוֹעַ. If קוֹל means "voice," what would קוֹלְנוֹעַ mean?

Seven different words were once used for an ordinary household object, but the word גַפְרוּר from גָפְרִית—sulphur, proved most popular and lasting. Can you guess what the object was?

When Israel launched her first space rocket in 1961, engineers went back to Bible roots for "rocket," "satellite," and "fuse." From a well-known story about Saul and David, they used טִיל for "missile." Look up I Samuel, 18:11—what did the original word mean?

Sometimes, Israelis simply translate a foreign expression to its Hebrew equivalent. If שְׁמַר means "take care of" and טַף is a young child, have *you* ever been a שְׁמַרְטַף?

Scholars seeking a good Hebrew word for "garage" finally found one in II Kings, 16:18. Look it up and see what a biblical "garage" was like.

A popular new *adult* word for "teen-ager" uses עֲשָׂרָה for the "teen" and טִפֵּשׁ—fool, to make טִפֵּשׁ־עֲשָׂרָה—an "idioteen."

What Hebrew word do you know for Bible, law, the Jewish way of life, that Israelis also use for a scientific law of physics or chemistry? Many old, familiar religious words are used this way for non-religious meanings.

Modern Hebrew "borrows" many colloquial words from Arabic, Yiddish, and English—sometimes with amusing results. For instance, Israelis say "beck-ex" for the back axle of a car: a front axle then becomes a "front beck-ex." You'll find other entertaining examples in *Israel Without Tears* by Ruth Gruber.

R'ee: רָאִי   Noa: נוֹעַ   R'eenoa: רָאִינוֹעַ   Kol: קוֹל   Kolnoa: קוֹלְנוֹעַ

Gafrur: גַפְרוּר   Gafrit: גָפְרִית   Til: טִיל   Shemar: שְׁמַר   Taf: טַף

Shemar-taf: שְׁמַרְטַף   Esreh: עֲשָׂרָה   Tipesh: טִפֵּשׁ   Tipesh-esreh: טִפֵּשׁ־עֲשָׂרָה

Today we speak foreign languages; tomorrow we shall speak Hebrew!

—Eliezer ben Yehudah, 1880

YOU'LL ENJOY READING

How the Hebrew Language Grew, by Edward Horowitz

YOU'LL ENJOY SEEING

The Aleph Bet and the Book (filmstrip: Jewish Education Committee)
Hayim Nahman Bialik (filmstrip: Jewish Agency)
Eliezer ben Yehudah (filmstrip: Jewish Agency)

chapter 15

Culture, Science and Sports

At every Independence Day celebration, a popular ceremony is "The Parade of Wisdom," when prizes are awarded to the outstanding men of the year in literature, science, art, law, and scholarship. These prizes are symbols of gratitude. Israel was created not only by farmers, workers, and fighters; writers and artists, scholars and scientists, helped too.

Most early Zionist settlers were educated men. Culture for them was a necessity, not a luxury. The major scientific institution, theater company, athletic clubs, newspapers, art school, symphony orchestra, all existed long before the State itself. They were all important in the Zionist ideal of a "normal people in its own land."

In Israel, culture and science have always been closely connected with the daily lives of the common people. The typical hero of Israel is a man of many talents. The first three presidents were a chemist, an expert in Oriental Jewish history, and a scholar and editor. The first Prime Minister was a diligent student of the Bible. The most famous army commander resigned to become an archeology professor at the Hebrew University.

ISRAELI ARCHITECTURE. This striking example is one of the buildings of the Technion, Israel's "M. I. T." in Haifa. Many of Israel's buildings were designed by Technion teachers and graduates.

(opposite page) MUSIC IN THE AIR. An American trio plays Beethoven at Caesarea. Visiting performers say Israeli audiences are unusually warm and understanding. What was this location probably used for in ancient times?

171

Reading and Writing

1966. The Nobel Prize for Literature was awarded to S. Y. Agnon, distinguished Israeli novelist and short story writer.

★ Translated books and plays, and foreign movies, are more popular in Israel than "originals." Can you explain this situation? Why will it probably change over the years?

Israelis enjoy all forms of culture and entertainment, but their three biggest favorites, in order, are reading, music, and theater.

Israeli best-sellers include not only translations of American and English best-sellers, but Jewish classics and reference books. Bible commentaries, poetry collections, and dictionaries—especially English-Hebrew dictionaries—are so popular that newspapers offer them as gifts to attract new subscribers. Every city has many small bookstores, all doing good business. Most homes have sizable book collections, and books are popular birthday and Bar Mitzvah gifts. Over a hundred new Hebrew books for children are produced every year by the foremost writers of the country.★

TEL AVIV NEWS-STAND. How many familiar American publications can you find? The Israeli newspaper best known to Jews of other lands is the *Jerusalem Post,* an English paper for tourists, diplomats, students, and businessmen. Thousands of American Jewish subscribers receive it by air mail a day or two after it appears. News-stands in the immigrant settlements display non-Hebrew newspapers in twelve different languages, including Arabic, Yiddish, and Ladino. *Omer* is a daily paper especially for new immigrants, with easy Hebrew, vowels, and footnotes translating hard words into six different languages.

Twenty-five different newspapers appear every day on the newsstands. Over 325 magazines, from weeklies to annuals, cover every conceivable subject from agriculture to zoology. *Life, Time,* and *Newsweek* are the most popular foreign magazines, along with similar publications from England and France. Most newspapers give little space to crime, gossip, or sensational events. They stress news of politics, cultural events, and economics. One oddity, to us, is the placing of family announcements—births, engagements, weddings, deaths—on the front page.

Three-fourths of the papers are connected with political parties or other organizations. They are read mainly by members and express the party's ideas on the country's problems. The three papers with the largest circulation, however, are independent.

A newspaper sometimes appears with words, sentences, or paragraphs blacked out. This is military information, like the location of camps or the sums spent for defense, which the Army feels should not be published. Otherwise there is no government censorship. Criticism of the government is frequent and strong. Newspapers from other countries are freely displayed for sale. Israel has the only free press in the whole Middle East.

Newspapers do not appear on Saturday. An extra large Friday edition includes articles, stories, and poems by outstanding writers, book reviews, features for women, sports, and translations of important articles in the major newspapers of other lands.

SHRINE OF THE BOOK. Home of the Dead Sea Scrolls (see pages 36-37) and the Bar Kochba letters (see pages 35 and 38-41), and part of the new Israel Museum in Jerusalem. The visitors above are German youth (see pages 254 and 256).

Only in Israel

Israeli Hebrew is usually printed without vowels. As a result, Israelis sometimes read *Hamlet* as "Ha-melet"—Hebrew for "cement"—or call a certain famous fictional sleuth "Sheerluck Holmas." A typist, till now, had to strike a letter first, then go back and strike the vowel under it. In 1962, an Israeli invented "the impossible"—a Hebrew typewriter that could produce a letter and its vowel sign at the same time. Now typists can go twice as fast in preparing reading matter for students, immigrants, visitors, and radio commentators trying to pronounce foreign names.

THE MANN AUDITORIUM, in Tel Aviv, is named for an American Jew whose contribution helped to erect it. Concerts here are always "sold out."

Only in Israel

Issachar Miron, Israeli composer of the hit song, *Tzena, Tzena,* was assigned by the government in 1953, to start choirs in the new settlements. The Yemenites, though quite musical, were too afraid of ridicule to sing with Europeans. So Miron learned a few Yemenite songs, and presented them in choir concerts *to* the Yemenites. They laughed at the Europeans' mistakes, tried to teach them how to do it "right"—and before they knew it were singing with Europeans and liking it. In choirs all over the land today, Yemenites sing along with other Israelis.

THE MANN AUDITORIUM, in Tel Aviv, is named for an American Jew whose contribution helped to erect it. Concerts here are always "sold out."

The Sound of Music

Music in Israel can be anything from rock-and-roll or cha-cha to experimental modern music—and in between, American and European hit tunes, popular Israeli songs, old-style synagogue chants, classical compositions, and opera.

Israeli jazz fans have a weekly radio hour, an annual one-night Jazz Festival in Haifa, and two jazz clubs in Haifa and Tel Aviv. A Kibbutz high school in Galilee gives a jazz appreciation course, conducted by an American music teacher who wrote his own textbook.

In Tel Aviv, its "home" town, the Israel Philharmonic plays each concert twice in order to present every program for all subscribers. Even at that, Tel Avivans have found a way to double the audience. At intermission, listeners come out and hand over their ticket stubs to friends and relatives, who go inside for the second half of the program.

Israel's radio symphony broadcasts weekly, each time featuring new original music and a new performer. The new villages, often distant and isolated, are entertained regularly by symphony orchestras from Haifa, the Kibbutzim, and the Gadna youth club of the Army. An opera company and a string quartet perform for large audiences.

THE HORA. This well-known dance actually comes from the Balkan countries, but has become so popular in Israel that we usually associate it with that country. Many Israeli composers have made up tunes purposely for Hora dancing. Here, an Army unit of soldier-farmers helps celebrate the opening of a new settlement in the Aravah canyon in the Negev.

★ Before 1948, most Israeli songs were about farmers and shepherds. Today, only one new song out of twenty is of this type. The favorites now are songs of love, "life" in general, the Army, humor, and tragedy. Can you explain this change?

In dozens of villages, settlers from twenty or more different countries gather one night a week to sing the songs each group brought to Israel, and the popular songs of all Israelis. At regional gatherings, ten or twenty village choirs combine voices, and at national contests 200 such choirs compete for trophies.★

Stage and Screen

Israel's four major theater companies present several hundreds of performances a year to audiences totaling over a million. Their productions include classics like Shakespeare and Ibsen, "Broadway hits" from New York, and original plays about Israel.

The world-famous Habimah ("The Stage"), now Israel's national theater, supported by the government, has made several tours of the United States.

In addition, Israel has over 200 amateur theater groups, including one maintained by the Army. In nearly every village a hard-working חוּג—circle, presents both published and original plays.

Israelis of all ages also love the movies. Over 200 motion picture theaters—sixteen in Jerusalem alone—show films in all languages, from all lands.

"The Voice of Israel"*

Kol Yisrael, Israel's radio, made its first broadcast on May 14, 1948, from Tel Aviv, with the official reading of Israel's Declaration of Independence. Today, it offers many different types of programs, to reach the old settlers, the new immigrants, Arab countries, and other foreign lands.

In addition to music, Kol Yisrael provides regular news bulletins, interviews, drama, language lessons, and religious programs. It is owned and managed by the government. To help pay expenses, it accepts advertising on some programs, but has strict rules about commercials—length, repetition, "phony" dramatizations, and program interruptions.

There is no censorship, no favoritism to the political parties in power. The better educated Arabs in nearby countries trust Israel's news broadcasts more than they do their own. The king of Jordan had to ban public listening to the Israel radio because it became too popular in his country.

SCREEN AND STAGE. (Above) Movie theater in Beer Sheva. (Below) Habimah actors in the famous play, *The Dybbuk*. Most movies and plays are foreign imports, but Israeli productions are increasing. The first Israeli-made full-length film appeared in 1964.

Chug: חוּג   *Kol Yisrael: קוֹל יִשְׂרָאֵל

Israel hesitated over television for several years. Several thousand TV sets in 1962, mostly in Arab homes and restaurants, were usually tuned to telecasts from Arab lands. Some Israelis argued for a TV station of their own, to provide more jobs, improve education, and answer Arab propaganda. Others felt that Israel was too poor to afford TV, as she had too many other more important needs. In 1963, the Knesset authorized educational TV to telecast science, language, and other lessons to the nation's classrooms.★

Land of the Bible

Bible study takes up almost one-third of the entire curriculum in every grade and school. An adult Bible study group meets every two weeks in the home of the President of Israel—attended not only by Bible scholars, but by a university president, a supreme court judge, a former commander-in-chief of the Army, and a newspaper editor.

INBAL. a unique Yemenite group, uses dance, speech, song, pantomime, and primitive instruments like drums, flutes, ankle-bells, tambourines, gourds, cymbals. Among their most popular numbers are "The Song of Deborah," a campfire celebration of the ancient Israelite victory over the Philistines, and "Yemenite Wedding," a dance interpretation of the seven-day oriental celebration of marriage. Why do you think they chose, for their name, a word meaning the clapper or tongue of a bell?

1966. Televised lessons began in English, biology, and math for Grades 7 and 9 in 32 schools and 60 classes. In 1968, Israel had 22,000 TV sets, with 5,200 more in areas occupied in the Six Day War (see Chapter 25). General TV began in 1968.

STANDING ROOM ONLY, in Jerusaem's huge Convention Center for the Annual Bible Quiz. Many in the audience check questions and answers in their own Bibles. Radio listeners stay up till two or three in the morning to find out who wins.

Many thousands of Israelis eagerly follow the nightly Bible reading on the radio. Thousands of others take a Bible correspondence course, or belong to the Israel Bible Research Society and attend its annual conference and smaller discussion groups. Bible themes appear in countless stories, poems, plays, ballets, operas, concerts, paintings, statues. Ancient Bible objects—menorah, Torah, ark, shofar, and others—often appear on Israeli stamps.

The Bible has been a practical guide for Israelis. The earliest settlers, for instance, followed Bible farming practices—they planted grain crops in the fall at the start of the rainy season, and vegetable crops in the winter. They planted vineyards too, because these are mentioned so frequently in the Bible. When Israelis wondered what would grow in the sandy soil around Beer Sheva, they found the answer in the Bible: Abraham planted tamarisk trees there.

In the War for Independence, army units imitated the surprise attacks of Gideon and Judah the Maccabee. They moved swiftly, made night raids, dodged through mountains and valleys, and changed tactics, suddenly. They used forgotten paths, mentioned in the Bible, to make surprise raids and escape from encirclement. They planned whole campaigns just like those of the Bible's first great military genius—Joshua.

Art in Israel

ISRAELI STAMP FOR HEROES AND MARTYRS DAY shows a flaming torch made up of the letters of what familiar Hebrew words? Why are these words appropriate?

In 1906, Boris Schatz, "the Father of Israeli Art," founded the Bezalel Art School in Jerusalem. (For the name, see Exodus 35:30-36:1.) He wanted to provide beauty for the settlers, stimulate them to produce their own art, and make the Jewish homeland a world art center. Today, the school and its museum, supported by Jews of many lands, are world-famous.

Jerusalem, Tel Aviv, and Haifa have fine art galleries, general museums, and special museums for modern art, ancient art, folk art—even Japanese art. New museums and galleries go up all the time, especially in the various art colonies throughout the country. Tel Aviv is a major art center, where some of Israel's best-known painters live and work. Every year, ten or twelve new "galleries" open in empty stores, hotel lobbies, or even on the open street. Tourists are the best customers, but Israelis buy many paintings, too—often on the instalment plan. Israel has a professional painter or sculptor for every 2,000 people—a high percentage compared to many other lands—besides thousands more of amateurs drawing and designing for the fun of it.

A LAND OF ART. (Left) Avraham Gilboa, noted Israeli painter, captures street scene in Safed. Here, in one of Israel's oldest towns, with many synagogues and holy sites along its narrow, curved streets, about 100 artists have set up their studios. At Ein Hod, in the Carmel hills near Haifa, about seventy artists have established a cooperative art community whose annual exhibit brings on a countryside traffic jam. In 1962, Israel brought in twelve sculptors from various lands to carve giant statues half-way down the Beer Sheva-Eilat Road—for a touch of beauty in one of the Negev's most desolate spots. (Below) Israelis of all ages throng to an exhibit in the Tel Aviv Museum. Look for Israeli art in your school and temple.

מוזיאון תל-אביב
TEL-AVIV MUSEUM
HELENA RUBINSTEIN PAVILION

*Science will bring to this land both peace and a renewal of its youth,
creating here the springs of a new spiritual and material life.*

—Chaim Weizmann

Science

MEET "WEIZAC." Electronic computer built by scientists of the Weizmann Institute is a "cousin" of our own country's ENIAC, MANIAC, and UNIVAC. Its 1800 tubes can memorize 32,000 words, do 250,000 arithmetic operations a second, and print 100 lines a minute. A music-minded engineer, noticing a humming sound between certain operations, "programmed" WEIZAC, by a special perforated tape, to turn its hum into the melody of *Hatikvah*.

A few years ago, delegates from many nations came to Israel for an international conference on using science to develop new countries. Israel was the ideal place for such a meeting. Her stress on science gave her a head start on most other undeveloped countries, and also made her an acknowledged leader among scientific nations.

The Beer Sheva Institute for Arid Zone Research is the world leader in studying plants, food, housing, clothes, and rest periods for desert living. The Hebrew University-Hadassah Medical School conducts research in thirty different branches of medicine, from anatomy to X-rays. The Technion, Israel's Institute of Technology, was nicknamed—by an American scientist—"the M.I.T. of the Middle East."

The laboratories of the Weizmann Institute of Science are world-famous. Many nations buy its "heavy" oxygen, which has the highest percentage of purity in the world. They exchange scientists with the Institute, and hold international science conferences there.

The United Nations, the United States, and other countries often employ Israel's laboratories to do research for them, and help to support these institutions with generous money grants. In 1964, the United States joined forces with Israel to find a cheap method of desalting ocean water.

HIKE-LOVERS. Hiking is a favorite sport and pastime with many Israelis. These men, who are finishing up their annual four-day hike from Tel Aviv to Jerusalem, are bus drivers.

Only in Israel

Chaim Weizmann, Zionist leader and Israel's first President, was also a noted chemist whose discoveries aided the western nations in both World Wars. He insisted that science would enable Palestine to support millions of people. The stubborn British authorities kept announcing that Palestine had no more "absorptive capacity"—could not take in more immigrants.

One day in 1936, a British official visited Weizmann in his laboratory at Rehovot. After watching him at his test-tubes a while, the visitor asked what he was doing.

Weizmann looked up at him, and replied gravely: "I am creating absorptive capacity!"

At the opening of the new Institute of Nuclear Science at Rehovot, a visiting scientist hemmed and hawed a little, then blurted out the question that was bothering him.

"How far is it here," he asked, "from the nearest Arab bomber base?"

"Six minutes!" snapped an Israeli scientist. "But it's 2,000 miles from any research laboratory like it!"

Sports

Israel bristles with athletic leagues of all kinds, but has no professional sports. Every athlete is an amateur, who plays not for money, but for fun, and to improve his mind and body. One daily paper and another coming out three times a week are devoted exclusively to sports. The regular press and the radio are also full of sports news.

Israelis grow up with soccer, and love it the most. But basketball runs soccer a close second in popularity, and may some day surpass it. Outdoor courts dot the entire countryside. They are cheap and easy to lay out, and the game's speed and excitement fit right in with the Israeli temperament. Swimming, the third-ranking sport, is made easy by the long seashore along the Mediterranean, and by the eight months of pleasant weather.

Other sports favorites include hockey, tennis, ping-pong, rowing, gymnastics, wrestling, weight-lifting, judo, cricket, sailing, fencing, track-and-field events. Volleyball and handball are especially liked by farmers and soldiers, and especially in the Kibbutzim—they take up so little space and need little field upkeep. Army stress on physical fitness carries over to the rest of the nation. Marksmanship is especially popular because of the Army. New sports—golf, bowling, water-skiing, skin-diving, surf-casting—are spreading rapidly.

Marching and hiking are national sports in Israel. Bus drivers, bank clerks, youth groups, Kibbutzniks—all take regular hikes. On Passover, thousands of Israelis of all ages revive the ancient custom of עֲלִיָה לְרֶגֶל—the pilgrimage to the Temple, with a four-day "Jerusalem March" of fifty to ninety miles, depending on each group's starting point.

HAVE YOU WONDERED . . . ?

. . . how Israel compares in culture with other countries?

In proportion to her population, Israel:
- —is second among all countries in the number of books published and imported each year
- —publishes eight times as many books a year as the United States
- —has a symphony orchestra with the most subscribers and the longest concert season—nine concerts every two weeks for ten months
- —is the second highest country in percentage of people attending the movies regularly
- —has one professional painter or sculptor for every 2,000 people—a high percentage compared to most countries
- —ranks third in the world in number of scientists and technologists, fifth in atomic research, and is among the leading countries in cancer research
- —is one of only four nations producing their own Salk polio vaccine, and one of only four nations developing sunlight as a source of power
- —does more science translation, in more languages and in more branches of science, than any other country

YOU'LL ENJOY READING

The History of Israel's Postage Stamps, by Harold U. Ribalow
Children of Freedom, by Libbie L. Braverman

Aliyah Leregel: עֲלִיָה לְרֶגֶל

Only in Israel

Israelis usually show good sportsmanship toward foreign teams, but sometimes lose their heads over local contests. Once a Gedera soccer team traveled to Haifa for a game. The bus driver was an ardent supporter of the Gedera team. As he watched the game, he became angrier and angrier with the referee who seemed to favor the Haifa team. At half-time, he could stand it no longer. In disgust, he threw a soda-water bottle at the referee, went off to his bus, and drove all the way home. When the game was over, the Gedera team had to find its own way home.

Try This: A committee job: Write to American Friends of the Hebrew University, American Friends of the Technion, and American Friends of the Weizmann Institute (addresses in the *American Jewish Year Book*). Ask for information about their work and about the institution itself in Israel. Look also in *Facts About Israel,* Israel Office of Information, 11 East 70th Street, New York, N.Y. 10021 (latest issue), under "Research," and in Jewish encyclopedias. Then: (1) Give a class or assembly talk on why your Keren Ami should contribute to an "American Friends" organization. (2) For one institution that interests you, make a poster chart of its departments, activities, accomplishments. (3) Describe a few recent science projects that might interest the class.

Israel is determined . . . to conquer the desert and make it flourish by the power of science and the pioneering spirit, and to transform the country into a bastion of democracy, liberty, and universal cultural values based on the teaching of Israel's prophets and achievements of modern science.

—David Ben-Gurion

YOU'LL ENJOY SEEING

The Earth Sings (film: Brandon Films)
Ein Breirah or Song of the Negev (film: United Israel Appeal)
Vistas of Israel (film: Center for Mass Communications)

YOU'LL ENJOY HEARING

Recordings of Israeli music, available in most stores selling records.

Try This: Write to America-Israel Cultural Foundation, 4 East 54th Street, New York, N. Y. 10022. Ask about Israeli institutions which this organization supports, its cultural exchange program, and scholarship awards. Prepare a class report or display using the materials you receive. Ask especially about Neot Kedumim (Israel's ancient culture park) and the new filmstrip, *Sukkoth and the Four Species.*

BIBLE ZOO, popular visiting spot in Jerusalem, has seventy-five of the eighty-five animals mentioned in the Bible, each with an appropriate biblical passage attached to its cage. The verse here, from Proverbs 28:15, compares a wicked ruler of hungry people to a roaring lion or a greedy bear.

Israel will witness a famine not for bread, and a thirst not for water, but for learning the words of the Lord.

—Amos 8:11

chapter 16

In Search of Faith

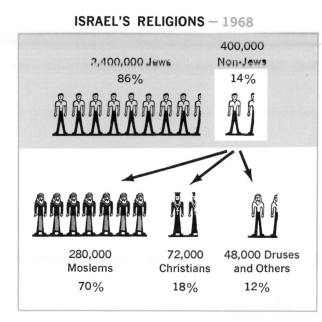

2,400,000 Jews
86%

400,000 Non-Jews
14%

280,000 Moslems
70%

72,000 Christians
18%

48,000 Druses and Others
12%

Religious Liberty—for Non-Jews

Israel allows full freedom of worship to the non-Jewish faiths. The government shows them respect and consideration, and aids them with money and advice.

Israel's government helps non-Jewish religious communities to look after their holy places and cemeteries, maintain orphanages and old-age homes. It pays the salaries of religious officials, remodels old churches and mosques, and builds new ones. It aids worshipers, both Israeli and foreign, to make pilgrimages to their sacred sites and hold ceremonies there. Often Israel builds new and better roads for this purpose. On the government radio, religious programs are broadcast for Moslems and Christians as well as for Jews. Despite strong opposition from some Israeli Jews, the government does not interfere with Christian missionaries trying to convert Jews to their religion.

Religious Liberty—for Jews

Only the laws concerning the official day of rest apply to the country as a whole. Each city, town, and village makes its own decisions on specific points like halting cars and taxis on Saturday. Accordingly, the rules of Sabbath observance vary from place to place.

ISRAEL'S RELIGIONS. Though ninety percent Jewish, and a small country, Israel has a bewildering variety of religious sects in her 4,500 synagogues, 200 churches, and 120 mosques. For the first time in 2,000 years a Jewish majority must deal with the problem of religious freedom for minorities. (Opposite page) Orthodox yeshivah students. What book are they studying?

1967. After the Six Day War (see Chapter 25), on uniting Jerusalem and occupying Arab territory, Israel immediately announced full religious liberty and protection of holy places for all faiths.

185

The State of Israel . . . will guarantee freedom of religion, conscience, language, education, and culture; it will safeguard the Holy Places of all nations.

—Israel Declaration of Independence, 1948

(Opposite page) Moslem mosque in Acre, 200 years old, where worshipers use prayer-rugs instead of seats. (Above left) Samaritans, though not considered Jewish, use the Torah scroll. This one, in Jerusalem, may be the oldest in the world. (Above right) Druse priests, at a holy shrine near the Sea of Galilee. The ancient mysterious Druse customs are unknown even to most of their own worshipers. (Left) A group of Roman Catholics in Jerusalem. Other interesting Israeli religions: (1) the Karaites, only two families in 1948 but now several thousand, date back to a "revolt" against the Talmud in Babylonia 1,200 years ago. (2) Bahai, the world's newest religion, hardly a hundred years old, and its smallest, with only a few hundred followers, has its world headquarters in Haifa.

187

Government operations observe the Sabbath strictly. Warships at sea continue to move, but the daily cleaning or painting jobs are cancelled. Ships do not leave port or arrive on the Sabbath, even in foreign countries. The Border Patrol makes its rounds, but other soldiers have no drills or maneuvers. Meals are prepared on Friday and kept warm over the Sabbath. Except for the essential duties or emergencies, all army personnel have a full thirty-six hour rest day —for worship, lectures, study, discussion, and festive meals. Leaves are timed so that no travel on the Sabbath is necessary. Recruits may choose separate mess kits for meat and milk foods, or one mess kit for both. The food itself is kosher; meat and dairy foods are not served together.

The traditional dietary laws are also observed in most hotels and cafes. Inspectors travel on all passenger ships to supervise the preparation of kosher food. Bread and beer, which contain yeast, are not sold anywhere during Pesach week. The post office will not deliver a food package then, as it might contain items that observant Jews may not eat on Passover. Otherwise, each community decides its own degree of kashrut enforcement.

Try This: Compare Israel's Sabbath with Sunday observances in your own community. Ask your parents if any disputes have arisen over opening stores or showing movies on Sunday.

SABBATH IN ISRAEL. (Below left) The Mea Shearim section of Jerusalem (woodcut by artist Jacob Steinhardt) observes the strictest, most Orthodox Sabbath in the world. (Right) Tel Aviv's beach is crowded on the Sabbath with swimmers and bathers. The Israeli Sabbath closes down most public transportation, stores, army, factory and farm operations, movies, theaters, schools, and offices. Restaurants, hotels, hospitals, electric and water stations, museums and zoos are open. You may use taxis and private cars (in most places), telephone, attend soccer games in bigger cities.

ORTHODOX: Observe strictly the traditional Sabbath, dietary laws, and other practices, though differing considerably among themselves.

TRADITIONAL: Observe Sabbath "more or less," attend synagogue several times a year, prefer Orthodox ceremonies for births, Bar Mitzvahs, weddings, divorces, and deaths, and may or may not keep kosher.

LIBERAL OR PROGRESSIVE: Resemble our Reform and Conservative groups, and have organized several new synagogues of these types. Believe in a religious life, but one that emphasizes discussion, self-expression, freedom, and experimentation.

NON-RELIGIOUS: Do not care about religion one way or the other, ignore religious matters, and do not even want to talk about God, worship, prayer, or spiritual problems.

ANTI-RELIGIOUS: Oppose strongly all religious ideas and customs. Say that Jews elsewhere, as a minority group, may need religious life to hold them together but in Israel, the whole land is the "Temple" — its language and culture are all a Jew needs.

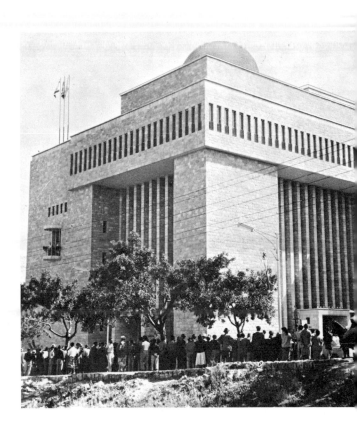

Israel's Religious Problem

An Israeli Jew has freedom of worship and belief in his private life. He can decide for himself about synagogue attendance, Sabbath and holiday observance, eating kosher foods, or sending his child to a religious or non-religious public school. He is also free to think and speak as he pleases about religion and to leave any community in which the regulations displease him.

Government affairs are a different matter—these generally follow the traditional Orthodox pattern. Some top government leaders, for example, are openly non-Orthodox. But on Independence Day, they join the other officials in attending an Orthodox synagogue for a special worship service.

A non-Orthodox Israeli Jew does not have a free choice in one very important part of his personal religious life, namely, that which deals with aspects of marriage and divorce.

Government and religion, church and state, are not completely separated in Israel. The government officially "recognizes" certain religious groups. Each group has its own religious councils, local

■ The tallest building in Jerusalem is the central headquarters of the government-supported Orthodox rabbis. Some Israelis jokingly call it "The Datican"— a pun on the Hebrew *dat* (religious law) and *Vatican*, the palace in Rome where the Pope "rules" over the world's Catholics. What do such Israelis object to—and why?

The State will satisfy the public religious needs of the people carefully, but will tolerate no force of whatever kind, from whatever source, in matters of religion.★

—Ben-Gurion, 1952

★ How far has Israel succeeded in carrying out these two promises? Which side did her first Prime Minister favor in the religious problem? What do you think of the word "public" in his statement?

THE NEW. . . . Children of a "non-religious" Kibbutz use an "original" Haggadah for their Pesach Seder. Hundreds of such Haggadahs have been created in Israel—a Kibbutz writes in its own troubles and triumphs, problems and hopes, history and adventures. At first, these Haggadahs omitted the word "God" and religious terms, but now use some traditional prayers and religious content. Why has Passover such a strong personal meaning for settlers in Israel, old and new?

and national, to run its religious affairs. A special cabinet post, the Ministry of Religious Affairs, has separate departments for each of the "official" groups. The government pays the expenses of these religious councils, such as the salaries of officials, out of local and national taxes. The government also gives each of these religious groups full control over marriage and divorce among its members.

For Jews, the only group recognized by the government is Orthodox Judaism. To be legal, therefore, a Jewish marriage or divorce in Israel must be performed by an Orthodox rabbi, according to Orthodox law. A Jew cannot marry a non-Jew, for instance. Government officials cannot marry a couple—there is no civil marriage. The state courts cannot grant a divorce. This situation often makes life unpleasant for non-Orthodox Jews, and sometimes causes needless heartbreak.

Orthodox law forbids descendants of priests to marry a divorced woman, and accepts a child as Jewish only if its mother is Jewish. One man changed his name (Cohen, meaning "priest"), so that the

rabbi would not know he was marrying a "priest" to a divorcee. The deception was found out, and the man punished—with three months in jail.

Some young people who were born in Israel and brought up in a Kibbutz, risked their lives in the Defense Forces—then found they could not get married because their mothers had not been Jewish. Their own children, in turn, could never hope to be buried in a Jewish cemetery—unless, of course, they went through a formal ceremony of conversion to Orthodox Judaism.

Samaritans and Karaites have considered themselves Jews for many centuries. They follow the laws of the Torah, but they do not accept the Talmud and later rabbinic laws. The Samaritans are not considered as Jews, and Israel's rabbis would not perform marriages between them and "true" Jews. The Karaites constitute themselves as a separate sect, with their own institutions and religious leaders.

The B'nai Israel, a group that came originally from India, encountered difficulties with some Orthodox rabbis when they asked them to officiate at their weddings. This group fought hard against such treatment and appealed to the Knesset, to the Ministry of Religious Affairs, and to the Jewish Agency for Israel. Finally, after careful study of the matter, the Chief Rabbinate gave in and declared the B'nai Israel full and equal Jews, who could marry and divorce other Jews.

. . . .AND THE OLD.   Scribes (*sofrim*) at work on new Torah scrolls. They are specially trained, and must follow strict traditional rules for the parchment, ink, pen, spacing, shape of letters, and so on. Orthodox Kibbutzim have revived many ancient Bible farming ceremonies, others have created new modern ones. The government has inaugurated a new ceremony for the last day of Pesach, held on the seashore of Tel Aviv, to commemorate the crossing of the Red Sea.

■ Relay runners of the Maccabi sports association carry the Chanukah torch from the town of Modin to Jerusalem where they hand it to Israel's President. (Why Modin?) An Israeli Chanukah is bright with flags hanging from every window and balcony. Traditional small lights burn in every home, school, public building. Giant electric menorahs glow atop synagogues and other buildings—an idea popular now too in our own country. Candlelight parades fill the streets. Israeli youngsters adore Chanukah—schools close down for a whole week.

■ While we are still bracing ourselves against winter winds, spring comes to Israel. Young people pour out into the countryside on Shevat 15th (Chamishah Asar, or Tu Bi-Shevat) to plant trees and flowers. Besides eating Israeli fruits and enjoying Israeli songs and dances, how do American Jewish children join their Israeli cousins in celebrating this festival?

■ A pious Jew kisses the tombstone of Rabbi Shimon Bar Yohai, at Meron. On Lag Ba-omer (33rd Day of Counting Omer, or Grain-sheaves) thousands of Israelis gather here to light candles, pray, sing, dance. Huge bonfires go up in many other places. This is also a time for picnics and outings, as it is in our own country for many Jewish religious schools. See what you can find out about Rabbi Shimon Bar Yohai, and why Lag Ba-omer is called "The Scholars' Holiday."

■ Tel Aviv's *Adloyada* (Purim Carnival) inspired the masquerades and carnival booths of many a religious school's Purim celebration. Ask your rabbi or Hebrew teacher what "adloyada" means.

■ The whole family helps build the Sukah for "the Feast of Booths." All our holidays have taken on a special meaning for Israeli Jews—can you see why, in each case?

■ Dancing and singing for Simchat Torah—"Rejoicing over the Torah." All holidays are exciting in Israel. For example, find out about the Bikkurim ceremony on Shavuot.

■ The Druses, though not Jewish, are among Israel's most loyal citizens, and take part enthusiastically in celebrating Yom Ha-atzmaut, Israel's Independence Day (Iyyar 5—April-May)—a new Jewish holiday. It begins with a sunset memorial service at Herzl's tomb, amid huge torches. Newcomers to Israel that year come to a microphone, state their name, original country, and date of arrival. Then all recite the Shehecheyanu, thanking God for bringing them alive to this joyful day. Next day, all over Israel, there are parades, flag-raisings, speeches, and special synagogue services. In the afternoon, the annual Israel Awards are presented. Compare this holiday with our own Fourth of July.

1968. Recent Supreme Court decisions have tended to weaken some of the Orthodox control over the daily life of Israelis. Also, new combinations of political parties have reduced the number of Knesset seats of Orthodox political parties.

To many Israelis, it seems wrong for the government to aid *any* religious groups—and unfair to recognize officially only *certain* ones. Only the Orthodox Jews, the Moslems, the Druses, and four Christian sects have religious courts and control over marriage and divorce. Only these groups get government funds for their religious expenses and salaries. Reform and Conservative Jews do not have these privileges. Neither do one-fourth of Israel's Christians, including 1,500 Protestants. All non-religious citizens, and members of non-recognized religious groups, must thus support, through taxes, certain "official" ways of religious living.

Perhaps a third of all Israeli Jews are Orthodox. Yet they often try to make an entire city—even the whole country, when they can—follow traditional practices. For example, Orthodox groups have used political and business pressures to keep new Reform congregations from renting a hall or obtaining a Sefer Torah. They have boycotted farms and factories that do not operate strictly by Orthodox Judaism. They say that community life in Israel should be Orthodox—that a man should not be allowed to do anything publicly that offends Orthodox religious feelings.

Orthodox Israelis maintain their own political parties, elect their own candidates to the Knesset (Parliament), and play a strong role in the country's government. A tug-of-war goes on between those trying to get more Orthodox Judaism in Israel, and those wanting less of it or none at all.

Because religion is involved in politics, the well-organized, determined Orthodox group can force some of their *religious* practices on the whole country, or prevent another group from following their religious practices with complete freedom and equality. In most places, Jews cannot choose among several varieties of Judaism —they must follow only one kind or none at all.

Why Israel Has a Religious Problem

Israel was not created overnight. The early Zionist settlers found a religious pattern that was centuries old. Orthodox Jews and other religious communities enjoyed certain rights and privileges under the Turks. Each group was responsible for its own members in matters of birth, marriage, divorce, burial, education, wills, adoptions, and charity. Each maintained its own courts, whose judges were religious leaders with full legal authority in these matters. The new governments—such as England in 1920, the Yishuv as organized in 1928, and the State of Israel in 1948—took some rights away from the religious communities, and provided some services to people not members of these communities. But the basic pattern remained: the religious communities retained some of their exclusive rights.

The State of Israel thus inherited an ancient and accepted system. Moslems, Christians, and Orthodox Jews expected their former rights to continue and objected strongly to any change. A new government with much to do and many problems to solve, naturally wants to keep things as they are until changes can be made smoothly. It is hard to take away suddenly all long-standing rights and privileges. The religious groups are part of the nation; they have votes and can influence the affairs of the country. The government needs their support.

Israel's pattern is still wide-spread in Oriental and European countries—even in democracies. England, for example, has an "established" or official government religion. Holland, Ireland, and several Canadian provinces provide two kinds of public school, religious and non-religious. Many people believe a government *should* provide for their religious needs, as well as for their education, health, safety, social security, and so on. Such people, when they speak of "religious equality," usually mean equality among the old, established religious groups. These have special rights and powers not granted to newer groups. In religion, education, and in other ways, many Israelis accept these ideas.

But many do not. They prefer the American pattern—complete personal religious freedom, public education without religion, separation of government from religion, *individual* freedom rather than group equality. Even a few Orthodox leaders want this in Israel, too.

Try This: Ask your parents how they feel about government aid, in our own country, to parochial schools. Find out how many Jewish schools of this type your community has, and how many Jewish parents might benefit financially from such government aid. Why do most American Jews oppose the idea? Why do most Israeli Jews accept it, even if not in favor of it?

ISRAEL'S NEW PRAYERS. Israel's rabbis have composed special soldier's prayers—before entering battle, parachuting, flying in a plane, submerging in a submarine. Other new prayers include a Yom Kippur blessing for young children, a Sukot prayer for world peace, prayers for Jews murdered by the Nazis, for raising the flag, and for the welfare of the new State. For our new prayers to honor Israel, see *Union Songster* (Reform), page 372, or *A Book of Prayer for Junior Congregations* (Conservative), p. 88.

THE OLD. . . . Orthodox Jews gather for prayer in Tel Aviv's Great Synagogue. Most of Israel's 4,000 Orthodox synagogues are small, often with congregations of less than thirty people. They are not social centers, like most of our synagogues, but intended only for worship and study. Can you see why?

Try This: Choose one of the holidays and plan an Israeli-style festival this year for your class or school. Use ideas from the pictures in this chapter. Make up your own ideas, too. Try to get some new, fresh, *personal* way to celebrate the festival.

The Israelis "in the middle" do not want complete Orthodox control of religious life, but neither do they want to remove it or even reduce it. They neither like nor dislike the present system, but are used to it. They want the country to have what they consider an Orthodox "flavor"—even though they themselves are not strictly Orthodox.

Israel inherited a mixture of Turkish, British, and traditional Jewish law. She is still a mixture of Orthodox and non-Orthodox Jews, of Eastern and Western ideas, of European and American styles of democracy, of ancient Jewish traditions and modern attitudes. Israelis believe in religious liberty and try to achieve it. They have much to be proud of, but also much that disturbs them.

Some day, Israelis will have to solve the conflict between personal religious freedom and government-sponsored religion. But feelings run high at the moment. Since earliest Zionist days, this problem, serious as it is, has had to take "a back seat" for the more pressing problems of immigration, development, and defense. Today also, most Israelis feel that they should not take time and energy away from these problems to fight among themselves on still another "front." Occasionally, Israeli tempers flare up—over a convert to Christianity who still wants to call himself a Jew, or a couple that wants to marry without an Orthodox ceremony, or fanatics who try to force their ideas on the public at large. But reluctance to change the present religious pattern will continue for many years to come.

HAVE YOU WONDERED . . . ?

. . . how the government treats the new congregations?

The Israel government itself shows no prejudice or unfairness. It never interferes with Reform congregations, and even helps them. For example, the government sold to the Jerusalem group the land and buildings for its permanent location. The state courts uphold Reform groups suing for equal rights and fair treatment.

A Reform leader asked Ben-Gurion, then Prime Minister, what would happen if a Reform rabbi applied to the government for a license to perform weddings and other ceremonies. He said he would use all his influence to get the rabbi such a license, as long as he was an Israeli citizen.

Ben-Gurion criticized American Reform leaders for not working *harder* to spread Reform Judaism in Israel. He invited them to confer with him and make plans "to bring more non-religious Israelis into synagogue life."

196

Ben-Gurion considers himself—and the Orthodox consider him—"anti"-religious. Can you think of a better way to describe his attitude, and that of other Israelis like him, toward religion?

YOU'LL ENJOY READING

Feast of Leviathan, by Leo W. Schwarz, pp. 207–291

YOU'LL ENJOY SEEING

As Long As I Live (film: United Israel Appeal)
Israel: Holidays and Festivals (filmstrip series: Jewish Agency)—
1. Sukkot and Simchat Torah. 2. Hanukah and Tu Bi-Shevat.
3. Purim and Passover. 4. Lag Ba-omer and Shavuot.

Only in Israel

A Reform group at Kfar Shmaryahu, a suburb of Tel Aviv, had to fight vigorously for the same rights as the "official" Orthodox congregation to rent space from the town council. It would rent a place, get all ready for services, then be locked out at the last minute. It had to smuggle in a Torah scroll, and bring a lawsuit against the town. "Worship," said Israel's Supreme Court, "is a matter of the heart, and each worshiper knows for himself what he needs or doesn't need." The Court ordered the town council to rent city property to "Progressives," as Reform Jews are called in Israel, the same as to other religious groups.

. . . .AND THE NEW. Open-air dedication exercises, April 14, 1962 of the new Reform center in Jerusalem, Har-El Synagogue. It represents the first permanent site for a Reform house of worship in Israel and serves as the Israel headquarters of the World Union for Progressive Judaism. A generous gift from an American philanthropist, as well as the enthusiasm of "progressive" Israelis, made this center possible. Reform worship in Israel differs from American Reform worship in several ways: for instance, they are all-Hebrew, and males wear head-covering. Do you think the new Israeli Hebrew Reform prayer book may influence worship in our own country?

chapter 17

Democracy in Action

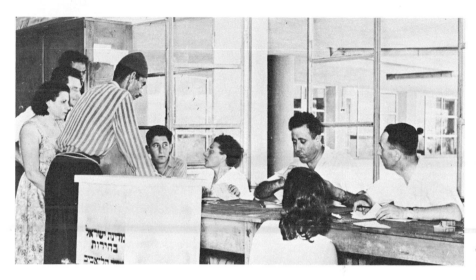

Election Time

Every Israeli citizen over the age of eighteen may vote regardless of religion, race, color, or sex. Any citizen over twenty-one may run for election, except judges, senior Army officers, and government employees—three groups expected to stay out of politics. Elections are unusually free of charges of bribery or graft, and the vote count is accepted with confidence by all concerned. Election time is lively and full of argument, but with little disturbance.

Israel law controls what the parties may do during a campaign, in order to prevent the wealthier or larger ones from having too many advantages. Thus, a party may provide no entertainment, gifts, food, or drink, and may not use loudspeakers in the street. It may not make or show any movies. During the last month before Election Day, no candidate may appear in a newsreel. Each party gets altogether only twenty-five minutes of radio time, plus four extra minutes for each candidate who won in the previous election. In the Army, political parties may post their list of candidates, a statement of principles, and notices of meetings—but may do nothing more.

THE CITIZENS VOTE. (Above) An Israeli voter enters a private booth containing a stack of ballots for each party, each ballot clearly marked with the party symbol. He folds and seals a ballot of the party he prefers, comes out, drops his ballot into a ballot box. Compare this procedure with American voting.

WHEN THE KNESSET MEETS. (Opposite page) Following the European pattern, members sit in a semicircle—the largest party on the right, the next largest to its left, and so on. A member addressing the Knesset sits on a platform, next to the Speaker conducting the session. Cabinet members sit at an oblong table in the center. Knesset sessions, three days a week, and open to the public, are conducted in Hebrew, though Arab members may use Arabic. Earphones bring each member instant translation of either language. Including what you see in the picture, what are the differences from a session of our Congress? Any similarities?

Try This: Compare and contrast an election in Israel with one in the United States.

Political parties spend huge campaign sums for such a small country. Some Israelis think this money should be put into schools, hospitals, and houses. But most of them believe that the political campaigns are a necessary form of education. They give the newcomers a practical lesson in democracy. They arouse the citizens to discuss the country's problems and to form their own conclusions. They review past achievements and future hopes. Some parties even arrange guided tours for voters to see what is going on in various parts of the country.

All campaigning stops at seven o'clock the night before Election Day. This is a public holiday, with all offices, stores, factories, and schools closed. From seven in the morning until midnight, Israelis vote at 2,500 voting stations throughout the country. Four out of five eligible voters cast their ballots—a high percentage compared to other democratic lands.

Each party offers the voters a list of candidates for the 120 seats in the Knesset. An Israeli votes for a party, not for individual candidates. He cannot "split" his ticket among candidates of different parties. Each party arranges its candidates in order of importance. Those at the top, therefore, have the best chance of becoming Knesset members.

A party wins a number of seats in the Knesset in proportion to its votes. If it wins one-fourth of the votes, its first thirty candidates (one-fourth of 120) become Knesset members; if it wins one-tenth of the votes, its first twelve candidates are elected. All parties win *some* representation in the Knesset as long as they get at least one per cent of the total votes. This method of "proportional representation" is also used in Holland and some of the Scandinavian countries.

Israel's Parliament*

Israel's system of government, in some ways, resembles the United States. In other ways, it resembles England, France, and other European democracies.

The Knesset elects the President, supervises the government, and makes the nation's laws. It is chosen every four years, but can also be dissolved at any time and new elections held. It can ask for reports from the government, and can approve or disapprove of them. Any party in the Knesset can call for a vote of "no confidence" in the Prime Minister and his Cabinet. When that happens, the Knesset must put aside all other business and decide at once whether or not to keep the government in office.

---

*Knesset Yisrael: כְּנֶסֶת יִשְׂרָאֵל

Only in Israel

Israelis love to trace their Knesset back to אַנְשֵׁי כְּנֶסֶת הַגְדוֹלָה—the Men of the Great Assembly, who began to meet 2,500 years ago in the days of Nehemiah. That body also had 120 members, and made laws and decisions for the Jewish people for several centuries. It developed the Judaism that we practice today. Members of the modern Knesset are proud of their role in developing the Jewish state and building a new Jewish life, and they hope their work will last a long time too.

Israel has no written constitution which the Knesset must follow in making laws. No official or court can veto any Knesset law or declare it invalid.

In most countries, members of parliament are mainly lawyers. In the Knesset, however, only a tenth are lawyers—the rest are farmers, rabbis, scholars, bankers, community leaders, and professional politicians. Israel's Jews are about evenly divided into three groups of citizens: those born in Europe, Israel (Sabras), or Asia and Africa. Most of the present Knesset members are European. The Sabras are next in number, and only a small percentage is of Asian or African background.

Of course, many Sabras are under twenty-one, too young to run for office. The Oriental immigrants are unfamiliar with Israeli life. But the pattern is gradually changing. With each new election, the Knesset becomes more representative of the country as a whole. It also grows "younger" all the time; the average age has dropped, within a few years, from fifty-four to forty-four.★

★ In what ways is the Knesset far more powerful than the Congress of the United States?

The President*

Israel's President, unlike our own, has no real power. He is a "symbol" of the whole country and does not represent a political party.

Any ten Knesset members may nominate a candidate for President. There are no special requirements. Israel's President can be a man or a woman, Jewish, Christian, Moslem, or Arab—he need not even be a citizen of Israel, or be born there. Once, for example, the position was offered to Albert Einstein. The Knesset holds a special session to elect the President, by majority vote, for a term of five years. He can be reelected indefinitely, but the Knesset can depose him at any time for "unbecoming conduct."

He carries out his duties "on advice"—that is, he must act as directed by the Knesset or the government. He welcomes foreign diplomats, formally signs treaties and laws, appoints ambassadors and judges, pardons criminals or shortens their sentences.

*Ha-nasi: הַנָּשִׂיא

Only in Israel

Yitzhak Ben-Zvi, returning home after election as second President of Israel, found a soldier standing guard in front of his house. He felt ill at ease, and told the soldier he didn't need him.

"Sorry," said the soldier, "but I have orders to guard the President."

Ben-Zvi went inside. But the soldier out in the cold worried him. He went outside again. "Maybe you'll come in and have a cup of tea?"

"Sorry," said the soldier, "but that would be a violation of my duties as a sentry."

The third time Ben-Zvi came outside, he was wearing a heavy overcoat. "I'll tell you what," he said. "You go in and have some tea. Give me the gun—I'll stand guard for you."

Israel's Government**

■ In 1963, Levi Eshkol followed David Ben Gurion as Prime Minister of Israel. He had served in the cabinet for several years as Minister of Finance and earlier as Minister of Agriculture.

רֹאשׁ הַמֶּמְשָׁלָה—the Prime Minister, has the real power in Israel's government. He carries out Knesset decisions, presides over the Cabinet, and speaks for the government.

After the election, the President invites the leader of the largest political party to become Prime Minister, choose a Cabinet, and draw up a statement of policies. If his party has not won a majority of the votes, the Prime Minister invites other parties to join with him in a "coalition" government.

Cabinet ministers are usually Knesset members, although not necessarily so. They are chosen by the various parties of the "coalition."

The Prime Minister presents his Cabinet and policy statement to the Knesset, which conducts a "vote of confidence." Since the coalition represents a majority of the votes, the new government is always accepted, and then legally takes office. The Prime Minister, his assistants, and the Cabinet all take oaths of office.

A government usually stays in office for four years, but it may be replaced at any time. If the "coalition" parties disagree, or the Prime Minister resigns, or the Knesset itself votes "no confidence," a new election must be held.

An important official, the State Controller, has the power to investigate everything going on in the government from the Prime Minister's office down. He may probe any government department he wants, whenever he chooses. His office also receives and investigates nearly 1,500 complaints against the government from citizens each year.

The Knesset chooses the Controller every five years. He is responsible only to the Knesset—no official or judge can silence or fire him. He publishes his findings at least once a year, more often if he wants to. Usually his reports reveal little graft, corruption, or dishonesty but much carelessness and inefficiency—from wasting water in army camps to building Western-style homes for Arabs instead of the kind they are used to. These reports stir up so much discussion that most complaints are soon corrected. The State Controller is probably the most respected fault-finder in the world.

In 1948, Israel began with only thirty-four local units of self-government. Today she has 185 city councils, village councils, and regional councils.

Only in Israel

Israelis like raffles and lotteries, especially for a good cause. The government sells tickets for a national lottery every week, using the profits for education and health services. To encourage savings, it awards a free home and other prizes to the winners among bank depositors who have saved certain amounts of money. The National Council for Accident Prevention offers an all-expense vacation trip in a lottery open to every driver with a perfect record for the year.

**Memshelet Yisrael: מֶמְשֶׁלֶת יִשְׂרָאֵל   Rosh Ha-Memshalah: רֹאשׁ הַמֶּמְשָׁלָה

These local units hold democratic elections every four years—for mayor, councilmen, and so on. They are responsible for the community's schools, cultural activities, health and sanitation, water supply, roads, and parks. Local governments impose their own taxes and carry out their own improvements, with the approval and help of the central government.

Plenty of Parties

The Yishuv developed self-government twenty years before the State of Israel. The Jews elected an Assembly, imposed their own taxes, made their own community laws, conducted departments of education, health, and so on. Various Zionist parties campaigned in Palestine for election to the Assembly. Each party was a combination of several smaller groups. Often, two or more parties cooperated for a time in order to control more votes. Each group in a party, and each party in a coalition, had proportional representation on councils and committees. The new State continued this system.

No party has ever won a majority of Knesset seats. The largest party over the years has been Mapai (Israel Labor Party). Mapai is socialist, but accepts a "mixed" economy of socialism and capitalism, and sides with the Western nations. This party generally wins only about a third of the votes, or about forty seats in the Knesset. To control a majority vote of sixty-one, Mapai teams up with three or four other parties. These disagree with Mapai on some of the country's basic problems—the Arab nations, siding with Russia or the United States, labor, religion, taxes, immigration, developing the Negev, education, and so on. But they agree sufficiently with Mapai to join its coalition government.

An Israel coalition usually includes the same "middle-of-the-road" parties, with some variations from election to election. The Achdut Ha-avodah (Labor Unity) Party is more socialist than Mapai, favors neutrality between Eastern and Western nations, and represents younger voters, especially in the Kibbutzim. Two religious parties—the National Religious Party and the Poalei Agudat Yisrael (Workers' Religious League)—want Israel governed strictly by traditional laws of Orthodox Judaism. The second of these is also a socialist party, and not as willing as the first one to cooperate with other parties. Two small Arab parties also usually join the coalition.

The remaining parties have extreme policies that usually keep them out of a coalition. Mapam (United Workers' Party) is very strongly socialist and anti-religious, and urges closer cooperation

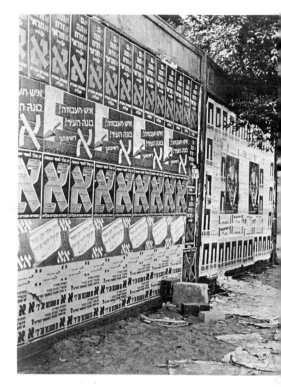

DEMOCRACY IN ACTION. For weeks before an election, Israel's twelve or more political parties work hard to persuade the country's million-and-a-half voters to choose their ballots. Each party publishes ads, puts up posters, holds meetings, mails leaflets, sends out door-to-door teams. Each party's symbol—a Hebrew letter—appears everywhere on walls and sidewalks and in flashing signs. Voters argue vigorously—at home, on the streets, at work, in restaurants. (Above) The "alef" —meaning "Number 1," belongs to Mapai, the largest party. The "chet" is the first letter of "Herut"—the "Freedom" Party.

1965. Certain parties combined—like the Herut-Liberal Party and the Mapai-Achdut Ha-avodah Party—and a new Rafi Party formed. Israel tends to have many parties that keep shifting, splitting, combining. After the Six Day War (see Chapter 25), "splinter" parties tended to come back together in a new spirit of unity. In 1968, Rafi, Mapai, and Achdut Ha-avodah joined into a combined party called MAI (initials of "Mifleget Avodah Yisraelit," the Israel Labor Party).

★ In every election, the various parties gain or lose a few seats, but the general balance of power has remained the same. Mapai continues to be the leading party, as it was for thirty-one years before the State. How do you explain these two facts, considering Israel's tremendous population increase, varied immigration, and many new problems?

1968. The Knesset is working on its last group of laws considered "basic." These will round out all similar laws passed since 1948, and become Israel's "constitution." Instead of designing a constitution at the start of their country, the Israelis decided to let it grow gradually out of specific "basic" laws passed from time to time. Why?

with Russia. It consists mainly of farmers and villagers, but also includes factory workers. The Communist Party, anti-Zionist and strongly for Russia, has both Jewish and Arab members. The Liberal Party favors the Western nations, private business, and foreign investment, and represents middle-class and working-class city people. The Herut (Freedom) Party, a militant group, proposes more territory for Israel, strongly opposes socialism, and sides with the Western nations.

Israelis see both advantages and disadvantages in their party system. Some want changes to make it more like our own American system. Two large parties competing for votes, rather than from ten to twenty small parties, would do away with coalitions and permit more unity in the government. Another recommended change would allow voters to choose candidates from different parties, and not be limited to a single party list. A third suggestion is for voters in the various sections of the country to elect their own representatives, instead of voting only for national candidates.

The three largest parties—Mapai, Liberal, and Herut—would benefit from these changes. But the smaller parties would have less power, and some of them might even go out of business. Some Israelis think this would make their government less democratic and less representative.

Israelis take their politics very seriously. A political party is more than an organization to win votes. It starts farm settlements, sponsors a youth movement and athletic teams, mixes religious, socialist, or capitalist ideas into its policies—it actually represents a complete way of life.★

Country Without a Constitution

Knesset or Cabinet members who sponsor a new law must show either that it is based on a traditional Jewish law, or that it uses a legal principle accepted in some other country. Israel's laws and court decisions are unusual for the way they quote, for their support, the laws and decisions of England, France, the United States, Canada, and other countries. At the same time, Israel's law schools require a course in the principles of ancient Jewish law.

The Knesset has passed over a thousand laws since 1948. These include guarantees of freedom of speech, worship, assembly, and the press, and the right to legal arrest and a fair trial, to follow any occupation, to own property. Some Israel laws are unique. For example, a citizen can sue the government even without the government's permission. Some laws are designed to protect Jewish and

It is exciting to be in Israel, which is one of the newest, yet in a broader sense one of the oldest nations on earth. It is comforting to see such emphasis still placed upon the Law — not merely the domestic law of the land, nor the law of nations, but the basic laws of civilization, the laws that flow from moral, ethical, and religious concepts of civilized people in determining the relationship of man to man and of man to God.

—Earl Warren, Chief Justice, U.S. Supreme Court

Zionist ideals—the Days of Rest Law, for example, or the Law of Return. Welfare laws, for health, labor, social security, and so on, are liberal and progressive. They compare well with the advanced nations of the world.

Israeli judges and lawyers often call their legal system a "patchwork." Israel law today includes traditional British laws, Turkish laws (often based on French and Arab laws), laws of both the Yishuv and the British authorities in Palestine, religious laws of Moslems, Christians, and Jews, and new Knesset laws. Judges must spend much time deciding which kind of law to use, and law cases often involve much delay and confusion. Sometimes the law books are in Turkish or other languages which the judges may not understand.

A clear, practical legal system takes a long time to develop. Israeli law-makers have not had enough time, and have had to work under great pressure. Gradually, the "patchwork" will become a smooth, orderly pattern.★

★ Israel in 1948 had the same problems as the American colonies in 1776: Should all previous laws be scrapped? All kept? Some kept, others abolished? Both countries decided on the same answer: all existing laws remain in force —unless changed later, or unless contradicting a new law. Why was this solution accepted in both situations?

Israel's Supreme Court*

Israel does not have a jury system. All cases are decided by a judge, or by a panel of three judges. Minor disputes and crimes come before the twenty Magistrates Courts located in the main cities and towns. Major disputes and serious crimes are heard in the three District Courts in Jerusalem, Tel Aviv, and Haifa. Matters of marriage and divorce are in the hands of the religious courts.

---

*Bet Ha-din Ha-elyon: בֵּית הַדִּין הָעֶלְיוֹן

ISRAEL'S TWO TYPES OF LAW COURTS

	State Court	Jewish Religious Court
JUDGES	Lawyers appointed by government, state court judges, and other lawyers	Orthodox rabbis appointed by other Orthodox rabbis and government
SALARIES	Paid by government, out of taxes	Paid by government, out of taxes
TYPES OF CASES	Criminal cases	Marriage and divorce matters for all Jews whether Orthodox or not
	Wills, adoption, custody of a child, etc., if **either** side prefers a state court	Wills, adoption, custody of a child, etc., if **both** sides prefer a religious court
	Cases not specifically reserved for a religious court	Cases not specifically reserved for a state court if both sides prefer a religious court
	Government law violations	Purely religious and ceremonial matters
POWERS	Arrest, summoning witnesses, fines, imprisonment	Arrest, summoning witnesses, fines, imprisonment
	No powers in cases reserved only for a religious court	No powers in cases reserved only for a state court
	Decision may be appealed only to a higher state court	Decision may be appealed only to a higher religious court

■ Like her two kinds of public school, Israel has two kinds of law court: state and religious. The "official" religions—Orthodox Judaism and a variety of Moslem and Christian groups—have their own judges. In some matters, a person can choose which court tries his case; in other matters, he *must* use one and not the other. This system goes back to Turkish rule, and even to medieval times. Why did the British government, and later the State of Israel, retain this system of courts?

Cases may be appealed to higher courts, up to the Supreme Court in Jerusalem. The nine members of this Court are appointed, for life, by Israel's President, "on the advice" of a special committee of Supreme Court judges, Gabinet and Knesset members, and representatives of Israel's lawyers. Usually, three judges try a case, but for exceptional or very difficult cases, five judges may be used. Citizens who feel that a government department or a public organization has acted illegally toward them may bring their cases directly to the Supreme Court. Supreme Court judges cannot decide whether a Knesset law is acceptable or not; they can only determine whether or not it has been obeyed.

In the neighboring Arab lands, judges are completely under control of the government, which in turn is controlled by the army, a dictator, or a monarch. In Israel, all judges are completely independent of government control, and the army is completely controlled by the elected government.

HAVE YOU WONDERED . . . ?

. . . why Israel has no constitution?

In 1947, experts prepared a constitution for the State of Israel, to be ready for discussion and approval when the new State began. The First Knesset hesitated over this for more than a year, then decided to proceed without a written constitution—following the pattern of England rather than the United States. With all the problems and changes facing Israel, her legislators preferred to be free to experiment. Also, there were sharp disagreements on various points. The Knesset, to avoid splitting the country, decided to make only specific laws that would some day be combined into a constitution.

YOU'LL ENJOY READING

Facts About Israel, latest edition (Israel Office of Information, 11 East 70th Street, New York, N.Y. 10021)

Ben-Gurion, Fighter of Goliath, by Gertrude Samuels

YOU'LL ENJOY SEEING

Modern Israel (View-Master Stereo Pictures, Sawyer's, Portland 7, Oregon)

Try This: The following statements were both issued in 1948:—

Israel's Declaration of Independence promised to "be open for Jewish immigration . . . foster development of the country for the benefit of all inhabitants . . . be based on freedom, justice, and peace as envisaged by Israel's prophets . . . ensure complete equality of social and political rights of all inhabitants irrespective of religion race or sex . . . guarantee freedom of religion, conscience, language, education, and culture . . . safeguard the holy places of all religions . . . be faithful to the principles of the Charter of the United Nations."

The United Nations Declaration of Human Rights called for "equality of all human beings regardless of race, color, sex, language, religion, politics, or other opinion . . . dignity of treatment as a human being . . . equality before the law the right to remedies against government injustice or unfairness . . . the right to own property, and freedom of thought, religion, opinion, and speech . . . the right to refuge and citizenship from a country of oppression . . . social security, and the right to work, get an education, and participate in cultural life."

List specific examples to show how Israel has carried out the U. N. principles as well as those contained in its own Declaration of Independence.

chapter 18

Providing for the Common Welfare

The new State of Israel faced many serious difficulties in 1948— war, lack of resources, huge immigration. But one of the gravest problems was health and welfare. Many of the new immigrants were poor, sick, handicapped, or helpless. Overcrowding in certain regions endangered health and safety. Lack of food and an unbalanced diet caused wide-spread malnutrition and weakened the people, especially children and infants. Thousands of youngsters were homeless. Deaths from diseases like tuberculosis, diphtheria, and typhoid fever, and the death rate of infants, rose rapidly in those first few years. So did juvenile delinquency and adult crime.

Israel still has much to do to improve health, especially in rural districts, and among immigrants, the elderly, and the Arabs. But today it is the healthiest spot in the whole Middle East—and healthier in some ways than many of the advanced Western nations. The average life span—71 years for men, 74 for women—is equalled only by Holland, Norway, and Sweden. Israel's annual death rate of five deaths for every thousand people is one of the lowest in the world. For the size of her population, Israel has the highest proportion of doctors in the world, more dentists than England or France, more nurses than Norway, Sweden, or the United States. Diseases once wide-spread in Palestine, and still raging in nearby Arab countries, have been reduced or completely wiped out. The amount of crime and juvenile delinquency has dropped.

For Health and Life

Poor food, poor housing, and hard work plagued the early Zionist settlers. Some sickened and died of malaria, dysentery, tuberculosis, and other ills. Often the sick had no one to care for them—they lay alone in a crude hut, enduring discomfort, hunger, and pain.

CHILDREN FROM EVERYWHERE. (Opposite page) These youngsters have come to Israel from many countries, many backgrounds. In Chapter 7 read about Jewish immigrants from oriental lands and the kind of life they led. Besides providing a good modern education, what other needs of these children does Israel have to meet?

209

Try This: What other voluntary organizations have you read about in previous chapters that also helped the settlers, and still serve as "partners" to the government?

1967. Since the State of Israel was declared in 1948, over 1,250,000 immigrants arrived from 80 different countries, mostly lands of persecution. 500,000 of these immigrants were refugees from Arab countries.

THE GREAT INGATHERING. On a "peak" day after 1948, a thousand newcomers arrived in Israel—ten families every hour. The population doubled in three years, tripled in ten. Never before in history had such a huge migration taken place in so small a country in such a short time. Does large immigration help or hinder a country? Does it make a difference whether immigrants come in at a steady rate—about the same number each year—or in large numbers some years, small numbers other years? Which way has it been for Israel and her immigrants?

Getting to a hospital took days of rough riding over bad roads. Even the best hospital was a primitive place, without heat, electricity, or running water, with little equipment, and few trained workers.

In 1911, these settlers organized Kupat Cholim, the Sick Fund. Each contributed a little of his hard-earned savings to pay for medical care when needed. When the fund saved up enough money, they employed a doctor and a nurse full time. In 1920, the Histadrut Labor Federation took over Kupat Cholim, expanded it, and increased its medical benefits. Today, it is the country's largest health care institution.

In 1913, two American-trained nurses arrived in Palestine. They were sent by Hadassah, the Women's Zionist Organization of America, to set up a health center in Jerusalem. Immediately after World War I, in 1918, Hadassah's first full medical unit of forty-five doctors, nurses, dentists, and technicians arrived. They were welcomed by the settlers like rescuing angels, as they took over old hospitals. They not only introduced modern medical methods, but attended to everything from replacing broken window panes to firing inefficient cooks. They also established a new hospital, opened a nurses training school, and set up the country's first infant welfare station. Thus began the great humanitarian project of American Jewish women, still going on, to heal the sick and strengthen the healthy in the Jewish homeland.

In 1939, the Hebrew University became a partner in the Rothschild-Hadassah Hospital. Ten years later, just as the new mass immigration was beginning, these two institutions opened Israel's first medical school in Jerusalem. Within a few years, its graduates were helping to heal the sick immigrants.

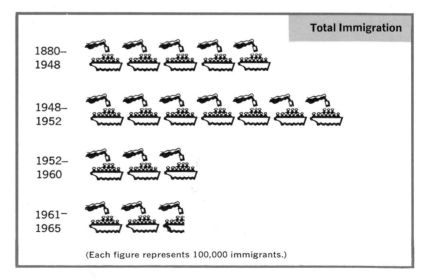

Total Immigration

1880–1948

1948–1952

1952–1960

1961–1965

(Each figure represents 100,000 immigrants.)

During British rule, the government contributed less than five per cent of the costs for health, education, and welfare services. The Yishuv levied its own high taxes, and maintained superior health services. Other voluntary health organizations grew up—such as מָגֵן דָּוִד אָדוֹם–the Red Shield of David, or the Israel Red Cross. Since 1930, this organization has maintained first-aid stations, ambulance service, and blood banks.

Operation Ship-to-Shore

Jewish communities in the Arab lands of North Africa and the Middle East had lived there as strangers, unwelcome "guests," for centuries. After 1948, and Israel's victories in the War for Independence, the Arab governments began to persecute them even more severely. In Europe, many homeless Jews, survivors of Nazi cruelty, waited in refugee camps as "displaced persons." The new Jewish State drew all these Jews like an irresistible magnet. Despite hardship and suffering, even danger to their lives, they headed for the Jewish homeland. Israeli and American Jews went to their aid and transported them "home"—across borders, deserts, mountains, lands, and seas.

But "home" wasn't ready for them. Immigrant families were herded into a crowded city slum, or a מַעְבָּרָה—temporary camp. They lived in broken-down shanties, tents, wood or tin shacks—and

---

Magen David Adom: מָגֵן דָּוִד אָדוֹם   Ma-barah: מַעְבָּרָה

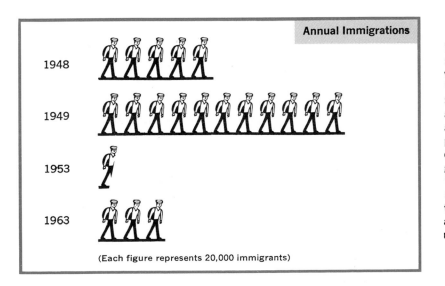

Annual Immigrations

1948

1949

1953

1963

(Each figure represents 20,000 immigrants)

■ Israel's immigration is higher in some years, lower in others. Why? Even when immigration drops, Israel cannot "relax" and catch her breath. Why not? See if you can find out why 1952 was a "peak" year, and what Israel's latest annual immigration has been, for comparison. Why do most other countries control the number and kind of immigrants they let in, whereas Israel keeps "an open door"? Of course, a certain amount of emigration *from* Israel also takes place—what can you find out about the number and reasons of Israel's emigrants?

BERUCHIM HA-BA-IM—BLESSED ARE THOSE WHO COME. Colorful newcomers from (1) Morocco, (2) Iraq, (3) Yemen, and (4) Kurdistan. According to Israel law, any Jew may move to Israel and become a citizen there, no matter how old or young, sick or handicapped —unless he is considered a traitor to the Jewish people, or has a contagious disease, or is a lawbreaker trying to escape justice. This "open door" policy is one of the finest examples of the ideals of Judaism carried out in practice.

1

2

3

4

waited a long time for a home, a job, and care for the sick, the old, and the children. Today, some newcomers still go to a Ma-abarah, especially in times of "peak" immigration. Some still experience difficulties, disappointments, mistakes. But since 1954, Israel's "Operation Ship-to-Shore" has taken care of most immigrants swiftly and smoothly.

When a group of immigrants leaves for Israel, a Jewish Agency "selection board" travels along on the ship or plane. It collects information about every family and advises them about new towns and job openings. Immigrants are urged to decide promptly where they want to settle—with the right to change their minds later. The selection lists are radioed to Israel, where government and Jewish Agency teams go into action. A few hours after they arrive, some immigrants enter a bright new village, complete with homes, stores, roads, synagogues, farmlands, water-sprinklers. Each family goes to its own modern cottage, all furnished. Inside, a woman soldier of the Defense Forces greets them with sweets, shows them around, and answers questions.

Meanwhile, others stay in a reception camp, starting classes in Hebrew, farming, or factory work. Still others go directly into the Army, or to a job. The widow with young children, the family with a crippled father, the people needing a doctor, surgeon, or psychiatrist, are taken to special homes, schools, and hospitals. Doctors, lawyers, engineers, and other professionals begin an "Ulpan" course.★

★ With all her pressing problems as a new State, and with all the special difficulties created by the newcomers, Israel did not regulate immigration as other countries have done. Why not? These two quotations may help you think of two reasons—perhaps more:

"All Jews are responsible for one another."
—Talmud

"It is for immigration alone that the State was established, and it is by virtue of immigration alone that it will stand."
—Ben Gurion

Partners in Welfare

The new State accepted its responsibility to look after all the people —to protect the healthy and to aid those not able to help themselves. But the government could not afford to do this big job all by itself. Kupat Cholim, Hadassah, and others became "partner" organizations, and continued their welfare work. The government had new "partners" too.

One of these was not a new organization for world Jewry. For almost seventy years before the Jewish State, ORT (Organization for Rehabilitation through Training) gave vocational training to Jews of Europe and Africa who had learned no modern trade or occupation.

213

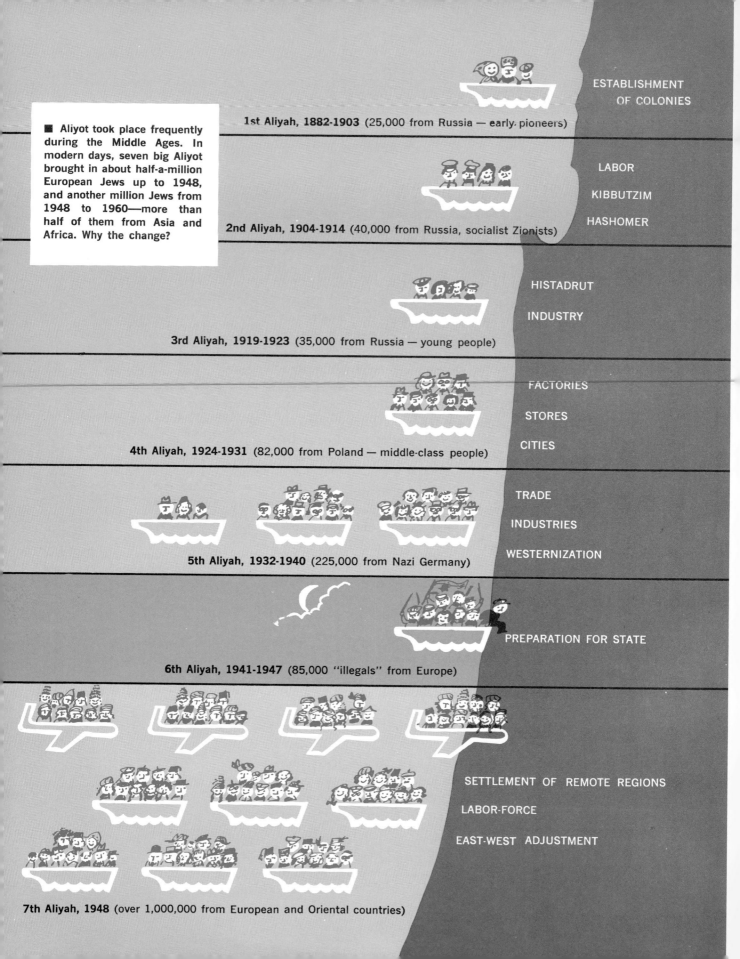

■ Aliyot took place frequently during the Middle Ages. In modern days, seven big Aliyot brought in about half-a-million European Jews up to 1948, and another million Jews from 1948 to 1960—more than half of them from Asia and Africa. Why the change?

ESTABLISHMENT OF COLONIES

1st Aliyah, 1882-1903 (25,000 from Russia — early pioneers)

LABOR

KIBBUTZIM

HASHOMER

2nd Aliyah, 1904-1914 (40,000 from Russia, socialist Zionists)

HISTADRUT

INDUSTRY

3rd Aliyah, 1919-1923 (35,000 from Russia — young people)

FACTORIES

STORES

CITIES

4th Aliyah, 1924-1931 (82,000 from Poland — middle-class people)

TRADE

INDUSTRIES

WESTERNIZATION

5th Aliyah, 1932-1940 (225,000 from Nazi Germany)

PREPARATION FOR STATE

6th Aliyah, 1941-1947 ("illegals" from Europe)

SETTLEMENT OF REMOTE REGIONS

LABOR-FORCE

EAST-WEST ADJUSTMENT

7th Aliyah, 1948 (over 1,000,000 from European and Oriental countries)

The well-being of the soul can be obtained only after that of the body has been secured.

—Moses Maimonides

After 1948, ORT expanded rapidly in Israel. It now conducts its largest single program there, and provides the country's largest vocational school system. About 20,000 Israelis attend its schools for both trade courses and a general high school education. The organization is supported by Jewish communities throughout the world, the governments of many nations—including sixty-five undeveloped countries—and the American Joint Distribution Committee. It has erected vocational schools in the immigrant centers, and sponsors clinics, libraries, sports, and summer vacations for its students. By training men, women, and children in over sixty modern skills and crafts, ORT benefits both its students and the whole country—which badly needs skilled workers of all kinds.

In 1950, the American Joint Distribution Committee and the United Jewish Appeal started an unusual project called Malben (from the Hebrew initials standing for Organization to Aid Handicapped Immigrants). It maintains old-age homes and villages, workshops for the handicapped, and hospitals. It lends the handicapped money to start a business or enter a profession, and teaches them how to earn a living and support their families. Especially in its care of the aged, it has attracted world-wide attention among doctors, social workers, and government experts.

The government cooperates with these organizations, supervises their work, makes them part of the general welfare program. Gradually, it also takes over some jobs these organizations were doing. Some day, with continuing peace and more prosperity, the government will do most of Israel's welfare work, though the organizations will still be there to help out. The organizations themselves want this. Health and welfare are basically a government's responsibility. Voluntary organizations fill in gaps, take care of special groups, experiment in new ideas and methods. This is the pattern in our own country, and in all modern democratic nations.

The government or the organizations, or both together, try to give prompt relief—but they also think ahead to when people will not need help. Thus, new immigrants receiving a home, furniture, and money are asked to sign contracts and receipts. Some day soon, they are told, they will be earning enough money to repay loans, start paying rent, and if they wish, buy their home and own their own land. The helpless are aided without question—but the healthy are encouraged to make their own way and not depend indefinitely on hand-outs and doles.

HOMECOMING. In Iran, this was a family of Marranos—Jews forced to convert to Islam and become Moslems, but maintaining a secret Jewish life. In Israel, they now live openly as Jews. In how many different ways does the term Aliyah ("Going up") fit what has happened to them? (Hint: see Chapter 7, *How Zionism Regained a Land*, the "Have You Wondered—?" section.)

How the Government Helps

The Israel government has a Cabinet department for Health and one for Social Welfare. Each of the three large cities, and about 200 smaller communities, have their own welfare departments or offices. These help poor people with money loans and grants, and advice on jobs, hospital care, and so on. Government child welfare officers work with teachers and parents, and organize youth clubs and centers. The government operates many institutions for vocational training, handicapped children, and problem children. There are probation officers for both children and adults who break the law. There are also special government services for the blind, handicapped, aged, new immigrants. Such people, for example, can get job training and loans to start their own business. Unemployed workers get a certain amount of work each month on government

A NEW LIFE. Immigrant women are taught sewing, knitting, and curtain-making by a Jewish Agency instructor. Many immigrants are handicapped physically as well as educationally. Many Israeli organizations train the blind, for instance, to become self-supporting. Israel has the world's only "Village of the Blind," supported by Malben, the Joint Distribution Committee's agency to aid the handicapped. Here the blind learn trades and also create their own community life. A blind director supervises 500 villagers and their children, most of whom are sighted. World-famous Helen Keller, visiting this unique community, renamed it "Village of Light."

216

projects, and help in finding permanent jobs. The money for all this comes from taxes, especially from one on all restaurant bills and amusement tickets.

Since 1951, the government has passed many important labor laws about working hours, rest days, paid vacations. There is no child labor. Workers between fourteen and eighteen and all women workers are carefully supervised. The government inspects safety and sanitation in all shops and factories.

The National Insurance Law, passed by the Knesset in 1953, was the first step in a "master" plan to give all Israelis full social security. It provides pensions for the elderly, insurance for widows and orphans, benefits for injured workers, pregnant mothers, and fathers with large families to support. Employers, people working for themselves, and housewives are included, as well as wage-earners. It is paid for partly by the government, and partly by workers and employers contributing a certain percentage of their income.

Try This: In *Facts About Israel,* look up either the labor laws (under "Labour") or the social insurance laws (under "National Insurance"). With the help of your public library, see if you can find some differences from American labor and social security laws.

Youth Aliyah*

In 1942, electrifying news spread through Palestine and among the Jews of the world. More than three years earlier, in 1939, thousands of Jewish children in Poland had fled from the German Army. They had walked eastward to Russia, and then southward. Somehow, they stayed together, found lodging and food. Almost 200 of them had parents with them, the rest were led by eighteen-year-olds. They were all ages—down to one toddler under two—all hungry, half naked, weak, and sick, waiting in Teheran, Iran, to come to Palestine.

Jews everywhere, almost as one man, turned to Youth Aliyah. For eight years this world-wide organization had brought thousands of Jewish youngsters out of the Nazi nightmare in Europe to a new life in Palestine's Kibbutzim. Youth Aliyah rushed workers, food, medicine to Teheran, and hired special trains. But the Iranian government refused to let the band travel across its country. So Youth Aliyah had to take them the long way around—to India, then across the sea to the Suez Canal, and finally to Palestine by train.

> ### *Only in Israel*
>
> At Suez, a group of Jewish combat engineers heard that the refugee children from Teheran were coming. They raised money, bought food packages, and wrapped a gift for each child. Here is the note one child found when she opened her gift package:
>
> "To you, my child, going up to the Land!
>
> "This is the name by which I wish to call you. I will not call you a refugee child, for from this moment on, you are a builder and a pioneer. You will work in the Land and build it and love it. And so you will forget the cup of grief which you have drunk to the full."
>
> —"A Jewish Soldier"

*Aliyat Ha-noar: עֲלִיַּת הַנֹּעַר

YOUTH ALIYAH GROUP FROM GERMANY, 1937. The first arrivals before World War II were usually well-dressed, well-equipped, well-trained. Later, thousands of war orphans had to be taken in without preparation. Some arrivals still wore the striped concentration camp uniform.

In 1960, the one hundred thousandth Youth Aliyah child arrived in Israel—and was met by a woman who had been one of the first Youth Aliyah children years before. The organization accepts about 250 children a month, between the ages of twelve and sixteen. Three times that number apply, in various countries—but there just isn't enough money for them all. All sick children are immediately accepted—then as many of the healthy ones as Youth Aliyah can provide for. Support comes from Hadassah, the Mizrachi Women's Organization of America, the Pioneer Women of America, and the Jewish Agency—and there is plenty of heartbreak among their members and the Youth Aliyah workers over the 500 children who must be rejected every month.

218

Teen-agers with a variety of difficult problems have to be cared for—and quickly. Some are alone, without parents; others have parents who can't take care of them. Many, after much wandering around, are like little hunted animals—full of hatred, bitterness, fear. Others come from modern well-to-do homes but know nothing of Jewish life—some don't even know they are Jews. Some have studied Jewish books but have no modern education. Families in unsafe countries, fearing future persecution, send just one child to Israel—lonely, bewildered, frightened. Normal children come, children from broken homes or mixed marriages, children whose parents want temporary help but soon demand their children back to help support the family. Children come from foreign countries, and from Israel's crowded cities, new towns, temporary immigrant camps.

Youth Aliyah teachers, nurses, social workers are trained to deal with all kinds of children. A Youth Aliyah worker, fifteen years ago, cared for children from Morocco and India. Five years ago, the same worker had to help children from Tel Aviv's slums. Next year, he might have to know and understand—and love—still a different kind of child.

YOUTH ALIYAH GROUP FROM INDIA, 1956. Before 1948, Youth Aliyah saw heartbreaking scenes. In 1946, for instance, an "underground" or "illegal" group came without British permission. Armed British soldiers "welcomed" the homeless children, and detained them on the island of Cyprus. Youth Aliyah promptly set up its own children's village there, until the gates of Israel opened in 1948. By 1960, Aliyah youngsters were coming not only from Europe and the orient, but from Israel herself—from the slums and temporary immigrant camps. Their Aliyah was not to a new land—but to a new life of health, education, freedom, and happiness.

219

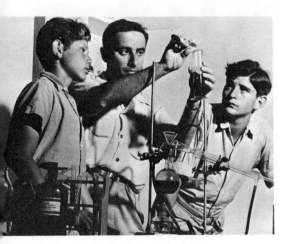

YOUTH ALIYAH "GRADUATES" LEARNING TO BE SKILLED FARMERS AND TECHNICIANS. All Youth Aliyah boys and girls go first to Ramat Hadassah-Szold, a reception center near Haifa. Here they are examined and assigned to their proper groups. The center has nine houses, a large dining room, an infirmary, a synagogue. The youngsters go to school half a day, work the other half. Eventually, they go on to a children's village, a Kibbutz, a Moshav, a trade school, or a special school.

Try This: Write to Junior Hadassah, 65 East 52nd Street, New York, N.Y. 10022, for information about Meier Shefeyah, the children's village this organization sponsors in Israel. When you receive the material, prepare a display or give a talk comparing a child's life in this village with your own.

Youth Aliyah works with the government, with Hadassah and other organizations, with the schools. It has also established its own schools, parents' clinics, teacher-training schools, day-care centers, and special institutions for retarded or handicapped children.

An unusual creation of Youth Aliyah is the children's village. Here the only adults are teachers, nurses, and counselors. Children help manage the village and decide many matters for themselves. Israel has about 250 of these villages, including some operated by Hadassah and Israel's various religious and political parties. Which village a youngster goes to depends on his family, his health and education, his needs and interests. On "graduation" from Youth Aliyah at sixteen, a youngster goes into Gadna, the Army's youth club, or to a school, a settlement, factory work—whatever he chooses.

From its beginning, in 1934, Youth Aliyah has stressed, for its wards, education and participation in group activities—to help a troubled youngster to become a responsible citizen, and to develop his pride and self-respect. Youth Aliyah workers—many of them "graduates" themselves—are selected for their love of children and are encouraged to express this love openly and warmly. Youth Aliyah also stresses vocational education—training for specific farm and factory work, or for professions. The Hebrew University provides special Youth Aliyah scholarships for gifted "graduates," named after Henrietta Szold—a founder of both Hadassah and Youth Aliyah, and their leading spirit for many years.

One out of every twenty Israelis is either a graduate or a ward of Youth Aliyah. Its graduates have fought in World War II, in the War of Independence, in the Sinai Campaign. They are nurses, teachers, farmers, factory workers, army officers. They make up one-fourth of the young fighter-farmers in the border villages.

Youth Aliyah is a unique achievement of the Jewish people. Great world leaders have supported it—Eleanor Roosevelt, for example, was one of its patrons. Educators and social workers from many lands come to Israel to see Youth Aliyah in action and learn its methods.

Youth in Trouble

Many different kinds of people tried to live together in a tiny land. Some newcomers lacked the Zionist ideals of sacrifice and pioneering. Those who came only because they had no other choice felt unhappy and frustrated. Others could not make ends meet in their daily struggle for a livelihood. Slum problems in the cities bred trouble, too. Village people, mostly newcomers, drifted back from the settlements to crowd together in crumbling buildings, alleys, "temporary" camps. For all these reasons, crime and especially juvenile delinquency increased in the new State.

Israelis are gravely concerned over their juvenile delinquency rate, even though it is about equal in proportion to other countries. Young offenders steal and rob, break into houses, destroy property, and annoy adults at movies or on the streets. But they seldom commit actual violence in the form of beatings or murder.

Delinquents usually come from poor homes and Oriental communities, but not always from the new immigrant families. Sometimes children of well-to-do families are also brought into the juvenile courts. They attend good high schools, make high marks, are children of prominent citizens, have almost everything they want. Yet they steal cars and car parts—for "thrills" and "kicks."★

★ In 1945, Jews were about one-third of the population, but committed only about one-tenth of the serious crimes. How would you explain the small number of Jewish criminals before the State was formed?

Rehabilitating the Offenders

The police and the courts pay special attention to young offenders—who are considered juveniles until the age of twenty-two. They are tried privately, in special juvenile courts. Fingerprints are not taken except for major crimes. The sentences are usually indefinite, their length depending on behavior in prison. Young criminals are put on probation, or sent to youth institutions. Unfortunately, there are not enough of these. Some youngsters go to regular prisons where they sometimes pick up wrong ideas from older criminals. But usually prison experience helps to rehabilitate them.

The Israelis want to educate and reform their prisoners, not merely punish them. Through various tests, a convicted criminal finds out what jobs he is best fitted for. He is then encouraged to start his sentence with a definite plan for rehabilitation. He knows his case will automatically be reopened when two-thirds of his sentence is up, and he can then go free if he deserves it.

All the prisons are called "camps," and their "officers" must respect a prisoner's dignity, protect his health, train him for a job. The prison schedule includes time for classes, reading, entertainment, job training, and actual work.

Maasiyahu Camp has few guards, some of whom are themselves prisoners, and they carry no weapons. Prisoners share in the managing of the institution. The prison bulletin board is labeled "Notices to Residents." The "residents" learn various trades. Those with good records are allowed to work and shop without guards, in the nearby town of Ramle. The Histadrut Labor Federation conducts classes, gives job tests, and issues, to released prisoners, a "diploma" from the "Ramle Trade School."

Only in Israel

Israel began an unusual experiment in 1958. Selected prisoners received passes permitting them to go home, unguarded, for a brief visit with their families. Every one of these prisoners returned on time. Later, two-day, three-day, and four-day "leaves" were granted—for joining the family at a birth, Bar Mitzvah, wedding, and so on. Despite the fears of many people, prisoners on leave behave properly, and return by themselves, and nearly always on time. One man, who stayed with his family a bit too long, stole a car in order to get back to prison before the deadline.

1966. Israel had a police force of about 9,000, of whom 600 were women, and 600 were Arabs and Druses. Many of them were immigrants, and besides police training had to have education in citizenship, history, customs — and, of course, Hebrew. Is it an advantage or a disadvantage for a country to be made up of so many immigrants?

221

★ With so many chances to escape, why do most Israeli prisoners obey the rules and voluntarily remain or return? (Several reasons!)

Prisoners live in small homes around an open square. They eat in a central dining room, move freely around the camp, and can walk away from it almost any time they want to. Visitors do not face them across glass or wire barriers, but sit and stroll with them among lovely flower beds—the pride of the "camp" and often prize-winners at flower shows. Children visiting a parent meet him in the home of the warden.

Over twenty social workers in the "camp" try to help prisoners change their lives. Of course, not all respond. Some are hopeless cases; others seem "cured," are released, then return because of new crimes. Some Israelis object to this camp's "coddling" of prisoners— but it seems to reform most of them and increase the number of Israel's law-abiding workers.

The authorities of one prison ask neighboring villagers to visit teen-age "pupils" once a week. The villagers bring books, show films, give lectures, conduct athletic events. Later on, the teen-agers get a day's leave to visit a family of their choice. Not one of these young prisoners has ever tried to escape.★

Keeping Youth Out of Trouble

In Israel, as in other lands, trained youth workers join street corner gangs. The worker wins their friendship, and then persuades them to get into athletics and club activities instead of mischief.

The Youth Departments of the government and the Jewish Agency have also begun to train professional youth leaders to run youth centers all over the country. These provide sports, games, outings, festival celebrations, and discussions. They also offer classes in music, art, drama, and handcrafts, at very low rates. Gradually, the new youth centers have become a familiar part of the Israeli scene. Youth Aliyah, the YMHA, the Mizrachi Women's Organization, and the American Jewish Congress Women's Division, as well as many private donors, have also opened such youth centers.

HAVE YOU WONDERED . . . ?

. . . about Israel being a "welfare state"?

Throughout Zionist history, many a person found protection in his own particular group against the troubles of life. His Kibbutz or his trade union, for example, helped him overcome poverty, provided for his health, employment, old age, retirement. The government of the new State was expected to do likewise—to care for the

> *There are eight rungs in the ladder of Tz'dakah. The highest rung is to help a man help himself so that he no longer needs Tz'dakah.*
>
> —Maimonides

underprivileged, provide social security for all. Israel is thus a "welfare state." Most modern democracies, including our own country, have been moving in the same direction.

A welfare state may turn into a "charity" state—where everything is handed to people whether they work or not, and no matter how hard they work. Some Israelis claim they see this trend coming in their country, just as some Americans do here. Most Israelis think they have many people to help, problems to solve, and jobs to do, that they needn't worry about getting "soft" and helpless. They are far from wealthy. They make great sacrifices to help the needy, work long hours and hard, and never forget the huge development job ahead of them—or the unyielding pressure of enemy Arabs. They do not *feel* like "charity cases"—they feel like people sharing with one another, in the age-old Jewish tradition of צְדָקָה—righteousness, justice, which means much more than caring for the needy. It also means treating the unfortunate with respect, and getting them to solve their own problems as far as possible.★

★ Do Israel's government and welfare organizations carry out this ancient Jewish ideal of social welfare? Can you give specific examples?

YOU'LL ENJOY READING

Destination Palestine: The Story of the Haganah Ship Exodus 1947, by Ruth Gruber
Home at Last, by Gloria Hoffman
Meir Sh'feya: a Children's Village in Israel, by Sonia Gidal
Miriam Comes Home: a Story of Our Israel Cousins, by Yehuda Harry Levin
To Build a Land, by Sally Watson

YOU'LL ENJOY SEEING

A Day of Deliverance (film: Joint Distribution Committee)
Fifty Miracle Minutes (film: Hadassah Film Library)
Hands of the Builders (film: Mizrachi Women's Organization)
Horizons of Hope (film: Women's Labor Zionist Organization)
I Came to Beersheba (film: Hadassah Film Library)
This Is the Way We Learn to Live (film: Hadassah Film Library)

Tzedakah: צְדָקָה

chapter 19

The Army: School for Citizens

Defenders of Israel

Speed, stamina, spirit—these made world headlines in 1956 when the Israel Defense Forces swept through the Sinai Peninsula to the Suez Canal in one hundred dramatic hours. In one week Israel smashed the murderous guerilla bands sent by some of the Arab countries into her territory. She broke their blockade of her Red Sea port of Eilat, and wrecked their plan, openly announced, to invade her at any moment. Jewish courage and toughness proved that Israel was here to stay, and would not be crushed.

But Israel's Army is more than a powerful fighting force. Some of its features make it one of the most unusual armies in the world.★

Youth Serves the Nation

All Israelis enter the Army at the age of eighteen, but some start at fourteen in גַדְנָ"ע—an abbreviated name for גְדוּדֵי נֹעַר or "Youth Corps." Sponsored jointly by the Army and the government's Ministry of Education, it has a double purpose. The boys and girls who join Gadna gain four years of preparation for regular army service. They also benefit from a well-rounded educational program.

Gadna's 20,000 members spend two hours every week, one full day a month, and two or three weeks each year, on one of the four Gadna farms. Here they learn physical endurance, ju-jitsu and other forms of self-defense, handling rifles, hand grenades, and mortars. Each Gadna group is attached to a different branch of the Defense Forces—Marines, Air Force, Engineers, Medical Corps, and so on. Members can thus begin quite early in their army training to specialize for a possible future career.

1967. Israel's Army, in the Six Day War, aroused the world again with a lightning campaign that crushed Arab armies and frustrated Russian plans to become the main power in the Middle East.

★ Israel's soldiers are usually outnumbered. Israel is a hard country to defend, and the Arab nations keep enlarging armies and equipment. Why, then, did Israel win in the War for Independence in 1948, the Sinai Campaign in 1956, and the Six Day War in 1967?

(Opposite page, top) GADNA (ARMY YOUTH CORPS) REHEARSES FOR A DEMONSTRATION (Bottom) ARMY GIRLS LEARN MACHINE GUN OPERATION. Women between 18 and 26 years old are drafted for 18 months, unless married, or from Orthodox families with religious objections to military service. Men between 18 and 29 are drafted for two years and 2 months. Draftees may be excused for a major physical handicap, or deferred if preparing for certain professions like medicine.

Gadna: גַדְנָ"ע   Gedudei Noar: גְדוּדֵי נֹעַר

They often take two-day cross-country hikes, covering about forty miles each time. On these trips, they get acquainted with the land. They learn about the past and current history of every place they may some day have to defend. They also help new settlers plant trees, lay roads and pipelines, and build homes.

Gadna members have considerable freedom to conduct their own affairs. Their program of activities aims to develop love and knowledge of the country, discipline, fair play, love of nature and physical work, punctuality, team spirit, tolerance, and a desire to improve oneself. Gadna brings together young people from the various communities to enjoy one another's company, to work and play in friendship.

The countries of Asia and Africa send teachers, gym instructors, and youth leaders, both men and women, to study Gadna's operations. The visitors enroll for special four-month courses at the Gadna farms, where they learn to supervise young people in camping, scouting, handcrafts, sports, folk songs, and dances.

Fighters All—Even the Girls

Israel differs from the United States in her policy on the draft. Her Army has rejected over the years only one out of ten draftees. In contrast, the United States, during World War II, turned down three out of ten soldiers for various reasons. Flat feet, color blindness, low I.Q., or a poor education do not disqualify anyone in Israel. Such persons are accepted—and then helped in various ways. They study basic subjects, learn how to work with others, and acquire new skills and grades. Simply by being in uniform, they can develop the self-confidence so vital to them. The Army keeps track of their progress, checking up on each one after a year or so. They return home not only able to help defend the nation, but much better equipped to lead a normal life of work and play.

Israel is the only country in the world that drafts women during peacetime. Her main reason is that she *must*. In case of war, this tiny, hard-pressed country will need everyone—and so every citizen must be trained for defense. Also, the women have a good influence on Israel's Army. When they're around, the men are neater and have better manners. The camp life in this tough, battle-ready army has the atmosphere of a co-ed school.

The Women's Corps—חֵיל נָשִׁים, is better known by its abbreviated name, חֵ״ן. Its members like the fact that the word "Chen" also

Try This: You're an Israeli boy or girl who has informed your American pen-pal about joining Gadna. Your pen-pal knows about Gadna activities, but wants to find out *why* you are joining— what you expect to get out of it. Give your answer—with *several* reasons.

1968. The U. S. Army now also educates, retrains, and rehabilitates certain types of rejectees. Why did Israel do so from the beginning?

1968. Israel drafts: all men 18-26, for 30 months; all men 27-29, if not previously drafted, for 24 months; unmarried women 18-26, for 20 months, unless they claim exemption for religious convictions against war. Arabs and Druses are not drafted, but may volunteer. After Army service, Israeli men and women go into reserve units, as explained on Page 233.

Cheil Nashim: חַיל נָשִׁים   Chen: חַ״ן

226

means "charm." Army women are clerks, teachers, telephone and radio operators. They pack parachutes, check instruments, drive and repair machinery, or do welfare and nursing work. They represent about one-fourth of all the Army's soldiers, freeing many men for the fighting jobs. But the women also get military training, so that in an emergency they can give a good account of themselves.

From the earliest pioneering days, women were regarded as equal to men, with the same privileges and duties. During the years of "underground" resistance against the British, women took part in many dangerous expeditions. They smuggled weapons and raided British posts, along with the men. In World War II, they parachuted behind enemy lines as secret agents. In the War for Independence, a number of young girls died on the road to Jerusalem, escorting military vehicles. The women, however, were taken out of the fighting units as soon as men could replace them.

Women recruits today receive special care and protection. Only a certain percentage may be assigned to each unit. They live in special quarters, do night duty in pairs, and can be punished only by their own officers.★

MILITARY UNIT ON PARADE. The women can handle the guns they carry, but use them only in an emergency. What is the main role of women in Israel's Army?

★ Is Israel's Army more than an ordinary fighting force? What is its second main purpose? What civilian institution does it resemble?

227

Poor Man's University

Try This: Design a poster showing an Israeli Army recruit with his hands outstretched to two officers. One officer is putting something in his hand that represents his basic task of defending his country; the other officer, something that represents his *second* task of . . . what? After you've decided on the two objects, and have finished the poster, add a paragraph explaining it.

In 1948, new immigrants began arriving from undeveloped Oriental lands. Many had to learn how to use a toothbrush, sleep on a bed, or wear shoes—to master a new language, accept women as equals, and walk upright without fear. Usually, an army is not asked to worry about such matters. But the Israel Army found itself not merely training fighters; it had to teach the young Oriental recruits to become modern Israelis, and the young Sabras to accept them as equals. The Army soon became the country's largest educational institution.

It offers the recruits courses in Bible, history, geography, social studies, and Hebrew for about one-fourth of their time. The aim is to develop thinking soldiers who know what they are defending as well as how to fight. Courses are flexible, tailored to fit whatever a particular unit needs. Immigrants are helped to master Hebrew; recruits who already know Hebrew choose and plan their own subjects.

Israel's soldiers also learn many trades and crafts. The Army tries to assign recruits to the kind of work they plan to do in civilian life. Future scientists serve in laboratories. Mechanics and accountants practice in machine shops and offices. Would-be farmers are assigned to border settlements, where they learn agriculture and defense at the same time. Recruits who can't read or write get special attention. New textbooks are prepared for whatever courses the recruits need—the Army is actually the biggest textbook publisher in the country.

In this way, Army service helps a soldier's career plans, instead of interfering with them. The country also benefits because recruits leave the Army better able to work and build up the land.

The young citizens train in different places to know their country first-hand. For ten days before maneuvers in a region, lectures and films inform them about what happened there in various periods of history, the plants, animals, and other features. As they march through the territory, they continue studying and taking examinations. In the evenings, they learn new songs connected with places seen that day. The officers retell ancient legends around the campfires, discuss the government's newest plans for the region.

An Israel Army camp is as busy with cultural activities as with military ones. The Army publishes its own magazines and has its own broadcasting station. Everything possible is done to encourage education. Soldiers in the regular Army pay only half tuition at the universities. Any group can organize its own evening study circle,

STUDENT SOLDIERS—SOLDIER STUDENTS. Hebrew lessons at an Army camp. Are these immigrants or native-born Israelis? Can you make out what the wall decorations are for?

and get free books and teachers. Nearly a thousand girl recruits have been trained to become school teachers when they leave. Nobody in Israel is surprised to find in an Army magazine a series of articles by twenty different writers on "How Can We Bring about a Mass Return to Judaism?"

Minutemen of Israel

After several months of military training, recruits may either continue in the regular Army or join נַחַ״ל—an abbreviation of נֹעַר חֲלוּצֵי לוֹחֵם, or "Fighting Pioneer Youth." This unit trains farmer-soldiers for duty in the border settlements.

A Nachal unit has thirty to fifty members, equally divided between men and women. They take advanced military courses, including commando tactics, and advanced studies in modern agriculture. Half-way through their term of service, they are sent to a border spot considered too dangerous for civilians. Here they join civilian settlers to help establish a village; often they start one of their own. They live close to unfriendly Arab guns, but they're as expert in firearms as in driving tractors.

Israel has a chain of such settlements stringing the border "like a necklace." They have well-trained commanders and fighter-workers, and all the weapons, food, medicine, and fuel needed for survival. They are strongly fortified with underground shelters and bunkers. Many are located on invasion routes, where the enemy is most likely to come. The farmer-pioneers will absorb the first blows and delay the invaders while the rest of the country mobilizes. The settlers are ready on a minute's notice to set fire to their green fields and comfortable homes and barns, leaving only scorched earth, in order to slow down the enemy. Should the Army be needed somewhere else, it may not be able to send help. Then the village will have to face whatever comes—by itself.

When their Army term ends, Nachal members can go back home, to college or to a job. But most of them prefer to live in a defense village. They plow and plant and harvest, marry and bring up children. They fight against spies, smugglers, saboteurs. They train constantly, ready to stand as a human wall to hold back an invading host. They are the Minutemen of Israel.★

"HIS SWORD AT HIS SIDE." On night patrol in a kibbutz near the Gaza Strip border, this modern fighter-farmer in a Nachal unit reminds us of the farmer-fighters of Bible days. Read the story in Nehemiah, Chapter 4.

★ If you ask Nachal members *why* they lead this kind of life, they shrug and answer with a favorite Israel saying: אֵין בְּרֵירָה "There's no other choice!" Can you explain what they mean?

Nachal: נַחַ״ל   Noar Chalutzi Lochem: נֹעַר חֲלוּצֵי לוֹחֵם

1

3

DEFENDERS OF ISRAEL. (1) The story of Israel's Army begins with Hashomer—"The Watchman." This group organized in 1909, in the home of Yitzhak Ben-Zvi, later Israel's President, and included Ben Gurion, later Prime Minister. Their purpose was to defend Jewish settlements against Arab raiders. They grew into a force of about 80, including 18 women and several young boys, who scattered among the settlements and single-handedly outfought the Arabs against great odds. Their daring exploits made them legendary heroes of pioneer days. (2) The Haganah—"Defense"—was a secret force of volunteers started in 1921 to protect the growing settlements in defiance of a British ban against Jews owning weapons. Within a short time, 800 men and officers were training secretly in school yards and vacant lots, early in the morning and late at night. Only 80 of them had guns—the rest trained with sticks and knives. In time, the Haganah became a well-organized, modern "underground" army. They brought in many "illegal" immigrants despite Jewish blockades. (3) When Arab nations attacked the new State of Israel in 1948, the Haganah came out into the open as the country's official Defense Forces. The Army trounced four invading armies, and in 1956 defeated Egypt in the Sinai Campaign. In 1967, against the massed Arab forces threatening "destruction" once again, the Army defeated them in just six days. Ben Gurion himself designed the Army's insignia: the old sword of the Haganah insignia, entwined with olive leaves. Why is this a fitting symbol for Israel's Army?

Leading by Example

Israel's Army officers are not professional soldiers. They are mostly farmers, engineers, and scholars who sign a contract with the government for a certain number of years. They may go back to their own work whenever they choose. The chiefs of staff since 1948 have served for an average of only two years. Every one of them left his high position to attend a university in Israel or abroad.

Officers are taught not to "pull rank," but to win the respect of enlisted men by their intelligence, character, and behavior. There are very few formal barriers between officers and soldiers, who are about the same age.

Officers and men wear the same kind of uniform. Separate dining rooms were set up only after long hesitation and debate. An officer is saluted only inside Army bases, and only the first time a man meets him during the day—after that, they simply exchange a שָׁלוֹם—Hello! Soldiers do not address an officer in the usual military manner, as "Sir." Instead, they use his title, such as "Commander" —or more often, his first name or even his nickname. Friendships are allowed between officers and men. There is little formal punishment—officers consider education and private conferences the best ways to straighten out a trouble-maker.

Officers get no special privileges at any time. During forced hikes they do not ride behind their men in jeeps, but walk along with them. They march ahead of their units in battle, and they never command קָדִימָה—Forward!—but אַחֲרַי—Follow me! Of the 170 men killed in the Sinai Campaign, half were officers—a remarkably high proportion, compared to other armies.

Army Life—Israeli Style

The training is harder than in the American forces. The soldiers do not spend much time in camps and are not bothered with "spit and polish" inspection. Mostly they are on maneuvers, out in the open country, often carrying live ammunition. Recruits who want to become non-commissioned officers have to march forty or fifty miles across hills with a light pack, for three days in a row. As fighting men, Israel's soldiers must be tough and alert to danger every second.

Israel's soldiers have a fine spirit of comradeship. Members of a youth club often join the Army as a group and do most of their

Try This: Present an interview between an American reporter and an Israeli officer. The reporter would like to know why this Army is so "unmilitary," how an officer controls his men, and whether there is much disobedience. Think of other questions.

Try This: An American and an Israeli officer are comparing their two outfits. The American argues that life in the Israel Army is more "civilian" than in any other Army in the world. The Israeli officer insists that this very civilian character makes it a *better* Army. What points does each use to prove his statement?

Shalom: שָׁלוֹם   Kadimah: קָדִימָה   Acharai: אַחֲרַי

service together. They naturally continue some of their former youth club activities.

For example, such a group may spend evenings on maneuvers as they used to spend them at a youth center back home. They sit around a small campfire and sing folk songs, accompanied by an accordion or a חָלִיל—flute, munching roast potatoes and candy. These "platoon evenings," like the club meetings of former days, bind them very close together.

The soldiers are taught to be considerate of one another, to feel they are members of a team and responsible for its welfare. On long marches, a unit will carry home those who were not able to finish the hike on their own legs. Competition is not pushed. No medals or special awards are given—only a simple blue ribbon to every soldier who fought in the War for Independence.

When the training period ends, the soldiers hold a מְסִיבָּה—a "sitting together." The commander makes a speech, and volunteers read Bible passages or Hebrew poetry. Candy, soft drinks, or wine are the usual refreshments. Then humorists entertain with "tall" stories, and the ceremony ends with folk songs and dancing. Without the uniforms, this could be a civilian youth gathering.

Citizens' Army

When soldiers finish their Army service, they go into reserve units— men until the age of forty-nine, women until thirty-four. Each man must spend a full month in training every year until he is forty, then two weeks a year for the last nine years. Reserve officers sometimes have to drop their civilian work for two months or more.

In their training periods, reservists live as though the country were at war. It is a tough, grueling session—an Israeli cannot afford to soften up after he leaves the Army, or forget what it has taught him. Nowhere in the world is so much asked of men in the reserves. The Israeli civilian will tell you, with a straight face, that he is a regular soldier with eleven months' leave.

The result is that Israel is always ready for total mobilization. In an emergency, she can raise a trained Army of about 250,000 people in just forty-eight hours. On "M"-Day, the reserves leave their homes, shops, factories, or fields. Every bus, taxi, truck, and auto in the land is requisitioned. Every hospital goes on a war alert, all roads and railroads become military routes, food and oil supplies

THE VOICE OF THE LORD . . . In 1961, two Navy crews graduated from a special training course. Ceremonies at Haifa included a procession escorting the crews on board Israel's two new submarines, to military music. Heading the procession, the Navy's Commander-in-Chief and the Army's Chief Chaplain carried Torah scrolls— gift of Israel's President to the world's first underwater synagogue. See Psalm 29:3.

1967. Israel's mobilization plans were tested in May and June with the Six Day War—and succeeded brilliantly.

Chalil: חָלִיל   Mesibah: מְסִיבָּה

233

Everyone worked with one hand, held his weapon with the other—every builder working with his sword at his side.

—Nehemiah 4:11-12

DEFENDERS OF ISRAEL

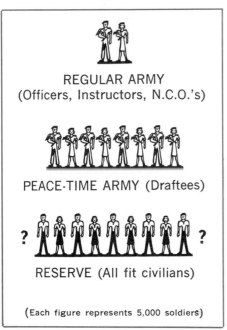

REGULAR ARMY
(Officers, Instructors, N.C.O.'s)

PEACE-TIME ARMY (Draftees)

? RESERVE (All fit civilians) ?

(Each figure represents 5,000 soldiers)

■ The permanent forces are about 11,000 "career" soldiers, all volunteers, who train the others and are responsible for the nation's security. About 40,000 young men and women recruits are drafted into the peace-time army. Supporting the regulars and recruits are the reserves or part-time soldiers—civilians who have had army training. They come back for "refresher" training once a year, and are on call in case the country is attacked. All three groups are vitally important. What is each group's special function in preparing the country for possible attack? Why such a relatively small regular army, and such relatively big reserves?

are tightly rationed. Every village unlocks its secret arsenal, and the people take their prearranged defense positions. This mobilization system is one of the fastest in the world.

Israel's Army reserves are as large as those of the United States, except for the National Guard in the various states. The Arab countries have no such trained reserves, and so Israel can match their regular armies. Yet Israel has one of the smallest regular armies in the world. She depends, if attacked, on a citizens' Army—an Army that consists of the entire nation.

Sons and Daughters of Israel

The Army is part of everything going on in Israel. It helps archeologists, educates immigrants, helps agriculture, promotes Hebrew and Jewish culture, supports religious life, teaches youth, and trains workers.

This Army has never lost its ties with the people. Israel is so small that most soldiers can go home on week-ends. Nearly every Israeli has been in the Army, and still serves once a year. The white-jacketed waiter in the restaurant may have carried ammunition to the front lines in the War for Independence. The clerk adding up the bill in a store may have parachuted down in the desert to capture fleeing Egyptians in the Sinai Campaign.

Israelis love and admire their Army. They do not look down on vacationing soldiers as loafers with a soft job, but treat them with respect and love. The only medal that former Prime Minister Ben-Gurion ever wore is the olive leaf given to graduates of the Army's officer school.

Israelis are not happy about those chapters in Jewish history when our people suffered bitterly and helplessly. They feel they are no longer weak and defenseless like their ancestors in the ghettos, but can strike back when attacked. They can live in dignity and, if necessary, die as free men, unafraid. This, too, the people owe to their beloved Army.

234

HAVE YOU WONDERED . . . ?

. . . about Israel's flag?

It was first displayed at the First Zionist Congress in Basle, Switzerland, in 1897. Here is the story as told by David Wolffsohn, a friend and supporter of Theodor Herzl.

"Among the many problems that occupied me then [preparing for the Congress] was one which was neither important nor unimportant, but which contained something of the essence of the Jewish problem. What flag should we hang in the Congress Hall? For we had no flag. This difficulty greatly vexed me. A flag must be created. But what colors should we choose? Would our nation make any distinction between colors, being a people that is so careful never to feast its eyes on any image or picture?

"Then an idea struck me. We have a flag, and it is blue and white. The טַלִּית?—prayer-shawl, with which we wrap ourselves when we pray, that is our symbol. Let us take this Talit from its bag and unroll it before the eyes of Israel and the eyes of all nations. So I ordered a blue and white flag with the Shield of David painted upon it. That is how our flag, that flew over Congress Hall, came into the world. And no one expressed any surprise or asked whence it came, or how."

Actually, others had already had the same idea: the Rishon L'Tzion colony in Palestine in 1885; the B'nai Zion Educational Society in Boston in 1891; and a Russian Jewish artist in London in 1893. But their ideas did not "catch on." It took the right moment, Wolffsohn's inspiration, and the appeal of Herzl's personality to get Jews to accept this flag without surprise or question.

YOU'LL ENJOY READING

The Army of Israel, by Moshe Pearlman

YOU'LL ENJOY SEEING

Edge of Danger (film: United Israel Appeal)

Try This: Israel's Army songs are popular with civilians, too. Ask your music teacher to teach one or two to your class, and explain what they mean.

Only in Israel

LOYALTY PLEDGE OF THE DEFENSE FORCES OF ISRAEL

I swear on my honor to keep faith with the State of Israel, her laws, and her elected officials; to accept completely the discipline of the Defense Forces of Israel; to obey all orders and instructions issued by its duly authorized officers; and to use all my strength, even to sacrifice my life, for the defense of the homeland and the freedom of Israel.

Israel's Army changed reception practices for volunteers from an Orthodox yeshivah (Talmudic Academy). Men clerks received them instead of women, as they celebrated the occasion with spirited Chassidic dances. These recruits substituted "undertake" for "swear" in their loyalty pledge, and ended it with ". . . in the spirit of the Torah and tradition." On receiving two mess-kits, one for meat foods, the other for dairy, they demanded a *third* one, and got it—in case something should happen to one of the other two.

Talit: טַלִּית

A BARRIER THAT HAS FALLEN. Until the Six Day War (see Chapter 25) all Arab frontiers were closed to Israel, except the Mandelbaum Gate in Jerusalem on the Jordan frontier. After the Six Day War, Jerusalem was reunited and everyone moved freely between the Old and the New City. Some travel began between the Israeli-occupied west bank of the Jordan River and the Arab east bank. People in Israeli-occupied territory are generally allowed to move freely in and out of Israel. On her new frontiers, of course, the old Arab restrictions continue.

chapter 20

Israel and Her Neighbors

Life with Neighbors

Four Arab countries hold Israel tightly between them as if in a vise. No Israeli may legally cross their frontiers. Farmers, manufacturers, merchants cannot do business with one another. Border guards are posted everywhere. A traveler whose passport has been stamped by Israel may not enter an Arab country: he needs *two* different passports, one for Israel, one for the Arab countries.

Each year, Israel admits about seventy foreign Arabs, especially from Jordan and Lebanon, for special medical treatment, to attend funerals, and similar reasons. But the Arab countries do not permit Israeli Arabs, though Israel does so freely, to make a pilgrimage to the holy Moslem city of Mecca, in Saudi Arabia.

Once, Israel suggested a direct telephone line between Israel and Egyptian guard posts on the Gaza border. This would prevent incidents due to misunderstanding or mistake. But Egypt turned the idea down—because, said her government, Israelis might use the phone to trick military secrets out of the Egyptian officers.

Israel's victory in the Six Day War (see Chapter 25) pushed border clashes farther back from Israeli territory, but did not end them. The United Nations has observers who investigate such incidents and try to prevent worse violence. Israeli civilians are fired on from across the border, and border patrols run into foreign Arabs who have crossed over to spy and sabotage. Border villagers live under constant tension.

The Arab Boycott

The Arab League—twelve nations, with central headquarters in Cairo and branches all over the Arab world—conducts a boycott against Israel. Foreign ships that stop at Israeli ports cannot do business with Arab countries, or even get service in their harbors. If a

★ Why would nearly all Israel's problems become easier to solve if the Arab nations made peace with her?

freighter carrying goods to or from Israel enters Arab territory, its merchandise is confiscated and the ship is barred from future Arab business. The world's governments protest half-heartedly, but actually do nothing about such acts of piracy.

After Egypt took over the Suez Canal in 1956, she allowed no Israeli ship to pass through. Long ago, the nations agreed that every country must be allowed to use Suez at all times, in war or peace. Israel complained to the United Nations, which twice directed Egypt to end her unfair policy. Egypt still keeps Israeli ships out.

The boycott has been carried over to other countries. Several companies closed their factories in Israel or stopped doing business with her, so as not to lose Arab customers. The boycott includes firms that have nothing whatever to do with Israel but are owned by Jews or employ Jews. Even in international sports and athletics, Arab teams sometimes walk out if they must compete against Israelis or teams with Jewish members.

The Arab boycott has failed several times. When Germany decided to pay reparations to Israel, the Arabs threatened to stop trade with Germany and break off diplomatic relations. Germany went ahead with her agreement—and her trade with Arab countries *increased*. Arab governments tried to bar airlines from flying over their territory or using their airports if they landed their planes in Israel. But the airlines threatened to use jet planes to by-pass them —which would lose them most of their tourist trade. The Arab governments gave in. They even allowed tourist ships to dock at their ports after stopping at Haifa.

Business firms in many lands no longer frighten as easily as they once did at Arab threats. Travel agencies, for example, advertise tours to both Israel and the Arab lands. The European Common Market, a union of six countries, has ignored Arab protests and agreed to work out some trade arrangements with Israel. Some large firms evade the boycott by organizing new companies under different names to trade with Israel.

Sometimes the Arab rulers cannot even persuade their own people to observe their "blacklist." The popular singer, Frank Sinatra, is so openly pro-Israel that the Arabs have blacklisted him for many years—but Cairo shops still sell his records in great numbers. Recently a blacklisted freighter brought a shipload of wheat to Lebanon. The other Arab governments demanded that the ship be sent

Only in Israel

A few years ago, Egypt wanted to buy a water-desalting device made by an American firm. She was told that Israel had invented it and had kept the marketing rights in the Eastern hemisphere—hence she would have to deal directly with Israel. Egypt dropped the whole idea, and even denied it had ever happened. Israel, on hearing of the incident, promptly offered to sell her desalters to Egypt or to any other Arab nation. No reply.

away, its wheat untouched. Lebanon officials ordered the wheat unloaded, called the boycott "fantastic," and called for a revision of its rules. A major Lebanon newspaper urged a complete end to the "ridiculous" boycott.

Israel has adopted a "get tough" policy against the boycott. A Dutch firm refused to build ship engines for her for fear of losing Arab business. But Israel threatened to withdraw all her shipbuilding business from Holland, and to explain why to the other shipbuilders. She got her engines. Israel's protest had Indonesia expelled from the Olympic Games because she had kept Israel out of international athletics in her country. Later, Indonesia was readmitted.

But the boycott has cost Israel great losses over the years, and is still strong enough to damage her considerably.

The Arab World

The Middle East is a glaring contrast between great wealth and frightful poverty. This is oil-rich land. Under its surface lie nearly half the world's known oil reserves, and no one knows how much more is yet to be discovered. One-fifth of the world's oil is produced here. The American and European companies developing these fields pay fantastic sums each year to the various governments. But most governments do not use this money to provide schools, hospitals, clinics, roads, or housing. Usually it goes into the king's treasury or the pockets of a few wealthy landowners—for luxuries and rich living.

Arab governments have made many promises—and even some attempts—to improve living conditions. Yet most people are still wretchedly poor. The average worker earns from $50 to $300 a year. Nine out of ten people suffer from one or another of the local diseases. Eight out of ten cannot read or write. In some countries, from one-third to one-half the children die at birth. Only half the usable land is farmed, and only three main crops are produced— cotton, corn, beans. Most of the land is owned by a few families, even though two out of three people live on farms. The absentee landlords take most of the produce for themselves, leaving the villagers barely enough to live on.

All the Arab countries have had a violent history, full of plots and assassinations. Out of a dozen independent Arab nations, hardly two have the same form of government. Some are ruled by dictators or army officers. Others are ruled by all-powerful kings; in two such countries, human slavery is legal. In the republics of the region, powerful governments permit no opposition, criticism, or freedom

Try This: Study a map of Israel and her neighbors. Then sketch a large map of your own, using sketches, arrows, and words to answer these questions for the class: (1) Why does Israel stress air and water transportation? (2) Why did Israel build an oil pipeline from Eilat, at the southernmost tip of the Negev, all the way up to Haifa in the north? (3) Why did Israel, in her Sinai Campaign in 1956, make a special drive to the Gulf of Aqaba and capture an Egyptian fort there?

HOW ISRAEL COMPARES — 1965

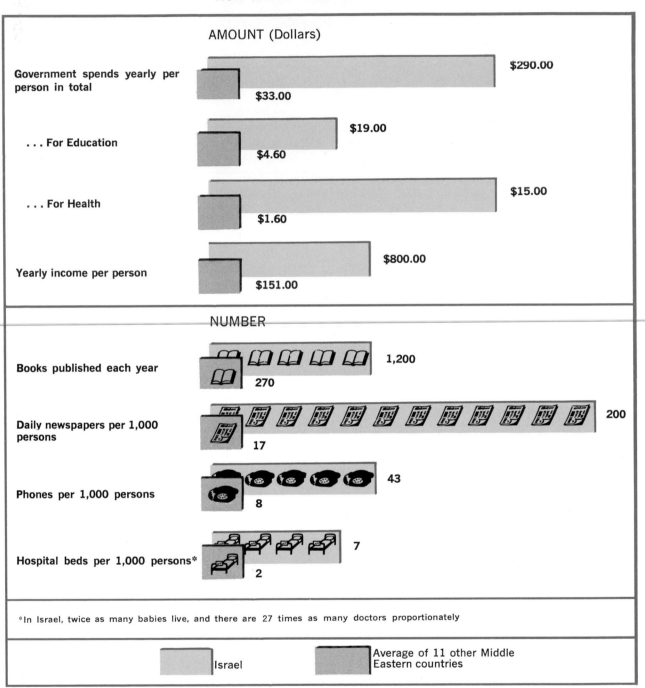

AMOUNT (Dollars)

Government spends yearly per person in total
$290.00
$33.00

. . . For Education
$19.00
$4.60

. . . For Health
$15.00
$1.60

Yearly income per person
$800.00
$151.00

NUMBER

Books published each year
1,200
270

Daily newspapers per 1,000 persons
200
17

Phones per 1,000 persons
43
8

Hospital beds per 1,000 persons*
7
2

*In Israel, twice as many babies live, and there are 27 times as many doctors proportionately

Israel

Average of 11 other Middle Eastern countries

■ In Israel: 90 per cent of the land is public property. Nine out of ten people can read and write . . . eight out of ten children go to school . . . government is democratic, everyone votes. In a typical Arab country: 10 per cent of the population owns half the land privately . . . two out of ten people can read and write . . . two out of ten children go to school . . . government, a dictatorship . . . women may not vote, men voters must meet special requirements. (Only one country where everyone votes; in one country—nobody votes.)

There are more special experiments and more diverse economic projects today in Israel than, to my knowledge, exist in any other part of the world. What gives cause for alarm is the difference between this and what is happening in the rest of the Middle East—the progress of Israel compared with the backwardness of the surrounding countries.

—Aneurin Bevan, Leader
British Labor Party

of the press, and can suspend the constitution any time they please. Most governments are shaky, and many rulers actually seem to fear their own people.

The people in most Arab countries know little about democracy, have little personal interest in the government. The rulers fill them with slogans, with grand ideas of conquest and expansion. A leader who talks of uniting all Arabs may actually be interested only in advancing his own career. Arab farmers and tribesmen like to lean on a "strong" leader, and quickly get used to whoever is in power.

Can the Arabs Work Together?

Arab leaders like to give the impression that their countries form one united family, but this is far from the truth. Often, various countries try to form a union. Each time, so far, the attempt has failed.

Arabs are united, of course, by their common Moslem religion and Arabic language. They also share a common memory of past greatness—of the time, a thousand years ago, when Arabs ruled a large part of the world and Arab scholars, poets, and scientists taught wisdom to all mankind. Arabs are much alike, too, in culture and manners. Certain traits are everywhere—gracious hospitality to strangers, a feeling for poetic language, a love of bargaining, the habit of not being on time, unconcern about the future. Everywhere, the shape of minarets and mosques, the colorful date palms along the roads, the crowded hidden alleys in the cities, the food, dress, and furniture are very much alike.

But despite all this, they do not get along peacefully; important differences separate them. Some countries are still in the Middle Ages, a few already have institutes of nuclear physics. The countries that own most of the region's oil are not eager to share their prosperity with the others.

Try This: Governments and alliances change so rapidly among the Arab states that it is impossible to describe them individually in this book without being out-of-date. Organize a committee to learn what is going on among these states right now. Use up-to-date encyclopedias and current almanacs to find out which states belong to the "Arab League," "Arab Federation," or "United Arab Republic," what governments are in power, and what "unions" are being tried.

241

Try This: Find out how these governments feel toward one another right now—Egypt, Syria, Jordan, Saudi Arabia, Yemen.

The various rulers do not agree politically. The Arab League, at times, speaks as with one voice, yet never really hides the quarreling that goes on all the time. Kings do not like leaders of republics, and vice versa. In public, rulers exchange polite compliments, but plot against one another behind the scenes. The smaller nations fear one another and the larger nations. These, in turn, compete for leadership of the Arab League, and bargain for Russian or American support. Old feuds, new rivalries, shifting alliances, fickle friendships, conspiracies, assassinations—these mark the Arab "family" of nations.

Because Arab rulers do not trust one another, every country feels unsafe. Governments are unsteady, changing rapidly, so that planning ahead or making agreements stick is difficult.

★ Israel has solved, or is solving, many of the same problems that concern the Arab nations. Why don't they follow her methods?

Even ordinary citizens cannot develop close ties with their neighbors. Free movement from one country to another is most difficult. There is no customs agreement, and trade cannot flourish. It takes several days longer for a letter to go from Egypt to Iraq than from either country to New York or London. Each nation has some group that considers itself a separate community, different from other Arabs, entitled to be an independent nation by itself.★

Land and Water

The biggest resource of the Arab lands is oil. Their biggest need is water. So far, the one has not been able to provide for the other.

Once, this whole region was a place of plenty. During the Roman Empire, it supported far more people than live there today, and at a fairly high standard of living. The Romans had a good system of irrigation, terraces, tree-planting, and a town or city every twenty miles, a day's march for soldiers. The land produced so much extra food for people in other countries that it was called "the granary of the world." The region declined about 700 years ago because of wars, invasions, and neglect of the land.

Try This: Make a list of needs common to both Israel and the Arab countries. Why can these needs be met more easily by all the countries working together than by each alone? (Several answers!) If your committee is studying the current Middle East conditions, be sure to include the Jordan River situation.

Today, ninety-five per cent of the land is desert, sheer wilderness. One state, larger than all western Europe, has fewer people than Holland. Another, bigger than Texas or Alaska, has a smaller population than New York City. The whole Middle East just barely supports its inhabitants—each country must actually import food for its people.

The same ancient rivers flow through this part of the world. Properly used, they could irrigate eight million acres of new land. In this climate, three crops could be grown annually, feeding the population the year round. Two million more families could be supported—ten million more persons. Every Arab nation could take a big step forward on the road to prosperity and independence.

The key to the Arab future is not oil, but water for the parched land. Of course, the oil money could be distributed more evenly so that all the people could benefit. But in the long run, green grass and fertile soil must replace the dry, brown desert. The basic question is how to capture and hold the precious rain water, how to get the most out of the river water. Engineers of various countries have drawn up plan after plan; western nations have offered many millions of dollars in loans and gifts.

In 1953, United States experts worked out a brilliant plan for the Jordan River. Dams, pumps, canals, tunnels, would bring water to hundreds of acres of dry land, open up thousands of new farms, create many new towns and industries. Two years later, everything was ready—plans, money, support of the leading nations. Arab and Israel water experts agreed on the technical details of the plan. Then the Arab League, led by Egypt, turned it all down.

The plan required Jordan, Lebanon, Syria—and Israel—to work together for the good of all four countries. The idea horrified Arab leaders. Helping other Arab countries was bad enough—but it would also help Israel. It would prove that Israel and Arab countries could work in harmony. It would clear the air of hatred, and remove a scapegoat whom the Arab rulers could blame for all their troubles. The very life of their people depends on water—but the Arab governments decided against their own people in order to hurt Israel. And so, year after year, millions of tons of water roll down the Jordan River to be wasted in the salt of the Dead Sea—mainly to spite Israel.

Why They Hate Israel

Many years ago, the king of Jordan began to discuss, with Israel, a peace treaty, trade agreements, and mutual help. He was assassinated by unknown killers. Since then, Arab leaders have not dared to make any move toward peace with Israel, even if they desire it. More than one Arab leader admits privately that peace with Israel would help his people; but publicly he must keep denouncing Israel if he wants to stay in power—or stay alive.

Arab leaders benefit personally from promoting tension with Israel. They have a grievance always ready to use. They are always able to get world attention by complaining, threatening, demanding, blackmailing.

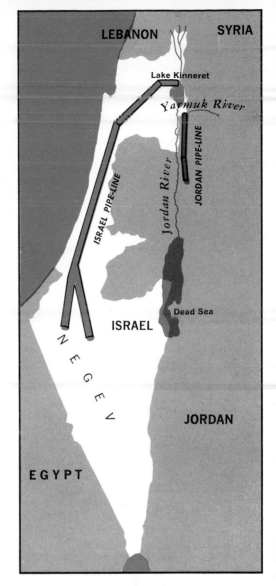

WATER PROBLEM. Israel, though small and limited, more than doubled her farmland without using Jordan River water. But her need became so great she carried out her part of an international water plan rejected by the Arabs—a 155-mile pipeline from Lake Kinneret down into the dry Negev. Meanwhile, Jordan dug her own canal from the Yarmuk River, though Israel promised to leave plenty of water available for her neighbor. Arab nations organized a special agency to "take action" against Israel's pipeline, but said nothing about Jordan's canal. What are the latest developments in this water dispute?

The successful, democratic country of Israel impresses the under-developed people of the Arab world. Not only are Israelis far better off than they are, but Arabs in Israel are far better off than Arabs anywhere else. Israel brings new ideas into the Arab world: respect for human rights, enlightened labor laws, decent wages, social insurance, equality of women. Such ideas are disturbing to those who live on oil income and the labor of starving tenants. They might stir up the restless Arab peasants against their own leaders. And so, in bitter harangues against Israel, these leaders inflame the people's feelings, take their minds away from their poverty and misery. Both rulers and people find it easier to blame an outside "enemy" for their nation's troubles than to try to solve problems through democracy, intelligence, and hard work.★

★ According to the Arab version of history, England and France "robbed" them of Palestine and gave it to the Jews—who are the "tools" of these nations and intend to expand and conquer the entire Arab world. What arguments and historical facts can you offer against this version?

Is Peace Possible?

Arab pressures, in a way, have actually helped Israel all through the years. Attempts to prevent immigration forced the Yishuv to fight all the harder for independence. The invasions of 1948–1949, and the continuing border raids for years afterward, forced Israel to build up a very efficient citizens' Army. The boycott and blockade made Israel work even harder to win friendship and trade with more distant nations. And perhaps the biggest boost the Arabs gave the Israelis was to strengthen their unity and their determination not to be surpassed in any way. The best answer to Arab charges and slanders was to show the world what a free Jewish nation could accomplish.

A few years ago, *Life* magazine addressed an editorial directly to the Arab nations, speaking to them as a "friend . . . gently but bluntly." Here is an interesting passage from this editorial:

> Until you, the Arabs, accept deep in your hearts the fact that Israel *is* here to stay, there can be no real peace in the lands of either. It is you, the Arabs, who insist there is no peace. Israel does not say she intends to destroy the Arab world, but it is you who proclaim your intention to destroy Israel. It is your holy men who cry out for holy wars against her. It is your spokesmen who talk of driving the last Israeli into the sea. It is you who refuse to accept Israel's right to existence. Until you do accept it, you will have no moral case before the world.

This statement comes from a world-famous magazine, not Jewish, and with no special feeling for Jews or for Israel. It discusses the Israel-Arab situation clearly and correctly.

Only in Israel

A Jewish family in a Jerusalem border neighborhood has hens that keep strolling across the border and laying eggs in Jordan territory. Jordanian guards, gathering the eggs, sometimes give them to the family's children. In return, the Jewish mother sends the "enemy" soldiers home-made cakes and cookies.

Recently, the family celebrated a child's birthday. During the party, the Jordanian soldiers came up to the border and handed across, as gifts, two of their own army headdresses. They called out: "May Allah grant you a long life!" The Jews called back: "May Allah grant you every blessing."

The peace we look forward to between us and our neighbors will surely come. Now, as in the past, we stretch out our hands for peace towards them. We pray that, in the course of time, they will realize that only mutual understanding and cooperation with Israel can bring about enduring security, progress, and well-being for the lands of the entire region.

—From the late President Ben-Zvi's Independence Day, 1963, Greetings, made public a few days after his death.

At the U.N. Conference in Geneva in February, 1963, on helping the less developed countries, Israel and Egypt participated without incident or outward signs of enmity. This conference's resolution on disarmament was transmitted by Abba Eban of Israel to Omar Loutfi of Egypt, who received it on behalf of the Disarmament Conference. In typical diplomatic fashion, they shook hands when the document was handed over.

As long as there is peace, Israel prospers and becomes more accepted by the world's nations. The very passage of time may slowly change the unreasonable stubbornness of the Arab governments. Incidents like the one above are hopeful signs, some observers say. Others see no significance in them, and predict that Arab hostility will sooner or later break out into all-out war.

For peace in the Middle East, the whole region must be modernized, irrigated, industrialized. But it lacks the money and resources for this. Also, old traditions and economic habits make it hard to build factories or divide the land among the peasants. The governments will have to find money, as Israel has done, to explore and pioneer, to search for new minerals, start new industries, improve transportation and communication, increase water, health, education, democracy, science.

The Arabs will have to show more respect for physical labor, as the Israelis have done. Until now, Arabs have looked on the landowners, traders, bankers, professionals, as their leaders. But prosperous farmers and productive factory workers also help make a country's future. The educational level of the workers must be raised, their families helped to a more decent life. The Arab countries must plan ahead for growth of population, which will double in the next twenty-five years.

Of course, many hard problems must be solved. Arab farmers are leaving the land to crowd into the cities, thus creating new slums. The governments have to make small and medium-sized towns more

Try This: Prepare a letter from your class to the President of the United States and to the Secretary-General of the United Nations. Ask them to take certain specific steps for peace in the Middle East and for improving living conditions in Arab lands.

attractive, get more people to stay on the land or return to it, and keep the bigger cities from becoming over-crowded. People coming from undeveloped villages to work in modern factories will have to be taught many things: to read and write, to handle money, to be clean and sanitary, to form their own opinions, and to behave in general like dignified human beings and responsible citizens. People moving from towns to farms must be taught how to work with land, animals, and farm tools, lead an active outdoor life and yet have cultural interests, and find ways to entertain and improve themselves. All this will require a complete revolution in habits and ways of thinking. But Israel can help—she has been through all this, and can show others what mistakes to avoid, what methods will work.

YOU'LL ENJOY SEEING

Israel (filmstrip: *Life* Filmstrips)

chapter 21

Israel Among the Nations

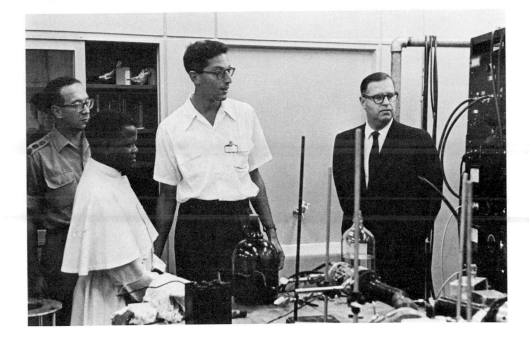

Good Neighbor

Israeli visitors to certain border villages in Burma are welcomed by children singing Hebrew songs—*Hevenu Shalom Aleichem, Havah Nagilah, David Melech Yisrael*—and the villages themselves turn out to be modeled on a Kibbutz or a Moshav. In Nepal, co-ops organized by Israelis run bus lines and banks. A Histadrut type of labor federation protects workers and develops resources in Tanganyika. Spectators in a Ghana stadium (Israeli-built), rising to sing their national anthem (accompaniment tape-recorded in Israel by the Kol Israel Radio Symphony Orchestra in an arrangement made by its director), salute their flag presented by a unit of the Builders' Corps (modeled after the Israel Gadna youth club). Scholars in India are applying "Zionist" methods to make Hindi the common language of all India. Made-in-Israel jeeps and station wagons run on Kenya's roads, an Israel-Japan Friendship Society in Tokyo offers films and lectures on Israel, and Nigerians live in planned regions like Israel's Lachish area.

ISRAEL TO THE RESCUE. President of Congo Republic in Africa visits an Israeli nuclear laboratory. Only a few months before, Israel had literally saved his country's life. When the Congo declared its independence in 1960, all Belgian doctors pulled out, leaving fourteen million people without any medical or sanitation services, facing epidemics amidst war and violence. The U. N. called on Israel—and a team of doctors and nurses flew in. In town after town, they took over the hospital, reopened it, reorganized sanitation services—the first outside help to a new nation in deep trouble. Can you recall a medical team from one country to another forty-two years earlier, in 1918? What countries, what organization? Any connection or similarity between the two acts?

247

ISRAEL THE TEACHER. Israeli engineer teaching students in the University of Liberia. Besides teacher and student exchanges with developing nations, Israel holds international meetings. In 1960, in the Weizmann Institute in Rehovot, 120 delegates from forty Afro-Asian lands came to the world's first International Conference on Science for the Advancement of New States. Visitors in tribal robes and velvet headresses learned from the world's top scientists how to build industries and find new sources of food. They also toured Israel's farms, laboratories, factories. Said the Sierra Leone Delegate: "When I came here, it was night, it was dark. When I leave here, it will be light." Look up Isaiah 2:3—how does Israel fulfill this ancient prophecy?

Try This: Ben Gurion has said that Israel's aid to new nations is based on ideals expressed in these three passages from Isaiah: 43:5-6; 42:6; 2:4. Look them up, also 41:6. Can you express the ideals in your own words? Find specific examples, in this chapter, of aid projects in line with these ideals.

In these and other Afro-Asian lands, Israel has built hotels and trained hotel managers, constructed roads, dams, and water pipelines, demonstrated modern farming methods. People in these countries use Israeli methods in manufacturing, mining, fishing, shipping, meat packing, dropping paratroopers, handling feuding desert tribes—and even operating soft-drink stands. Several Israeli professors are college department heads, government advisers, business consultants.

Over 800 Israeli experts are "on loan" to foreign countries, helping other undeveloped countries to use the latest modern ideas and methods. These experts take on foreign jobs at a fraction of the pay demanded by Americans or Europeans. They eat the same food, wear the same clothes, sleep in the same kind of bed as the local people—and don't seem bothered about unfamiliar customs or politics different from their own. In fact, they say they feel quite at home. The climate, the land and water problems, the mixture of peoples—it all resembles just what they left back home in Israel.

They know all kinds of short-cuts, ingenious ways to do things quickly and cheaply with whatever materials happen to be handy. They don't stay permanently, or try to grow rich and powerful—they get the local people started in modernizing their country, and then leave promptly when no longer needed or wanted. And they seem to *enjoy* helping new young nations like their own, small and struggling, to establish themselves.

248

I spent two months in the United States on a study tour. I went to many towns. At the end they asked me what I thought of America, and I answered: Wonderful! Fabulous! Fantastic! Then they asked me what I had learned, and I said: Nothing! You see, America is too big for us. The smallest project I saw cost millions. Israel is closer to the problems we are up against.

—Pham Minh Dvong, Director, South Vietnam Public Works Department

Afro-Asians today need education and health care more than anything else—the very two "exports" in which few modern nations can compete with Israel. Hospitals, clinics, and sanitation systems organized by Israel's medical men are ending age-old tropical diseases, lengthening life, increasing the population. Even Egypt, Israel's bitterest enemy, fights its deadly "Nile Fever" disease with information from an American organization which paid Israel to do its research. Israeli disaster teams show up immediately after earthquakes, fires, outbreaks of plague.

In Nigeria, American experts made fun of jungle magic and witch doctors—and were asked to leave. Israeli experts who replaced them explained they too had powerful "magic." After local witch doctors failed to produce rain to break a dry spell, the Israelis turned on the water-sprinklers they had been installing, and sent up a plane with scientific rain-making equipment. When a chief's son swallowed a needle, an Israeli ambulance brought an Israeli surgeon—who X-rayed and operated on the spot, and saved the boy's life. The natives accepted Israel's "new magic," and gradually learned about modern science and medicine.

Come and Learn!

Almost a thousand students from over fifty new nations study every year in Israel. Proportionately, this is larger than our own country's student exchange program. Students stay in Israel from three months to a year. Most of them study agriculture. But many are learning to be doctors, nurses, engineers, teachers, youth leaders, radio broadcasters, bankers, housing and sanitation experts, policemen, army officers, government officials, labor leaders, and tourist experts—as well as scientists, historians, mathematicians, artists. About one-fourth of these students live and work in Kibbutzim, Moshavim, and other farm settlements.

1968. The first 7 African students ever to do so completed 6 years at the Hebrew University — Hadassah Medical School and began interning in their own African hospitals.

Try This: Here are a few of the more than seventy countries that Israel helps. Locate them on an outline map of the world, and draw arrows connecting them with Israel. Select, from this chapter, some Israeli projects you think most important or most interesting, and list them along the side of your map. Perhaps you can sketch some drawings to illustrate the projects you select.

Bangui	Japan
Burma	Kenya
Cameroons	Liberia
Ceylon	Mozambique
Congo	Nepal
Costa Rica	Nigeria
Cyprus	Nyasaland
Dahomey	Philippines
East Africa	Rhodesia
Ethiopia	Ruanda
Ghana	Sierra Leone
Guinea	Tanganyika
India	Togo
Iran	Turkey
Ivory Coast	Upper Volta

1966. Israel had 620 experts working in 55 developing countries in 4 continents, either through the U.N. or by request of the country itself. About 1,600 from these countries attended 32 courses in Israel.

1966. Israel signed agreements with the Organization of American States for new cooperative projects in Latin America.

1968. Israel planned a major water supply and sewage project for the country of Ghana. (See "Only in Israel," Page 250.)

★ Trade and business arrangements help Israel become more self-supporting. What is another important reason Israel has tried to make friends with so many Afro-Asian countries?

Only in Israel

At a 1955 conference of Afro-Asian nations, Egypt's Nasser persuaded the delegates from Ghana to vote for his resolution denouncing Israel. On their way home, these delegates decided to visit Israel and see for themselves how "dangerous" she was. What they found changed their minds completely. Ghana and Israel became good business partners, exchanged many students and experts. In 1958, Ghana kept several other African nations from signing Nasser's annual resolution against Israel. In 1963, for the first time, Nasser did not offer such a resolution—because he knew most Afro-Asian nations would vote against it, and he would "lose face."

The Israel government gives foreign students free scholarships. The Histadrut Labor Federation has a special Afro-Asian Institute for sixty students a year. The Hebrew University—Hadassah Medical School conducts classes for the visitors in English and French. ORT provides every year for forty foreign students in its Technical High School. The Hebrew University, the Technion, the Weizmann Institute, and others all welcome and help foreign students.

Israel's "Partners"

Israel's Department of International Cooperation uses two other methods of working with a new nation. Through trade agreements, she obtains foods for her people, raw materials for her factories, and customers for her own products. In business partnerships, an Israeli firm joins the local government in a business venture. The Israelis own forty per cent of the new company; the local government, sixty per cent. Israelis start the business, supply managers and know-how, and if necessary, lend money and equipment. Meanwhile, local people go to Israel and learn all operations of the business. Israelis also start training schools in the country itself. In three or four years, the country has enough trained people and enough profits to buy out the Israelis and become the sole owner and manager.★

No Easy Road

All Asian nations except the Philippines voted against the 1947 U.N. resolution for an independent Jewish homeland. Neither Asians nor Africans had had much contact with Jews. They both considered the Jews part of the white race—European conquerors and oppressors, "imperialists," not to be trusted. The Afro-Asians did not know how the Zionist settlers struggled against the British government, how they had to fight for national independence just like other new nations.

The biggest African obstacle to Israel has been Egypt. Her present ruler, Nasser, still pictures his country as "protector" of the whole continent, guarding its northern gate from "colonialism" and invasion by Israel. Nineteen countries, including the twelve Arab League members, still refuse to recognize Israel. Several Afro-Asian countries still bar her from conferences, trade, fairs, and athletic meets, and sign frequent declarations against her. Indonesia, Pakistan, Mauretania, and Somalia, for example, still threaten to boycott any gathering to which Israel is invited, or to leave unless Israeli delegates are expelled. Others, like Ghana, Guinea and Mali, recognize Israel and accept and appreciate her cooperation. But they also want to work closely with Egypt, the other Arab nations, and Russia. They sign resolutions against Israel, and sometimes cancel a joint project with her before it can be completed.

India and Iran are examples of countries who are friendly to Israel, but would probably be even more friendly if they could afford to ignore Russia and the Arab nations. They recognize Israel, and exchange delegates or consuls with her—but not ambassadors. They ask and accept her aid, and do business with her—but as quietly as possible, without publicity.

Israel still has a long, hard battle to fight against prejudice, hostility, and misunderstanding. Out of more than 120 free nations in the world, Israel seems to be the only one that still has to explain or justify her existence.★

1967. During the Six Day War (see Chapter 25), Guinea broke off diplomatic relations with Israel, then tried to persuade 7 Israelis, part of a U. S. aid team, not to leave. They left anyhow.

★ Some Israelis want to stop helping countries that do not support Israel openly and firmly. Why does the government try to keep as many contacts as possible with such countries? Which approach is right?

A Sorry Game

In the summer of 1948, when the Arab nations were at war with Israel, Tel Aviv was so crowded that representatives of the Soviet Union and the United States actually slept under the same hotel roof. The Stars and Stripes and the Hammer and Sickle fluttered side by side on two flag poles. Israel had the support of both countries in those days. Both had voted for the Jewish State, and were the first to recognize its new government—one of the few times in recent history that these two powers voted the same way in the U.N.

Then came the "cold" war between Russia and the United States, and their struggle for control of the Middle East. Russia, who for a time seemed ready to develop friendly relations with Israel, now turned against her.

An arms race began in this part of the world by the Arabs—as they openly announced—to attack and destroy Israel; by Israel, to defend herself. Both Russia and the U.S. tried to win Arab friendship, because Arab countries have so much oil, territory, and population. Israel remained almost alone. She had little to offer besides democracy and friendship. Western nations that might have wanted to help Israel sometimes held back in order to stay on good terms with the Arabs and prevent Russia from gaining too much influence over them. Russia has been ruthless in her propaganda against Israel, though she still recognizes Israel and exchanges ambassadors with her. Her leaders claim Israel is being "used" by the West. Thus she covers up her own efforts to gain a foothold in the Middle East by arming Egypt.

Israel would like to soften the hostility of communist countries. Their powerful support of the Arab rulers greatly increases her

Try This: Political parties in Israel disagree over whether their government should take sides in this struggle, or try to stay neutral. Glance back at Chapter 17, and see whether pro-Russian, neutral, or pro-American parties get most votes.

1967-68. For Russia's most recent role and attitude, see Chapter 25.

1967-68. For the change in France's attitude to Israel with the Six Day War, see Chapter 25.

danger. Russia and Rumania especially have many Jews who would find a welcome in Israel, and would like to go there—if only they were allowed to emigrate.

In 1957, Israeli students at a youth conference in Moscow distributed to Russian Jews 5,000 souvenir pencils—each inscribed, in Russian, English, and Hebrew, with "Brotherly Greetings from Israel." The pencils became so popular that people wanted to buy them—for as much as $75 apiece. The Russian government called the pencils "anti-Communist Zionist propaganda intended to turn Soviet citizens into hirelings and agents of imperialism." It ordered all "propaganda pencils" to be handed over, and even searched suspected homes. After four years, the authorities gave up—having discovered not a single one of the 5,000 pencils.

The competition for the friendship of the Arab countries helped build up their military strength. Israel, on the other hand, had to rely on the few who supported her loyally, and on her own courage and intelligence.

If not for the help of Canada and France, Israel would have had trouble building up her armed forces. When Israel, in self-defense, fought the Sinai Campaign in 1956 against Egypt, most nations voted against her. Then they continued doing nothing about Arab boycotts and blockades, illegal seizure of ships, and refusal to even discuss a peace treaty with Israel.

More recently, as the Arab nations grew stronger and more aggressive, the Western powers gave Israel more support. But she is still caught in a global tug-of-war between East and West.★

★ In the voting at the United Nations, Arab nations usually line up with Russia, Israel with the United States. Two points to explain: (1) Why does the United States handle the Arabs so gently, and even sometimes side *against* Israel? (2) Why does Israel nevertheless usually still side with the United States?

Israel in the U. N.

Israel has diplomatic relations—ambassadors, consuls, and so on—with over eighty countries. A number of them have defied Arab threats and propaganda. Especially Turkey, Burma, Japan, Thailand, Ethiopia, Tanganyika, and Nigeria have dealt openly with Israel, and defended her when unfairly criticized.

Israel does not belong to any of the three "blocs" of nations—neutral, western, and communist. When a dispute arises, she tries to vote for her own best interests, or for the side she feels is right. But whichever way she votes, she may antagonize friends as well as enemies. By siding with France, England, and the United States, as she often does, she sometimes loses ground with the Afro-Asians and Russia. When she sometimes votes the other way, her western friends are annoyed. If she does not vote at all, or tries to arrange a compromise, then all three "blocs" may hold it against her.

Only in Israel

An international Protestant church organization established a Moshav in Israel, for Jews and Arabs together. Dutch members provided farms and factories; Swiss members, the houses, roads, water system, electricity. Purpose: not to make converts to Christianity, but to increase understanding among people.

In spite of this problem, Israel's international prestige has steadily increased. She is represented on the U.N.'s main committees, its special agencies for health, education, and welfare, and others. U.N. agencies often use Israeli experts in their projects in undeveloped lands. The U. N. has given Israel large sums for water research and development. In 1961, eight African and eight other countries requested the U. N. to call on the Arab governments to make peace with Israel. A year later, twenty-one nations—African, South American, and European—made the same request. Neither resolution passed. But every year the nations show more sympathy for Israel.

In 1962, a world-wide trade organization accepted Israel against Egyptian threats and demands, put an Israeli delegate on its acceptance committee, and refused to expel him from the room when Egypt presented her application to join. Egypt is still only a temporary member, until she drops her boycott and blockade of Israel. The next year, the World Health Organization chose an Israeli delegate to represent the Middle East, in preference to an Egyptian.

Israel and Europe

Most European countries have befriended Israel, sometimes against strong Arab protests and threats. About two-thirds of Israel's foreign trade is with European countries, and she is one of *their* best customers, buying from them about twice as much as she sells to them.

1967. Israel's mutual aid program with other developing nations was 13 years old. At U.N. debates on the Six Day War (see Chapter 25), 15 Afro-Asian countries receiving Israeli aid sided with the Arabs, but 19 others and 22 Latin American countries refused to condemn Israel.

OPEN HOUSE. Catholic bishop, returning to his own country from meetings in Rome, stops off in Israel to plant trees near Nazareth. There is much coming and going of visitors in Israel. Her location between East and West is one reason. Another is her high reputation in certain fields of work—for instance, education, health, and social welfare. In 1961, the International Union for Child Welfare, for its first meeting of Afro-Asian delegates, wanted a model country to inspire the new nations—and selected Israel. After their meetings and tours, the delegates had many good ideas to try out in their own lands. The Turkish delegate, for example, hurried home to organize all her countrywomen into a "Turkish Hadassah."

Europe's socialists and trade unions support Israel in their newspapers and devote much space to Israeli life and events. Israeli tourists, students, businessmen are welcomed in European towns. The smaller countries—like Sweden, Norway, and Denmark—are all Israel's sincere friends.

Israelis, in turn, have a special place in their hearts for these three nations. In World War II, their people, at the risk of their lives, saved many Jews from the Nazis. France is another special friend. With England, she sent armies during the Sinai Campaign to take Suez. France has consistently helped Israel with weapons for self-defense. England buys more Israeli goods than any other nation in the world.

★ Israelis feel closely tied to Europe. Can you give several reasons? Consider, for instance, Israel's history, population, science, culture, politics, government, business.

Israel and Germany

Most of Germany's reparation money paid for machinery built in Germany and then shipped to Israel, representing about a third of all her imports. German ships and harbor equipment helped Israel become a major seafaring nation in the Middle East. She was also able to modernize and expand her electric power industry, railway, and post office, and improve her steel, food, textile, chemical, and mining industries. Israel buys spare parts from Germany, who in turn is Israel's third largest customer after England and the United States, for Israeli foods, diamonds, clothing, chemicals—and even guns and ammunition.

Only in Israel

In 1963, twenty Germans arrived in Jerusalem to build a home for the blind for fifty cents pocket-money a day—and to atone for the Nazi crimes against the Jews. They were members of German Evangelical Churches, which sent similar groups to France, Belgium, Greece, and Norway, as part of their "Operation Reconciliation."

An order of German Protestant nuns —the Ecumenical Sisterhood of Mary— includes among its vows one to help Jews in repentance for Nazi acts. Seventy-five of the Sisters take turns, in groups of four, coming to Israel to serve as nurses in hospitals and old-age homes. In Germany, these nuns burn an eternal light in memory of the six million Jews slaughtered by the Nazis, read Hebrew prayers on Yom Kippur, and hold special services on Yom Ha-Atzma-ut, Israel's Independence Day. They are not interested in converting Jews, but in making their own kind of "reparations."

Israel and the United States

Our country's friendship is one of the foundations of Israel's existence. Israel might never have been established in the first place without American support in the U.N. In 1950–1951, the new state seemed about to collapse under the weight of a vast immigration. Our Congress passed a special law granting Israel millions of dollars in loans and gifts to help her with her development problems. In the next few years, our government continued to aid Israel with money and food.

Equally important, our country gave much "technical" aid. Thousands of Israeli students came here to study, and hundreds of American experts were sent to Israel. Her scientists, doctors, engineers learned a great deal, in those early days, from American advisers.

1964. The United States and Israel agreed on a joint project for desalinization (obtaining fresh water out of sea water) to be completed by 1972. The international magazine on desalting water, *Desalination,* is published in Israel.

Israel made good use of this vast aid from the American people. Within ten years, she was able, because of her record, to borrow millions of dollars from the World Bank to expand factories and build harbors and roads.

Many non-Jewish organizations in this country support and aid Israel. Labor unions especially buy Israel bonds, give scholarships, and speak up for Israel to our government. Our unions help many foreign countries, but are especially interested in Israel—they consider it a country where the ideals of the labor movement are fully carried out.

More than fifty buildings in Israel were erected partly with money from American unions. One of the biggest gifts—over a million dollars—went to the Histadrut's Kupat Cholim (Sick Fund) for a large modern hospital in Beer Sheva. Other buildings include medical clinics, children's homes, housing projects, libraries, vocational training schools, cultural centers, rest homes, youth clubs, a cold storage plant, a woodworking mill, a metal shop, and a sports arena.

Trade between our country and Israel grows every year. Americans buy most of Israel's diamonds, cement, raincoats, arts and crafts, stamps, chocolates, wines—and of course, Jewish religious objects. More and more American investors, too, put their money into Israeli business enterprises.

Some Americans feel our government, in trying to win over the Arab nations, does not help Israel enough, and helps the Arabs too much. At times, our country has refused to sell Israel weapons, in order to prevent war in the Middle East. But all the time, Russia was furnishing weapons to Egypt. Recently, against Arab opposition, our government did supply weapons to Israel, to help her defend herself against the growing power of the Arabs. The United States has always told the Arabs openly that she will not permit any aggression against Israel. This promise has helped to protect Israel and keep peace in the Middle East. ★

AMERICA'S HELPING HAND. United States official speaks at the opening of the Beer Sheva—Dimona Road, a joint Israel-America project. For eleven years, from 1951 to 1962, U. S. O. M. —the United States Operations Mission to Israel—helped the new Jewish State deal with its many problems and plan its development program. American loans, grants, and experts helped Israel to grow rapidly and successfully. When Israel seemed able to "go it alone," both nations cancelled the operation. Now Israel does business with our country as an equal—and extends the same kind of help to other new nations.

★ How does our country gain by helping Israel? (More than one answer!)

1965-66. Israel and Germany established diplomatic relationships, exchanged ambassadors, and signed a trade agreement as German reparations ended. In 1967, about 16,000 Germans visited Israel, more than half of them to help build homes and institutions and to work in kibbutzim as in atonement for Nazi crimes. More and more Israelis have been trying to forget the past and accept the new German attitude. Eighteen Israelis, 20 to 30 years old, went to Germany for a conference with German youth, and a committee of Israeli educators went there on a similar mission.

Only in Israel

Kol Israel regularly broadcasts programs to many other countries in English, French, Yiddish, and other languages. But Israel is especially interested in reaching Afro-Asian peoples. As many of these love the Bible deeply, she succeeds.

Here are two of the many letters from Africans received by Kol Israel:

"When I heard broadcasting from Zion, I fell on my knees and thanked God!"

"I always thought Jerusalem existed only in the next world. I heard your program, and now please tell me whether I tuned in to this world or the world to come?"

HAVE YOU WONDERED . . . ?

. . . how Israelis feel about accepting Germans?

Israeli feeling runs high against Germany, because of the Nazi persecutions. Many Israelis cannot forget the horrors they went through, the torture and death of their loved ones.

Sometimes, they boycott German films, books, music, artists. Jerusalem rejected an offer of cultural exchanges from the German city of Munich. German Boy Scouts were not welcomed at an international jamboree in Haifa. Sometimes musicians of other countries who have performed in Germany are greeted coldly or even with hostility. The Cabinet has banned German-made movies—though not German-language movies made by others. German tourists in Israel—whose number increases every year—are sometimes treated coldly, though they are carefully screened to make sure none of them has ever harmed the Jews. Exchange of visits by Israeli and German government leaders stirs up bitter complaints and demonstrations.

Many Israelis have accepted German goods and money because they need them, and because they feel the Germans are only giving back what they took from the Jews. But they cannot "live" with Germans—share with them anything cultural, or spiritual, or personal. The government therefore moves very cautiously in relations with Germany. It has not exchanged consuls or ambassadors with Germany, or encouraged Israeli teachers and students to study there. Real friendship with Germany may take many, many years—if it comes at all.

Ask your parents how they feel about Germany and the Germans. What German products have they bought or refused to buy? How do *you* feel about this question?

YOU'LL ENJOY READING

Modern Jewish Life in Literature, by Azriel Eisenberg, pp. 147–206

YOU'LL ENJOY SEEING

The Highest Commandment (film: American Friends of the Hebrew University)

chapter 22

The Arab Refugees

While the Jewish State was being established in 1948, hundreds of thousands of Arabs left the country. Many of them still live in "temporary" quarters, waiting for an end to their distress.

These refugees are a disturbing problem. Year by year, suspicion, fear, and hatred increase among them. Contradictory statements fly back and forth—as to how many refugees there are, who is to blame, who should care for them, who should take them in. The United Nations supports and aids them. Israel, though not to blame for the situation, has done all she can to help. The Arab countries caused the problem in the first place, by going to war against a U. N. decision. But they have done little about it—in fact, they have done their best to aggravate it.

A LIFE OF WAITING. Arab refugee camp in Damascus, Syria. The children go to school or play. The women keep busy all day with chores around their huts. But the men sit idle. Bored, frustrated, disgruntled, they listen eagerly to agitators and troublemakers, to curses and threats against the United Nations, the United States, Israel— and even against the Arab governments. Most refugees once farmed their own land, owned their own shops, served in their own professions. Why do such people call refugee camp existence "a living death"?

How Many Refugees?

Nobody knows exactly how many refugees there are. The U. N. estimates them at over a million—but this is a doubtful figure. Officially, a refugee is someone who has lived in a country at least two years before leaving it. About 500,000 such Arabs left Israel during 1947–49. Counting the new children born, there should be about 700,000 refugees today.

The U. N. figure includes Arabs who never lived in Palestine, but who moved in with the refugees to get free support from the U. N. A new-born infant among the refugees is often passed from one family to another, to get an extra U. N. ration card. The dead are often buried secretly, to avoid giving up their ration cards. A 1962 U. N. report admitted at least 100,000 dead persons on the relief rolls. Even when a refugee gets a job, he holds on to his ration card as long as he can, to add to his food supply.

The Arab governments encourage this fraud. They try to get as many ration cards issued as possible, and interfere whenever U. N. officials try to cancel them. They do not permit the U. N. to conduct an accurate census of the refugees or of those really needing support. Apparently, they do not want the world to find out the truth.

Try This: Find out about the forty million refugees in the world, where they are, how many in each group, what is being done about them, who is doing it. Why are there actually many more Jewish refugees in the world than the official figures indicate?

Life in the Refugee Camps

About two-thirds of all Arab refugees registered with the U. N. have found new homes in four Arab countries. The other third lives in about sixty refugee camps, located along the Israeli border.

The U. N. gives the refugees food, shelter, clothing, medical care, social workers, clubs and recreation facilities, schools, teachers, and textbooks. They are better off in many ways than they were in Palestine before the Jewish State, and are probably better off than the average Arab citizen. They get more to eat and are healthier than ever before. Pregnant and nursing women get extra rations. Other Arabs are actually jealous of the refugees because a U. N. ration card means many free benefits. It can always be sold or pawned for a large sum. Children get midday meals and vitamins, and a better education than the average Arab child. A few hundred even attend universities on scholarships.

But the refugees are not happy. Three of the four Arab governments do not grant them citizenship, work privileges, or the right to live where they choose. Refugees find little work to do outside the camps—they are the last to be hired for any job, and the first to be fired. They do not have permanent homes, jobs, or future prospects. They feel bitter and hopeless, like men without a country.

The Arab governments keep telling them that Israel "drove them out," and that they will soon go back for revenge and booty. This idea has been dinned into them for many years. It is taught to children almost from birth, through all their school days and adult lives. Textbooks in refugee schools, maps and pictures in the schoolrooms, call the Jews "wicked criminals," promise "a Holy War" to destroy them. The governments plant secret agents in the refugee camps, to keep this idea boiling. They recruit guerrilla fighters from the refugee camps, and train them to make raids into Israeli territory to kill, burn, and rob. They instigate refugee riots whenever U. N. officials try to take a census or put up permanent buildings in place of tents.

How They Got There—The Arab View

Arabs blame the U. N. for the situation because of its 1947 decision to divide Palestine between the Jews and the Arabs. They do not admit that their war of invasion against Israel caused the trouble.

The Arabs also blame the United States because of her important part in creating the State of Israel. Actually, over thirty nations, including Russia, approved the partition of Palestine.

REFUGEE SCHOOL. This school for elementary and high school pupils in Lebanon is one of about 400 such schools in which U.N.R.W.A. (United Nations Relief and Works Agency for Palestine Refugees) provides twelve years of education for about 190,000 refugee children. The Arab nations insist that the U. N., the U. S., and Israel are responsible for the Arab refugees and must take care of them. The U. N. apparently accepts this responsibility. Aside from humanitarian reasons of kindness, charity, generosity, why does the U. N. support these refugees as it does no other refugee group? For example, the half million Jewish refugees who fled from Arab lands to Israel are not supported or helped by the U.N. Why not?

★ Many Arabs could not or would not leave Palestine. If charges of Jewish terrorism are correct, what should logically have happened to them?

Finally, the Arabs claim that the Jews forcibly expelled their Arab neighbors from their homes. And that rioting Jewish terrorists cruelly threatened, tortured, and killed the Arabs until they ran for their lives. These charges are completely false. Jewish and Arab official documents, statements by neutral British officials and Christian churchmen, public statements in Arab newspapers and magazines and on the Arab radio, all prove the exact opposite.★

How They Got There—the Facts

In November, 1947, the U. N. voted to divide Palestine into separate Jewish and Arab states. Arab terrorists all over Palestine began to riot, burn, torture, and murder in violent attacks on the Jews. Arab countries mobilized armies to "exterminate the Jews" and take over their land and possessions.

For the Arab civilians in Jewish territory, these were months of confusion, doubt, and danger. Arab terrorists continued to commit horrible atrocities. In self-defense, the Haganah struck back at their posts, often located in Arab towns. The Arab civilians sometimes helped the terrorists—willingly, or out of fear. Sometimes, they tried to stay neutral, or even to help their Jewish neighbors. They were caught in the middle.

Some Jewish terrorist groups, without official authority or approval, raided Arab villages. One such group cruelly massacred an entire Arab village near Jerusalem. Jewish authorities bitterly condemned this action—the only Jewish atrocity in the whole sad affair, compared to hundreds of cases of Arab brutality, then and in the later war.

The wealthier, better-educated Arabs and the community leaders were the first to leave Jewish territory. They wanted to wait out the coming violence in a safer place in some Arab country. This left the Arab peasants even more frightened—they felt deserted and helpless.

Arab leaders in other lands, over the Arab-language radio, magnified the one Jewish atrocity. They pictured *all* Jews as utterly merciless and fanatical, but said nothing of the Haganah's efforts to suppress Jewish terrorists and to protect Arab life and property.

Arab terrorists and armies had shot down civilian Jews riding in buses and walking the streets. They had horribly cut up wounded Jewish fighters and left them to die, had killed all Jewish prisoners by torture, and had even peddled photograph albums of the mutilated bodies of dead Jews. Arab civilians in Jewish territory knew all this. They knew their leaders were calling for the extermination of every Jew in the land. They expected the Jews to take revenge. As the war developed, and Jews pushed back the Arab invaders, Arab civilians grew even more fearful that the Jews would punish *all* Arabs.

Armies, in all wars, always want civilians out of their way. Arab villagers and townspeople found themselves ordered out by Arab or Jewish fighters or both, to clear the way for troops. Some people fled to safer places on their own.

Harvest of Hate

The Arab Higher Committee, representing the Arab nations, repeatedly ordered all Arabs to pack up and leave Israel. In their own words, they had three purposes. They wanted to clear the roads and villages ahead of their armies mobilizing on Israel's borders. They wanted to demonstrate that Arabs would never accept a Jewish government. And they wanted to ruin all government services following the end of British control.

The leaders denounced Arabs who remained among the Jews, threatened to punish them as traitors. They promised that the Arab armies would "drive the Jews into the sea" within just a few weeks. Then the Arab refugees could go back and take over all Jewish property and wealth. The British, eager to pull out, also advised the Arabs to go—even offered them transportation.

Beginning in April, 1948, and continuing for many months, a mass panic seized the Arabs. Hundreds of thousands of men, women, and children—whole villages, towns, and city communities—hysterically poured across the borders into Arab territory, abandoning homes, jobs, friends, and even relatives.

ONE CAUSE OF THE ARAB REFUGEES. A group of Palestine Arab Volunteers in 1947, ready with Bren guns and rifles to start attacking anything Jewish on Israel's roads. They told Arab villagers to run away before the Jews came to destroy them in revenge—to wait outside Israel until the Jews were wiped out. Then they could return and take over Jewish land and wealth. If they stayed, they would be considered traitors to the Arab cause, and executed. On the next two pages, read what actually happened to the 100,000 Arabs who defied these warnings, promises, and threats, and remained in Israel.

261

The Haifa Story

At Haifa, the British troops secretly planned to turn over all their forts, police stations, and weapons to the Arab forces, and then leave the city. Haganah agents had tapped British telephone lines and overheard these plans. When the British left, the Haganah, in a surprise midnight raid, attacked the Arab headquarters. In surrendering, the Arab leaders asked permission to evacuate the 80,000 Arabs of Haifa and take them to Lebanon.

Jewish leaders begged the Arab civilians to stay—promised not to harm them, guaranteed them equal rights and protection as full citizens. Seventy-five thousand Haifa Arabs would not listen, and were allowed to go. Five thousand believed the Jews, and remained.

At Tiberias, Safad, Jaffa, and other places, this pattern was repeated. The Jews, after a victory, invited Arab civilians to remain in peace. But Arab military leaders insisted that they go—and they went, reluctant and bewildered. Every Jewish government agency issued public announcements of friendship for neighbors. The Jewish radio repeated official promises of safety and equality. Jewish agents even risked their lives to spread leaflets in Arab towns under the very noses of Arab army officers, but it was no use. The Arabs were either too frenzied to listen to reason, or too frightened by the threats of Arab leaders, or too greedy for Jewish possessions.★

Only in Israel

In 1949, Israel and Jordan signed an armistice. Jordan agreed Israel should have the "Little Triangle"—a narrow border strip holding 33,000 Arabs in over thirty villages. The agreement gave these Arabs two choices. Israel would pay them for their land and they could move to Jordan, or they could stay and live under the Jewish State. An overwhelming majority voted to stay. Within ten years, this was the most prosperous and progressive Arab region in Israel. The first joint Arab-Jewish business firm opened a canning factory there in 1959.

The Supreme Proof

More than 100,000 Arabs did *not* leave Israel, and about 40,000 others returned soon after the war ended. These Arabs were not harmed or mistreated in any way. The new Jewish State gave them full citizenship rights. Today, these Arabs still own their homes, shops, farms, factories. They share with Israel's Jews the highest standard of living in the Middle East. They have more education, job opportunities, and participation in government than most Arabs elsewhere in the Middle East.

The fact that there are these refugees is the direct consequence of the action of the Arab States in opposing partition and the Jewish State. The Arab States agreed on this policy unanimously, and they must share in the solution of the problem.

—Emile Ghoury, Secretary of the Palestine Arab Higher Committee, in an interview published in the Beirut (Lebanon) *Telegraph*, September 6, 1948

Whole Arab villages chose to stay in Israel, though "surrounded" by Jewish settlements which could easily have destroyed them. They are still there, happy and prospering. In 1956, Israel launched her Sinai Campaign against guerrilla raiders from Egypt. Israel's Arabs, who are concentrated mainly in one border region, could have revolted and caused trouble—but they didn't.

Over 200,000 Arabs live peacefully in Israel today. But the part of Palestine assigned by the U. N. to the Arabs has not a single Jew.

What the U. N. Did

The U. N. took immediate charge of the refugees, as if responsible for their situation. It sent money and officials, encouraged volunteer welfare organizations to help. To this day, the U. N. supports these refugees completely. It has looked after no other refugee group in such a manner and for so many years.

The U. N. spends for this purpose about thirty million dollars a year. Most of the money comes from the United States and some from England. Only a third of the U. N. members help out—Russia and her allies do not participate at all.

Besides food, clothing, and shelter, the U. N. has given the refugees the best school system in the entire Arab world. In the U. N. schools, open to any Arab refugee child, the refugees themselves decide on teachers, courses, and texts. Nearly 200,000 children attend, including all the boys and about one-fourth of the girls. The U. N. also provides nearly 4,000 doctors, nurses, and aides to run hospitals, clinics, and pharmacies, and to supervise sanitation. The refugees suffer less from disease than Arabs elsewhere—their death rate is lower, too.

But in finding homes and jobs, and starting the refugees on a new life, the U. N. has not accomplished much. It has tried many times to reduce relief expenses, develop unused Arab lands, start projects that would create jobs, build homes, and develop towns. It offers money and makes suggestions, but is weak and hesitant in dealing with the Arab governments. They stall, put obstacles in the way,

CEREAL AGAIN. Refugee Arab mother feeds her child at a U. N. refugee camp near Damascus. A special food center in each camp provides a daily hot meal for undernourished children, and extra monthly rations for pregnant or nursing mothers and tuberculosis patients. This is in addition to the basic U. N. rations providing 1,500 calories a day (1,600 in winter). For comparison, look up, in the latest U. N. Yearbook, the average daily consumption of calories in our own country, in Israel, in Arab countries. What conclusions do you draw?

★ The U. N. and the U. S. are not really responsible for the refugees. Why then do they spend so much money taking care of these refugees? (More than one answer!)

think up reasons for delay. The official U. N. report each year since 1948 has usually complained of organized, deliberate resistance by Arab governments.★

What the Arab Governments Did

Lebanon and Syria impose heavy taxes on U. N. supplies coming into their countries for the refugees. In Lebanon, 100,000 refugees are not allowed to become citizens or vote, because that would upset the delicate balance in that country between Christian and Moslem voters. Refugees are treated like foreigners. They must get all kinds of licenses and permits, and cannot move about freely. In Gaza, under control of Egypt, refugees outnumber native Arabs by more than two to one—yet they are "second-class" citizens without rights of any kind. Saudi Arabia refuses to admit any refugees altogether.

Jordan is the only Arab country that has tried to welcome and absorb her refugees—500,000 of them. She has given them citizenship rights, privileges, and duties. Some have risen to important government positions—one even became Prime Minister.

★ This statement appeared in an Arab refugee camp newspaper, addressed to the Arab government: "You brought us here to our misfortune, you spread us over the face of your countries, and now you are going to destroy us." Why do many refugees hate Arab leaders, and Arab leaders often act coldly to their refugee "brothers"?

The Arab nations use the refugees to prolong their one-sided "war" against Israel. They want to squeeze the last ounce of propaganda value out of this situation, and to keep around Israel a tight ring of hatred and anger. The Arab states actually benefit from refugee aid supplied by the U. N., the Red Cross, the Quakers, and others. Much free food, clothing, medicine, and other supplies come into their countries. The U. N. makes many purchases in each country, employs local people for its camps, builds roads and houses, plants forests, improves factories and towns.★

What Israel Did

After the 1947 U. N. decision, 500,000 Jews living in Arab countries suffered boycotts, arrests, pogroms. Iraq, Yemen, Syria, and especially Egypt confiscated their homes, land, and savings. The Arab governments did not urge them to stay, or promise them safety and equality. Instead, these Jews were forced to leave under peril of imprisonment and death. Israel, helped by Jews the world over, airlifted many of them and took them in.

The U. N.'s reports on the world's refugees never mention these Jews driven out of the Arab countries. The U. N. did not offer to support them—nor did Israel ever ask it to help. They, too, abandoned homes, shops, and farms, and needed food, clothing, medicine, education, jobs. Israel never demanded that the Arab countries take them back, or pay for their confiscated property. She accepted the 500,000 Jews so quickly and successfully that nobody thinks of them as refugees any more—they were immigrants at first, but soon became Israelis.

Israel contributes her fair share every year to U. N. funds for Arab refugee relief. She helped, and accepted as citizens, many thousands of Arab refugees who sneaked back into Israel when they realized their mistake. She arranged with a refugee committee to return many millions of dollars the refugees had left behind in Israeli banks.

In return, Israel asks the Arabs to stop their boycott of her products, to allow her ships in the Suez Canal, to join her in land and water projects, to work out a peace treaty and officially end the war.

But all this means recognizing the existence of Israel as an independent Jewish State—something the Arab leaders will not do. They will not even talk with Israel's leaders about common problems and ways to solve them. Year after year, they reject pleas from Israel and various world organizations to discuss the best way to help the Arab refugees.★

★ What should Israel have done about the Arab refugees? What should the Arab countries have done?

Should Israel Take Back the Arab Refugees?

Arab leaders insist that Israel must immediately take back all the Arab refugees and restore them to their former lands and jobs. But Arab newspapers openly describe the Arab refugees as a "Fifth Column"—a powerful group trained to undermine Israel if allowed to return, and to prepare for "the day of revenge and reckoning." Many would return not as peaceful, law-abiding citizens, but as enemies eager to destroy Israel. Asking Israel to let them back is like asking her to commit suicide.

In the many years since the refugees left, Israel has greatly changed. Huge post-war immigration has doubled her population, making her one of the most densely populated regions of the Middle East. She is a modern, scientific and industrial country, and no longer an undeveloped peasant country. Many refugees could not fit in with the new Israeli life. They could not make a living, or raise their families as they used to. They would not feel at home, or be happy. Even some Arab authorities have recently admitted this obvious fact.

When Israel agreed to let those refugees return who had families in Israel, almost half the approved applications were never used. Neutral observers of the refugee camps report that many refugees don't really want to return to Israel, but dare not say so—they

★ Some Arab leaders admit—privately —that refugee resettlement in Israel is not practical. But publicly these leaders demand a complete return. Why do they act in this contradictory way?

would be persecuted as traitors by the Arab governments. Others, asked if they would return to live under an Israeli government, do not give a direct yes or no answer. They talk about the *right* to go back even if they *don't want* to.★

The Only Solution

The best answer is to integrate most of the refugees in the countries where they live. This is the solution accepted today by most nations, international organizations, and experts.

Resettlement has worked out well with other refugee groups. Two million Greeks driven out of Turkey found new, happy homes in Greece within a few years. Half a million Armenians, fleeing from Turkey, resettled successfully in Syria and Greece. Finland, Austria, West Germany, and others have absorbed refugees in great numbers, without asking the world's help, without aid from the U. N., without insisting on a return of all refugees. Only the Arab governments have stubbornly refused to solve their refugee problem in a normal, natural manner.

Resettling Arab refugees in Arab lands would be an easy matter. The refugees resemble the native Arabs in religion, language, race, customs, attitudes. They would have no trouble fitting in. Arab lands, in contrast to Israel, have plenty of space and proportionately few people.

Iraq has immense natural resources of land and water, and a serious manpower shortage. Two-thirds of Syria's vast usable lands lie empty and wasted. Only five million Arabs live there—yet long ago, in Roman times, nine million people lived there, producing enough grain to become world-famous.

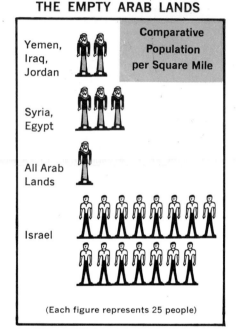

THE EMPTY ARAB LANDS

Yemen, Iraq, Jordan

Comparative Population per Square Mile

Syria, Egypt

All Arab Lands

Israel

(Each figure represents 25 people)

■ 1968. Unused land in the various Arab countries is one hundred times larger than all of Israel. These countries have from two to four times as much room for people as Israel does. Libya, Sudan, and Saudi Arabia have even fewer people per square mile than the Arab lands in the chart. In all the Middle East, only Lebanon is more crowded than Israel, with 600 people per square mile to Israel's 375. Experts say that because Israel is more densely populated, and more developed, it costs far more to settle new people there than in the more open, less developed Arab lands. If the world is to solve the Arab refugee problem, what new policies must be accepted by the Arab nations? By the U. N. and the U. S.? By the Soviet Union and her allies? By Israel herself?

Is There Hope?

Each year, old and new "solutions" are brought up in the U. N. Israel is willing to take back as many refugees as she can—provided the Arab countries accept her, make peace, end their war threats. The Arabs demand that Israel first take back all refugees, meanwhile insisting they are still at war with her and intend to destroy her. The U. N., the United States, and various world organizations have drawn up plans for water and land projects in the Middle East, for international funds, to resettle most of the refugees and return the rest to Israel. Israel has accepted most of these plans— but the Arabs have persistently rejected any plan that means cooperating with her.

ARAB HOMECOMING. Within three months after winning the War for Independence in 1949, Israel was letting Arab refugees come back to their homes. Here, a Greek Orthodox bishop at the Lebanon-Israel frontier welcomes a busload of Arab girls about to rejoin families in Israel. Through the Family Reunion Scheme and other programs, Israel has allowed 40,000 Arab refugees to come back. She has offered to take back more, but many eligible refugees do not apply for the privilege. What requirements does Israel want "returnees" to meet? Why are many refugees not eligible—or, if eligible, not willing?

Is it hopeless? Many people think so, in Israel and elsewhere. But others see a few hopeful signs. Some Arab leaders, for example, are beginning to cooperate more in smaller U. N. resettlement projects. A group of African nations, growing in number every year, keeps asking the Arab countries to settle their complaints against Israel through peaceful discussion and compromise. World pressure may force the Arab states to deal more fairly with Israel, and to think of their refugees as human beings in trouble instead of pawns in a cruel game of blackmail against Israel and the Western nations. Perhaps, if all men and nations of good will keep working in their behalf, the Arab refugees will at last find happiness in the new homes they need and deserve so much.

1968. As he had done a few times before, President Bourguiba of Tunisia urged Arab countries to recognize Israel, and make peace with her. In 1967, he was the first modern Arab ruler ever to enter a synagogue.

YOU'LL ENJOY READING

The Story of Modern Israel, by Dorothy F. Zeligs, pages 378–382

Israel: Idea and Reality, by Emil Lehman, pages 205–209

Write to Israel Office of Information, 11 E. 70th St., New York City, for pamphlets on the Arab refugee problem—especially "The Jewish Exodus from the Arab Countries and the Arab Refugees" and "The Arab Refugees: Arab Statements and the Facts," two that will provide many pictures and quotations for a good bulletin board display.

chapter 23

The Ties That Bind Us

Two Great Centers

For several centuries, the great centers of Jewish life were in Eastern Europe. After 1880, to escape bitter persecution, millions of Jews left Russia and Poland—most of them coming to the United States and some to Palestine. Many Jews perished in World War I (1914–1918), and the German Nazis killed six million more by the end of World War II (1945). Russia still has many Jews, but does not allow them to practice Judaism or maintain Jewish culture.

The great European Jewish communities have been destroyed. The Jewish future is now mostly in the hands of American and Israeli Jews. What Jews do here, and Israelis there, will determine Jewish life in the next few centuries. And how we feel about each other is vitally important—to both of us.

American Jews feel much love and responsibility towards Israel. Many Israelis deeply appreciate what American Jews have done for them. But some Israelis think that Jews elsewhere live as strangers and foreigners, and cannot be safe or happy. They cannot understand why more of us do not go to live in Israel. They consider our Jewish lives colorless and incomplete.

We American Jews do not believe we are in exile—the United States is our safe and happy home. We feel that Israeli and American Jews need each other. American Jews, as well as others, were always important to Israel—and still are. Israel might never have existed or survived without us. Israel, we think, also needs our ideas and opinions, and our personal help. On the other hand, we need Israel—not, like some Jews, as a place to live, but as a source of help and inspiration in Jewish living. As *the* Jewish country, we expect Israel to give us new Jewish ideas, institutions, art, culture.

IN HONOR OF ISRAEL. (Opposite page) A parade of the Jewish War Veterans of the United States of America, on Israel Independence Day. Our country has many groups with "ties" to another land, another culture—Irish, Italians, Chinese, and so on—who honor the country of their ancestors. They celebrate the country's holidays, study its language, visit it, enjoy its art, literature, and music, contribute money to it, and urge our government to befriend it. Yet they are all loyal, patriotic Americans. A few Jews say that supporting Israel is *unpatriotic*. How would you prove that they are wrong?

1966. Over 200 American college students and graduates, paying their own expenses, went to Israel for the Jewish Agency's Sherut La-am (Volunteer Service Corps for Israel). They worked in villages, settlements, kibbutzim, and Youth Aliyah centers as teachers, social workers, technicians, nurses, mechanics, and others. Purpose—to help immigrants from countries where they had no modern education. The Sherut La-am program began in 1965.

★ Do you agree with the following statement? How would you explain or prove it?

"Everything that has been created in this country is the common possession of the Jews of all lands."

—Ben Gurion, Independence Day Message, 1957

1967. Opinion polls found 99 per cent of American Jews supported Israel over the Six Day War (see Chapter 25). Even the anti-Zionist Council for Judaism issued no statement until after the war. Since then, some of their leaders have resigned and have begun to support Israel vigorously.

Try This: Interview your rabbi, principal, teacher, and parents on changes in your synagogue, school, and home because of Israel. Post your results on the bulletin board. What other Israeli patterns of living would you like to see added to your list?

Try This: Find out about three small groups of Jews who bitterly oppose Zionism and the Jewish State: (1) The Neturay Karta, an Orthodox group in Jerusalem; (2) The Bund, an organization of Jewish workers in several countries; (3) The American Council for Judaism. What objection does each group have? Can you answer their arguments?

On the other hand, we occasionally have wrong ideas about Israelis. We sometimes exaggerate their achievements, consider everything they do perfect, and object to any criticism of them. Or, we find fault because Israelis do not follow our own particular way of doing things.★

Zionists All

Practically all American Jews are firm supporters of Israel—including Orthodox, Reform, Conservative, "non-religious" socialist and labor groups, and "unattached" Jews who belong to no special group. All of us give generously to the United Jewish Appeal, the Jewish National Fund, and about seventy-five other pro-Israel organizations in our country. We buy Israel bonds, invest in Israeli enterprises.

Zionism and Israel have greatly changed American Jewish life. Winning and preserving a Jewish homeland brought together all sorts of Jews, despite their disagreements. Each group conducted its own Zionist efforts, but also joined with the others in general projects. The Zionist Organization, Hadassah, the United Jewish Appeal campaigns, and other organizations united American Jews for a common cause. They became acquainted with one another, and learned more about the Jewish people as a whole.

American Jews had always united for charity and welfare work, and for defense against anti-Semitism. But unity for Zionism did something that welfare and defense activities could not do. For example, Israel interests more Jews in Hebrew and Jewish history, in Jewish music, literature, art, dance, crafts. Because of Israel, a growing number of American Jews give their children Hebrew names, study Hebrew in public high schools and colleges, dance the *hora* at weddings, try Israeli recipes in new Jewish cookbooks. The Hebrew language, Zionist ideas, Israeli songs and dances are studied in all types of Jewish schools. This very book you are reading, for instance, was published by the Reform movement to meet the requests of its religious schools. Many synagogues use Israeli music in worship, raise funds for Israel, exhibit Israeli art, buy Torah covers and ornaments from Israel, offer courses on Israeli life and problems. Books, articles, movies, radio and TV programs, news reports about Israel appear almost daily around us.

Since 1948, American Jews in many cities have taken the Jerusalem Examination—a test given by the Hebrew University to Jews the world over. These include not only Hebrew teachers, but ordinary Jewish men and women, of all ages, of all occupations. In the examination, they write an original Hebrew essay, translate or summarize Hebrew literary selections, and answer questions, in Hebrew, on certain books. If they pass, they proudly display their certificate granting them the title of עָמִית—friend, associate, "fellow."

Jewish families in America display Israeli art and religious symbols, hear Israeli recordings, eat and drink Israeli-made foods and wines, or American products with Hebrew names. Hebrew books from Israel appear in Jewish homes and religious schools—and in the public libraries and general bookstores of our big cities. Jewish graduate students do research on Israeli life for their degrees. Businessmen, fund-raisers, community leaders, ordinary families travel to Israel. Many rabbis conduct an annual pilgrimage of their members, and various organizations offer annual summer tours for adults and young people. All types of synagogues, and other organizations in their summer camps, provide for Hebrew and Israel-centered activities.

All this has given American Jews a tremendous boost in morale. So have Israel's achievements in all fields, showing what Jews as a nation could do. Israel's story has made us more willing, more proud, to be Jews. Jewish life has become more interesting, exciting, rewarding. We have learned new ways of practicing Judaism, new songs and prayers and ceremonies. From our contacts with the Yishuv and with Israel, we have learned about new ways of working, governing people, new forms of democracy, new kinds of freedom. Zionism and Israel have helped make us better Jews, better Americans, better people.

Reform Judaism and Zionism

The Jews were not always so unanimous for Zionism. Orthodox and Conservative Jews, when Herzl established the Zionist Organization in 1895, accepted the *idea* of Zionism. They all believed the Jews were a people as well as a religious group, that Zionism was part of Judaism, and that Jews should have a homeland in Palestine. But some Orthodox Jews opposed Zionist action. They believed Jews should leave the return to Palestine entirely up to God—human beings could not and should not try to hurry His plans.

This idea gradually disappeared as settlements grew in Palestine and living conditions in Eastern Europe became intolerable. For many years, other Orthodox groups objected to Zionism because

---

amit: עָמִית

Mordecai Emanuel Noah (United States, 1785-1851). The first American Zionist, wrote and pleaded for a Jewish return to Palestine. He worked out a complete plan, and tried to start a training settlement at Buffalo, N.Y.—but failed.

Louis M. Marshall (1856-1929). Lawyer, Jewish community leader. Though a "non-Zionist," he supported the Balfour Declaration, the Jewish Agency, and the upbuilding of Palestine.

Louis Dembitz Brandeis (1856-1941). Supreme Court judge.

We share the joy, gratitude, and pride felt by Jews everywhere over the growth and progress of the State of Israel. We hail the heroism and sacrifice of its builders and of all who are struggling to maintain its security and further its development. The State of Israel has been the great refuge for our oppressed. It has established a center for a dynamic Hebrew culture. It has translated some of the prophetic ideals of Judaism into living forms and institutions. It has been a source of living inspiration to all our people. It offers great promise in the future.

As we acknowledge our responsibilities towards all Jews everywhere, we affirm our special obligation to provide the fullest measure of brotherly support and assistance —material and moral—for the people of the State of Israel.

—Statement on Reform Judaism and the State of Israel, adopted by the Central Conference of American [Reform] Rabbis, 1962

Only in Israel

About 10,000 Americans, including some non-Jews, have settled in Israel—about 1,600 each year. Almost half of them change their minds after a time and go back. Main reasons: they expect Israel to be a romantic place of heroes and Kibbutzniks, always dancing the *hora,* and they can't take the uncomfortable housing. The others, the majority, stay for good.

One-fourth of Israel's American Jews are in farming villages of all types. They have introduced more family life into some Kibbutzim. One all-American co-operative village pioneered in producing Israeli frozen turkeys. A Detroit businessman opened Israel's first supermarket in Tel Aviv. An American photographer bought a rusted printing press and built up a thriving printing plant. An American professor opened Israel's first and only institute of applied psychology—the science of figuring out what makes people think and act as they do.

its prominent leaders were socialists and non-religious. But most of these objectors eventually agreed with the Orthodox majority, and learned to work with all others to build the homeland.

The early Reform Jews opposed the Zionist idea of a Jewish people and a Jewish homeland. When Reform Judaism began, in Germany in the early 1800's, democracy was spreading in Europe. Jews were winning freedom and citizenship in western countries after centuries of ghetto life and persecution. The early Reform Jews considered themselves permanent citizens, not temporary visitors waiting to go back to "Zion." Their leaders declared that Jews were no longer a separate nation, but only a religious group within each nation. They felt that they should therefore not separate themselves from other citizens except in religious matters. In revising the traditional prayer book, the early Reform leaders eliminated references to the Messiah, restoration of ancient temple sacrifices, and return of the Jewish people to Palestine.

Reform Jews came to this country during the second half of the 19th century. Here, they found freedom such as Jews had never enjoyed anywhere else. They felt that their future was tied up with America, not Palestine. Besides, there was no organized Zionist movement at this time.

As Zionist ideas spread and the Zionist movement began, some leading Reform rabbis became active Zionists. They were among the organizers of the first American Zionist Organization in 1897. But officially, the Reform movement rejected Zionism as part of Judaism.

In the twentieth century, Reform Jews gradually changed their views. Growing anti-Semitism in Europe, the horrible persecutions in Russia, showed that the nations were not really willing to treat Jews as equal citizens. More and more, persecuted and homeless Jews needed a safe place of refuge—land, houses, jobs.

The achievements of the Yishuv in Palestine impressed all Jews, Reform included. The Balfour Declaration, the League of Nations approval, the support of many governments and leading Christians —all this put Zionism in a new light.

The Nazi terror after 1932 made a Jewish homeland more necessary than ever. Thousands of Jews poured into Palestine to escape Hitler. The inhuman Nazi atrocities shocked all Jews everywhere. The Yishuv took in more Jewish refugees than all the nations of the world combined. Zionism offered hope and new life to homeless Jews. Jews in the free countries, whether Reform, Conservative, or Orthodox, felt a solemn duty to help their European brothers by supporting Palestine as a Jewish homeland. Many Reform rabbis supported Zionist organizations and projects. Several became accepted Zionist spokesmen here and throughout the world. But others still objected to Zionism. Reform leaders had a great many discussions—even long quarrels—over the relationship between Zionism and Judaism.

In 1937, the Reform Movement officially withdrew its opposition to Zionism and its rabbis called on their congregations to help rebuild Palestine. Eight years later, the president of the Zionist Organization of America and one of the world's most powerful Zionist leaders was a Reform rabbi.

The long debate over Zionism among Reform Jews ended almost completely when the new State was established. After 1948, the Reform Movement enthusiastically joined all American Jews in helping the new State. In 1962, the Reform rabbis, at their 73rd Annual Convention, officially recognized the strong attachment of Reform Jews toward the State of Israel.

The New Worship in Israel

An American Reform or Conservative Jew would feel quite at home in a similar Israeli congregation. He would hear familiar ideas about God, the meaning of prayer, the place of religion in our lives. Most of the prayers, music, and customs—and in some cases, even the prayer book—would also be familiar. But there would be differences, too.

Henrietta S. Szold (1860-1945). Founder of Hadassah (the Women's Zionist Organization of America) and leader of the Youth Aliyah movement to bring Jewish refugee children to Palestine.

Richard J. H. Gottheil (1862-1936). Rabbi (Reform). First president of Zionist Organization of America.

Stephen Samuel Wise (1874-1949). Rabbi (Reform), community leader, social reformer. A founder of Zionist Organization of America, American Jewish Congress, World Jewish Congress. Leader in many Zionist organizations. Helped achieve the Balfour Declaration, and won many American Jews to the cause of Zionism.

HONOR ROLL

The question is not only how to conserve the existence of the Jewish people . . . but—what is more difficult—how to perpetuate Judaism, Jewish culture, Jewish existence in the modern world. . . . You have marvelous institutions of Jewish learning, which will perpetuate the Jewish heritage in the framework of modern America, modern Western life. We try to do the same as a nation in the framework of modern international life.

—Binyamin Eliav, Israel's Consul-General in New York, addressing the first international assembly of the World Council of Synagogues in Jerusalem, 1962

Try This: Review all the different names for Jews and the Jewish land at the end of Chapter 1. Can you be an Israeli without being a Jew? A Jew without being an Israeli? Pick out chapters of this book that deal with experiences common to Israelis and Americans in general. Express in your own words what *kind* of experience binds us *as Jews* to the Israelis, and what kind binds us to them *as Americans*.

1967. The Rabbinical Council of America, an Orthodox group, announced plans for an educational and religious center in Jerusalem, where new rabbis will study for a year before returning to congregations here.

★ Are any of the new Israeli worship procedures—or anything like them—used in your synagogue? What distinctive custom of your synagogue might appeal to Israel's new congregations?

At the Reform synagogue in Jerusalem, for example, almost the entire service is sung by the whole congregation. At certain points, members of the congregation rise quietly from their seats, without introduction, and give readings of inspirational poetry and Bible selections. Modern original melodies are woven into the service. Occasionally, a worshiper delivers an impromptu prayer—his thoughts of the moment expressed in whatever words come to him. This group, after studying all kinds of prayer books from all over the world, composed its own Sabbath prayer book.

The Haifa Conservatives group developed their own Bar Mitzvah service, to combine ancient tradition with modern ideas. A procession of thirteen persons brings the Bar or Bat Mitzvah symbolic gifts. A younger brother and sister, for example, offer cedar saplings; an older sister and brother present, with a blessing, bread and salt. Mothers bless their boy or girl with a spice-box. Younger friends, not yet Bar Mitzvah, bring forward Kiddush cups; older friends, prayer books; the youth group leader, Bibles. Finally, each father blesses his child and places his own *Talit*, or prayershawl, on his child's shoulders.

An American Jew would not find, in Israel's "Progressive" congregations, some activities that are all-important here. The government, the Histadrut, the political parties, and other organizations provide religious education, social and cultural activities, welfare and social action, rather than the synagogues. In our country, the synagogue offers Jews as a minority group a place to do things together, apart from the non-Jewish majority. In Israel, one is always with other Jews, and does not need a synagogue for this kind of group association.★

274

Can We Teach Israel?

Every Reform service attracts a few curious Israelis who want to "see for themselves." They are usually surprised to find the service all in Hebrew, and the worshipers wearing yarmulkes. Out of ignorance, or from false impressions given by the Orthodox, Israelis expect Reform worship to be "foreign," "un-Jewish." The average Israeli, though he finds little appeal in Orthodox Judaism, knows no other kind. He thinks Orthodoxy—and all religion—is unchanging, stubborn, out-of-date. The Progressive congregations show him there are different kinds of Judaism, from which he can choose the one that most appeals to him and best meets his religious needs. He begins to think and question, instead of simply rejecting.

An Orthodox synagogue usually attracts only one group of Jews —Yemenite, Persian, German, Moroccan, Sefardic or Ashkenazic. The newer synagogues bring together a cross-section of Israel's entire population in the same religious community. In the Jerusalem services, for example, a Yemenite student at the Hebrew University read the Sabbath portion from the Torah for several years. Even some B'nai Israel—a group not fully accepted by the Orthodox rabbis until a few years ago—can be found at a Reform service. The new Reform congregations also began interfaith activities with Christians and Moslems. Above all, Progressive congregations offer Israeli girls and women a new role of equality with men in religious education, worship, leadership.

How We Help

A new Progressive group usually has trouble financing a congregation. It gets no government aid as Orthodox groups do—everything has to come out of its own pockets.

A new congregation usually meets in rented quarters, often bare and unappealing, without religious symbols or inspiring atmosphere, without a permanent rabbi. It seems temporary and insecure. Often, Israelis attracted by the new approach do not join—explaining that they will wait until it really "works." The Jerusalem Reform group found that permanent quarters greatly increased attendance and membership. In religion, as in building up the land, pioneers are few, and have to prove they are succeeding before most people will follow them.

Religious American Jews have supported such pioneers. The World Union for Progressive Judaism sent two American Reform

Judah Leon Magnes (1877-1948). Rabbi (Reform), community leader, first president of the Hebrew University, and supporter of Jewish-Arab unity.

Meir Bar-Ilan (Berlin, 1880-1949). Rabbi (Orthodox), editor, scholar. World leader of Mizrachi Zionists. Member of First Knesset for the religious parties.

James G. Heller (1892-). Rabbi (Reform). Former president of Labor Zionist Organization of America. His father (Maximilian H.) was also a Reform rabbi and early Zionist leader.

HONOR ROLL

275

★ What other lessons—in religion, politics, education, welfare, and so on—can Israel learn from American life? From Jewish life in America? Can you balance each answer with a lesson *we* can learn from Israel?

rabbis to Israel to start new worship groups, conduct village services, give religious guidance, and preach sermons. The Leo Baeck School —a twelve-year-old Liberal educational institution in Haifa—was started by a European Reform rabbi who still directs it. The World Union lent money for a new building for this school. It also sent an American rabbi to teach Bible there and start a Reform religious youth movement, while serving the Nazareth Reform congregation. The Hebrew Union College-Jewish Institute of Religion recently established a School of Archaeology in Jerusalem.★

REFORM LINK TO ISRAEL. Many forests have been planted in Israel in honor of special persons, groups, or ideas. Israel has forests named after Balfour, Einstein, Washington, Kennedy; a Forest of Six Million, for the Jews murdered by the Nazis of Germany; a Freedom Forest, for the friendship between Israel and the United States; a Children's Forest, planted by boys and girls of Hebrew schools and Jewish religious schools in this country. The Union of American Hebrew Congregations, with one forest already completed on Mt. Atzmon, began a new one in 1963. This is the Bar Kochba Forest, located on a stony hill southwest of Jerusalem. Reform Jews, congregations, schools, classes began subscribing for 100,000 trees. How did your school take part in this or other Israeli forest projects? What advantages will such a forest bring to the people of Jerusalem and Israel? What religious beliefs do we express by planting trees in Israel?

The Conservative Jews in America established a fine synagogue in Jerusalem about thirty-five years ago. They help support the new congregation in Haifa, and their rabbis take turns spending a year in Israel serving this group. The Conservative movement has a building and cultural center in Jerusalem. The Jewish Theological Seminary of America has a dormitory in Jerusalem for American rabbinical students studying at the Hebrew University. These students will help stimulate and guide Conservative groups.

These two American synagogue groups believe in cultural ties with Israel, and strongly support her with funds for immigration and development. But they also want to strengthen our *religious* ties with Israeli Jews, and to support their *religious* growth.

YOU'LL ENJOY SEEING

Rabbi Stephen S. Wise: A Twentieth Century Prophet (filmstrip: Union of American Hebrew Congregations)

Try This: In 1968, Israel had 7 Progressive (Reform) congregations, in Haifa, Jerusalem, Kfar Shmaryahu, Nahariya, Ramat Gan, and Tel Aviv. Each is "adopted" by a different regional council of the Union of American Hebrew Congregations. Find out which one "belongs" to your own region, and what connections your own congregation has with it. Or, get the name and address of the rabbi there, and write him a letter asking about conditions.

Abba Hillel Silver (1893-1963). Rabbi (Reform). Former president of Zionist Organization of America, leader in many Zionist organizations. Helped win United States support for partition of Palestine.

Israel Goldstein (1896-). Rabbi (Conservative). Former president and leader of Zionist Organization of America, and numerous other Zionist bodies.

Golda Meir (Meyerson) (1898-). Leader in Histadrut, Jewish Agency, Israel government. One of the two women signers of Israel Declaration of Independence, first ambassador to Russia, and world's only woman to hold office of foreign minister.

HONOR ROLL

chapter 24

Yesterday and Tomorrow

November 29, 1947—a day of suspense, for Jews in Palestine and the world, for Arabs and other nations. The United Nations was voting on the partition of Palestine.

For two years after World War II, Palestine rocked with violence. Hundreds of thousands of Jewish refugees wanted to come in, but the British insisted they could not. The Haganah, the secret Jewish defense force, brought in the "illegal" immigrants anyhow. The British arrested, expelled, blockaded. Arabs, both inside and outside the land, raided and rioted. The British put the country under military law, arresting anyone carrying a weapon, searching houses and buildings. Somehow, arrested Arabs were soon released, Jews were treated harshly. The Haganah fought back, bombing British radar and other installations designed to keep out ships with "illegal" immigrants.

Arabs demanded the end of Jewish immigration, and an independent Arab state. Jews demanded unlimited immigration, and an independent Jewish state. The British decided they had had enough—and tossed "the Palestine problem" to the United Nations.

A U. N. committee, representing eleven countries, spent two months in Palestine. It recommended that the British leave, and the country be divided between Jews and Arabs. This recommendation came up before the U. N. for debate and voting. If the U. N. passed this resolution, declared the Arab leaders, they would make war on the Jews of Palestine and destroy them. The Jews accepted the proposal to divide Palestine. They offered the Arabs peace and friendship, a chance to work together to rebuild the whole Middle East.

THE GREAT DAY. (Opposite page) News that the U. N. had voted for an Independent Jewish State in Palestine sparked celebrations everywhere. In Rome, Jews gathered at the triumphal arch erected long ago by Emperor Titus to mark his "permanent destruction" of the Jewish state. In Tel Aviv, Jews wild with joy danced, sang, cheered in the streets all that night and the next day. But not all of them. Thousands of Haganah men and women were mobilizing. Smoothly, swiftly, according to plan, they brought secretly hidden weapons to assembly points, readied truckloads of soldiers to rush promptly to meet any Arab riot or attack. Military headquarters went into action at strategic spots. Guards took their posts in hidden defense positions near towns and cities. Kol Yisrael, the Haganah's secret radio, checked and coordinated. The Arabs had threatened war—and the Haganah got ready for them.

How shall we sing the Lord's song
In a foreign land?
If I forget thee, O Jerusalem,
Let my right hand forget its cunning.

Let my tongue cleave to the roof of my mouth,
If I remember thee not;
If I set not Jerusalem
Above my chiefest joy.

—Psalm 137:4-6

A Jewish Land—Always

The Jews claimed a historic right to the land of Palestine. It was the birthplace of their faith and nation, thousands of years ago. It was taken from them by force, and they had never given up their right to it.

From Abraham's time onward, some Jews always lived in Palestine—sometimes independent, other times a conquered people. The Romans took away their independence in 70 C.E., and exiled most of them, but Jewish communities still continued there. The Jewish population was sometimes larger, sometimes smaller, depending on conditions. But the Jewish community of Palestine never died out, and Jews all over the world never gave up the idea that Palestine was still their homeland.

After the Jews lost Palestine, no new independent government was established there—except for one brief time during the Crusades. After 70 C.E., Palestine was conquered and reconquered many times. First, it was part of the Roman Empire, which became Christian in the fourth century. Three hundred years later, Moslems took over. In the eleventh century, Moslems and Christians fought back and forth over it. Various nations had their turn—even Egypt, for about a hundred years. Finally the Turks conquered it in 1516 and held it until defeated by the British in 1918. Through all the centuries, Palestine remained only a province, the possession of a larger empire. No one people or nation lived there, or "owned" it.

The Jews never gave up the idea that Palestine was still their homeland. At times, men announced themselves as messiahs—sent by God to lead the Jews back to Palestine, as a step toward freedom, justice, and peace for the whole world. In days of bitter suffering, many Jews believed such men—the hope of rescue and return was so strong. They sold or gave away their homes and possessions, packed and stood ready to go at once to Palestine.

The messiahs turned out to be false; the nations would not give Palestine back to the Jews. The disappointment each time was intense—but the longing to go back never weakened.

Over the years, thousands of Jews went to live in Palestine, often at the risk of their lives. As far back as 1121, a group of 300 French

Try This: A committee report: (1) Look up "Aliyah" in a Jewish encyclopedia, and find dates, leaders, countries, purposes of various groups from 1121 to 1880. (2) Joseph Nasi, in 1561, tried to establish farms and factories worked by Jews. Find out what happened with this pioneer's attempt to rebuild a ruined country. (3) From Palestine, in 1565, came the basic law-book of Jewish life still followed by Orthodox Jews—the *Shulchan Aruch* (Prepared Table). Look up Joseph Caro and Moses Isserles for a fascinating tale of Sefardic-Ashkenazic conflict in those days. (4) Sabbatai Zevi, greatest of the false messiahs, persuaded thousands of Jews to follow him to Palestine—then turned Moslem in 1666. Find out why—and what became of his followers.

In the East, in the East is my heart,
And I dwell at the end of the West;
How then shall I join in your feasting,
How then shall I share in your jest? . . .

All the beauties and treasures of Spain
Are worthless as dust, in mine eyes;
But the dust of the Lord's ruined house
As a treasure of beauty I prize!

—Judah Halevi, 1085–1140

and English Jews made the "Aliyah." Other groups arrived—hundreds of years apart, from different countries, for different reasons. Some were expelled and had nowhere else to go. Others came to live out their lives in study and prayer. Important scholars settled in Palestine, bringing along families, students, and friends. They wrote important books that influenced Jews everywhere. Some groups even came as colonists—to start farming and business enterprises, and build a self-supporting Jewish community. But these attempts usually failed—they were ahead of their time.

All through the centuries, Jews outside the country never forgot about it. Wherever they lived, they celebrated Pesach, Shavuot and Sukot according to the seasons in Palestine—spring, early harvest, fall harvest. Sometimes amidst snow and icy winds, Jews celebrated Tu Bi-Sh'vat—tree-planting time in Palestine. Even during downpours of rain, they prayed *for* rain—in Palestine's dry season. Living in crowded city ghettos, they counted the "Omer" from Pesach to Shavuot—as the farmers of ancient Palestine counted the days when they brought their grain offering to the Temple. Every Chanukah, they recalled their ancestors' heroic fight for religious freedom and political independence. At Lag Bo-omer, they recalled Bar Kochba's rebellion against Rome, his great try for independence. On Tisha B'Av and other days, they fasted, mourned, wept for the Jewish land.

When they prayed—in daily services and on Sabbath and holidays—they faced toward Jerusalem. Again and again, in their prayers, they spoke and dreamed of the Holy Land—beseeching God to "return to Jerusalem," reminding themselves that "out of Zion shall go forth the Torah, and the word of the Lord from Jerusalem." On New Moons and most holidays, they recited the *Hallel*, a collection of psalms sung in the ancient Temple. They ended the Passover Seder and the final service of Yom Kippur with the cry לְשָׁנָה הַבָּאָה בִּירוּשָׁלַיִם—Next Year in Jerusalem! They began the בִּרְכַּת הַמָּזוֹן—the Grace After Meals, by chanting Psalm

Try This: Look up Psalm 137:1-6. When was it composed, and why? Has the Jewish people kept this vow of our ancestors? How have you personally kept this vow?

Leshanah haba-ah biyerushalayim: לְשָׁנָה הַבָּאָה בִּירוּשָׁלַיִם

Birkat hamazon: בִּרְכַּת הַמָּזוֹן

126: "When the Lord brought back those who returned to Zion. . . ." Later, in the Grace, they called on God to "rebuild Jerusalem, the holy city, speedily in our very own days!" Even at times of mourning, they consoled the bereaved family with the words: "May God comfort you along with all the mourners of Zion and Jerusalem!"

To remind themselves of their lost homeland, Jews developed dramatic customs. At weddings, the groom smashed a glass. Painting a home, a Jew left one spot untouched. A bit of "holy earth" from Palestine, obtained at great expense and risk, was treasured in every household. When a person died, this soil was placed in his grave.

Jews everywhere kept close contact with Palestine, always knew what went on there. Letters came and went. Pilgrims traveled there and returned, helped along the way by Jewish communities. Messengers from Palestine's Jewish communities regularly visited synagogues in every country, reporting conditions.

A Land Built Only by Jews

Jewish spokesmen told the U. N. this moving story of a people who could not and would not forget their homeland. They presented two other strong claims.

As a nation, Jews had no home, and suffered deeply for it—always a minority, often "inferiors" even when tolerated, at times inhumanly persecuted. The world's leaders, from Herzl's time on, had admitted this often. Most nations had encouraged Zionism and the Jewish homeland—in the Balfour Declaration, in the vote of the League of Nations. Many impartial committees—including the latest one from the U. N. itself—had praised Jewish achievements in Palestine and their contribution to modern democracy, and had admitted the Jewish need for a refuge from persecution.

Arabs in Palestine had done nothing with the land. It remained a desert for centuries—until Jews made it fertile again. Jews did not take land away from Arabs. They bought it—at high prices, and only land *not* used by the Arabs themselves. On land the Arabs thought worthless, Jews established a modern community that benefited the Arabs too—improved their health, increased their income, gave them new hope of a better life for their children. Jews could point to thriving farms where swamp land used to be, modern schools and hospitals, Tel Aviv, Kibbutzim, the Histadrut, community organizations, scientific laboratories, expressions of art and culture, new villages even in the Negev. All that took years of courage, hard labor, aid from other Jews. Arabs in Palestine and elsewhere had not been willing to make such sacrifices.★

★ Palestine's Arabs benefited from Jewish settlement. The Jews promised them full equality in the Jewish State. The U. N. offered them a separate Arab State in their portion of the country. Why, then, all the Arab resistance to the partition plan? (Hint: Who among the Arabs might lose something if Jews and the Arab population benefited?)

The Arab Claim

During World War I, Britain wanted the Arabs to revolt against their Turkish rulers. She promised, if victorious, to give the Arabs about a million square miles of territory taken from the Turks—embracing the whole Arabic-speaking population in Asia. Here, Arabs could set up their own new independent nations. The British later explained that they never included Palestine in this promise. But the Arabs insist to this day that they did.

The Arabs interpreted the Balfour Declaration of 1917 to mean that Jewish refugees could come to live in Palestine in small numbers, as citizens of an *Arab* state. Eventually, the League of Nations placed Lebanon and Syria under French control, Palestine and Iraq under British control. This was the start of Arab bitterness toward the Western countries—and toward the Jews. In the Arabs' opinion, the Western nations had "stolen" their lands, and "given" Palestine to the Jews.

The Arabs claimed they had lived in Palestine for over a thousand years. When Britain took charge of it, Arabs made up ninety per cent of the population. Now, in 1947, they were still two-thirds of the population. In contrast, 95 per cent of the Jewish people lived outside of Palestine. Arabs owned all but a small fraction of the actual soil of the country.★

★ Can you answer the Arab arguments? For example, how did most of the world's nations interpret the Balfour Declaration? Who actually owned the "Arab" land of Palestine? How did Arab people actually get along with Jews when not stirred up by their leaders' appeals and accusations?

The War for Independence*

Almost to the final moment, no one was sure how the U. N. vote would go. The United States and other friends of the Jewish State were about evenly balanced with the Arab nations and their friends. All day long, delegates met, telephoned, argued, pleaded. In Palestine, Jews gathered all day around loudspeakers broadcasting the latest news. Elsewhere, Jews waited nervously.

The word came: a stunning victory of 33–13 for a Jewish state.

Within a few days, Jewish rejoicing ended. Arab bands ambushed buses, shot up passengers, set buildings on fire. A large Arab guerrilla force attacked Jewish settlements. Five Arab armies outside the country mobilized for invasion.

The War for Independence lasted a year-and-a-half—a time of daring attack and stubborn defense, suicide missions, suffering, heroism, and death. The "illegal" immigrants were called, in

---

*Milchemet Ha-Atzmaut: מִלְחָמָת הָעַצְמָאוּת

283

Hebrew, מַעְפִּילִים—adventurers, fighters against great odds. In those days, thousands of Ma-apilim moved from ship to fighting lines. But all Jews of the country deserve to be called Ma-apilim—at the front or at home, they risked everything in a daring fight for freedom.

All the odds seemed to be against the Jews. Their enemies outnumbered them sixty to one in population, three to one in military forces. The Arab countries had hundreds of warplanes, tanks, armored cars, heavy cannon, and fourteen warships. Against these "heavy" weapons, Israel had a few thousand rifles and machine guns, a few hundred light and medium mortars, a few anti-tank guns.

For the first five months of the struggle, the Jews had to fight the British as well as the Arabs. The British refused to cooperate with a U. N. committee sent to help the change in government. They ignored the Arab attacks, but tried to suppress the Haganah, confiscate its weapons, arrest its leaders. The British kept up their blockade against immigrants, weapons, reinforcements. But they sold weapons freely to the Arab nations, even helped them train their armies.

The Jews had other disadvantages. Living mostly in the towns, they had to move through Arab territory to join one another. Arabs could easily cut off the roads they had to use. The Arab nations could attack almost anywhere they choose on the long, twisting border. The Jews were locked into the center of the vast Arab semicircle, with the sea at their backs. Besides the Haganah, several secret terrorist groups fought the enemy. They disliked one another, were not used to obeying the central command of a single fighting force. Jewish civilians were without government, food, community services—and under constant attack.★

★ Within two weeks after Israel's Declaration of Independence, May 14, 1948, six nations officially recognized Israel: the United States, Russia, Poland, Czechoslovakia, Uruguay, South Africa. During this time, Arabs conquered border towns, forced the heroic Jewish forces in the old section of Jerusalem to surrender, and seemed to have every advantage. Why, then, did these nations act as if Israel were here to stay?

Why Israel Won

The British left in May, 1948. At the same moment, the five Arab nations attacked. The U. N. arranged several temporary truces during the war. Israel badly needed the first of these, to catch her breath and reorganize. But all the other truces helped the Arabs, and actually prevented Israel from trouncing them completely. For after a poor start, the Israelis began to win. They recaptured Jewish towns and roads, pushed the enemy back to the borders and beyond. Only Jordan's Arab Legion, trained by the British, was able to

Ma-apilim: מַעְפִּילִים

stand up against the Israelis. They besieged Jerusalem for months, conquered half of it, and resisted all attempts to force them out. Jordan controlled half the divided city until the Six Day War in 1967 (see Chapter 25).

Israel could even have invaded some of her "neighbors"—but was held back by appeals and warnings from Britain and the United States. One by one, the Arab nations signed an armistice with Israel. By July, 1949, the War for Independence was over. Israel's army, tripled in size, had destroyed, damaged or captured much Arab military equipment. Israel also had about twenty per cent more territory than the U. N. had originally suggested, mostly in Western Galilee.

ISRAEL FIGHTS. A unit moves out to relieve Jerusalem under siege. Israelis explain their victory quite simply: they *had* to think straighter, move faster, fight harder—or be driven into the sea. When the Arabs cut off Jerusalem, Israelis built a secret road around them—working nights, with dim flashlights and hand tools, close to the Arab lines. They supplied food, weapons, reinforcements to the city's defenders, until they could drive off the attackers. In a dozen "operations" just as spectacular, Israelis outsmarted, outfought the enemy.

One reason for Israel's victory was Arab mistakes and over-confidence. The invaders were not a united fighting force. Each country tried to cut off a big piece of land for itself. The Arab governments were weak and dishonest, always having to suppress rebellions and riots of their own. Arab soldiers had no real heart for fighting, no real cause to die for. They were promised quick, easy victories. In defeat, they simply collapsed and quit.

The Israelis made mistakes too—but corrected them more quickly. They established a single united army with a single master war plan. Excited by the dream of centuries coming true, by the knowledge that everything now depended on them, they worked and fought with courage, intelligence, and faith. They had a cause they believed in—and they refused to give up.

They also had outside help. Jews in other lands had taken Arab threats quite seriously. As the U. N. debated the Palestine question, thousands of officers and men were training in fifty-two different camps in Europe alone. After the British left, Jewish volunteers poured into Palestine to make up about one-fifth of Israel's fighting forces. The Jews of South Africa, though not a large community, sent Israel more trained volunteers than any other country. Thousands of American Jewish volunteers arrived, and American Jews sent Israel many millions of dollars, too. Jewish communities in over a dozen other lands did their part—even in "Iron Curtain" countries like Poland, Rumania, and Russia herself.★

★ Arab leaders say they are still at war with Israel and intend to attack her again. Their forces are now well-trained, well-equipped. What makes Israelis confident that they can win again? (Several answers!)

How Israel Built for the Future

In these eighteen months of danger and doubt, Israel prepared for peace and independence. Even before the British left, the Jews set up a temporary government and their own postal service.

On May 14, 1948, Iyyar 5, 5708, thirty-nine Jewish leaders gathered in a museum near Tel Aviv. They sang *Hatikvah,* recited the Shehecheyanu blessing, broadcast Israel's Declaration of Independence, and proclaimed מְדִינַת יִשְׂרָאֵל—the new State of Israel, to be in existence.

The Declaration guaranteed freedom and equal rights for all, regardless of religion, race, or sex, and full support of the U.N. The Declaration also called on Israel's Arabs (at that moment rioting, pillaging, or racing out of the country) to accept equal citizenship and representation in the new government.

MEDINAT YISRAEL. (Opposite page) Ben Gurion signs Israel's Declaration of Independence. The document was immediately buried in a secret underground vault—to preserve it for future historians if Israel were destroyed. Egyptian planes were on the way to bomb the city, and things looked dark. But the signers went on building a state, in the concluding words of the Declaration, "with faith in the Rock of Israel."

Medinat Yisrael: מְדִינַת יִשְׂרָאֵל

286

בארץ-ישראל קם העם היהודי, בה עוצבה דמותו הרוחנית, הדתית והמדינית, בה חי חיי קוממיות ממלכתית, בה יצר נכסי תרבות לאומיים וכלל-אנושיים והוריש לעולם כולו את ספר הספרים הנצחי.

לאחר שהוגלה העם מארצו בכוח הזרוע שמר לה אמונים בכל ארצות פזוריו, ולא חדל מתפלה ומתקוה לשוב לארצו ולחדש בתוכה את חירותו המדינית.

מתוך קשר היסטורי ומסורתי זה חתרו היהודים בכל דור לשוב ולהאחז במולדתם העתיקה, ובדורות האחרונים שבו לארצם בהמונים, וחלוצים מעפילים ומגינים הפריחו נשמות, החיו שפתם העברית, בנו כפרים וערים, והקימו ישוב גדל והולך השליט על משקו ותרבותו, שוחר שלום ומגן על עצמו, מביא ברכת קדמה לכל תושבי הארץ ונושא נפשו לעצמאות ממלכתית.

בשנת תרנ"ז (1897) נתכנס הקונגרס הציוני לקול קריאתו של חוזה המדינה היהודית תיאודור הרצל והכריז על זכות העם היהודי לתקומה לאומית בארצו.

זכות זו הוכרה בהצהרת בלפור מיום ב' בנובמבר 1917 ואושרה במנדט מטעם חבר הלאומים, אשר נתן במיוחד תוקף בין-לאומי לקשר ההיסטורי שבין העם היהודי לבין ארץ-ישראל ולזכות העם היהודי להקים מחדש את ביתו הלאומי.

השואה שנתחוללה על עם ישראל בזמן האחרון, בה הוכרעו לטבח מיליונים יהודים באירופה, הוכיחה מחדש בעליל את ההכרח בפתרון בעית העם היהודי מחוסר המולדת והעצמאות על ידי חידוש המדינה היהודית בארץ-ישראל, אשר תפתח לרוחה את שערי המולדת לכל יהודי ותעניק לעם היהודי מעמד של אומה שוות-זכויות בתוך משפחת העמים.

שארית הפליטה, שניצלה מהטבח הנאצי האיום באירופה ויהודי ארצות אחרות, לא חדלו להעפיל לארץ-ישראל, על אף כל קושי, מניעה וסכנה, ולא פסקו לתבוע את זכותם לחיי כבוד, חירות ועמל-ישרים במולדת עמם.

במלחמת העולם השניה תרם הישוב העברי בארץ את מלוא-חלקו למאבק האומות השוחרות חירות ושלום נגד כוחות הרשע הנאצי, ובדם חייליו ובמאמצו המלחמתי קנה לו את הזכות להמנות עם העמים מייסדי ברית האומות המאוחדות.

ב-29 בנובמבר 1947 קיבלה עצרת האומות המאוחדות החלטה המחייבת הקמת מדינה יהודית בארץ-ישראל, העצרת תבעה מאת תושבי ארץ-ישראל לאחוז בעצמם בכל הצעדים הנדרשים מצדם הם לביצוע ההחלטה. הכרה זו של האומות המאוחדות בזכות העם היהודי להקים את מדינתו אינה ניתנת להפקעה.

זוהי זכותו הטבעית של העם היהודי להיות ככל עם ועם עומד ברשותו עצמו במדינתו הריבונית.

לפיכך נתכנסנו, אנו חברי מועצת העם, נציגי הישוב העברי והתנועה הציונית, ביום סיום המנדט הבריטי על ארץ-ישראל, ובתוקף זכותנו הטבעית וההיסטורית ועל יסוד החלטת עצרת האומות המאוחדות אנו מכריזים בזאת על הקמת מדינה יהודית בארץ-ישראל, היא מדינת ישראל.

אנו קובעים שהחל מרגע סיום המנדט, הלילה, אור ליום שבת ו' אייר תש"ח, 15 במאי 1948, ועד להקמת השלטונות הנבחרים והסדירים של המדינה בהתאם לחוקה שתיקבע על-ידי האספה המכוננת הנבחרת לא יאוחר מ-1 באוקטובר 1948 – תפעל מועצת העם כמועצת מדינה זמנית, ומוסד הביצוע שלה, מנהלת-העם, יהווה את ממשלת המדינה היהודית, אשר תקרא בשם ישראל.

מדינת ישראל תהא פתוחה לעליה יהודית ולקיבוץ גלויות, תשקוד על פיתוח הארץ לטובת כל תושביה, תהא מושתתה על יסודות החירות, הצדק והשלום לאור חזונם של נביאי ישראל, תקיים שויון זכויות חברתי ומדיני גמור לכל אזרחיה בלי הבדל דת, גזע ומין, תבטיח חופש דת, מצפון, לשון, חינוך ותרבות, תשמור על המקומות הקדושים של כל הדתות, ותהיה נאמנה לעקרונותיה של מגילת האומות המאוחדות.

מדינת ישראל תהא מוכנה לשתף פעולה עם המוסדות והנציגים של האומות המאוחדות בהגשמת החלטת העצרת מיום 29 בנובמבר 1947 ותפעל להקמת האחדות הכלכלית של ארץ-ישראל בשלמותה.

אנו קוראים לאומות המאוחדות לתת יד לעם היהודי בבנין מדינתו ולקבל את מדינת ישראל לתוך משפחת העמים.

אנו קוראים – גם בתוך התקפת-הדמים הנערכת עלינו זה חדשים – לבני העם הערבי תושבי מדינת ישראל לשמור על השלום וליטול חלקם בבנין המדינה על יסוד אזרחות מלאה ושווה ועל יסוד נציגות מתאימה בכל מוסדותיה, הזמניים והקבועים.

אנו מושיטים יד שלום ושכנות טובה לכל המדינות השכנות ועמיהן, וקוראים להם לשיתוף פעולה ועזרה הדדית עם העם העברי העצמאי בארצו. מדינת ישראל מוכנה לתרום חלקה במאמץ משותף לקידמת המזרח התיכון כולו.

אנו קוראים אל העם היהודי בכל התפוצות להתלכד סביב הישוב בעליה ובבנין ולעמוד לימינו במערכה הגדולה על הגשמת שאיפת הדורות לגאולת ישראל.

מתוך בטחון בצור ישראל הננו חותמים בחתימת ידינו לעדות על הכרזה זו, במושב מועצת המדינה הזמנית, על אדמת המולדת, בעיר תל-אביב, היום הזה, ערב שבת, ה' אייר תש"ח, 14 במאי 1948.

Our people once gave the world a spiritual message fundamental to civilization. The world is watching us now to see the way we choose in ordering our lives, how we fashion our State. The world is listening to hear whether a new message will go forth from Zion, and what that message will be.

—Chaim Weizmann, addressing first session of the
Knesset, February 19, 1949

The next day, on May 15, the first immigrants entered the country freely and openly. Within three weeks, all government departments were operating—including a school to train young men and women to become consuls and ambassadors in foreign countries. One of the government's first acts, still during the fighting, was to set up departments for Moslem and Christian religious affairs—to help these communities maintain their religious life without interruptions from the war.

INAUGURATION OF WEIZMANN AS ISRAEL'S FIRST PRESIDENT, 1949. Israel then was the U. N.'s youngest, smallest, least-known member. Today, her position in the U. N. is firm and respected.

That summer, Israel established a merchant fleet, offered to discuss peace terms with the Arabs (who declined), issued her first money (printed in both Hebrew and Arabic), and installed her Supreme Court. In the fall, Israel again offered peace to the Arabs (again declined), and established El-Al, her first commercial airline. Seven months after the State began, 102,000 new immigrants had arrived and been cared for.

In 1949, the United States Export-Import Bank lent Israel a hundred million dollars. They new nation held elections for the First Knesset—by secret ballot, Arabs voting as well as Jews, women as well as men.

On being accepted into the U. N., Israel again offered Arab countries an honorable peace and partnership in improving the whole region (again declined). A month later, Israel established her Research Council, to supervise science and technology in the new State. In July, the war officially ended—but the Arab countries kept up their boycott, Suez Canal blockade, border raids, threats. Israel offered permanent peace, discussion of all questions, treaties —all declined.

Throughout 1950, the Arab countries continued to harass Israel in every possible way short of actual war. The Knesset passed its famous Law of Return. Israel airlifted 47,000 Yemenite Jews out of persecution to safety in "Operation Magic Carpet." She also established, for Arabs, twenty-eight health clinics, four traveling clinics, a tuberculosis hospital, thirty welfare offices, and free medical services for school children. She began her seven-year Huleh drainage project, and by the end of the year had taken in 70,000 more immigrants.★

HAVE YOU WONDERED . . . ?

. . . about Israel's main problems:—

Peace with Arab Neighbors. Their war threat forces her to concentrate on defense at the expense of other vital needs. Can she persuade them—or get the other nations to persuade them—to become partners instead of enemies?

Water and oil. These are absolute musts for modern agriculture and industry, yet still quite scarce in Israel. Can she increase her supply fast enough and high enough for her development plans?

Self-support. Israel still depends on foreign aid, loans, gifts. Can she increase her exports over her imports, take in more money than she pays out, and support herself completely? Can she do it *soon*?

Only in Israel

After the proclamation, two government officials picked up the parchment scroll and a stenographic record of official discussions leading up to the Declaration. They hurried down a narrow staircase to a deep vault, where they locked the scroll and the folder in a steel safe.

Israel's leaders were preparing for the worst—the bombing of Tel Aviv from air or sea, and the death of everyone who had prepared the Declaration and organized the new State. Even if all Israel were wiped out, the records of the great event would remain safely hidden. Some day someone would find them, and other Jews would try again.

It was Friday afternoon—Erev Shabbat—and Israel's leaders hurried home to enjoy the Shabbat meal with their families. Come what may, Jews must not worry or be sad on Shabbat!

★ Israel won a fighting war against the Arab nations. What other war did she begin to fight, against what enemies, in the very first hours of her existence? Does this help explain why she quickly gained the respect and admiration of so many nations? Has she won *this* war yet?

We have established a state; we have not yet built a nation.

—Abba Eban

World relations. Israel must get along with the western democracies, the "neutrals," and the Communist countries. Should she continue to walk alone, depending not on alliances with one group but on the friendly feelings of all three? Should she take sides, or avoid "entanglements"?

Jewish relations. Israeli Jews have much in common with the Jews of America and other lands—but are also very different from them. Can Israel maintain her bonds with other Jewish communities despite the differences? Can she prevent the misunderstandings and hard feelings that sometimes crop up?

Pioneering ideals. Israel was built by hard work, personal sacrifice, and high ideals. With growing prosperity, many Israelis seem to be mainly interested in money, conveniences, luxuries. Can Israel retain the original pioneer drive—continue to inspire her young people and the Jews of other lands?

Religious freedom. Israel neither governs herself completely by Orthodox Jewish law, nor allows everyone complete personal religious freedom. Can she retain this mixture of two opposite ways of life? Can she try one or the other without splitting the country into two violent factions? Can she survive the contradictory challenge of Orthodox tradition and modern ideas?

Integrating European and Oriental Jews. The "first" Israel—light-skinned, with advanced education and the top jobs—is gradually becoming a minority. The "second" Israel—dark-skinned, backward, poor, underprivileged—is becoming the majority. Can Israel unite the two into one nation before trouble breaks out between them? Can she prevent serious conflict of race and color, harmonize the East and the West in Jewish life?

Education. Israel's schools are "bursting at the seams" with her population "explosion." Can she provide full, free education for every child? Can she close her big gaps in high school and vocational education soon enough to produce all the educated workers she needs?

Immigration. Israel needs—expects—and must be ready for more immigrants. Can she take in a million more Jews? Two million more? Can she stand the tremendous strain this puts on her resources, on her people?

290

Now, let's see if you can answer some questions:

1. The ten problems are not listed in any special order. How would you arrange them by importance? Be ready to explain your reasoning.

2. A job for committees: Review the chapter dealing with each problem. Why is a solution to the problem vital? What is Israel doing about it? How can we help her with it?

3. The problems are all connected—solving one will help solve others. Give some specific examples to prove this statement. Can Israel work on one problem at a time—or must she tackle them all at once?

YOU'LL ENJOY READING

Cast a Giant Shadow, by T. Berkman. The life story of Colonel David Marcus, American Jewish soldier, who was the Haganah's military adviser, and was killed in action in the War for Independence.

YOU'LL ENJOY SEEING

Beyond the Wilderness (film: National Committee for Labor Israel)
Israel Among the Nations (pictorial wall newspaper; Jewish Agency)
Years of Destiny (film: Keren Hayesod, United Israel Appeal, Jewish Agency—American section)

chapter 25

A New Israel?

This chapter was written in May, 1968, and is up-to-date to that time. Since the Six Day War of June, 1967, the situation in the Middle East has been indefinite and changeable. As you study this chapter, watch for the latest news and changes.

A Time of Peril

1957—No sooner is Suez Campaign over than the Arabs start their aggressions again. Palestine Liberation Organization renews acts of sabotage inside Israel. Most of the guerillas are "refugees" supported by U.N. funds.

1957-1967—Egypt and Syria get 3 billion dollars worth of military equipment from Russia. Israel, to keep up, buys arms from the United States and France.

1965—Nasser and other Arab leaders call for a "holy war" to destroy Israel and "drive the Jews into the sea." Israel, the United States, and Great Britain urge the U.N. to act to prevent invasion of Israel. Russia and the Arabs insist Israel's charges are false. Nothing is done.

1965-1966—Continuing raids and sabotage inside Israel's borders. She answers by attacking Jordanian village used by terrorists. U.N. criticizes Israel, but overlooks Arab invasions. Trouble grows along Israel-Syria border—main Israeli roads are mined, Israeli villages are shelled, border kibbutzim are frequent targets.

May, 1967—Arab leaders say Israel is massing 13 brigades on Syrian border to attack Damascus and overthrow Syrian government. U.N. observers on the spot say charge is false. Egypt sends troops into Sinai Peninsula, and demands the U.N. withdraw its Emergency Force from the Egypt-Israel border.

■ After bitter fighting and heavy losses, Israeli paratroopers approached the Western Wall on June 7, 1967. This wall is the only remnant of the Second Temple of ancient times, destroyed by the Romans in 70 C.E. Jews have prayed throughout the centuries at this holy shrine. For 20 years, since 1948, the Jordanians had allowed no Jew to come to it. Now, steel-helmeted soldiers leaned on the ancient stones, and wept. General Moshe Dayan, following an ancient tradition, wrote out, on a slip of paper that he wedged among the stones of the wall, this prayer: "May peace come to Israel." Then he pronounced this vow: "We have returned to the holiest of our holy places, never to depart from it again." On Shavuot, a week after the war ended 200,000 Jews worshiped at the Western Wall. (Opposite page)

The U.N. gives in to Nasser and withdraws its troops. Egypt blockades the Gulf of Aqaba and takes positions along the Strait of Tiran and the Gaza Strip.

Nasser over the Cairo radio: "We know that closing the Gulf of Aqaba might mean war with Israel. . . . It will be a total war and the objective will be to destroy Israel."

Arab nations, until now bitter enemies among themselves, sign military pacts. Their troops mass on Israel's borders. Arab voices call louder and louder for a "holy war" to wipe out the Jews.

June 1-5, 1967—The U.N. seems helpless to interfere. Russia warns Israel against "aggression." The United States urges her to show "restraint." Much talk, no action, no offers of help. Jews the world over fearful and angry over each day's news. Israelis calm, begin getting ready. For the third time in twenty years, events move rapidly to a final show-down.

June 5, 1967—Egyptians bomb Israeli villages.

Try This: Bring this list up to date by adding later events in Israel and the Middle East.

The Six Day War

In 1948, the United States and Russia both supported independence for Israel. In 1956, France and England joined her in the Suez Campaign against Egypt. In 1967, no one seemed to be on Israel's side. The communist nations, and France, openly sided with the Arabs. The United States and other Western countries pressured Israel to "hold back," to "wait." All the while, Arab armies were growing stronger, coming closer. Israelis decided they had only themselves to count on, and on June 5 they went into action.

What followed amazed the entire world. With incredible speed, Israeli forces wiped out Egypt's air force and smashed her invasion troops in Sinai. Jordan and Syria began shelling Israel heavily, and she went after them too.

Six days later it was all over. Israel had broken Egypt's blockade, reunited Jerusalem, and occupied Arab territory on nearly every border.

As in 1949 and 1956, with the Arabs going down to disgraceful defeat, the U.N. called for a cease-fire. Israel and the Arabs accepted, and the whole world caught its breath.

Once again, Israelis rejoiced over victory, lamented over death and destruction, faced new problems, discovered new opportunities. The Arabs, once again, pulled back defeated and disheartened, ashamed and angry, worried, frightened—and burning for revenge.

When the war broke out, Israel urged Jordan to stay out of it. Jordan ignored this warning and began bombarding the Jewish por-

> *"Now we know that we have built a structure that can be protected. We know that the opportunity for the dignity of freedom is in our own hands."*

—Levi Eshkol, Prime Minister of Israel,
January, 1968, New York City

tion of Jerusalem. Israel counterattacked and captured the Jordanian portion, uniting the Old City and the New City. Israelis, and Jews everywhere, were stirred with deep feeling.

Jerusalem is, of course, a sacred city to three major religions. For Christians it is the city where Jesus preached and taught; for Moslems, it contains a mosque called the Dome of the Rock, holiest of their shrines after Mecca and Medina; and for Jews, it is the site of the Temple and its Western Wall. But as a national capital, Jerusalem has belonged only to the Jewish people. Twice they were exiled from Jerusalem, and twice they returned. In June, 1967, the Western Wall became a symbol to all Jews—perhaps even more than the establishment of Israel herself—of a final return from two thousand years of exile.

The U.N. condemned Israel for "annexing" the Old City—completely ignoring the facts of the previous twenty years. In 1948, the U.N. decided to partition Palestine into a Jewish state and an Arab state, with Jerusalem an international city. The Arab nations rejected this decision and attacked Israel. Jordan besieged Jerusalem and captured the Old City—by war and conquest. They did not "own" it or have any right to it.

Jerusalem stayed divided for the next nineteen years—with borders running through houses and yards, walls, armed sentries facing each other across barbed wire, Arab sniping and terror.

The 1949 armistice granted Israelis the right to visit holy places and cultural institutions in the Old City. Jordan never lived up to this agreement. For the first time in two thousand years, Jews were barred from visiting and praying at their holiest shrine. Even Israeli Arabs were not allowed to come to worship at their holy places. Jordan destroyed or vandalized every Jewish institution, every synagogue, in the Old City. They bulldozed ancient graves in the Jewish cemetery on the Mount of Olives and built a road through it. The Hebrew University and the Hadassah Medical Center on Mt. Scopus were closed down and abandoned. But the nations and many Christian groups remained silent—until Israel, attacked by Jordan, took the Old City back and set it free for all religions. Then, the world protested.

Try This: Ask your teacher to play a recording of "Jerusalem of Gold." Learn the words and the music, and enjoy singing this beloved song.

295

■ One of several Jewish cemeteries in the Old City, vandalized by the Jordanians between 1949 and 1967. How do you explain the 20-year silence of nations in the U. N.—and of Christians in our own country — over Jordan's armistice violations (see page 295) and the outcry against Israel reuniting Jerusalem in 1967.

★ Do you think Israel's victory in the Six Day War was a "miracle"? Why or why not?

The government officially declared all Jerusalem, Old and New, a united Israeli city. Holy places of all faiths were guaranteed total respect. They were to be open to all, with complete freedom of worship. Arabs in the Old City had full rights of Israeli citizenship.

Israel has declared that she will never give up Jerusalem. Her men fought a bitter, bloody battle for it. Jordan's troops had deliberately placed their cannon in or near the holy places of Christians and Moslems. To avoid damaging these places, Israel's men did not use air power or artillery. Instead, they fought in hand-to-hand combat that cost them many extra lives. Israel had paid too great a price for something far too precious to "give it back."

"If I Forget Thee, O Jerusalem...."

What happened in Israel in June, 1967, according to many Jews, was a miracle. If so, there was another miracle—what happened among the Jews of the world, especially the younger Jews, mostly in the United States, Canada, and Latin America. *

296

"Suddenly I realized that Israel was more important than anything else in my life."

—Young Italian Jewish volunteer, June, 1967

Thousands of visitors in Israel stayed on, refusing to go home, volunteering to work in place of those who had gone to war. They worked at their own special skills and occupations, or they helped to plant trees, clear rubble, drive trucks—anything. Many of them kept right on with their two hours a day of Hebrew study—a true act of Jewish faith.

On the first day of the war, 10,000 Jews volunteered to work in Israel. In more than 30 countries, over 23,000 people, of all ages and backgrounds, registered with the Jewish Agency and at Israeli embassies. About 7,000 could be accommodated, and these joined their fellow-Jews in Israel for the emergency.

The Israel Emergency Fund of the United Jewish Appeal raised over $100 million within a few days—the largest private welfare fund ever collected in the United States. Some Jews gave their entire life's savings. Communities, synagogues, organizations, individuals did not wait to be asked—they acted on their own. Many Jews who never before took part in Jewish life came to a synagogue or a Jewish building, or telephoned, or wrote, offering what they had, asking what they could do.

No other event—not even the establishment of Israel in 1948— brought such unity, devotion, sacrifice among Jews everywhere. The younger generation surprised many Jews, including those who knew and worked with them. Even those with limited Jewish education, with little interest in Israel or in Jewish life, joined in this mass movement of world Jewry to aid Israel. Despite all appearances, they still felt strong ties to the Jewish people and its fate, to the land and people of Israel, to their own identity as Jews. Everyone knew what was in their minds: Destruction of Jews as under the Nazis must not happen again. The threat to Israel brought out their inmost loyalties, their feeling of belonging to a worldwide people, of not being able to be silent and passive while Jews of another country faced destruction.★

In Russia, the government for many years has made it difficult for anyone to live openly as a Jew—to worship, celebrate holidays, study, show interest in Israel. In 1967, with Russia thundering away at Israel as "the aggressor" and accusing "Zionists" of being "as bad as Hitler," Russian Jews had to be even more careful of what they said and did. But we know—from letters, secret conversations, and other sources—that deep inside their hearts they thrilled at Israel's magnificent stand, that once again they felt like Jews.

★ (1) Two days after the war, a large gathering of Jewish leaders from all over this country took place. Many of them did not belong to a synagogue, did not consider themselves "religious." Yet at the final blessing, thanking God "for keeping us alive and enabling us to reach this day," almost everyone in the room burst into tears.

(2) The American Council for Judaism says that Israel and Zionism are not part of Judaism, that the Jewish religion has nothing to do with being a nation, having a homeland and an independent government, and so on.

What conclusions do you draw from these two facts?

297

"In our nation's long history there have been few hours more intensely moving than the hour of our reunion with the Western Wall. A people had come back to the cradle of its birth."

—Abba Eban

Problems of Victory

Try This: Select an earlier chapter of this book with a topic that especially interests you. In connection with that topic, did the Six Day War solve any of Israel's problems, make them easier, make them harder, or add new problems? Make a poster with two columns: "What Israel Gained" and "What Israel Lost."

■ Jews gather at the Western Wall—to pray, to weep, to sing, rejoice, or keep silent out of emotion too deep for words. What do you think of the traditional custom of writing a prayer on a piece of paper and putting it into a crevice among the stones? Is this merely a superstitious act or does it have meaning for an intelligent modern Jew?

It was a short war. It saved Israel from invasion and possible destruction and brought other important gains. But the cost was high and tremendous new problems developed.

Now that she controls new territory, Israel is safer from attack. Syrian guns can no longer shell villages along the northern border. Jordan, from the present cease-fire lines, cannot open fire on Jerusalem or Tel Aviv. The Sinai Desert and Gaza stand between Israel and Egypt. The Strait of Tiran and the Gulf of Aqaba are free for Israeli ships, and her troops patrol the Suez Canal where Egypt has illegally kept out Israel ships for twenty years. Guerilla bands still raid and sabotage—but there is no immediate threat of an all-out war. Arab war plans have been set back for a few years at least.

The occupied territories bring new income to Israel, from tourists, trade, new customers, new jobs. She has the chance to win over many Arabs who can get to know Israelis better and perhaps become friends. She has a strong "bargaining point" with the Arab nations—if they want these territories back, they will have to give Israel something in return.

The war came at a time when Israel was in a "slump"—unemployment increasing, money value decreasing in American dollars, immigration declining, political parties wrangling, splitting and setting up new parties. The war changed much of this—new work was created, more visitors and immigrants came, political parties rejoined, and the general mood is one of building and planning for the future.

Businessmen of the world have certainly not lost faith in Israel. Even during the Six Day War she continued shipping exports as usual. Rumania—one communist country that did not follow Russia —agreed on trade and cultural exchange with Israel. A huge exhibit of Israeli industrial products in our own country attracted hundreds of visitors and buyers. Six members of the European Common Market organized to promote Israel as an associate member. Several large American firms opened new factories in Israel. Through 1967, applications for new business projects came in twice as fast as in 1965.

All the various gains of the war proved that Israel is here to stay— that she is alert, strong, and able to protect herself. This is a "psycho-

■ After the Six Day War, Israel controlled four times as much territory and almost 50 per cent more population. The occupied area includes four main parts: (1) Sinai Peninsula—mostly desert and wilderness; stretches between two great seas; dominates the Suez Canal, controls the Strait of Tiran; can supply twice as much oil a year as Israel consumes. (2) Western bank of the Jordan River—mountains, valleys, fertile land, desert areas; thickly populated, including 1948 Arab refugees; holy places of all three faiths that attract many tourists; high unemployment. (3) Syrian (or Golan) Heights—from here, artillery had frequently shelled Israeli border settlements across a very unsafe "neutral" zone; area includes some of the Jordan River's sources, and has fertile slopes. (4) Gaza Strip—small, but densely populated; used by Egypt to lock 1948 Arab refugees into a concentration camp highly dangerous to Israel; major source of citrus fruit exports. (5) Jerusalem—uniting the city has put holy places of three religions and many Arab city-dwellers under Israeli control. Why did Israel accept a cease-fire, stopping at these points, instead of going on to attack deeper in Arab lands? Why was she safer now from Arab attacks? Should she be willing to give up these areas?

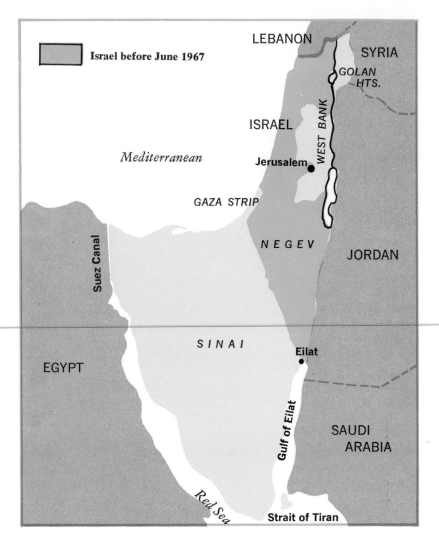

Israel before June 1967

LEBANON
SYRIA
GOLAN HTS.
ISRAEL
WEST BANK
Mediterranean
Jerusalem
GAZA STRIP
N E G E V
JORDAN
Suez Canal
SINAI
Eilat
EGYPT
Gulf of Eilat
SAUDI ARABIA
Red Sea
Strait of Tiran

logical" boost to Israelis' morale that enables them to face the future with courage and hope.

But for all this, Israel had to pay with the lives of over 800 of her best educated, most intelligent young men, an unusually high percentage of them officers. This, proportionally, is like a loss to the United States of 60,000 soldiers, or about three times the actual American losses in Vietnam.

Damage to Israel herself—mostly in Jerusalem and the border settlements—ran into hundreds of millions of dollars. Occupying new territory, with its large Arab population, is a heavy financial burden. Before the war, much of this territory received help from the United States, Great Britain, and charitable donations, and it did much business with surrounding Arab populations. Now, without this aid, and with all its own problems, Israel must keep peace there, be ready to defend it against attack, provide all government services, keep people at work. Experts say Israel will have to spend an extra $25,000,000 a year to govern the occupied territory.

Israel is counting on the Arabs wanting this territory back and making peace in order to get it. The Arabs are counting on Israel having so much trouble supporting this territory that she may give it back. As so often before, Israel faces another "impossible" job. We can only hope that once again with her own courage and intelligence, with the help of Jews elsewhere and the free nations, she will somehow get the job done.

Try This: Some of Israel's actions since the 1967 cease-fire have aroused criticism, even among Jews and Israelis. For instance, destroying a Jordanian village that she claimed harbored guerilla terrorists, or holding her 1968 Independence Day parade throughout Jerusalem despite U.N. and United States protests. Find out about such actions and Israel's motives in carrying them out, and then decide for yourself if Israel was right or wrong in each case.

Jews in Arab Lands

Israel's swift and crushing counterattacks brought great suffering to many Arab soldiers and civilians. This has blinded many people to certain Jewish victims of the Six Day War—the 100,000 Jews still living in the Middle East and North Africa.

These Jews were the last of great and ancient Jewish communities in this region. In 1948, there were about 700,000 of them. Since then, to escape Arab persecution, 600,000 have fled to Israel, France, Latin America—wherever a friendly country and a Jewish community welcomed them. They were refugees every bit as much as the 500,000 Arabs who fled from Palestine in 1948. They lost homes, possessions, and in many cases their citizenship.

But unlike the Arab refugees they were not put by their own people into crowded concentration camps. They were not used as political pawns to stir up hatred for neighboring countries. They were not even counted as refugees in U.N. censuses, and they got no U.N. aid. The Jewish world—especially Israel—took them in, gave them homes, jobs, training, and a new life.

The 100,000 Jews who stayed behind in Arab lands did so for many reasons. Some countries would not let them go. Many were too old to uproot themselves or refused to leave their sick or aging parents. Some lacked courage to start a new life in a strange land. Thousands, especially in North Africa, trusted their Arab rulers and expected no harm.

But with the June 1967 war, the Arabs exacted vengeance. Jews were brutally murdered in the streets of Tripoli and other places. Mobs burned down synagogues and shops in Tunisia. All of Aden's 200 Jews were expelled, ending a community two thousand years old. In Egypt, 2,000 Jews were arrested and tortured.

Nothing like this has happened to Arabs in Israel or in occupied territory. There have been "incidents" and complaints, and nobody

★ Why do you suppose that in May and June of 1967 there was no Arab uprising or revolt in Israel, and no attempt in 1948 as to get out of the country?

likes to be governed by a victorious enemy. But both the "occupied" Arabs and neutral observers agree that the Israelis have been as humane and as fair as possible. For example, they allowed Arabs on the bank of the Jordan to cross over and join the Jordanians if they wanted to and then allowed them to come back if they changed their mind. There have been no mass murders or executions, no wanton destruction, no expulsions, no mass arrests or torture.★

Israel and the Nations

Israel's Army captured or destroyed a vast amount of Arab military equipment. Most of it came from Russia, since 1955, at the cost of billions of dollars. Russian experts trained the Egyptian Army. Russian diplomats in the U.N. supported the Arabs at all times, and spoke of Israel like vicious bigots. Russian and Arab leaders frequently exchanged visits. Russia and most of her satellites broke off relations with Israel, clamped down on Jewish emigration to Israel. Russian propaganda compared Israel to the Nazi monsters, stirring up anti-Semitism in that country to even greater heights, surrounding Russian Jews in an atmosphere of even deeper hostility which they had to bear in bitter silence. The one exception among the communist nations has been Rumania, which has refused to support the Arabs against Israel and has continued to trade with her.

Try This: Find out about anti-Semitism in Russia—what forms it takes, the motives behind it, what anyone is trying to do about it. Write to: American Jewish Conference on Soviet Jewry, 55 W. 42nd St., New York, N. Y. 10036.

Russia, her allies, and Red China, India, Malaysia, and others—representing over half the world's population—joined the "crusade" against Israel. This hostility, on the surface, seems senseless. The Arab nations vastly outnumber Israel in size and population. They have the tremendous power of Russia behind them against any Israeli attack they might be afraid of. They are the ones constantly threatening to destroy Israel, while she is the one constantly asking for peace and friendship. Why are the pro-Arab nations apparently so afraid of one small country, so opposed to helping her, so eager to help her enemies?

Israel is the only nation created since World War II that is a true democracy; it proves that democracy can work in a developing nation. Also, the United States and many other Western democracies support Israel. These two facts probably explain the great fear and hatred of Israel in certain parts of the world that have failed to provide real freedom and security for their people. Israel represents a way of life that these governments wish to destroy. Israel's struggle to survive is a struggle to save democracy against its enemies.★

★ Some people think the United States supports Israel mainly because of the strong influence of Jews in American politics. On the other hand, a leading rabbi says: "Even if there were not one Jew in America, America should be committed to Israel . . . [because] it is a commitment not to Israel but to America itself." Think of several reasons why this statement is true.

Russia is trying to get power in the Mediterranean countries, by lining up with the Arabs against Israel and her Western supporters,

especially the United States. Many American non-Jews—statesmen, congressmen, editors, experts of all kinds—described Israel's victory in the Six Day War as a victory for our own country against Russia —a victory we won without having to fight for it. Thus, a leading editor wrote, in *The New York Times* (June 11, 1967): "The Israelis had the courage of our convictions and they won the war we opposed. Washington was saved because the Israelis didn't follow its advice." Intelligent Americans know that if Israel had lost the war, not only would she have been wiped off the map but the United States would have lost the entire Middle East to Russia.

France, though a democratic country, and formerly Israel's great friend, recently turned against her. She too called Israel the "aggressor" in the Six Day War, supported the Russians and Arabs, cancelled her sales of weapons to Israel, and began supplying weapons to Arab countries. The French government seems eager to regain influence with the Arabs and to weaken American influence any way it can. In a rather bitter gesture, Israel has insisted on paying for the cancelled airplanes, in the hope of arousing French conscience and

TOGETHER AGAIN. Jews and Arabs mingling in the Old City after Jerusalem was reunited in June, 1967. There is some tension, doubts about the future, and occasional resistance. But in the main, the two groups get along pretty well, and in many ways life is better for both of them. Think of several reasons why. Also, why is Israel determined at all costs to make a success of the new, united Jerusalem?

303

sympathy. But France seems set on trying to be a "third force" in the world, the equal of Russia and the United States, no matter which of its former friends gets hurt.

Israelis today are not afraid of Arab governments or Arab armies. They are disappointed in France. But they are gravely concerned about Russia—what she will do, how far she will go, how she can be stopped. And they are worried too about where they stand with the United States.

Most Americans were—and are—sympathetic to Israel. But they do not want our government to take any action against the Arabs that might risk war with Russia and possibly another world war. Our government tried to compromise with Nasser, to talk with him about agreements of various kinds. But only a few senators urged the President to use force to end Egypt's illegal blockade of the Gulf of Aqaba.★

Then Israel won her war, and the United States urged a policy in the U.N. that didn't exactly support Israel, but at least opposed the Arabs and the Russians. The American policy laid down five points, which are fully supported by American Jews and by Israelis as the only sensible way to real peace in the Middle East—recognizing the right of all nations to exist, justice for refugees, free passage of all ships through international waters, ending the arms race between the Arabs and Israel, independence and safety for all nations.

★ Israelis seem to be caring less and less about world opinion. Are they right or wrong? They claim the U.N. will never say anything against the Arabs no matter what wrongs they commit, but will always criticize Israel or keep silent. If this is so, how would you explain it?

The Days Ahead

The nations of the U.N. are divided on the future of the Middle East.

On one side: Israel, the United States, other Western democracies (except France). Their position: Arabs and Israelis must talk directly to each other and make peace. They must decide together on all problems of the region—the Arab territory Israel holds, the Arab refugees, Israeli shipping in the Gulf of Aqaba and the Suez Canal, guarantees against attacks by either side, cooperative projects for common welfare. Practically all American Jews support this program of direct negotiations between Israel and the Arab nations.

On the other side: the Arab nations, Russia, most communist governments, certain Asian and African nations. Their position: Israel must first withdraw her troops from all occupied territory, and only then might there be any discussion about the future. In other words—as in 1948 and 1956, the Arabs want everything back as it was before a war they forced on Israel and lost. But if the Middle East goes back to the very same conditions that led to war, there will not be peace.★

★ Nearly three-fourths of the world's oil reserves are in the Middle East. Almost all this oil is *outside* of Israel. The Suez Canal, so important for world shipping, has been under Egyptian control. How do these two facts help explain the interest, concern, and attitudes of various nations about the Middle East?

The Arabs make no promises, offer no terms. They keep talking of "another round," of defeating and destroying Israel "next time." Whatever they win in a war with Israel—like the Old City of Jerusalem in 1948—they claim as their permanent property; but what they lose to Israel must immediately be returned. Israel refuses to start all over again with the very same conditions that seem to bring war every ten years. Real peace in the region requires both sides to work together. Israel is willing to do this; the Arabs are not. They apparently just want to keep trying again and again to defeat and destroy Israel.

Israelis are not all of one mind about future relationships with the Arabs. They agree on just two things—direct peace talks before anything else and keeping a united Jerusalem. Beyond that, some would return the occupied territory if the Arabs accept peace; some want to keep it, or part of it, permanently for Israel; still others want to set up a new Arab state on the west bank of the Jordan River, or create "neutral" zones supervised by the U.N. Some say the only real solution is an all-out war in which Israel invades and occupies all Arab capitals, and then forces the Arab governments to make peace. Others say it all depends on cooperation between Russia and the United States—if these two great powers want peace there will be peace, but if both or one of them does not want peace there won't be any.★

★ Many people are speaking of "a new Israel" or "a greater Israel," on the ground that the Six Day War brought such radical changes that Israel will never be the same again—in geography, in world affairs, in government, business affairs, and so on. Do you agree?

As this chapter is being written, the situation is not clear, the future doubtful, the end not in sight. Arab guerillas raid Israeli settlements, Israeli military units hit back at Arab villages. Fighting between the armies keeps breaking out. The U.N. keeps trying to maintain some sort of cease-fire, get some kind of peace agreement. There are some hopeful signs. For example, a U.N. peace team circulating between the Israelis and the Arabs seems right now (May, 1968) to be making a little progress. But there are discouraging signs too. Russia has replaced 80 to 90 per cent of the Arab war machine destroyed by Israel in 1967. Israel's problems, old and new, seem overwhelming. Her need for help and support seems greater than ever.

Israelis are excited and proud over their victory—but sad, too. They don't hate the Arabs, or enjoy killing, wounding or humiliating them. Many are worried about their country becoming, in self defense, more and more warlike. Some ask: "Are we going to be the David who fought Goliath or the David who wrote the Psalms?" It's not easy to be both, but they know they have to try.

Have the Arabs learned their lesson? Will they talk with Israel and come to some kind of peace agreement? Or will they plan and prepare for "the next round"? Will Russia and the United States work together for a Middle East peace, or will they line up again on

Try This: Write to JNF Coordinator, UAHC, 838 Fifth Avenue, New York, N. Y. 10021, for information about the new Victory Forest planned for the barren hills near Jerusalem. Ask for posters, charts, coin cards, filmstrips, and so on for a class or assembly project to "kick off" tree purchases in your school.

opposite sides? If war comes again, can Israel still defeat the Arabs, and if so will it do any good? Is this the best we can hope for—war after war after war? Will one of these wars explode into another world war?

Nobody can answer these questions. We can only hope and work with patience, courage, and faith for the cause we believe in. That is how the Jewish people survived through the centuries, how they reestablished an independent homeland, and how they protected it against Arab attacks.

YOU'LL ENJOY READING

Some of the many books about the Six Day War and after the war in Israel. Ask your librarian to let you look over her collection. Be sure to consult the latest edition of *Facts About Israel,* available from an Israel information office or embassy.

YOU'LL ENJOY SEEING

Exciting new films and filmstrips about Israel during the last few years. Ask your teacher or principal for the latest annual issue of *The Jewish Audio-Visual Review* (101 Fifth Avenue, New York, N. Y. 10003), which has a whole section on Israel with complete descriptions and full information.

OTHER RESOURCES

For latest and various kinds of information on Israel, audio-visual aids, publications, bulletins, current news analyses and background, write to the following:

American Israel Public Affairs Committee, 1341 "G" Street, NW, Washington, D. C. 20005

B'nai B'rith Anti-Defamation League, 315 Lexington Avenue, New York, N. Y. 10016

American Jewish Committee, 165 E. 56th Street, New York, N. Y. 10022

American Jewish Congress, 15 E. 84th Street, New York, N. Y. 10028

Conference of Presidents of Major American Jewish Organizations, 515 Park Avenue, New York, N. Y. 10022

Israel Information Services, 11 E. 70th Street, New York, N. Y. 10021

Jewish Agency, 515 Park Avenue, New York, N. Y. 10022

National Community Relations Advisory Council (NCRAC), 55 W. 42nd Street, New York, N. Y. 10036

United Jewish Appeal, 1290 Sixth Avenue, New York, N. Y. 10019

Shalom

You have explored only a little of Israel in this book, learned only a fraction of her story. You are like an explorer who has rapidly surveyed a new territory and has a good general idea of it—but has to come back many times to learn more about it.

Wouldn't you like to go on exploring Israel, and helping her? There are many ways. Join a Zionist youth club, read books and magazines, keep up with Israeli news. Buy Israeli art, religious symbols, recordings, foods. Learn more Hebrew to understand your own religious and cultural heritage. Form your own Hebrew Club or join a Hebrew class. Plant a tree in Israel. Give to the Keren Ami and the U.J.A. Help the Leo Baeck School in Haifa, or some other Israeli institution. Support a pro-Israel organization of your community. Find an Israeli pen-pal.

Several American Jewish organizations sponsor summer camps in Israel especially for American young people your age. The Jewish Agency conducts a summertime Bar Mitzvah Pilgrimage for boys and girls just reaching thirteen. Dues paid over a three-year period to the National Bar Mitzvah Club are put aside to pay the cost of your trip to Israel when you are sixteen. Tours and trips, for study and fun, are offered to Jewish youth by various groups, with scholarship aid that keeps expenses low. For instance, when you are a bit older, you can spend your senior high school year, or your junior college year, studying in Israel. Or you can spend a summer, with an American youth group, in a Kibbutz. Of course, you can visit Israel on your own, with your family.

Think of seeing for yourself the Negev, Jerusalem, border villages, a Knesset session, Israeli holidays, Jews of all colors and races—and many, many other fascinating sights!

The Jewish people has an exciting history, a proud heritage of literature, customs, ideas. Its homeland, Israel, is an exciting place, part of *your* Jewish heritage.

■ **Outside the town of Kiryat Gat in the Negev (see page 20).**

1968. Several organizations, including the Union of American Hebrew Congregations, now sponsor summer camps for teen-agers in Israel, and there is also a program for taking your second year of high school in Israel with full credit. For more information, write to: Jewish Agency, 515 Park Avenue, New York, N. Y. 10021; UAHC, 838 Fifth Avenue, New York, N. Y. 10021.

CREDITS

American Friends of the Hebrew University   pp. 31, 35, 39, 40.

Fred Csaznick, Jerusalem   p. 197.

Al Goldman   p. 187 (upper right).

Government Press Office, Tel Aviv   pp. 51, 123, 130, 152 (top), 153 (top left, lower left), 172, 179 (top), 183, 187 (bottom), 190, 202, 230, 247, 248, 255.

Hazel Greenwald   pp. 48 (lower), 219.

Hadassah   p. 4 (middle, lower).

Israel Government Tourist Office   pp. 138, 176.

Israel Office of Information   pp. 14, 15, 16, 17, 19, 20, 30, 37, 38, 41, 43, 45 (top), 47, 48 (top), 50, 52, 54, 55, 56, 57, 58, 65 (right), 66, 79, 80 (lower left, center right), 81 (lower left, center right), 90, 94, 96, 97, 98 (left), 99, 100, 101, 104, 112, 121 (right), 128, 129, 131, 133, 134, 135, 137, 146, 149, 152 (bottom), 153 (right), 157, 161 (bottom), 170, 171, 174, 175, 177, 178, 179 (bottom), 181, 186, 188, 189, 191, 192 (upper, lower), 193, 196, 198, 199, 201, 203, 216, 224, 227, 228, 229, 233, 253, 287, 288, 292, 303.

Louise Jefferson   pp. ii, iii.

Jewish National Fund   p. 4 (top).

Press Association, Inc.   pp. 261, 268, 278.

David Rubinger   p. 180.

Herbert Sonnenfeld   pp. 67, 218.

Leni Sonnenfeld   pp. iv, v, xvii, xviii, xix, xx, xxi, xxii, xxiii, xxiv, 72, 75, 83, 86, 102, 108, 140, 173, 184, 208, 296, 299, 307.

UAHC   pp. 275, 276, 277 (top).

United Nations   pp. 257, 259, 263.

Whitestone Photo   p. 117.

Wide World Photos   pp. 231, 267.

Zim Lines   p. 161 (top).

Zionist Archives and Library   pp. 21, 24, 26, 28, 33, 45 (lower), 80 (upper left, center, upper right), 110, 118, 120, 121 (left), 163, 164, 187 (upper left), 192 (center), 194, 195, 212, 215, 220, 271, 273, 275, 277 (lower), 285.

Zionist Organization of America   pp. 60, 61, 62, 64, 65, 69, 81 (upper left, center, top center, lower right), 91.

INDEX AND GLOSSARY

NOTE: Dashes indicate English translation of preceding Hebrew term. This index does not cover the new Chapter 25.

Religion, religious attitudes, liberty, problems, official religions, political parties, 72–3, 113, 184–97, 203, 206, 220, 233, 288, 290

Religious Zionism, movement to establish Jewish homeland as center of Orthodox Judaism, 62

Resources, 48–52, 124–7, 242–3, 289

Revisionism, movement to establish Jewish homeland based on capitalism, free enterprise, and strong opposition to British and Arabs, 64

Rishon Letzion—First for Zion—town, 20–21; nickname of Kalischer, Zionist leader, 24

Rosh Ha-Memshalah—Head of the Government—prime minister, 202

Rothschild, Zionist leader, 28

Russia, 251–2, 255

Rutenberg, Pinhas, businessman, 121

Sabbath (see Shabbat)

Sabra, fruit, Israeli-born Jew, 97, 105–6

Safed, town, xxi, 20, 179

Samaritans, religious sect, 187, 191

Schapira, Hermann Tzevi, Zionist leader, 118

Science, xxii, 180–2, 248

Scouts, scouting (see Tzofim)

S'dom, industrial settlement, 49

Seas, xix, 9–12, 18, 53–4, 121, 225

Sefardim, Jews of southern Europe and North Africa, 71–85, 166–7, 211–3, 280, 290

Shabbat—Sabbath, 13–5, 148, 185–9, 205, 289

Shalom—peace, 2, 10–1, 13, 33, 43–4, 92–3, 127, 150, 225–46, 251, 264–5, 275, 283–9

Shazar, Zalman, third President, 1963– , 20

Shomrim—Guards—members of Hashomer, early defense organization, 150, 231

Shulchan Aruch—Prepared Table—basic Orthodox law book of Jewish life, 280

Simchat Torah, festival, 193

Silver, Abba Hillel, Zionist leader, 277

Sinai Campaign, 1956, against Egypt, 3, 43–4, 225, 231, 239

Smolenskin, Peretz, Zionist leader, 28

Sochnut, Jewish Agency, world-wide organization to aid Israel, 117, 161, 213, 216, 218, 222

Socialism, 109–16, 118–21, 143

Socialist Zionism, movement to establish a Jewish homeland governed by socialist principles, 62–3

Social security, justice, welfare (see tzedakah)

Sodom, Bible town, 22

Songs, 111, 174, 291

Spiritual Zionism, movement to establish Palestine as a Jewish cultural center, 62

Sports, 100–1, 146, 181–2

Stamps, 136, 178

Sukot, festival, 193

Synagogues, 189, 196–7, 273–7

Szold, Henrietta, founder of Hadassah and Aliyat Noar, 218, 220, 273

Tabor, Mt., 22

Talmud, Jewish literary classic, completed about 550 C.E., 14, 213

Taxes, 132

Technion (Institute of Technology), "Israel's M.I.T.," 135, 163, 165, 171, 180

Tel Aviv, city, 16–8, 20, 32, 123, 128, 132, 172, 174–5, 178, 188, 196–7

Tel Aviv University, 107

Television, 177

Tel Hai, kibbutz, 22

Tiberias, town, 20

Timna, copper mines, 48, 50

Theater, 147, 176

Totzeret Ha-aretz—products of the land, 3, 5, 136–7, 139, 293

Towns, xx, xxi, 20–2, 49, 101, 134, 170, 179, 186, 192, 221, 253, 275, 277

Transportation, ii–iii, 19–20, 53–4, 128–9, 156, 255, 289

Travel, 1, 138–9, 237, 293

Trumpeldor, Joseph, chalutz, 60

Tu Bi-Shevat (Chamishah Asar Bishevat), festival, 192

Tzahal (Tzeva Haganah Leyisrael—Israel Defense Forces) (Army), 182, 201, 224–35, 285–6

Tzedakah—charity—welfare, social justice, 76–84, 87–96, 142–3, 158, 216–7, 222–3, 262–5

Tzion (Zion), symbolic term for Jewish homeland, 7

Tzofim—Scouts, 103–4

Ulpan, residential Hebrew college, 165–6

Union of American Hebrew Congregations (UAHC, Reform), 6, 276

United Jewish Appeal (UJA), 130–1, 139, 215

United Nations (U.N.), 207, 237, 245, 250, 252–3, 257–60, 263–4, 266–7, 278–9, 283–6, 288–9

United States, 3–4, 10, 254–5, 257, 259, 266

Uriel, village, 22

Villages, 4, 21–2, 44, 48, 109–11, 114, 118–21, 127–8, 136, 140–69, 156–9, 174, 179, 182, 192, 216–7, 220, 247, 249, 252

War for Independence (see Milchemet Ha-Atzmaut)

Water, 51–2, 242–3, 289

Wolffsohn, David, Zionist leader, 235

Weizmann, Chaim, Zionist leader, first President of Israel, 66, 89, 117, 180–1, 288

Weizmann Institute, 107, 180–1, 248

Welfare, welfare organizations, welfare state, 155–8, 208–23, 253

World and Israel, 2–3, 181–2, 209, 250–6, 279, 283, 290

World Union for Progressive Judaism (Reform), 275–6

Worship, 189, 196–7, 273–7

Yad Mordechai, kibbutz, 43

Yarden—descender, Jordan River, ii–iii, 11–2, 121, 243, 262

Yarkon River, 51

Yarmuk River, 243

Yavne, urban settlement, 22

Yehudah, Yehudi, Yehudim, Judah, Jew(s), 8

Yemenite Jews, 75–6, 174, 177, 289

Yerushalayim—Jerusalem, 13–5, 20, 178, 187–9, 196–7, 274–5, 284–5

Yeshivah, academy stressing Talmud study, 20, 184

Yishuv—Settlement—Jewish community of Palestine, 61, 66–9, 109–18, 163–7, 203

Yisrael—Israel, 7

Yom Ha-Atzmaut—Independence Day, 17, 171, 194, 286, 289

Yotvata, kibbutz, 44, 48

Youth, youth clubs, 99–106, 217–22

Youth Aliyah (see Aliyat Ha-noar)

Zichron Ya-akov, Moshavah village, 22

Zim (Zi Mischari), Israel Navigation Company, 156, 161

Zion (see Tzion)

Zionism, Zionists, Zionist movement, Zionist organization, effort to regain and rebuild the Jewish homeland, 4, 8, 23–9, 56–70, 108–18, 131, 143, 147, 171, 203, 209–10, 220–1, 270–3

Zion, Mt., 15

312